Prisoners of War i 1756 to 181b

A record of their lives, their romance and their sufferings

Francis Abell

Alpha Editions

This edition published in 2024

ISBN 9789362516633

Design and Setting By
Alpha Editions
www.alphaedis.com
Email - info@alphaedis.com

As per information held with us this book is in Public Domain.
This book is a reproduction of an important historical work.
Alpha Editions uses the best technology to reproduce historical work
in the same manner it was first published to preserve its original nature.
Any marks or number seen are left intentionally to preserve.

Contents

PREFACE	- 1 -
CHAPTER I INTERNATIONAL RECRIMINATIONS	- 3 -
CHAPTER II THE EXCHANGE OF PRISONERS	- 28 -
CHAPTER III THE PRISON SYSTEM—THE HULKS	- 40 -
CHAPTER IV LIFE ON THE HULKS	- 59 -
CHAPTER V LIFE ON THE HULKS—(continued)	- 80 -
CHAPTER VI PRISON-SHIP SUNDRIES	- 96 -
CHAPTER VII TOM SOUVILLE A FAMOUS PRISON-SHIP ESCAPER	- 107 -
CHAPTER VIII THE PRISON SYSTEM THE PRISONERS ASHORE. GENERAL	- 118 -
CHAPTER IX THE PRISONS ASHORE 1. SISSINGHURST CASTLE	- 128 -
CHAPTER X THE PRISONS ASHORE 2. NORMAN CROSS	- 138 -
CHAPTER XI THE PRISONS ASHORE 3. PERTH	- 166 -
CHAPTER XII THE PRISONS ASHORE 4. PORTCHESTER	- 177 -
CHAPTER XIII THE PRISONS ASHORE 5. LIVERPOOL	- 200 -
CHAPTER XIV THE PRISONS ASHORE 6. GREENLAW—VALLEYFIELD	- 209 -
CHAPTER XV THE PRISONS ASHORE 7. STAPLETON, NEAR BRISTOL	- 220 -
CHAPTER XVI THE PRISONS ASHORE 8. FORTON, NEAR PORTSMOUTH	- 228 -
CHAPTER XVII THE PRISONS ASHORE 9. MILLBAY, NEAR PLYMOUTH	- 233 -
CHAPTER XVIII THE PRISONS ASHORE 10. DARTMOOR	- 247 -

CHAPTER XIX SOME MINOR PRISONS	- 279 -
CHAPTER XX LOUIS VANHILLE: A FAMOUS ESCAPER	- 295 -
CHAPTER XXI THE PRISON SYSTEM PRISONERS ON PAROLE	- 301 -
CHAPTER XXII PAROLE LIFE	- 318 -
CHAPTER XXIII THE PRISONERS ON PAROLE IN SCOTLAND	- 335 -
CHAPTER XXIV PAROLE PRISONERS IN SCOTLAND (continued)	- 358 -
CHAPTER XXV PRISONERS OF WAR IN WALES	- 378 -
CHAPTER XXVI ESCAPE AGENTS AND ESCAPES	- 386 -
CHAPTER XXVII ESCAPES OF PRISONERS ON PAROLE	- 397 -
CHAPTER XXVIII COMPLAINTS OF PRISONERS	- 416 -
CHAPTER XXIX PAROLE LIFE. SUNDRY NOTES	- 433 -
CHAPTER XXX PAROLE LIFE: SUNDRY NOTES (continued)	- 455 -
CHAPTER XXXI VARIORUM	- 465 -

PREFACE

Two influences have urged me to make a study of the subject of the prisoners of war in Britain.

First: the hope that I might be able to vindicate our country against the charge so insistently brought against her that she treated the prisoners of war in her custody with exceptional inhumanity.

Second: a desire to rescue from oblivion a not unimportant and a most interesting chapter of our national history.

Whether my researches show the foregoing charge to be proven or not proven remains for my readers to judge. I can only say that I have striven to the utmost to prevent the entrance of any national bias into the presentation of the picture.

As to the second influence. It is difficult to account for the fact that so interesting a page of our history should have remained unwritten. Even authors of fiction, who have pressed every department of history into their service, have, with about half a dozen exceptions, neglected it as a source of inspiration, whilst historical accounts are limited to Mr. Basil Thomson's *Story of Dartmoor Prison*, Dr. T. J. Walker's *Norman Cross*, and Mr. W. Sievwright's *Perth Depôt*, all of which I have been permitted to make use of, and local handbooks.

Yet the sojourn among us of thousands of war prisoners between the years 1756 and 1815 must have been an important feature of our national life—especially that of officers on parole in our country towns; despite which, during my quest in many counties of England, Scotland, and Wales, I have been surprised to find how rapidly and completely the memory of this sojourn has faded; how faintly even it lingers in local tradition; how much haziness there is, even in the minds of educated people, as to who or what prisoners of war were; and how the process of gathering information has been one of almost literal excavation and disinterment. But the task has been a great delight. It has introduced me to all sorts and conditions of interesting people; it has taken me to all sorts of odd nooks and corners of the country; and it has drawn my attention to a literature which is not less valuable because it is merely local. I need not say that but for the interest and enthusiasm of private individuals I could never have accomplished the task, and to them I hope I have made sufficient acknowledgement in the proper places, although it is possible that, from their very multitude, I may have been guilty of omissions, for which I can only apologize.

FRANCIS ABELL

LONDON, 1914.

CHAPTER I
INTERNATIONAL RECRIMINATIONS

He who, with the object of dealing fairly and squarely with that interesting and unaccountably neglected footnote to British history, the subject of prisoners of war in Britain, has sifted to the best of his ability all available sources of information both at home and abroad, as the present writer has done, feels bound to make answer to the questions:

1. Did we of Britain treat our prisoners of war with the brutality alleged by foreign writers almost without exception?

2. Did our Government sin in this respect more than did other Governments in their treatment of the prisoners taken from us?

As an Englishman I much regret to say in reply to the first question, that, after a very rigorous examination of authorities and weighing of evidence, and making allowance for the not unnatural exaggeration and embellishment by men smarting under deprivation of liberty, I find that foreigners have not unduly emphasized the brutality with which we treated a large proportion of our prisoners of war, and I am fairly confident that after a study of the following pages my readers will agree with me.

Between our treatment of prisoners on parole and in confinement on land, and foreign treatment of our countrymen similarly situated, the difference, if any, is very slight, but nothing comparable with the English prison-ship system existed anywhere else, except at Cadiz after the battle of Baylen in 1808, and to the end of time this abominable, useless, and indefensible system will remain a stain upon our national record.

In reply to the second question, the balance appears to be fairly even between the behaviour of our own and foreign Governments—at any rate, between ours and that of France—for Britain and France practically monopolize the consideration of our subject; the number of prisoners taken by and from the United States, Spain, Holland, Denmark, and other countries, is comparatively insignificant.

Each Government accused the other. Each Government defended itself. Each Government could bring forward sufficient evidence to condemn the other. Each Government, judging by the numerous official documents which may be examined, seems really to have aimed at treating its prisoners as humanely and as liberally as circumstances would allow. Each Government was badly served by just those sections of its subordinates which were in the closest and most constant contact with the prisoners. It is impossible to read the printed and written regulations of the two Governments with regard to the treatment of war-prisoners without being impressed by their justness, fairness, and even kindness. The French rules published in 1792, for instance, are models of humane consideration; they emphatically provided that foreign prisoners were to be treated exactly as French soldiers in the matter of sustenance, lodging, and care when sick.

All this was nullified by the behaviour of subordinates. It is equally impossible to read the personal narratives of British prisoners in France and of French prisoners in Britain without being convinced that the good wills of the two Governments availed little against the brutality, the avarice, and the dishonesty of the officials charged with the carrying out of the benevolent instructions.

It may be urged that Governments which really intended to act fairly would have taken care that they were suitably served. So we think to-day. But it must always be borne in mind that the period covered in this book—from 1756 to 1815—cannot be judged by the light of to-day. It was an age of corruption from the top to the bottom of society, and it is not to be wondered at that, if Ministers and Members of Parliament, and officers of every kind—naval, military, and civil—were as essentially objects of sale and purchase as legs of mutton and suits of clothes, the lower orders of men in authority, those who were in most direct touch with the prisoners of war, should not have been immune from the contagion.

Most exactly, too, must it be remembered by the commentator of to-day that the age was not only corrupt, but hard and brutal; that beneath the veneer of formal politeness of manner there was an indifference to human suffering, and a general rudeness of tastes and inclinations, which make the gulf separating us from the age of Trafalgar wider than that which separated the age of Trafalgar from that of the Tudors.

It is hard to realize that less than a century ago certain human beings—free-born Britons—were treated in a fashion which to-day if it was applied to animals would raise a storm of protest from John o' Groats to the Land's End: that the fathers of some of us who would warmly resent the aspersion of senility were subject to rules and restrictions such as we only apply to children and idiots; that at the date of Waterloo the efforts of Howard and Mrs. Fry had borne but little fruit in our prisons; and that thirty years were yet to pass ere the last British slave became a free man. Unfortunates were regarded as criminals, and treated accordingly, and the man whose only crime was that he had fought for his country, received much the same consideration as the idiot gibbering on the straw of Bedlam.

It could not be expected that an age which held forgery and linen-stealing to be capital offences; which treated freely-enlisted sailors and soldiers as animals, civil offenders as lunatics, and lunatics as dangerous criminals; of which the social life is fairly reflected in the caricatures of Gillray and Rowlandson; which extolled much conduct which to-day we regard as base and contemptible as actually deserving of praise and admiration, should be tenderly disposed towards thousands of foreigners whose enforced detention in the land added millions to taxation, and caused a constant menace to life and property.

So, clearly bearing in mind the vast differences between our age and that covered in these pages, let us examine some of the recriminations between Britain and France, chiefly on the question of the treatment of prisoners of war, as a preparation for a more minute survey of the life of these unfortunates among us, and an equitable judgement thereon.

In Britain, prisoners of war were attended to by 'The Commissioners for taking care of sick and wounded seamen and for exchanging Prisoners of War', colloquially known as 'The Sick and Hurt' Office, whose business was, 'To see the sick and wounded seamen and prisoners were well cared for, to keep exact accounts of money issued to the receiver, to disburse in the most husbandly manner, and in all things to act as their judgements and the necessities of the service should require.' John Evelyn, Samuel Pepys, and Home, the author of *Douglas*, had been Commissioners. On December 22, 1799, the care of prisoners of war was transferred to the Transport Office, and so remained until 1817. In 1819 the Victualling Office took over the duty.

Throughout the period of the Seven Years' War—that is, from 1756 to 1763—there was a constant interchange of letters upon the subject of the treatment of prisoners of war. The French king had made it a rule to distribute monthly, from his private purse, money for the benefit of his subjects who were prisoners in Britain; this was called the Royal Bounty. It was applied not merely to the relief and comfort of the prisoners while in confinement, but also to the payment of their homeward passages when exchanged, and of certain dues levied on them by the British Government upon entering and leaving the country. The payment was made on a graduated scale, according to rank, by regularly appointed French agents in England, whose exact and beautifully kept accounts may be examined at the Archives Nationales in Paris.

This Royal Bounty, the French Government asserted, had been inspired by the continual complaints about the bad treatment of their countrymen, prisoners of war in England. To this it was replied that when the French prisoners arrived it was determined and arranged that they should have exactly the same victualling both in quality and quantity as British seamen, and this was actually increased by half a pound of bread per man per diem over the original allowance. It was asserted that all the provisions issued were good, although the bread was not always fresh baked. This should be remedied. The meat was the same in quality as that served out to British seamen—indeed it was better, for orders were issued that the prisoners should have fresh meat every meat day (six in the week) whereas British seamen had it only twice a week, and sometimes not so often.

The Commissioners of the Admiralty expressed their difficulty in believing that the French prisoners were really in need of aid from France, but said that if such aid was forthcoming it should be justly distributed by appointed agents.

They appended a *Table d'Avitaillement* to this effect:

Every day except Saturday every man received one and a half pounds of bread, three-quarters of a pound of beef, and one quart of beer. On Saturday instead of the beef he got four ounces of butter or six ounces of cheese. Four times a week each man was allowed in addition half a pint of peas.

For money allowance officers of men-of-war received one shilling a day, officers of privateers and merchant ships sixpence. These officers were on parole, and in drawing up their report the Admiralty officials remark that, although they have to regret very frequent breaches of parole, their standard of allowances remains unchanged.

With regard to the prison accommodation for the rank and file, at Portchester Castle, Forton Prison (Portsmouth), Millbay Prison (Plymouth), the men slept on guard-beds, two feet six inches in breadth, six feet in length, provided with a canvas case filled with straw and a coverlid. Sick prisoners were treated precisely as were British.

At Exeter, Liverpool, and Sissinghurst—'a mansion house in Kent lately fitted up for prisoners'—the men slept in hammocks, each with a flock bed, a blanket, and a coverlid.

All this reads excellently, but from the numberless complaints made by prisoners, after due allowance has been made for exaggeration, I very much doubt if the poor fellows received their full allowance or were lodged as represented.

This was in 1757. As a counterblast to the French remonstrances, our Admiralty complained bitterly of the treatment accorded to British prisoners in French prisons, especially that at Dinan. We quote the reply of De Moras, the French Administrator, for comparison. The French scale of provisioning prisoners was as follows:

On Sunday, Monday, Tuesday, and Thursday each prisoner received one and a half pounds of bread, one pint of beer at least, one pound of good, fresh meat, well cooked, consisting of beef, mutton, or veal, 'without heads and feet', soup, salt, and vinegar. On Wednesday, Friday, and Saturday, and 'maigre' days, half a pound of beans or peas well cooked and seasoned, and two ounces of butter. The same allowance was made in all prisons, except that in some wine took the place of beer.

The Administrator complained that he had great difficulty in getting contractors for provisioning prisoners—a fact not without significance when we note how eagerly the position of contractor for prisoners of war was competed for in England.

De Moras further stated that prisoners when sick were sent to the regular Service Hospitals, where they received the same attention as Frenchmen. Each officer prisoner received a money allowance of thirty sous—one shilling and threepence—a day, and renewed clothing when needed.

The following remonstrance, dated 1758, is one of many relating to alleged British peculation in the matter of the French Royal Bounty.

'Plusieurs Français enfermés dans le château de Portchester représentent l'excessive longueur de leur détention et ont fait connoître une manœuvre qui les prive d'un secours en argent que le Roy leur fait donner tous les mois; après avoir changé l'or et l'argent qui leur a été donné pour une monnoie de cuivre nommée *half pens* on en a arrêté le cours et on les a mis dans l'impossibilité de jouir du soulagement que le Roy avoit voulu leur accorder.'

Commenting upon this De Moras adds:

'Je suis instruit que les châtiments les plus rigoureux sont employés à l'égard des Français prisonniers pour la faute la plus légère et que celui qui cherche à s'évader est chargé de fers, mis en cachot, et perd toute espérance de liberté. Je sais que quelques paroles inconsidérées lâchées contre votre agent à Portsmouth ont excité sa colère au point de faire dépouiller 150 Français et de leur faire donner la bastonnade avec si peu de ménagements que quelques-uns sont morts des suites de cette barbare punition. Quant à la nourriture elle est assés décriée par tous les Français qui reviennent d'Angleterre, et il est vray que si on leur distribue souvent du biscuit aussy mal fabriqué que celuy que quelques-uns d'eux ont raporté, et que j'ay veu, l'usage n'en peut estre que désagréable et pernicieux. Ils disent aussy que la viande ne vaut pas mieux, et qu'il en est de même de toutes les espèces de denrées.

'Je ne l'attribue qu'à l'infidélité et à l'avidité des entrepreneurs.'

In 1758, as a reply to complaints made to the British Government about the treatment of prisoners at Portchester, a report to the following effect was made by De Kergan, an officer of the French East India Company on parole.

1. The chief punishment is the *cachot*, which is wholesomely situated above ground near the entrance gate. It is untrue that prisoners are placed there in irons.

2. Prisoners recaptured after escape are put in the *cachot* upon half-rations until the expenses of recapture and the reward paid for the same are made up, but prisoners are never deprived of the French King's Bounty or debarred the market.

3. Only three men have lost everything as a result of recapture: one was a lieutenant who had broken parole from Petersfield; the others were two sailors who defended themselves against Hambledon people who tried to capture them, and killed one.

4. It is utterly untrue that 150 prisoners have been flogged.

5. The biscuit sent to M. de Moras as a specimen of the prison food did not come from Portchester.

6. He reports well upon the food served out to the prisoners.

7. All complaints are listened to.

From the fact that De Kergan was shortly afterwards allowed to go home to France with his servant, it is difficult to resist the conclusion that it had been 'arranged' by the British authorities that he should have been selected to make the above report under promise of reward.

De Moras adds that although the number of English prisoners multiplies continually, it is owing to the slackness of exchange. On the part of France, he declares that they are all well treated, and asserts that the balance of prisoners due to France is 800. Complaints from France about the non-distribution of the King's Bounty are continued during the year 1758 and the following years, and a proposal is made that agents should be stationed in each county to attend solely to the proper arrangement and distribution of all charitable contributions, for the benefit of the prisoners.

'C'est le seul moyen,' says De Moras, 'qui puisse faire goûter aux officiers et aux soldats que le sort des armes a privés de la liberté quelqu'apparence des avantages de la Paix au milieu même des malheurs de la guerre.'

More complaints from our side brought an answer in which lay the kernel of the whole matter: 'L'exactitude des inférieurs demande à estre souvent réveillée.'

In 1759 the care of the French prisoners in England practically devolved entirely upon us, as their Government unaccountably withdrew all support. The natural consequence was that their condition became pitiable in the extreme—so much so that public subscriptions were opened on behalf of the poor fellows. A London Committee sat at the *Crown and Anchor* in the

Strand, and the sum of £7,000 was collected. With this sum were sent to different prisons 3,131 great coats, 2,034 waistcoats, 3,185 pairs of shoes, 3,054 pairs of breeches, 6,146 shirts, 3,006 caps, and 3,134 pairs of stockings. Letters of grateful acknowledgement and thanks were received from most of the dépôts. The following will serve as a specimen.

'*Cornwall* Man-of-War at Chatham, 13.1.1760.'

'Nous les prisonniers de guerre à bord du vaisseau du Roi le "Cornwall", dans la rivière de Chatham, reconnoissons d'avoir reçu chacun par les mains de notre bon commandant Guillaume Lefebre des hardes, consistant d'un surtout, une chemise, un bonnet, une paire de bas, de souliers et de coulottes. Nous prions MM. les Anglais qui out eu cette bonté pour infortunés presque dépourvus auparavant de quoi se garantir de la sévérité de la saison, et de grandes souffrances par le froid, d'être persuadés de notre vive reconnoissance qui ne s'oubliera pas.'

The letter of thanks from Sissinghurst contains excuses for some men who had sold the clothes thus supplied for urgent necessaries, such as tobacco and the postage of letters, and praying for the remission of their punishment by being put on half-rations. From Helston, the collector, W. Sandys, wrote that 'in spite of vulgar prejudices which were opposed to this charity, and the violent clamours raised against it by the author of a letter who threw on its promoters the accumulated reproach of Traitors, Jacobites and Enemies to their country,' he sent £32.

It was in allusion to the above act of public benevolence that Goldsmith wrote in the twenty-third letter of the *Citizen of the World*: 'When I cast my eye over the list of those who contributed on this occasion, I find the names almost entirely English; scarce one foreigner appears among the number.... I am particularly struck with one who writes these words upon the paper enclosing his benefaction: "The mite of an Englishman, a citizen of the world, to Frenchmen, prisoners of war, and naked."'

Even abroad this kindly spirit was appreciated, as appears from the following extract from a contemporary Brussels gazette:

'The animosity of the English against the French decreases. They are now supposed to hate only those French who are in arms. A subscription is opened in the several towns and countries for clothing the French prisoners now in England, and the example has been followed in the capital.'

In 1760 the French Government thus replied to complaints on our side about the ill-treatment of British prisoners at Brest.

'The castle at Brest has a casemate 22 feet high, 22 feet broad, and 82 long. It is very dry, having been planked especially and has large windows. Prisoners are allowed to go out from morning till evening in a large "meadow" [probably an ironical fancy name for the exercising yard, similar to the name of "Park" given to the open space on the prison hulks]. They have the same food as the men on the Royal ships: 8 ounces of meat—a small measure but equal to the English prison ration—the same wine as on the Royal ships, which is incomparably superior to the small beer of England. Every day an examination of the prisoners is made by the Commissioner of the Prison, an interpreter and a representative of the prisoners. Bedding straw is changed every fifteen days, exactly as in the Royal Barracks.'

Here it is clear that the Frenchman did exactly as the Englishman had done. Having to give a reply to a complaint he copied out the Regulation and sent it, a formal piece of humbug which perhaps deceived and satisfied such men in the street as bothered their heads about the fate of their countrymen, but which left the latter in exactly the same plight as before.

At any rate, with or without foundation, the general impression in England at this time, about 1760, was that such Englishmen as were unfortunate enough to fall into French hands were very badly treated. Beatson in his *Naval and Military Memoirs*[1] says:

'The enemy having swarms of small privateers at sea, captured no less than 330 of the British ships.... It is to be lamented that some of their privateers exercised horrid barbarities on their prisoners, being the crews of such ships as had presumed to make resistance, and who were afterwards obliged to submit: Conduct that would have disgraced the most infamous pirate; and it would have redounded much to the credit of the Court of France to have made public examples of those who behaved in this manner. I am afraid, likewise, that there was but too much reason for complaint of ill-treatment to the British subjects, even after they were landed in France and sent to prison. Of this, indeed, several affidavits were made by the sufferers when they returned to England.

'On the contrary, the conduct of Great Britain was a striking example of their kindness and humanity to such unfortunate persons as were made prisoners of war. The prisons were situated in wholesome places, and subject to public inspection, and the prisoners had every favour shown them that prudence would admit of. From the greatness of their number, it is true, they frequently remained long in confinement before they could be exchanged in terms of the cartel, by which their clothes were reduced to a very bad state, many of them, indeed, almost naked, and suffered much from the inclemency of the weather. No sooner, however, was their miserable condition in this respect made known, than subscriptions for their relief were opened at several of the principal banking-houses in London, by which very great sums were procured, and immediately applied in purchasing necessaries for those who stood in the greatest need of them.

'The bad state of the finances of France did not permit that kingdom to continue the allowance they formerly granted for the maintenance of their subjects who might become prisoners of war; but the nation who had acquired so much glory in overcoming them, had also the generosity to maintain such of these unfortunate men as were in her power at the public expense.'

The American prisoners conveyed to England during the War of Independence, seem to have been regarded quite as unworthy of proper treatment. On April 2, 1777, Benjamin Franklin and Silas Deane wrote from Paris to Lord Stormont, British Ambassador in Paris, on the subject of the ill-treatment of American prisoners in England, and said that severe reprisals would be justifiable. On this a writer in the *Gentleman's Magazine*, October 1777, commented:

'It must certainly be a matter of some difficulty to dispose of such a number of prisoners as are daily taken from captured American privateers; some of whom have from 100 to 300 men on board, few less than 70 or 80; against whom the Americans can have no adequate number to exchange.... Were the privateersmen, therefore, to be treated as prisoners of war, our gaols would be too few to hold them. What then is to be done? Not indeed to load them with chains, or force them with stripes, famine, or other cruelties, as the letter charges, to enlist in Government service; but to allow them the same encouragement with other subjects to enter on board the King's ships, and then they would have no plea to complain of hard usage.'

The letter referred to, sent on by Stormont to Lord North, contained the chief grievance that 'stripes had been inflicted on some to make them commit the deepest of all crimes—the fighting against the liberties of their country'. The reply to this was the stereotyped one 'that all possible was done for the prisoners: that they were permitted to receive charitable donations, and that complaints were attended to promptly'. A contemporary number of the *London Packet* contains a list of subscriptions for the benefit of the American prisoners amounting to £4,600. The Committee for the collection and administration of this money, who sat at the *King's Arms* at Cornhill, seem to have occupied themselves further, for in 1778 they call attention to the fact that one Ebenezer Smith Platt, a Georgia merchant, had been put in Newgate, and ironed, and placed in that part of the prison occupied by thieves, highwaymen, housebreakers, and murderers, without any allowance for food or clothes, and must have perished but for private benevolence.

The most absurd reports of the brutal treatment of French prisoners in England were circulated in France. It was gravely reported to the Directory that English doctors felt the pulses of French prisoner patients with the ends of their canes; that prisoners were killed *en masse* when subsistence became difficult; that large numbers were punished for the faults of individuals; and that the mortality among them was appalling. The result was that the Directory sent over M. Vochez to inquire into matters. The gross calumnies were exposed to him; he was allowed free access to prisons and prison ships; it was proved to him that out of an average total of 4,500 prisoners on the hulks at Portsmouth only six had died during the past quarter, and, expressing himself as convinced, he returned, promising to report to the French minister the 'gross misrepresentations which had been made to him'.

A good specimen of the sort of report which sent M. Vochez over to England is the address of M. Riou to the Council of Five Hundred of the 5th of Pluviôse of the year 6—that is January 25, 1798.

After a violent tirade against England and her evil sway in the world, he goes into details. He says that when his Government complained of the promiscuous herding together of officers and men as prisoners of war, the English reply was: 'You are republicans. You want equality, therefore we treat you here equally.' Alluding to the harsh treatment of privateersmen taken prisoners, he declares it is because they do more harm to England by striking at her commerce than any fleets or armies. He brings up the usual complaints about bad and insanitary prisons, insufficient food, and the shameful treatment of officers on parole by the country people. One hundred Nantes captains and officers had told him that prisoners were confined in parties of seventy-two in huts seventeen feet long and ten feet high, some of them being merely cellars in the hillside; that the water soaked through hammocks, straw, and bread; that there was no air, that all this was light suffering compared with the treatment they received daily from agents, officers, soldiers, and jailors, who on the slightest pretext fired upon the prisoners. 'Un jour, à Plymouth même, un prisonnier ajusté par un soldat fut tué. On envoie chercher le commissaire. Il vient: soulève le cadavre: on lui demande justice; il répond: "C'est un Français," et se retire!'

Alluding to the precautionary order which had been recently given in England that all parole should cease, and that all officers on parole should be sent to prisons and prison ships, he says: 'There is now no parole for officers. All are pell-mell together, of all ranks and of both sexes. A woman was delivered of a child, she was left forty-eight hours without attention, and even a glass of water was denied her. Even the body of a dead dog was fought for by the famished prisoners.'

He then describes in glowing terms the treatment of English prisoners in France; he suggests a tax for the relief of the French prisoners of war, a 'taxe d'humanité,' being one-third of the ordinary sumptuary tax, and winds up his attack:

'Français! Vous avez déposé une foule d'offrandes sur l'autel de la Patrie! Ce ne sera pas tromper vos intentions que de les employer au soulagement de l'humanité souffrante. Vous voulez combattre l'Angleterre: eh bien! Soulagez les victimes; conservez 22,000 Républicains qui un jour tourneront contre leurs oppresseurs leurs bras dirigés par la Vengeance! N'oubliez pas que le Gouvernement anglais médite la ruine de la République; que, familiarisé avec tous les crimes, il en inventera de nouveaux pour essayer de la renverser; mais elle restera triomphante, et le Gouvernement anglais sera détruit! Attaquez ce monstre! Il expirera sous vos coups! Quirot, Le Clerc (Maine-et-Loire), Riou.'

The Times of January 8, 1798, comments severely upon the frequent tirades of the Directory, ridiculing the attitude of a Government remarkable above all others for its despotic character and its wholesale violation of the common rights of man, as a champion of philanthropy, of morals, and of humanity, and its appeal to all nations to unite against the only country which protects the victims of Directorial anarchy. After declaring that the prisoners in England are treated better than prisoners of war ever were treated before, a fact admitted by all reasonable Frenchmen, the writer says:

'And yet the Directory dares to state officially in the face of Europe that the Cabinet of St. James has resolved to withdraw all means of subsistence from 22,000 Republican prisoners in England, and has shut them up in dungeons, as if such a measure, supposing it even to be true, could have any other object than to force the French Government to provide for the sustenance of the French prisoners in this country in the same manner as our Government does with respect to the English prisoners in France.'

In February 1798 the French Directory announced through Barras, the president, that it would undertake the subsistence of the French prisoners in England, meaning by subsistence, provisions, clothing, medical attendance, and to make good all depredations by prisoners.

The Times of February 27 said:

'The firm conduct of our Government in refusing any longer to make advances for the maintenance of French prisoners, has had the good effect of obliging the French Directory to come forward with the necessary supplies, and as the French agents have now the full management of this concern, we shall no longer be subject to their odious calumnies against the humanity of this country.'

Directly the French Government took over the task of feeding and clothing the prisoners in England, they reduced the daily rations by one quarter. This irritated the prisoners extremely, and it was said by them that they preferred the 'atrocious cruelty of the despot of London to the humanity and measures of the Five Directors of Paris'. A correspondent of *The Times* of March 16, 1798, signing himself 'Director', said that under the previous British victualling régime, a prisoner on his release showed the sum of four guineas which he had made by the sale of superfluous provisions, and the same writer declared that it had come to his knowledge that the new French provision agent had made overtures to the old British contractor to supply inferior meat.

In 1798 it was resolved in the House of Commons that an inquiry should be made to establish the truth or the reverse of the French complaints about the treatment of French prisoners in England. It was stated that the reports spread about in France were purposely exaggerated in order to inflame national feeling against Britain. Mr. Huskisson confirmed this and alluded to the abominable treatment of Sir Sydney Smith.

Colonel Stanley affirmed that the prisoners were generally well treated: he had lately been in Liverpool where 6,000 were confined, and found the officers had every indulgence, three billiard tables, and that they often performed plays.

In May 1798 the Report was drawn up. After hearing evidence and making every inquiry it was found that the French complaints were gross exaggerations; the Commissioners observed that 'our prisoners in France were treated with a degree of inhumanity and rigour unknown in any former war, and unprecedented in the annals of civilized nations', and reiterated the complaint that all British proposals for the exchange of prisoners were rejected.

The Report stated that there was good medical attendance given to prisoners in Britain; that there were constant checks on fraud by contractors and officials; that the prisoners appointed their own inspector of rations; that fraudulent contractors were proceeded against, and punished, giving as a recent example, a Plymouth contractor who, having failed in his engagements to supply the prisons with good provisions of full weight, was imprisoned for six months and fined £300.

The Report stated that the daily scale of provisions for prisoners in health was: one and a half pounds of bread, three-quarters of a pound of beef, one-third of an ounce of salt, and one quart of beer, except on Saturdays, when four ounces of butter and six ounces of cheese were substituted; and on four days of the week half a pint of pease, or in lieu one pound of cabbage stripped from the stalk.

The prisoners selected their own surgeons if they chose, and the same diet was given to sick prisoners as to sick British seamen. Each man was provided with a hammock, a palliasse, a bolster and a blanket, the straw of bolsters and palliasses being frequently changed.

A letter written in 1793 to the Supplement of the *Gentleman's Magazine*, holds good for 1798, as to the belief of the man in the street that the foregoing liberal and humane regulations were worth more than the paper they were written on:

'The Sans Culottes we hold in prison never lived so well in their lives before: they are allowed every day three-quarters of a pound of good beef, two pounds of bread with all the finest of the flour in it, the bran alone being extracted, two quarts of strong well-relished soup, one pound of cabbage with the heart included, and a quart of good beer. As a Frenchman can live upon one pound of meat for a week, this allowance is over-plenteous, and the prisoners sell more than half of it. With the money so obtained they buy as much strong beer as they can get leave to have brought them.... Such is the manner in which Englishmen are at this juncture treating their natural, inveterate, and unalterable enemies.'

On December 22, 1799, the French Government—now the Consulate—repudiated the arrangement made by the Directory for the subsistence of French war-prisoners in England, and the British Government was obliged to undertake the task, the Transport Office now replacing the old 'Sick and Hurt' Office. So the prisoner committees in the dépôts and prisons were abolished, and all persons who, under the previous arrangement, were under the French agents and contractors, and as such had been allowed passports, returned to their original prisoner status.

The Duke of Portland wrote thus to the Admiralty:

'It is less necessary on this occasion to recall the circumstances which gave rise to the arrangement under which the two Governments agreed to provide for the wants of their respective subjects during their detention, as they have been submitted to Parliament and published to the world in refutation of the false and unwarrantable assertions brought forward by the French Government on this subject; but His Majesty cannot witness the termination of an arrangement founded on the fairest principles of Justice and Protection due by the Powers of War to their respective Prisoners, and proved by experience to be the best calculated to provide for their comfort, without protesting against the departure (on the part of the French Government) from an agreement entered into between the two countries, and which tended so materially to mitigate the Calamities of War. To prevent this effect as much as possible with respect to the British prisoners now in France, it is His Majesty's pleasure that Capt. Cotes should be instructed to ascertain exactly the rate of daily allowance made to each man by the French Government, and that he should take care to supply at the expense of this country any difference that may exist between such allowance and what was issued by him under the late arrangement.

'With respect to all the prisoners not on Parole in this country, it is His Majesty's command that from the date of the French agent ceasing to supply them, the Commissioners of Transports and for taking care of prisoners of war shall furnish them immediately with the same ration of Provisions as were granted before the late arrangement took place.'

(Not clothing, as this had always been supplied by the French Government.)

Previous to this repudiatory act of France, the British Government made a similar proposal to Holland, accompanying it with the following remarks, which certainly seem to point to a desire to do the best possible to minimize the misery of the unfortunate men.

'We trust that your Government will not reject so humane a proposition, which, if accepted, will, of course, preclude the possibility of complaints or recriminations between the respective Governments, and probably meliorate the fate of every individual to which it relates. In health their mode of living will be more conformable to their former habits. In sickness they will be less apt to mistrust the skill of their attendants, or to question the interest they may take in their preservation. On all occasions they would be relieved from the suspicion that the Hand which supplies their wants and ministers to their comfort, is directed by that spirit of Hostility which is too often the consequence of the Prejudice and Enmity excited by the State of War between Nations.'

However, the Dutch Government, no doubt acting under orders from without, replied that it was impossible to comply. So Dutch prisoners became also the objects of our national charity.

The *Moniteur* thus defended the Act of Repudiation:

'The notification of the abandonment by the French Government of the support of French prisoners in England is in conformity with the common customs of war, and is an act of wise administration and good policy. The old Directory is perhaps the first Government which set the example of a belligerent power supporting its prisoners upon the territories of its enemies ... Men must have seen in this new arrangement a sort of insult. The English papers of that time were filled with bitter complaints, with almost official justification of this conduct, supported by most authentic proofs. Well-informed men saw with surprise the French Government abandon itself blindly to these impolitic suggestions, release the English from the expense and embarrassment of making burthensome advances, exhaust of its own accord the remains of its specie in order to send it to England; deprive themselves of the pecuniary resources of which they stood in such pressing need, in order to add to the pecuniary resources of its enemies; and, in short, to support the enormous expenses of administration.

'The English, while they exclaimed against the injustice of the accusation, gathered with pleasure the fruits of this error of the Directory; though our old Monarchical Government left England during the whole war to support the expenses of the prisoners, and did not liquidate the balance until the return of Peace, and consequently of circulation, credit, commerce, and plenty, rendered the payment more easy. The generally received custom of leaving to the humanity of belligerent nations the care of protecting and supporting prisoners marks the progress of civilization.'

The results of repudiation by France of the care of French prisoners in England were not long in showing themselves.

The agent at Portchester Castle wrote to the Transport Office:

'August, 1800.

'GENTLEMEN:

'I am under the necessity of laying before you the miserable situation of a great number of Prisoners at this Depôt for want of clothing. Many of them are entirely naked, and others have to cut up their hammocks to cover themselves. Their situation is such, that if not provided with these articles before the cold weather commences they must inevitably perish.

'I beg to observe that it is nearly eighteen months since they were furnished with any article of wearing apparel by the French Government, and then only a single shirt to each suit which must necessarily have been worn out long since.

JOHN HOLMWOOD.'

And again, later on:

'The prisoners are reduced to a state of dreadful meagreness. A great number of them have the appearance of walking skeletons. One has been found dead in his hammock, and another fell out from mere debility and was killed by the fall. The great part of those sent to the hospital die in a short time, others as soon as they are received there.'

These were written in consequence of letters of complaint from prisoners. The Agent in France for prisoners of war in England, Niou, was communicated with, but no reply came. Otto, the Commissioner of the Republic in England, however, said that as the French Government clothed British prisoners, *although they were not exactly British prisoners but allies*, it was our duty to clothe French prisoners. The British Government denied this, saying that *we* clothed our allies when prisoners abroad, and ascribed much of the misery among the French prisoners to their irrepressible gambling habits. Dundas wrote a long letter to the French Commissioners about the neglect of their Government, but added that out of sheer compassion the British Government would supply the French prisoners with sufficient clothing. Lord Malmesbury hinted that the prisoners were refused the chance of redress by the difficulty of gaining access to their Commissary, which Grenville stated was absolutely untrue, and that the commonest soldier or sailor had entire freedom of access to his representative.

On October 29, 1800, Otto, the French Commissioner in England, wrote:

'My letter from Liverpool states that the number of deaths during the past month has greatly exceeded that of four previous months, even when the depôt contained twice the number of prisoners. This sudden mortality which commenced at the close of last month, is the consequence of the first approach of cold weather, all, without exception, having failed from debility. The same fate awaits many more of these unfortunate beings, already half starved from want of proper food, and obliged to sleep upon a damp pavement or a few handfuls of rotten straw. Hunger and their own imprudence, deprived them of their clothes, and now the effect of the cold weather obliges them to part with a share of their scanty subsistence to procure clothing. In one word, their only hope is a change in their situation or death.'

In this account Otto admits that the prisoners' 'imprudence' has largely brought about the state of affairs. Rupert George, Ambrose Serle, and John Schenck, the Transport Office Commissioners who had been sent to inquire, report confirming the misery, and re-affirm its chief cause. About Stapleton Prison they say:

'Those who are not quite ragged and half naked, are generally very dirty in their scanty apparel, and make a worse appearance as to health than they would do had they the power in such a dress to be clean. Profligacy and gambling add to the distress of many, and it is perhaps impossible to prevent or restrain this spirit, which can exercise itself in corners. The Dutch prisoners at Stapleton (1800), being clothed by the Dutch Government are in much better health than the French.'

The Commissioners sent to Otto an extract of a letter from Forton, near Gosport. Griffin, the prison surgeon, says that 'several prisoners have been received into the Hospital in a state of great debility owing to their having disposed of their ration of provisions for a week, a fortnight, and in some instances for a month at a time. We have felt it our duty to direct that such persons as may be discovered to have been concerned in purchasing any article of provision, clothing or bedding, of another prisoner, should be confined in the Black Hole and kept on short allowance for ten days and also be marked as having forfeited their turn of exchange.'

Callous, almost brutal, according to our modern standards, as was the general character of the period covered by this history, it must not be inferred therefrom that all sympathy was withheld from the unfortunate men condemned to be prisoners on our shores. We have seen how generously the British public responded to the call for aid in the cases of the French prisoners of 1759, and of the Americans of 1778; we shall see in the progress of this history how very largely the heart of the country people of Britain went out to the prisoners living on parole amongst them, and I think my readers may accept a letter which I am about to put before them as evidence that a considerable section of the British public was of opinion that the theory and practice of our system with regard to prisoners of war was not merely wrong, but wicked, and that very drastic reform was most urgently needed.

Some readers may share the opinion of the French General Pillet, which I append to the letter, that the whole matter—the writing of the anonymous letter, and the prosecution and punishment of the newspaper editor who published it, was a trick of the Government to blind the public eye to facts, and that the fact that the Government should have been driven to have recourse to it, pointed to their suspicion that the public had more than an inkling that it was being hoodwinked.

In the *Statesman* newspaper of March 19, 1812, appeared the following article:

'Our unfortunate prisoners in France have now been in captivity nine years, and, while the true cause of their detention shall remain unknown to the country there cannot be any prospect of their restoration to their families and homes. In some journeys I have lately made I have had repeated opportunities of discovering the infamous practices which produce the present evil, and render our exiled countrymen the hopeless victims of misery....'

(The writer then describes the two classes of prisoners of war in England.)

'They are all under the care of the Transport Office who has the management of the money for their maintenance, which amounts to an enormous sum (more than three millions per annum) of which a large part is not converted to the intended purpose, but is of clear benefit to the Commissioners and their employers. The prisoners on parole receiving 1s. 6d. per diem produce comparatively little advantage to the Commissioners, who are benefited principally by the remittances these prisoners receive from France, keeping their money five or six months, and employing it in stock-jobbing. They gain still something from these, however, by what their agents think proper to send them of the property of those who die or run away. The prisoners in close confinement are very profitable. These prisoners are allowed by the Government once in eighteen months a complete suit of clothing, which however, they never receive. Those, therefore, among them who have any covering have bought it with the product of their industry, on which the Agents make enormous profits. Those who have no genius or no money go naked, and there are many in this deplorable state. Such a picture Humanity revolts at, but it is a true one, for the produce of the clothing goes entirely into the pockets of the Commissioners.

'A certain amount of bread, meat, &c., of good quality ought to be furnished to each prisoner every day. They receive these victuals, but they are generally of bad quality, and there is always something wanting in the quantity—as one half or one third at least, which is of great amount.

Besides, when any person is punished, he receives only one half of what is called a portion. These measures, whenever taken, produce about £250 or £300 a day in each depôt according to the number of prisoners, and of course, are found necessary very often. These are the regular and common profits. The Commissioners receive besides large sums for expenses of every description which have never been incurred in the course of the year, and find means to clear many hundreds of thousands of pounds to share with their employers.'

The writer goes on to say that

'the real reason for bringing so many prisoners into the country is not military, but to enrich themselves [i.e. the Government]. For the same reason they keep the San Domingo people of 1803, who, by a solemn capitulation of Aux Cayes were to be returned to France. So with the capitulation of Cap François, who were sent home in 1811 as clandestinely as possible. Bonaparte could say ditto to us if any of ours capitulated in Spain like the Duke of York in Holland.

'All this is the reason why our people in France are so badly treated, and it is not to be wondered at.

'HONESTUS.'

The Transport Office deemed the plain-speaking on the part of an influential journal so serious that the opinion of the Attorney-General was asked, and he pronounced it to be 'a most scandalous libel and ought to be prosecuted'. So the proprietor was proceeded against, found guilty, fined £500, imprisoned in Newgate for eighteen months, and had to find security for future good behaviour, himself in £1,000, and two sureties in £500 each.

I add the remarks of General Pillet, a prisoner on a Chatham hulk, upon this matter. They are from his book *L'Angleterre, vue à Londres et dans ses provinces, pendant un séjour de dix années, dont six comme prisonnier de guerre*—a book utterly worthless as a record of facts, and infected throughout with the most violent spirit of Anglophobism, but not without value for reference concerning many details which could only come under the notice of a prisoner.

'Mr. Lovel, editor of the *Statesman*, a paper generally inclined in favour of the French Government, had published in March 19, 1812, a letter signed "Honestus", in which the writer detailed with an exactness which showed he was thoroughly informed, the different sorts of robberies committed by the Transport Office and its agents upon the French prisoners, and summed them up. According to him these robberies amounted to several millions of francs: the budget of the cost of the prisoners being about 24,000,000 francs. Mr. Lovel was prosecuted. "Honestus" preserved his anonymity; the editor was, in consequence, condemned to two years imprisonment and a heavy fine. His defence was that the letter had been inserted without his knowledge and that he had had no idea who was the author. I have reason to believe, without being absolutely sure, that the writer was one Adams, an employé who had been dismissed from the Transport Office, a rascal all the better up in the details which he gave in that he had acted as interpreter of all the prisoners' correspondence, the cause of his resentment being that he had been replaced by Sugden, even a greater rascal than he. I wrote to Mr. Brougham, Lovel's Solicitor, and sent him a regular sworn statement that the prisoners did not receive one quarter the clothing nominally served to them, and for which probably the Government paid; that, estimating an outfit to be worth £1, this single item alone meant the robbery every eighteen months of about £1,800,000. My letter, as I expected, produced no effect; there was no desire to be enlightened on the affair, and the judicial proceedings were necessary to clear the Transport Office in the eyes of the French Government. Hence the reason for the severe punishment of Lovel, whose fine, I have been assured, was partly paid by the Transport Office, by a secret agreement.'

The General, after some remarks about the very different way in which such an affair would have been conducted in France, appends a note quoting the case of General Virion, who, on being accused of cruelty and rapacity towards the English prisoners in Verdun, blew his brains out rather than face the disgrace of a trial.

Pillet wrote to Lovel, the editor, thus:

'On board the prison ship *Brunswick*,

Chatham, May 19, 1813.

'Sir:

'Since I have become acquainted with the business of the letter of "Honestus" I have been filled with indignation against the coward who, having seemed to wish to expose the horrible truth about the character and amount of the robberies practised upon prisoners of war, persists in maintaining his incognito when you have asked him to come forward in your justification.... Unhappily, we are Frenchmen, and it seems to be regarded in this country as treason to ask justice for us, and that because it is not possible to exterminate France altogether, the noblest act of patriotism seems to consist in assassinating French prisoners individually, by adding to the torments of a frightful imprisonment privations of all sorts, and thefts of clothing of which hardly a quarter of the proper quantity is distributed....

'We have asked for impartial inquiries to be made by people not in the pay of the Admiralty; we have declared that we could reveal acts horrible enough to make hairs stand on end, and that we could bring unimpeachable witnesses to support our testimony. These demands, even when forwarded by irreproachable persons, have been received in silence. Is it possible that there are not in England more determined men to put a stop to ill-doing from a sense of duty and irrespective of rank or nation? Is it possible that not a voice shall ever be raised on our behalf?

'Your condemnation makes me fear it is so.

'If only one good man, powerful, and being resolved to remove shame from his country, and to wash out the blot upon her name caused by the knowledge throughout Europe of what we suffer, could descend a moment among us, and acquaint himself with the details of our miseries with the object of relieving them, what good he would do humanity, and what a claim he would establish to our gratitude!'

Pillet adds in a note:

'Lord Cochrane in 1813 wished to examine the prison ships at Portsmouth. Although he was a member of Parliament, and a captain in the navy, permission was refused him, because the object of his visit was to ascertain the truth about the ill-treatment of the prisoners. Lord Cochrane is anything but an estimable man, but he is one of those who, in the bitterness of their hatred of the party in power, sometimes do good. He complained in Parliament, and the only reply he got was that as the hulks were under the administration of the Transport Office, it could admit or refuse whomsoever it chose to inspect them.'

CHAPTER II
THE EXCHANGE OF PRISONERS

From first to last the question of the Exchange of Prisoners was a burning one between Great Britain and her enemies, and, despite all efforts to arrange it upon an equitable basis and to establish its practice, it was never satisfactorily settled. It is difficult for an Englishman, reviewing the evidence as a whole and in as impartial a spirit as possible, to arrive at any other conclusion than that we were not so fairly dealt with by others as we dealt with them. We allowed French, Danish, and Dutch officers to go on parole to their own countries, which meant that they were on their honour to return to England if they were not exchanged by a certain date, and we continued to do so in face of the fact that violation of this pledge was the rule and not the exception, and that prominent officers of the army and navy were not ashamed thus to sin. Or we sent over shiploads of foreigners, each of whom had been previously arranged for as exchanged, but so often did the cartel ships, as they were called, return empty or without equivalent numbers from the French ports that the balance of exchange was invariably heavily against Britain. The transport of prisoners for whom exchanges had been arranged, and of invalids and boys, was by means of cartel ships which were hired, or contracted for, by Government for this particular service, and were subject to the strictest regulation and supervision. The early cartel ports were Dover, Poole, and Falmouth on this side; Calais, St. Malo, Havre, and Morlaix in France, but during the Napoleonic wars Morlaix was the French port, Plymouth, Lynn, Dartmouth, and Portsmouth being those of England. The French ports were selected with the idea of rendering the marches of exchanged prisoners to their districts as easy as possible.

A cartel ship was not allowed to carry guns or arms, nor any merchandise; if it did the vessel was liable to be seized. The national flag of the port of destination was to be flown at the fore-top-gallant mast, and the ship's flag on the ensign staff, and both were to be kept continually flying. Passengers were not allowed to carry letters, nor, if from England, gold coin; the latter restriction being imposed so as partially to check the lucrative trade of guinea-running, as, during the early nineteenth century, on account of the scarcity of gold in France, there was such a premium upon British guineas that the smuggling of them engaged a large section of the English coast community, who were frequently backed up by London houses of repute. Passengers going to France on their own account paid £5 5s. each, with a deposit against demurrage on account of possible detention in the French port at one guinea per day, the demurrage being deducted from the deposit and the balance returned to the passenger.

The early cartel rates were, from Dover to Calais, 6s. per head; between all the Channel ports 10s. 6d., and to ports out of the Channel, £1 1s. For this the allowance of food was one and a half pounds of bread, three-quarters of a pound of meat, and two quarts of beer or one quart of wine, except between Dover and Calais, where for the meat was substituted four ounces of butter or six ounces of cheese. Commanding officers had separate cabins; a surgeon was compulsorily carried; officers and surgeon messed at the captain's table. It was necessary that the ship should be provisioned sufficiently for an emergency, and it was especially ruled that if a ship should be delayed beyond sailing time owing to weather or incomplete number of passengers, nobody upon any pretence was to leave the ship.

In 1808, on account of the discomforts and even the dangers of the cartel service, as well as the abuse of it by parole-breakers and others, a request was made that a naval officer should accompany each cartel ship, but this was refused by the Admiralty upon the ground that as such he might be arrested upon reaching a French port. As it became suspected that between the cartel shipowners and captains and the escape agents a very close business understanding existed, it was ordered in this same year, 1808, that all foreigners found about sea-port towns on the plea that they were exchanged prisoners waiting for cartel ships, should be arrested, and that the batches of exchanged prisoners should be timed to reach the ports so that they should not have to wait.

Later, when practically Plymouth and Morlaix had a monopoly of the cartel traffic, the cartel owner received uniformly half a guinea per man if his carriage-rate was one man per ton of his burthen; and seven shillings and sixpence if at the more usual rate of three men to two tons, and for victualling was allowed fourteen pence per caput per diem.

In 1757 much correspondence between the two Governments took place upon the subjects of the treatment and exchange of prisoners, which may be seen at the Archives Nationales in Paris, resulting in a conference between M. de Marmontel and M. de Moras, Minister of Marine and Controller-General of Finances, and Vanneck & Co., agents in England for French affairs. Nothing came of it except an admission by the French that in one respect their countrymen in England were better treated than were the English prisoners in France, in that whereas the French prisoners were provided with mattresses and coverlids, the English were only given straw. England claimed the right of monopolizing the sea-carriage of prisoners; and this France very naturally refused, but agreed to the other clauses that king's officers should be preferred to all other in exchange, that women and children under twelve should be sent without exchange, and that in hospitals patients should have separate beds and coverlids. But after a long exchange of requests and replies, complaints and accusations, England ceased to reply, and matters were at a standstill.

In 1758 there was a correspondence between M. de Moras and M. de Marmontel which shows that in these early days the principle of the exchange of prisoners possessed honourable features which were remarkably wanting on the French side during the later struggles between the two countries. Three French 'broke-paroles' who in accordance with the custom of the time should, when discovered, have been sent back to England, could not be found. M. de Moras suggested that in this case they should imitate the action of the British authorities in Jersey, who, unable to find nine English prisoners who had escaped from Dinan, stolen a fishing-boat, and got over to Jersey, had sent back the stolen vessel and nine French prisoners as an equivalent.

The following was the passport form for French prisoners whose exchange had been effected.

'By the Commissioners for taking care of sick and wounded seamen, and for Exchanging Prisoners of War.

'Whereas the one person named and described on the back hereof is Discharged from being Prisoner of War to proceed from London to France by way of Ostend in exchange for the British prisoner also named and described on the back hereof; you and every of you (*sic*) are hereby desired to suffer the said Discharged Person to pass from London to France accordingly without any hindrance or molestation whatever. This passport to continue in force for six days from the date of these presents.

'June 3rd. 1757.

'To all and Singular the King's officers Civil and Military, and to those of all the Princes and States in Alliance with His Majesty.'

In 1758 the complaints of the French Government about the unsatisfactory state of the prisoner exchange system occupy many long letters. 'Il est trop important de laisser subsister une pareille inaction dans les échanges; elle est préjudiciable aux deux Puissances, et fâcheuse aux familles', is one remark. On the other hand, the complaint went from our side that we sent over on one occasion 219 French prisoners, and only got back 143 British, to which the French replied: 'Yes: but your 143 were all sound men, whereas the 219 you sent us were invalids, boys, and strangers to this Department.' By way of postscript the French official described how not long since a Dover boat, having captured two fishing-smacks of Boulogne and St. Valéry, made each boat pay twenty-five guineas ransom, beat the men with swords, and wounded the St. Valéry captain, remarking: 'le procédé est d'autant plus inhumain qu'il a eu lieu de sang-froid et qu'il a été exercé contre des gens qui achetoient leur liberté au prix de toute leur fortune'.

This and other similar outrages on both sides led to the mutual agreement that fishing-boats were to be allowed to pursue their avocation unmolested—an arrangement which in later times, when the business of helping prisoners to escape was in full swing, proved to be a mixed blessing.

I do not think that the above-quoted argument of the French, that in return for sound men we were in the habit of sending the useless and invalids, and that this largely compensated for the apparent disproportion in the numbers exchanged—an argument which they used to the end of the wars between the two nations—is to be too summarily dismissed as absurd. Nor does it seem that our treatment of the poor wretches erred on the side of indulgence, for many letters of complaint are extant, of which the following from a French cartel-ship captain of 1780 is a specimen:

'Combien n'est-il pas d'inhumanité d'envoyer des prisonniers les plus malades, attaqués de fièvre et de dissentoire. J'espère, Monsieur, que vous, connoissant les sentiments les plus justes, que vous voudriez bien donner vos ordres à M. Monckton, agent des prisonniers français, pour qu'il soit donné à mes malades des vivres frais, suivant l'ordinnance de votre Majesté; ou, qu'ils soient mis à l'hôpital.'

It would seem that during the Seven Years' War British merchant-ship and privateer officers were only allowed to be on parole in France if they could find a local person of standing to guarantee the payment of a sum of money to the Government in the case of a breach of parole.

The parole rules in France, so far as regarded the limits assigned to prisoners at their towns of confinement, were not nearly so strict as in England, but, on the other hand, no system of guarantee money like that just mentioned existed in England.

On March 12, 1780, a table of exchange of prisoners of war, with the equivalent ransom rates, was agreed to, ranging from £60 or sixty men for an admiral or field-marshal to £1 or one man for a common sailor or soldier in the regular services, and from £4 or four men for a captain to £1 or one man of privateers and merchantmen.

In 1793 the French Government ordained a sweeping change by abolishing all equivalents in men or money to officers, and decreed that henceforth the exchange should be strictly of grade for grade, and man for man, and that no non-combatants or surgeons should be retained as prisoners of war. How the two last provisions came to be habitually violated is history.

On February 4, 1795, the Admiralty authorized the 'Sick and Hurt' Office to send a representative to France, to settle, if possible, the vexed question of prisoner exchange, and on March 22 Mr. F. M. Eden started for Brest, but was taken on to Roscoff. A week later a French naval officer called on him and informed him that only the Committee of Public Safety could deal with this matter, and asked him to go to Paris. He declined; so the purport of his errand was sent to Paris. A reply invited him to go to Dieppe. Here he met Comeyras, who said that the Committee of Public Safety would not agree to his cartel, there being, they said, a manifest difference between the two countries in that Great Britain carried on the war with the two professions—the navy and the army—and that restoring prisoners to her would clearly be of greater advantage to her than would be the returning of an equal number of men to France, who carried on war with the mass of the people. Moreover, Great Britain notoriously wanted men to replace those she had lost, whilst France had quite enough to enable her to defeat all her enemies.

So Eden returned to Brighthelmstone. Later, a meeting at the *Fountain*, Canterbury, between Otway and Marsh for Britain, and Monnerson for France, was equally fruitless, and it became quite evident that although France was glad enough to get general officers back, she had no particular solicitude for the rank and file, her not illogical argument being that every fighting man, officer or private, was of more value to Britain than were three times their number of Frenchmen to France.

In 1796 many complaints were made by the British cartel-ship masters that upon landing French prisoners at Morlaix their boats were taken from them, they were not allowed to go ashore, soldiers were placed on board to watch them; that directly the prisoners were landed, the ships were ordered to sea, irrespective of the weather; and that they were always informed that there were no British prisoners to take back.

In this year we had much occasion to complain of the one-sided character of the system of prisoner exchange with France, the balance due to Britain in 1796 being no less than 5,000. Cartel after cartel went to France full and came back empty; in one instance only seventy-one British prisoners were returned for 201 French sent over; in another instance 150 were sent and nine were returned, and in another 450 were sent without return.

From the regularity with which our authorities seem to have been content to give without receiving, one cannot help wondering if, after all, there might not have been some foundation for the frequent French retort that while we received sound men, we only sent the diseased, and aged, or boys. Yet the correspondence from our side so regularly and emphatically repudiates this that we can only think that the burden of the prisoners was galling the national back, and that the grumble was becoming audible which later broke out in the articles of the *Statesman*, the *Examiner*, and the *Independent Whig*.

From January 1, 1796, to March 14, 1798, the balance between Britain and Holland stood thus:

Dutch officers returned 316, men 416   732

British officers returned 64, men 290   354

Balance due to us   378

Just at this time there were a great many war-prisoners in England. Norman Cross and Yarmouth were full, and new prison ships were being fitted out at Chatham. The correspondence of the 'Sick and Hurt' Office consisted very largely of refusals to applicants to be allowed to go to France on parole, so that evidently the prisoner exchange was in so unsatisfactory a condition that even the passage of cartel loads of invalids was suspended.

In 1798 an arrangement about the exchange of prisoners was come to between England and France. France was to send a vessel with British prisoners, 5 per cent of whom were to be officers, and England was to do the same. The agents on each side were to select the prisoners. It was also ruled that the prisoners in each country were to be supported by their own country, and that those who were sick, wounded, incapacitated, or boys, should be surrendered without equivalent.

But in 1799 the French Republican Government refused to clothe or support its prisoners in Britain, so that all exchanges of prisoners ceased. Pending the interchange of correspondence which followed the declaration of this inhuman policy, the French prisoners suffered terribly, especially as it was winter, so that in January 1801, on account of the fearful mortality among them, it was resolved that they should be supplied with warm clothing at the public expense, and this was done, the cost being very largely defrayed by voluntary subscriptions in all parts of the Kingdom.

This was not the first or second time that British benevolence had stepped in to stave off the results of French inhumanity towards Frenchmen.

The letter before quoted from the agent at Portchester (p. 18) and the report on Stapleton (p. 19) in the chapter on International Recriminations have reference to this period.

This state of matters continued; the number of French prisoners in Britain increased enormously, for the French Government would return no answers to the continued representations from this side as to the unsatisfactory character of the Exchange question. Yet in 1803 it was stated that although not one British prisoner of war, and only five British subjects, had been returned, no less than 400 French prisoners actually taken at sea had been sent to France.

In 1804 Boyer, an officer at Belfast, wrote to his brother the general, on parole at Montgomery, that the Emperor would not entertain any proposal for the exchange of prisoners unless the Hanoverian army were recognized as prisoners of war. This was a sore topic with Bonaparte. In 1803 the British Government had refused to ratify the condition of the Treaty of Sublingen which demanded that the Hanoverian army, helpless in the face of Bonaparte's sudden invasion of the country, should retire behind the Elbe and engage not to serve against France or her Allies during the war, in other words to agree to their being considered prisoners of war. Bonaparte insisted that as Britain was intimately linked with Hanover through her king she should ratify this condition. Our Government repudiated all interest in Hanover's own affairs: Hanover was forced to yield, but Britain retaliated by blockading the Elbe and the Weser, with the result that Hamburg and Bremen were half ruined.

A form of exchange at sea was long practised of which the following is a specimen:

'We who have hereunto set our names, being a lieutenant and a master of H.B.M.'s ship *Virgin*, do hereby promise on our word of honour to cause two of His Christian Majesty's subjects of the same class who may be Prisoners in England to be set at liberty by way of Exchange for us, we having been taken by the French and set at liberty on said terms, and in case we don't comply therewith we are obliged when called on to do so to return as Prisoners to France. Given under our hands in port of Coruña, July 31, 1762.'

As might be supposed, this easy method of procuring liberty led to much parole breaking on both sides, but it was not until 1812 that such contracts were declared to be illegal.

During 1805 the British Government persisted in its efforts to bring about an arrangement for the exchange of prisoners, but to these efforts the extraordinary reply was:

'Nothing can be done on the subject without a formal order from the Emperor, and under the present circumstances His Imperial Majesty cannot attend to this business.'

The Transport Board thus commented upon this:

'Every proposal of this Government relative to the exchanging of prisoners has been met by that of France with insulting evasion or contemptuous silence. As such [*sic*] it would be derogatory to the honour of the Kingdom to strive further in the cause of Humanity when our motives would be misnamed, and the objects unattained.

'This Board will not take any further steps in the subject, but will rejoice to meet France in any proposal from thence.'

In the same year the Transport Office posted as a circular the Declaration of the French Government not to exchange even aged and infirm British prisoners in France.

In 1806 the Transport Office replied as follows to the request for liberation of a French officer on parole at Tiverton, who cited the release of Mr. Cockburn from France in support of his petition:

'Mr. Cockburn never was a prisoner of war, but was detained in France at the commencement of hostilities contrary to the practise of civilized nations, and so far from the French Government having released, as you say, many British prisoners, so that they might re-establish their health in their own country, only three persons coming under the description have been liberated in return for 672 French officers and 1,062 men who have been sent to France on account of being ill. Even the favour granted to the above mentioned three persons was by the interest of private individuals, and cannot be considered as an act of the Government of that country.'

(A similar reply was given to many other applicants.)

Denmark, like Holland, made no replies to the British Government's request for an arrangement of the exchange of prisoners, and of course, both took their cue from France. In the year 1808 the balance due from

Denmark to Britain was 3,807. There were 1,796 Danish prisoners in England. Between 1808 and 1813 the balance due to us was 2,697. As another result of the French policy, the Transport Office requested the Duke of Wellington in Spain to arrange for the exchange of prisoners on the spot, as, under present circumstances, once a man became a prisoner in France, his services were probably lost to his country for ever. Yet another result was that the prisoners in confinement all over Britain in 1810, finding that the exchange system was practically suspended, became turbulent and disorderly to such an extent, and made such desperate attempts to break out, notably at Portchester and Dartmoor, that it was found necessary to double the number of sentries.

At length in 1810, soon after the marriage of Bonaparte with Marie Louise, an attempt was made at Morlaix to arrange matters, and the Comte du Moustier met Mr. Mackenzie there. Nothing came of it, because of the exorbitant demands of Bonaparte. He insisted that all prisoners—English, French, Spanish, Portuguese, Italians—should be exchanged, man for man, rank for rank, on the same footing as the principal power under whom they fought; in other words, that for 50,000 Frenchmen, only 10,000 British would be returned, the balance being made up of Spanish and Portuguese more or less raw levies, who were not to be compared in fighting value with Englishmen or Frenchmen.

The second section of the fourth article of Mr. Mackenzie's note was:

'All the French prisoners, of whatever rank and quality, at present detained in Great Britain, or in the British possessions, shall be released. The exchange shall commence immediately after the signature of this convention, and shall be made by sending successively to Morlaix, or to any other port in the British Channel that may be agreed on, or by delivering to the French Commissioners, a thousand French prisoners for a thousand English prisoners, as promptly and in the same proportion as the Government shall release the latter.'

As neither party would yield, the negotiations were broken off. The *Moniteur* complained that some one of higher rank than Mr. Mackenzie had not been sent as British representative, and the British paper *The Statesman* commented strongly upon our non-acceptance of Bonaparte's terms, although endorsing our refusal to accede to the particular article about the proportion of the exchange.

General Pillet, before quoted, criticizes the British action in his usual vitriolic fashion. After alluding bitterly to the conduct of the British Government in the matters of San Domingo and the Hanoverian army—both of which are still regarded by French writers as eminent instances of British bad faith, he describes the Morlaix meeting as an 'infamous trap' on the part of our Government.

'We had the greater interest in this negotiation,' he says; we desired exchange with a passion difficult to describe. Well! we trembled lest France should accept conditions which would have returned to their homes all the English prisoners without our receiving back a single Frenchman who was not sick or dying ... it was clearly demonstrated that the one aim of the London Cabinet was to destroy us all, and from this moment it set to work to capture as many prisoners as possible, so that it might almost be said that this was the one object of the War!'

Las Cases quotes Bonaparte's comments in this matter:

'The English had infinitely more French than I had English prisoners. I knew well that the moment they had got back their own they would have discovered some pretext for carrying the exchange no further, and my poor French would have remained for ever in the hulks. I admitted, therefore, that I had much fewer English than they had French prisoners: but then I had a great number of Spanish and Portuguese, and by taking them into account, I had a mass of prisoners considerably greater than theirs. I offered, therefore, to exchange the whole. This proposition at first disconcerted them, *but at length they agreed to it*. But I had my eye on everything. I saw clearly that if they began by exchanging an Englishman against a Frenchman, as soon as they got back their own they would have brought forward something to stop the exchanges. I insisted therefore that 3,000 Frenchmen should be exchanged against 1,000 English and 2,000 Spaniards and Portuguese. They refused this, and so the negotiations broke off.'

Want of space prevents me from quoting the long conversation which was held upon the subject of the Exchange of Prisoners of War between Bonaparte and Las Cases at St. Helena, although it is well worth the study.

As the object of this work is confined to prisoners of war in Britain, it is manifestly beyond its province to discuss at length the vexed questions of the comparative treatment of prisoners in the two countries. I may reiterate that on the whole the balance is fairly even, and that much depended upon local surroundings. Much evidence could be cited to show that in certain French seaports and in certain inland towns set apart for the residence of Bonaparte's *détenus* quite as much brutality was exercised upon British subjects as was exercised upon French prisoners in England. Much depended upon the character of the local commandant; much depended upon the behaviour of the prisoners; much depended upon local sentiment. Bitche, for instance, became known as 'the place of tears' from the misery of the captives there; Verdun, on the other hand, after the tyrannical commandant Virion had made away with himself, was to all appearances a gay, happy, fashionable watering-place. Bitche had a severe commandant, and the class of prisoner there was generally rough and low. Beauchêne was a genial jailer at Verdun, and the mass of the prisoners were well-to-do. So in Britain. Woodriff was disliked at Norman Cross, and all was unhappiness. Draper was beloved, and Norman Cross became quite a place of captivity to be sought after.

CHAPTER III
THE PRISON SYSTEM—THE HULKS

The foreign prisoner of war in Britain, if an ordinary sailor or soldier, was confined either on board a prison ship or in prison ashore. Officers of certain exactly defined ranks were allowed to be upon parole if they chose, in specified towns. Some officers refused to be bound by the parole requirements, and preferred the hulk or the prison with the chance of being able to escape.

Each of these—the Hulks, the Prisons, Parole—will be dealt with separately, as each has its particular characteristics and interesting features.

The prison ship as a British institution for the storage and maintenance of men whose sole crime was that of fighting against us, must for ever be a reproach to us. There is nothing to be urged in its favour. It was not a necessity; it was far from being a convenience; it was not economical; it was not sanitary. Man took one of the most beautiful objects of his handiwork and deformed it into a hideous monstrosity. The line-of-battle ship was a thing of beauty, but when masts and rigging and sails were shorn away, when the symmetrical sweep of her lines was deformed by all sorts of excrescences and superstructures, when her white, black-dotted belts were smudged out, it lay, rather than floated, like a gigantic black, shapeless coffin. Sunshine, which can give a touch of picturesqueness, if not of beauty, to so much that is bare and featureless, only brought out into greater prominence the dirt, the shabbiness, the patchiness of the thing. In fog it was weird. In moonlight it was spectral. The very prison and cemetery architects of to-day strive to lead the eye by their art away from what the mind pictures, but when the British Government brought the prison ship on to the scene they appear to have aimed as much as possible at making the outside reflect the life within.

No amount of investigation, not the most careful sifting of evidence, can blind our eyes to the fact that the British prison hulks were hells upon water. It is not that the mortality upon them was abnormal: it was greater than in the shore prisons, but it never exceeded 3 per cent upon an average, although there were periods of epidemic when it rose much higher. It is that the lives of those condemned to them were lives of long, unbroken suffering. The writer, as an Englishman, would gladly record otherwise, but he is bound to tell the truth, the whole truth, and nothing but the truth. True it is that our evidence is almost entirely that of prisoners themselves, but what is not, is that of English officers, and theirs is of condemnation. It should be borne in mind that the experiences we shall quote are those of officers and gentlemen, or at any rate educated men, and the agreement is so remarkable that it would be opening the way to an accusation of national partiality if we were to refuse to accept it.

The only palliating consideration in this sad confession is that the prisoners brought upon themselves much of the misery. The passion for gambling, fomented by long, weary hours of enforced idleness, wrought far more mischief among the foreign prisoners in England, than did the corresponding northern passion for drink among the British prisoners abroad, if only from the fact that whereas the former, ashore and afloat, could gamble when and where they chose, drink was not readily procurable by the latter. The report of a French official doctor upon prison-ship diseases will be quoted in its proper place, but the two chief causes of disease named by him—insufficient food and insufficient clothing—were very largely the result of the passion for gambling among the prisoners.

A correspondent of *The Times*, December 16, 1807, writes:

'There is such a spirit of gambling existing among the French prisoners lately arrived at Chatham from Norman Cross, that many of them have been almost entirely naked during the late severe weather, having lost their clothes, not even excepting their shirts and small clothes, to some of their fellow prisoners: many of them also are reduced to the chance of starving by the same means, having lost seven or eight days' provisions to their more fortunate companions, who never fail to exact their winnings. The effervescence of mind that this diabolical pursuit gives rise to is often exemplified in the conduct of these infatuated captives, rendering them remarkably turbulent and unruly. Saturday last, a quarrel arose between two of them in the course of play, when one of them, who had lost his clothes and food, received a stab in the back.'

'Gambling among the French prisoners on the several prison-ships in the Medway has arrived at an alarming height. On board the *Buckingham*, where there are nearly 600 prisoners, are a billiard table, hazard tables, &c.; and the prisoners indulge themselves in play during the hours they are allowed for exercise.'

For the chief cause of suffering, medical neglect, there is, unhappily, but little defence, for, if the complaints of neglect, inefficacy, and of actual cruelty, which did manage to reach the august sanctum of the Transport Office were numerous, how many more must there have been which were adroitly prevented from getting there.

Again, a great deal depended upon the prison-ship commander. French writers are accustomed to say that the lieutenants in charge of the British prison ships were the scum of the service—disappointed men, men without interest, men under official clouds which checked their advance; and it must be admitted that at first sight it seems strange that in a time of war all over the world, when promotion must have been rapid, and the chances of distinction frequent, officers should easily be found ready, for the remuneration of seven shillings per diem, plus eighteenpence servant allowance, to take up such a position as the charge of seven or eight hundred desperate foreigners.

But that this particular service was attractive is evident from the constant applications for it from naval men with good credentials, and from the frequent reply of the authorities that the waiting list was full. If we may judge this branch of the service by others, and reading the matter by the light of the times, we can only infer that the Commander of a prison hulk was in the way of getting a good many 'pickings', and that as, according to regulation, no lieutenant of less than ten years' service in that rank could apply for appointment, the berth was regarded as a sort of reward or solatium.

Be that as it may have been, the condition of a prison ship, like the condition of a man-of-war to-day, depended very largely upon the character of her commander. It is curious to note that most of the few testimonies extant from prisoners in favour of prison-ship captains date from that period of the great wars when the ill-feeling between the two countries was most rancorous, and the poor fellows on parole in English inland towns were having a very rough time.

In 1803 the Commandant at Portsmouth was Captain Miller, a good and humane man who took very much to heart the sufferings of the war prisoners under his supervision. He happened to meet among the French naval officers on parole a M. Haguelin of Havre, who spoke English perfectly, and with whom he often conversed on the subject of the hard lot of the prisoners on the hulks. He offered Haguelin a place in his office, which the poor officer gladly accepted, made him his chief interpreter, and then employed him to visit the prison ships twice a week to hear and note complaints with the view of remedying them.

Haguelin held this position for some years. In 1808 an English frigate captured twenty-four Honfleur fishing-boats and brought them and their crews into Portsmouth. Miller regarded this act as a gross violation of the laws of humanity, and determined to undo it. Haguelin was employed in the correspondence which followed between Captain Miller and the Transport Office, the result being that the fishermen were well treated, and finally sent back to Honfleur in an English frigate. Then ensued the episode of the *Flotte en jupons*, described in a pamphlet by one Thomas, when the women of Honfleur came out, boarded the English frigate, and amidst a memorable scene of enthusiasm brought their husbands and brothers and lovers safe to land. When Haguelin was exchanged and was leaving for France, Miller wrote:

'I cannot sufficiently express how much I owe to M. Haguelin for his ceaseless and powerful co-operation on the numerous occasions when he laboured to better the condition of his unfortunate compatriots. The conscientiousness which characterized all his acts makes him deserve well of his country.'

In 1816, Captain (afterwards Baron) Charles Dupin, of the French Corps of Naval Engineers, placed on record a very scathing report upon the treatment of his countrymen upon the hulks at Chatham. He wrote:

'The Medway is covered with men-of-war, dismantled and lying in ordinary. Their fresh and brilliant painting contrasts with the hideous aspect of the old and smoky hulks, which seem the remains of vessels blackened by a recent fire. It is in these floating tombs that are buried alive prisoners of war—Danes, Swedes, Frenchmen, Americans, no matter. They are lodged on the lower deck, on the upper deck, and even on the orlop-deck.... Four hundred malefactors are the maximum of a ship appropriated to convicts. From eight hundred to twelve hundred is the ordinary number of prisoners of war, heaped together in a prison-ship of the same rate.'

The translator of Captain Dupin's report[2] comments thus upon this part of it:

'The long duration of hostilities, combined with our resplendent naval victories, and our almost constant success by land as well as by sea, increased the number of prisoners so much as to render the confinement of a great proportion of them in prison-ships a matter of necessity rather than of choice; there being, in 1814, upwards of 70,000 French prisoners of war in this country.'

About Dupin's severe remarks concerning the bad treatment of the prisoners, their scanty subsistence, their neglect during sickness and the consequent high rate of mortality among them, the translator says:

'The prisoners were well treated in every respect; their provisions were good in quality, and their clothing sufficient; but, owing to their unconquerable propensity to gambling, many of them frequently deprived themselves of their due allowance both of food and raiment. As to fresh air, wind-sails were always pointed below in the prison ships to promote its circulation. For the hulks themselves the roomiest and airiest of two and three deckers were selected, and were cleared of all encumbrances.

'Post-captains of experience were selected to be in command at each port, and a steady lieutenant placed over each hulk. The prisoners were mustered twice a week; persons, bedding, and clothing were all kept clean; the decks were daily scraped and rubbed with sand: they were seldom washed in summer, and never in winter, to avoid damp. Every morning the lee ports were opened so that the prisoners should not be too suddenly exposed to the air, and no wet clothes were allowed to be hung before the ports.

FRENCH SAILORS ON AN ENGLISH PRISON SHIP.

(*After Bombled.*)

'The provisions were minutely examined every morning by the lieutenant, and one prisoner from each mess was chosen to attend to the delivery of provisions, and to see that they were of the right quality and weight. The allowance of food was:

'Each man on each of five days per week received one and a half pounds of wheaten flour bread, half a pound of good fresh beef with cabbage or onions, turnips and salt, and on each of the other two days one pound of good salted cod or herrings, and potatoes. The average number of prisoners on a seventy-four was from six to seven hundred, and this, it should be remembered, on a ship cleared from all encumbrances such as guns, partitions, and enclosures.'

Dupin wrote:

'By a restriction which well describes the mercantile jealousy of a manufacturing people, the prisoners were prohibited from making for sale woollen gloves and straw hats. It would have injured in these petty branches the commerce of His Britannic Majesty's subjects!'

to which the reply was:

'It was so. These "petty branches" of manufactures were the employment of the wives and children of the neighbouring cottagers, and enabled them to pay their rent and taxes: and, on a representation by the magistrates that the vast quantities sent into the market by the French prisoners who had neither rent, nor taxes, nor lodging, firing, food or clothes to find, had thrown the industrious cottagers out of work, an order was sent to stop this manufacture by the prisoners.'

As to the sickness on board the hulks, in reply to Dupin's assertions the Government had the following table drawn up relative to the hulks at Portsmouth in a month of 1813:

Ship's Name.	*Prisoners in Health.*	*Sick.*	
Prothée	583	10	}
Crown	608	3	} = 1½%
San Damaso	726	32	}
Vigilant	590	8	}

Guildford	693	8	}
San Antonio	820	9	}
Vengeance	692	7	}
Veteran	592	7	}
Suffolk	683	6	}
Assistance	727	35	}
Ave Princessa	769	9	}
Kron Princessa	760	4	}
Waldemar	809	1	}
Negro	175	0	}
	9,227	139	

Dupin also published tables of prison mortality in England in confirmation of the belief among his countrymen that it was part of England's diabolic policy to make prisoners of war or to kill or incapacitate them by neglect or ill-treatment. Between 1803 and 1814, the total number of prisoners brought to England was 122,440. Of these, says M. Dupin,

There died in English prisons	12,845
Were sent to France in a dying state	12,787
Returned to France since 1814, their health more or less debilitated	70,041
	95,673

leaving a balance of 26,767, who presumably were tough enough to resist all attempts to kill or wreck them.

To this our authorities replied with the following schedule:

Died in English prisons	10,341
Sent home sick, or on parole or exchanged, those under the two last categories for the most part perfectly sound men	17,607
	27,948

leaving a balance of at least 94,492 sound men; for, not only, as has been said above, were a large proportion of the 17,607 sound men, but no allowance was made in this report for the great number of prisoners who arrived sick or wounded.

The rate of mortality, of course, varied. At Portsmouth in 1812 the mortality on the hulks was about 4 per cent. At Dartmoor in six years and seven months there were 1,455 deaths, which, taking the average number of prisoners at 5,000, works out at a little over 4 per cent annually. But during six months of the years 1809–1810 there were 500 deaths out of 5,000 prisoners at Dartmoor, due to an unusual epidemic and to exceptionally severe weather. With the extraordinary healthiness of the Perth dépôt I shall deal in its proper place.

I have to thank Mr. Neves, editor of the *Chatham News*, for the following particulars relative to Chatham.

'The exact number of prisoners accommodated in these floating prisons cannot be ascertained, but it appears they were moored near the old Gillingham Fort (long since demolished) which occupied a site in the middle of what is now Chatham Dockyard Extension. St. Mary's Barracks, Gillingham, were built during the Peninsular War for the accommodation of French prisoners. There is no doubt that the rate of mortality among the prisoners confined in the hulks was very high, and the bodies were buried on St. Mary's Island on ground which is now the Dockyard Wharf.

(*From a sketch by the author.*)

'In the course of the excavations in connexion with the extension of the Dockyard—a work of great magnitude which was commenced in 1864 and not finished until 1884, and which cost £3,000,000, the remains of many of the French prisoners were disinterred. The bones were collected and brought round to a site within the extension works, opposite Cookham Woods. A small cemetery of about 200 feet square was formed, railed in, and laid out in flower-beds and gravelled pathways. A handsome monument, designed by the late Sir Andrew Clarke, was erected in the centre—the plinth and steps of granite, with a finely carved figure in armour and cloaked, and holding an inverted torch in the centre, under a canopied and groined spire terminating in crockets and gilt finials. In addition to erecting this monument the Admiralty allotted a small sum annually for keeping it in order.

'The memorial bore the following inscription, which was written by the late Sir Stafford Northcote, afterwards Lord Iddesleigh:

Here are gathered together

The remains of many brave soldiers and sailors, who, having been once the foes, and afterwards captives, of England, now find rest in her soil, remembering no more the animosities of war or the sorrows of imprisonment. They were deprived of the consolation of closing their eyes among the countrymen they loved; but they have been laid in an honoured grave by a nation which knows how to respect valour and to sympathize with misfortune.

'The Government of the French Republic was deeply moved by the action of the Admiralty, and its Ambassador in London wrote:

The Government of the Republic has been made acquainted through me with the recent decision taken by the Government of the Queen to assure the preservation of the funeral monument at Chatham, where rest the remains of the soldiers and sailors of the First Empire who died prisoners of war on board the English hulks. I am charged to make known to your lordship that the Minister of Marine has been particularly affected at the initiative taken in this matter by the British Administration. I shall be much obliged to you if you will make known to H.M's Government the sincere feelings of gratitude of the Government of the Republic for the homage rendered to our deceased soldiers.

(Signed) WADDINGTON.

'In 1904 it became necessary again to move the bones of the prisoners of war and they were then interred in the grounds of the new naval barracks, a site being set apart for the purpose near the chapel, where the monument was re-erected. It occupies a position where it can be seen by passers-by. The number of skulls was 506. Quite recently (1910) two skeletons were dug up by excavators of the Gas Company's new wharf at Gillingham, and, there being every reason to believe that they were the remains of French prisoners of war, they were returned to the little cemetery above mentioned.'

MEMORIAL TO FRENCH PRISONERS OF WAR IN THE ROYAL NAVAL BARRACKS, CHATHAM

That a vast system of jobbery and corruption prevailed among the contractors for the food, clothing, and bedding of the prisoners, and, consequently, among those in office who had the power of selection and appointment; and more, that not a tithe of what existed was expressed, is not the least among the many indictments against our nation at this period which bring a flush of shame to the cheek. As has been before remarked, all that printed regulations and ordinance could do to keep matters in proper order was done. What could read better, for instance, than the following official Contracting Obligations for 1797:

'Beer:

to be equal in quality to that issued on H.M.'s ships.

Beef:

to be good and wholesome fresh beef, and delivered in clean quarters.

Cheese:

to be good Gloucester or Wiltshire, or equal in quality.

Pease:

to be of the white sort and good boilers.

Greens:

to be stripped of outside leaves and fit for the copper.

Beer:

every 7 barrels to be brewed from 8 bushels of the strongest amber malt, and 6 or 7 lb. of good hops at £1 18s. per ton.

Bread:

to be equal in quality to that served on H.M.'s ships.'

As if there was really some wish on the part of the authorities to have things in order, the custom began in 1804 for the Transport Board to send to its prison agents and prison-ship commanders this notice:

'I am directed by the Board to desire that you will immediately forward to this office by coach a loaf taken indiscriminately from the bread issued to the prisoners on the day you receive this letter.'

In so many cases was the specimen bread sent pronounced 'not fit to be eaten', that circulars were sent that all prisons and ships would receive a model loaf of the bread to be served out to prisoners, 'made of whole wheaten meal actually and bona fide dressed through an eleven shilling cloth'.

Nor was the regulation quantity less satisfactory than the nominal quality. In 1812 the scale of victualling on prison ships according to the advertisement to contractors was:

Sunday.

1½ lb. bread.

Monday.

½ lb. fresh beef.

Tuesday.

½ lb. cabbage or turnip.

Thursday.

1 ounce Scotch barley.

Saturday.

⅓ ounce salt.

¼ ounce onions.

Wednesday.

1½ lb. bread, 1 lb. good sound herrings, 1 lb. good sound potatoes.

Friday.

1½ lb. bread, 1 lb. good sound cod, 1 lb. potatoes.

In the year 1778 there were 924 American prisoners of war in England. It has been shown before (p. 11) how the fact of their ill-treatment was forcibly taken up by their own Government, but the following extract from a London newspaper further shows that the real cause of their ill-treatment was no secret:

'As to the prisoners who were kept in England' (this is the sequel of remarks about our harsh treatment of American prisoners in America), 'their penury and distress was undoubtedly great, and was much marked *by the fraud and cruelty of those who were entrusted with their government, and the supply of their provisions.* For these persons, who certainly never had any orders for ill-treatment of the prisoners by countenance in it, having, however, not been overlooked with the utmost vigilance, besides their prejudice and their natural cruelty, *considered their offices as only lucrative jobs which were created merely for their emolument.* Whether there was not some exaggeration, as there usually is in these accounts, it is certain that though the subsistence accorded them by Government would indeed have been sufficient, if honestly administered, to have sustained human nature, in the respect to the mere articles of foods, yet the want of clothes, firing, and bedding, with all the other various articles which custom or nature regards as conducive to health and comfort, became practically insupportable in the extremity of the winter. In consequence of the complaint by the prisoners, the matter was very humanely taken up in the House of Peers by Lord Abingdon ... and soon after a liberal subscription was carried on in London and other parts, and this provided a sufficient remedy for the evil.'

On April 13, 1778, a Contractors' Bill was brought in to Parliament by Sir Philip Jenning Clarke 'for the restraining of any person being a Member of the House of Commons, from being concerned himself or any person in trust for him, in any contract made by the Commissioners of H.M.'s Navy or Treasury, the Board of Ordnance, or by any other person or persons for the public service, unless the said contract shall be made at a public bidding'.

The first reading of the Bill was carried by seventy-one to fifty, the second reading by seventy-two to sixty-one. Success in the Lords was therefore regarded as certain. Yet it was actually lost by two votes upon the question of commitment, and the exertion of Government influence in the Bill was taken to mean a censure on certain Treasury officials.

So things went on in the old way. Between 1804 and 1808 the evil state of matters was either so flagrant that it commanded attention, or some fearless official new broom was doing his duty, for the records of these years abound with complaints, exposures, trials, and judgements.

We read of arrangements being discussed between contractors and the stewards of prison ships by which part of the statutory provisions was withheld from the prisoners; of hundreds of suits of clothing sent of one size, of boots supposed to last eighteen months which fell to pieces during the first wet weather; of rotten hammocks, of blankets so thin that they were transparent; of hundreds of sets of handcuffs being returned as useless; of contractors using salt water in the manufacture of bread instead of salt, and further, of these last offenders being prosecuted, not for making unwholesome bread, but for defrauding the Revenue! Out of 1,200 suits of clothes ordered to be at Plymouth by October 1807, as provision for the winter, by March 1808 only 300 had been delivered!

Let us take this last instance and consider what it meant.

It meant, firstly, that the contractor had never the smallest intention of delivering the full number of suits. Secondly, that he had, by means best known to himself and the officials, received payment for the whole. Thirdly, that hundreds of poor wretches had been compelled to face the rigour of an English winter on the hulks in a half naked condition, to relieve which very many of them had been driven to gambling and even worse crimes.

And all the time the correspondence of the Transport Office consists to a large extent of rules and regulations and provisions and safeguards against fraud and wrong-doing; moral precepts accompany inquiry about a missing guard-room poker, and sentimental exhortations wind up paragraphs about the letting of grazing land or the acquisition of new chimney-pots. Agents and officials are constantly being reminded and advised and lectured and reproved. Money matters of the most trifling significance are carefully and minutely dealt with. Yet we know that the war-prison contract business was a festering mass of jobbery and corruption, that large fortunes were made by contractors, that a whole army of small officials and not a few big ones throve on the 'pickings' to be had.

Occasionally, a fraudulent contractor was brought up, heavily fined and imprisoned; but such cases are so rare that it is hard to avoid the suspicion that their prominence was a matter of expediency and policy, and that many a rascal who should have been hanged for robbing defenceless foreigners of the commonest rights of man had means with which to defeat justice and to persist unchecked in his unholy calling. References to this evil will be made in the chapter dealing with prisons ashore, in connexion with which the misdeeds of contractors seem to have been more frequent and more serious than with the hulks.

If it is painful for an Englishman to be obliged to write thus upon the subject of fraudulent contractors, their aiders and abettors, still more so is it to have to confess that a profession even more closely associated with the cause of humanity seems to have been far too often unworthily represented.

Allusion has been made to the unanimity of foreign officer-prisoners about the utter misery of prison-ship life, but in nothing is their agreement more marked than their condemnation, not merely of our methods of treatment of the sick and wounded, but of the character of the prison-ship doctors. Always bearing in mind that Britain treated her own sailors and soldiers as if they were vicious animals, and that the sickbay and the cockpit of a man-of-war of Nelson's day were probably not very much better than those described by Smollett in *Roderick Random*, which was written in 1748, there seems to have been an amount of gratuitous callousness and cruelty practised by the medical officers attached to the hulks which we cannot believe would have been permitted upon the national ships.

And here again the Government Regulations were admirable on paper: the one point which was most strongly insisted upon being that the doctors should live on board the vessels, and devote the whole of their time to their duties, whereas there is abundant evidence to show that most of the doctors of the Portsmouth, Plymouth, and Chatham hulks carried on private practices ashore and in consequence lived ashore.

More will be found upon this unhappy topic in the next chapter of records of life on the hulks, but we may fittingly close the present with the report upon hulk diseases by Dr. Fontana, French Officer of Health to the Army of Portugal, written upon the *Brunswick* prison ship at Chatham in 1812, and published as an appendix to Colonel Lebertre's book upon English war-prison life.

He divides the diseases into three heads:

(1) *External*, arising from utter want of exercise, from damp, from insufficient food—especially upon the 'maigre' days of the week—and from lack of clothing. Wounds on the legs, which were generally bare, made bad ulcers which the 'bourreaux' of English doctors treated with quack remedies such as the unguent basilicon. He describes the doctor of the *Fyen* prison hospital-ship as a type of the English ignorant and brutal medical man.

(2) *Scorbutic diathesis*, arising from the ulcers and tumours on the lower limbs, caused by the breathing of foul air from twelve to sixteen hours a day, by overcrowding, salt food, lack of vegetables, and deprivation of all alcohol.

(3) *Chest troubles*—naturally the most prevalent, largely owing to moral despair caused by humiliations and cruelties, and deprivations inflicted by low-born, uneducated brutes, miserable accommodation, the foul exhalations from the mud shores at low water, and the cruel treatment by doctors, who practised severe bleedings, prescribed no dieting except an occasional mixture, the result being extreme weakness. When the patient was far gone in disease he was sent to hospital, where more bleeding was performed, a most injudicious use of mercury made, and his end hastened.

The great expense of the hulks, together with the comparative ease with which escape could be made from them, and the annually increasing number of prisoners brought to England, led to the development of the Land Prison System. It was shown that the annual expense of a seventy-four, fitted to hold 700 prisoners, was £5,869. Dartmoor Prison, built to hold 6,000 prisoners, cost £135,000, and the annual expense of it was £2,862: in other words, it would require eight seventy-fours at an annual expense of £46,952 to accommodate this number of prisoners.

The hulks were retained until the end of the great wars, and that they were recognized by the authorities as particular objects of aversion and dread seems to be evident from the fact that incorrigible offenders from the land prisons were sent there, as in the case of the wholesale transfer to them in 1812 of the terrible 'Romans' from Dartmoor, and from the many letters written by prisoners on board the hulks praying to be sent to prison on land, of which the following, from a French officer on a Gillingham hulk to Lady Pigott, is a specimen:

H.M.S. *Sampson.*

'MY LADY:

'Je crains d'abuser de votre bonté naturelle et de ce doux sentiment de compation qui vous fait toujours prendre pitié des malheureux, mais, Madame, un infortuné sans amis et sans soutiens se réfugie sous les auspices des personnes généreuses qui daignent le plaindre, et vous avez humainement pris part à mes maux. Souffrez donc que je vous supplie encore de renouveler vos demandes en ma faveur, si toutefois cette demande ne doit pas être contraire à votre tranquillité personnelle. Voilà deux ans que je suis renfermé dans cette prison si nuisible à ma santé plus chancellante et plus débile que jamais. Voilà six ans et plus que je suis prisonnier sans espoir qu'un sort si funeste et si peu mérité finisse. Si je n'ai pas mérité la mort, et si on ne veut pas me la donner, il faut qu'on me permette de retourner m'isoler à terre, où je pourrais alors dans la tranquillité vivre d'une manière plus convenable à ma faible constitution, et résister au malheur, pour vous prouver, my lady, que quand j'ai commis la faute pour laquelle je souffre tant, ce fut beaucoup plus par manque d'expérience que par vice du cœur.

'JEAN-AUGUSTE NEVEU.'

1812.

This letter was accompanied by a certificate from the doctor of the *Trusty* hospital ship, and the supplicant was noted to be sent to France with the first batch of invalids.

Many of the aforementioned letters are of the most touching description, and if some of them were shown to be the clever concoctions of desperate men, there is a genuine ring about most which cannot fail to move our pity. Lady Pigott was one of the many admirable English women who interested themselves in the prisoners, and who, as usual, did so much of the good work which should have been done by those paid to do it. It is unfortunate for our national reputation that so many of the reminiscences of imprisonment in England which have come down to us have been those of angry, embittered men, and that so little written testimony exists to the many great and good and kindly deeds done by English men and women whose hearts went out to the unfortunate men on the prison ships, in the prisons, and on parole, whose only crime was having fought against us. But that there were such acts is a matter of history.

CHAPTER IV
LIFE ON THE HULKS

From a dozen accounts by British, American, and French writers I have selected the following, as giving as varied a view as possible of this phase of the War Prison system.

The first account is by the Baron de Bonnefoux, who was captured with the *Belle Poule* in the West Indies by the *Ramillies*, Captain Pickmore in 1806, was allowed on parole at Thame and at Odiham, whence he broke parole, was captured, and taken to the *Bahama* at Chatham.

When Bonnefoux was at Chatham, there were five prison ships moored under the lee of Sheppey between Chatham and Sheerness. He describes the interior arrangements of a hulk, but it resembles exactly that of the painter Garneray whose fuller account I give next.

Writing in 1835, the Baron says:

'It is difficult to imagine a more severe punishment; it is cruel to maintain it for an indefinite period, and to submit to it prisoners of war who deserve much consideration, and who incontestably are the innocent victims of the fortune of war. The British prison ships have left profound impressions on the minds of the Frenchmen who have experienced them; an ardent longing for revenge has for long moved their hearts, and even to-day when a long duration of peace has created so much sympathy between the two nations, erstwhile enemies, I fear that, should this harmony between them be disturbed, the remembrance of these horrible places would be reawakened.'

Very bitterly does the Baron complain of the bad and insufficient food, and of the ill-fitting, coarse, and rarely renewed clothing, and he is one of those who branded the commanders of the prison ships as the 'rebuts'—the 'cast-offs' of the British navy.

The prisoners on the *Bahama* consisted largely of privateer captains, the most restless and desperate of all the prisoners of war, men who were socially above the common herd, yet who had not the *cachet* of the regular officers of the navy, who regarded themselves as independent of such laws and regulations as bound the latter, and who were also independent in the sense of being sometimes well-to-do and even rich men. At first there was an inclination among some of these to take Bonnefoux down as an 'aristo'; they 'tutoyer'd' him, and tried to make him do the fagging and coolie work which, on prison ships as in schools, fell to the lot of the new-comer.

But the Baron from the first took up firmly the position of an officer and a gentleman, and showed the rough sea-dogs of the Channel ports that he meant it, with the result that they let him alone.

Attempted escapes were frequent. Although under constant fear of the lash, which was mercilessly used in the British army at this time, the soldiers of the guard were ready enough to sell to the prisoners provisions, maps, and instruments for effecting escape. One day in 1807 five of the prisoners attempted to get off in the empty water casks which the Chatham contractor took off to fill up. They got safely enough into the water boat, unknown of course to its occupants (so it seems, at any rate, in this case, although there was hardly a man who had dealings with the hulks who would not help the prisoners to escape for money), but at nightfall the boat anchored in mid-stream; one of the prisoners got stuck in his water-cask and called for aid; this was heard by the cabin-boy, who gave the alarm, the result being that the prisoners were hauled out of their hiding places, taken on board, and got ten days Black Hole. The Black Hole was a prison six feet square at the bottom of the hold, to which air only came through round holes not big enough for the passage of a mouse. Once and once only in the twenty-four hours was this *cachot* visited for the purpose of bringing food and taking away the latrine box. Small wonder that men often went mad and sometimes died during a lengthened confinement, and that those who came out looked like corpses.

The above-mentioned men were condemned to pay the cost of their capture, and, as they had no money, were put on half rations!

The time came round for the usual sending of aged and infirm prisoners to shore prisons. One poor chap sold his right to go to Bonnefoux, and he and his friend Rousseau resolved to escape en route. Bonnefoux, however, was prevented from going, as his trunk had arrived from Odiham and he was required to be present to verify its contents.

In December 1807, three Boulogne men cut a hole just above the water near the forward sentry box on the guard gallery which ran round the outside of the ship, and escaped. Others attempted to follow, but one of them cried out from the extreme cold, was fired at and hauled on board. Three managed to get off to Dover and Calais, one stuck in the mud and was drowned, and the Baron says that the captain of the *Bahama* allowed him to remain there until he rotted away, as a deterrent to would-be imitators.

Milne, captain of the *Bahama*, the Baron says, was a drunken brute who held orgies on board at which all sorts of loose and debased characters from the shore attended. Upon one occasion a fire was caused by these revels, and the captain, who was drunk, gave orders that the prisoners should be shot at should the fire approach them, rather than that they should escape.

A rough code of justice existed between the prisoners for the settlement of differences among themselves. One Mathieu, a privateersman, kept a small tobacco stall. A soldier, who already had a long bill running with him, wanted tobacco on credit. Mathieu refused; the soldier snatched some tobacco off the stall, Mathieu struck him with a knife and wounded him badly. Mathieu was a very popular character, but justice had to be done, even to a captive. Luckily the soldier recovered, and Mathieu got off with indemnification.

During the very bad weather of March 1808, the sentries ordinarily on the outer gallery were taken on board. To this gallery a boat was always made fast, and the Baron, Rousseau, and another resolved to escape by it. So they cut the painter and got off, using planks for oars, with holes in them for handhold. They reached land safely, and hid all day in a field, feeding on provisions they had brought from the *Bahama*. At nightfall they started, and, meeting a countryman, asked the way to Chatham. 'Don't go there,' he replied, 'the bridge is guarded, and you will be arrested.' One of the prisoners, not knowing English, only caught the last word, and, thinking it was 'arrêtez', drew a piece of fencing foil, with which each was armed, and threatened the man. The others saved him, and in recognition he directed them to a village whence they could cross the Medway. They walked for a long time until they were tired, and reaching a cottage, knocked for admission. A big man came to the door. They asked hospitality, and threatened him in case of refusal. 'My name is Cole,' said the man, 'I serve

God, I love my neighbour, I can help you. Depend on me.' They entered and were well entertained by Cole's wife and daughter, and enjoyed the luxury of a night's rest in a decent bed. Next morning, Cole showed them how to reach the Dover road across the river, and with much difficulty was persuaded to accept a guinea for his services.

Such instances of pity and kindness of our country people for escaped prisoners are happily not rare, and go far to counterbalance the sordid and brutal treatment which in other cases they received.

That evening the fugitives reached Canterbury, and, after buying provisions, proceeded towards Dover, and slept in a barn. Freedom seemed at hand when from Dover they had a glimpse of the French coast, but fortune still mocked them, for they sought in vain along the beach for a boat to carry them over. Boats indeed were there, but all oars, sails, and tackle had been removed from them in accordance with Government advice circulated in consequence of the frequent escapes of French officers on parole by stealing long-shore boats.

So they went on to Deal, and then to Folkestone. Here they were recognized as escaping prisoners and were pursued, but they ran and got safely away. They held a consultation and decided to go to Odiham in Hampshire, where all of them had friends among the officers on parole there, who would help them with money. The writer here describes the great sufferings they underwent by reason of the continuous bad weather, their poor clothing, their footsoreness, and their poverty. By day they sheltered in ditches, woods, and under hedges, and journeyed by night, hungry, wet to the skin, and in constant dread of being recognized and arrested. For some unknown reason, instead of pushing westward for their destination they went back to Canterbury, thence to London, then via Hounslow Heath to Odiham, where they arrived more dead than alive, shoeless, their clothing in rags, and penniless. At Odiham they went to one of the little houses on the outskirts of the town, built especially for French prisoners. This house belonged to a Mr. R——, and here the three men remained hidden for eight days. Suddenly the house was surrounded by armed men, the Baron and his companions were arrested and put into the lock-up. Céré, a friend of the Baron's, believed that R—— had betrayed them, and challenged him. A duel was fought in which R—— was badly wounded, and when he recovered he found that feeling among the

Frenchmen in Odiham was so strong, that the Agent sent him away to Scotland under a false name. At Odiham lock-up, Sarah Cooper, an old friend of the Baron's when he was on parole there, who had helped him to get away, came to see him and left him a note in which she said she would help him to escape, and would not leave him until she had taken him to France. The escape was planned, Sarah contrived to get him a rope ladder and had a conveyance ready to take him away, but just as his foot was on the ladder the police got the alarm, he was arrested, chained, and shut up in the *cachot*.

For three days the Baron remained in irons, and then was marched to Chatham, so closely watched by the guards that every night the prisoner's clothes and boots were removed, and were not returned until the morning. They went to Chatham by way of London where they were confined in the Savoy prison, then used for British deserters. These men were friendly to the Frenchmen. All of them had been flogged, one had received 1,100 lashes, and was to receive 300 more.

On May 1, 1808, the unfortunate men found themselves once more on the *Bahama*, with a sentence of ten days in the Black Hole.

Captain Milne of the *Bahama* was exasperated at these escapes, and attempts to escape, and was brutal in his endeavours to get hold of the tools with which the prisoners had worked. He tried the effect of starvation, but this only fanned the spirit of revolt in the ship, the state of life in which became very bad, threats, disputes, quarrels and duels being of everyday occurrence. The climax came when bad weather prevented the delivery of bread, and the prisoners were put on biscuit. They assembled in the *parc*, the open space between the two batteries, forty feet square, and declared they would not disperse until other provisions were served out. Milne was mad with anger and drink, and ordered the soldiers to fire upon the prisoners, but the young officer in command would not respect the order, and, instead, counselled a more moderate action. Bonnefoux managed to calm the prisoners, and determined personally to interview Milne, and represented to him that to compel eight hundred desperate, hungry men to descend from the *parc* would mean bloodshed. The captain yielded, and peace was temporarily assured.

However, more hole-boring was discovered; Rousseau, the Baron's friend, slipped overboard and swam away, but was captured just as he was landing; the result being that the watch kept was stricter than ever.

The Baron here dilates upon the frightful immorality of the life on the *Bahama*. He says:

'Il n'existait ni crainte, ni retenue, ni amour-propre dans la classe qui n'avait pas été dotée des bienfaits de quelque éducation. On y voyait donc régner insolemment l'immoralité la plus perverse, les outrages les plus honteux à la pudeur et les actes les plus dégoûtants, le cynisme le plus effronté, et dans ce lieu de misère générale une misère plus grande encore que tout ce qu'on peut imaginer.'

There were three classes of prisoners.

(1) Les Raffalés. (2) Les Messieurs ou Bourgeois. (3) Les Officiers.

The Raffalés were the lowest, and lowest of the Raffalés were the 'Manteaux impériaux.' These had nothing in the world but one covering, which swarmed with lice, hence the facetious allusion in their name to the bees of the Imperial Mantle. These poor wretches eat nothing during the day, for their gambling left them nothing to eat, but at night they crept about picking up and devouring the refuse of the food. They slept packed closely side by side on the deck. At midnight the officer of the evening gave the word, 'Par le flanc droit!' and all turned on to their right sides. At 3 a.m. the word rang out 'Pare à virer!'[3] and all turned on to their left sides.

They gambled with dice for their rations, hammocks, clothes, anything, and the winners sold for two sous what often was worth a franc. They had a chief who was fantastically garbed, and a drummer with a wooden *gamelle*. Sometimes they were a terror to the other prisoners, but could always be appeased with something to gamble with.

Bonnefoux's companions worked in wood and straw. The *Bahama* had been captured from the Spaniards and was built of cedar, and the wood extracted by the prisoners in making escape holes they worked into razor-boxes and toilette articles. Bonnefoux himself gave lessons in French, drawing, mathematics, and English, and published an English Grammar, a copy of which is at Paris, in the Bibliothèque Nationale.

Gradually the spread of the taste for education had a refining and civilizing effect on board the *Bahama*, and when Bonnefoux finally obtained parole leave, the condition of affairs was very much improved.

In June 1809 the Baron left the *Bahama* for Lichfield, and with him was allowed to go one Dubreuil, a rough typical privateer captain, who never had any money, but had a constant craving for tobacco. He had been kind to Colonel and Mrs. Campbell, whom he had taken prisoners, and who had promised to befriend him should luck turn against him. Bonnefoux had helped him pecuniarily, and in return Dubreuil promised to teach him how to smoke through his eyes!

The next relation is that of Louis Garneray, a marine painter of some note, specimens of whose work during his nine years' captivity in England may still be found in Portsmouth and its neighbourhood, and one at least of whose later pictures is in the Marine Gallery of the Paris Louvre.

What follows is an analysis in brief of his book *Mes Pontons* (which is, so far as I am aware, the most complete picture of life on a prison ship yet published), and, being but a brief analysis, is incomplete as to numberless most interesting details, so that I would recommend any reader who wishes to be minutely informed upon the subject to read the original volume of 320 pages. It is caustically, even savagely written, but nine years cut out of a young man's life cannot serve to sweeten his disposition.

In May 1806 Garneray, who had been captured in the West Indies, was taken on board the hulk *Prothée* at Portsmouth, stripped, plunged into a cold bath, and clothed in an ill-fitting orange-yellow suit, on the back of which the large letters T. O. proclaimed him as under the care of the Transport Office. He describes the *Prothée*,—as he is hustled into the mob of 'dead people come out for a moment from their graves, hollow-eyed, earthy complexioned, round backed, unshaven, their frames barely covered with yellow rags, their bodies frightfully thin,'—as a black, shapeless sarcophagus, of which the only parts open to air was the space between the fo'c'sle and the poop and the fo'c'sle itself, which was unbearable from the smoke of the many chimneys on it. Each end of the ship was occupied by the garrison, the officers aft and the soldiers forward. A stout barrier divided the guard from the prisoners, which was so garnished with heavy-headed nails as to seem like iron, and was fitted with loop-holes for inspection, and, if needs be, for firing through. On the lower deck and in the lower battery were packed seven hundred human beings.

Only one ladder communicated between the lower deck and the lower battery. In the latter the only daylight came through port-holes, in the former through narrow scuttles, all of which had iron gratings.

All round the ship, just above the water-line, ran a gallery with open-work floor, and along this paced three sentries by day and seven by night. The ship was commanded by a lieutenant and a master, and was garrisoned by forty or fifty soldiers under a marine officer and about twenty sailors. The day guard consisted of three sentries on the gallery, one on the ladder communicating with the battery, one on the fo'c'sle, one on each gangway, and on the poop a dozen armed men ready for instant action. At night there were seven sentries on the gallery, one on the battery ladder; an officer, a sergeant, a corporal, and a dozen sailors were continually moving round, and every quarter of an hour the 'All's well' rang out.

The ship's boats were slung ten feet above the water, and one was chained to the gallery aft.

At 6 a.m. in summer and 8 in winter, the port-holes were opened, and the air thus liberated was so foul that the men opening the port-holes invariably jumped back immediately. At 6 p.m. in summer and 2 p.m. in winter, every wall and grating was sounded with iron bars, and one hour later all the prisoners were driven on deck and counted.

GARNERAY DRAWING AN ENGLISH SOLDIER.

(*After Louis Garneray.*)

The only furniture in the ship was a bench along each side and four in the middle, the prisoners squatting on deck at mess time. Each prisoner on arrival received a hammock, a thin coverlet, and a hair mattress weighing from two to three pounds. For a long time no distinction was made between officers and men, but latterly a special ship was allowed for officers. Some idea of the crowding on board may be gained from the facts that each battery, 130 feet long, 40 feet broad, and 6 feet high, held nearly 400 prisoners, and that the hammocks were so closely slung that there was no room to sleep on deck.

The alimentation of the prisoners, humane and ample as it looks on paper, seems to have been a gross sham. Not only did the contractors cheat in quality and quantity, but what with forfeitures on account of breaches of discipline, and observance of the law imposed by the prisoners on themselves, that, deductions or no deductions, no man should have a larger ration than another, and contributions to men planning to escape, it was impossible for all to touch full rations.

The prisoners elected their own cooks, and nominally a committee of fifteen prisoners was allowed to attend at the distribution to see that quality and quantity were just, but the guards rarely allowed them to do so. Six men formed a mess; no spoons, knives or forks were supplied, merely bowls and pannikins. The fish supplied on 'maigre' days—Wednesdays and Fridays—was usually uneatable, and the prisoners often sold the herrings at a penny each to the purveyors, who kept them for redistribution, so that it was said that some herrings had done duty for ten years! With the money thus made the prisoners bought butter or cheese. The cod they re-cooked; the bread was filthy and hard. Complaints were useless, and the result was constant hunger.

All but the Raffalés, the scum, occupied themselves with trades or professions. There were tobacco manufacturers, professors of dancing, fencing, and stick-play, who charged one sou for a lesson, which often lasted an hour. Mathematics and languages were taught at the same rate. Whilst these and many other occupations were busy, up and down the battery passed the 'merchants' crying their wares, hungry men who offered their rags for sale, menders of shoes, and the occupants of favourable positions in the battery inviting bids for them, so that despite the rags and the hunger and the general misery, there was plenty of sound and movement, and general evidence of that capability for adapting themselves to circumstance which so invariably distinguished the French prisoners in England from the British prisoners in France.

Garneray's chief friend on board was a sturdy Breton privateer Captain named Bertaud. Bertaud hated the English fiercely, and, being somewhat of a bruiser, had won the esteem of his companions quite as much by his issue of the following challenge as by his personal qualities.

'Challenge to the English! Long live French Brittany! The undersigned Bertaud, native of Saint-Brieuc, annoyed at hearing the English boast that they are the best boxers in the world, which is a lie, will fight any two of them, in any style with fists, but not to use legs.

'He will also, in order to prove his contempt for these boasters, receive from his two adversaries ten blows with the fist before the fight wherever his adversaries choose, and afterwards he will thrash them. Simply, he stipulates that as soon as he has received the ten blows and before the fight begins he shall be paid two pounds sterling to compensate him for the teeth which shall have been broken.

'Done on board the *Prothée* where Bertaud mopes himself to death!'

Garneray calls him a madman, and says that the ten blows alone will do for him. What is his game?

'I shall pocket two pounds, and that will go into our escape fund,' replied the Breton laughing.

Garneray and Bertaud had been saving up for some time for the escape they resolved to attempt, and, although Bertaud's challenge was not taken up, they at last owned forty-five shillings, to which Garneray's writing lessons at a shilling each to the little girl of the *Prothée's* commander chiefly contributed. Each made himself a bag of tarred cloth to hold clothes and provisions, they had bored a hole through the ship's side large enough to slip through, and only waited for a dark quiet night. As it was the month of July this soon came. Bertaud got through first, Garneray was on the point of following when a challenge rang out, followed by a musket-shot, and peeping through the hole, to his horror he saw poor Bertaud suspended over the water by the cord of his bag which had caught in an unnoticed nail in the ship's side. Then was a terrible thing done. The soldiers hammered the helpless Frenchman with their musket butts, Garneray heard the fall of something heavy in the water; there was silence; then as if by magic the whole river was lit up, and boats from all the other vessels put off for the *Prothée*. Garneray slipped back to his hammock, but was presently turned out with all the other prisoners to be counted. His anxiety about the fate of his friend made him ask a sailor, who replied brutally, 'Rascal, how should I know? So far as I am concerned I wish every Frenchman was at the bottom of the sea!' For a consideration of a shilling, however, the man promised to find out, and told Garneray that the poor Breton had received three bayonet thrusts, a sabre-cut on the head, and musket-butt blows elsewhere, but that the dog still breathed! For twenty days the man gave his shilling bulletins, and then announced that the Breton was convalescent.

Garneray and Bertaud made another attempt some months later. Garneray had saved money he had earned by drawing designs for the straw-workers among the prisoners, who had hitherto not gone beyond birds and flowers, and who readily paid for his ships in full sail and other marine objects.

It was mid-winter and bitterly cold, so the two adventurers prepared themselves by rubbing themselves with oil saved from the little lamp by which Garneray taught his pupils. Without attracting notice they slipped overboard, and swam for the muddy shore of an island. This they crossed on *patins* which Bertaud had provided, and reached the river by Gosport. Only occasional pulls at the rum flask prevented them from perishing with cold, and their second swim nearly cost both of them their lives. Each in turn had to support the other, and they were on the point of giving up when they reached an anchored vessel. Here a watchdog greeted them, and kept up his barking until he aroused the crew, who hailed them in what they thankfully recognized to be broken English. Alas! Their joy was short-lived. The skipper of the vessel was a Dane, and so far from promising to help them declared he would send them back to the hulk, abusing them violently. This was too much for the fiery Breton, who, seizing a knife, sprang upon the Dane and bore him to the ground. They tied and gagged him, and, said Bertaud, 'Now let us be off!'

But Garneray declared himself too exhausted to attempt another swim, even for liberty, and said he would go back to the hulk. The prospect of this was too horrible for Bertaud. 'Better be drowned and be done with it,' said he, 'than live to be killed by inches,' and before Garneray could remonstrate, to the amazement of the Danish sailors, he sprang overboard.

At four the next morning the Danes brought Garneray back to the *Prothée*. Instantly, although he was wet through and half dead with cold, he was put into the *cachot*, and but for the fact that the carpenters had been working there and had left a pile of shavings, amongst which he nestled, he could not have lived through the night. Next day he was released and sent back to the battery, but no fresh clothes were issued to him, and but for the charity of his fellow prisoners he would have gone naked.

Seeing all the prisoners peering excitedly through the grated port-holes, Garneray, sick in his hammock, asked the reason: 'See, the crows!' was the reply.

He joined the onlookers, and describes his feelings when he saw stretched on the mud of the Portchester river the body of Bertaud, already an attraction for the crows. On the brutal scene which followed, the dragging of the body to the ship, and the utterly inhuman response made to Garneray's prayer for the decent treatment of his friend's remains, it is as unnecessary as it is distasteful to dwell.

Garneray was now changed from the *Prothée* to the *Crown*—a ship with a bad reputation among the prisoners.

Captain R—— of the *Crown* was a brute in every sense of the word, and the prisoners maddened him by winning for the *Crown* the reputation of being the most unmanageable, because the worst managed, hulk in Portchester River. Bully, sot, and coward as he was, he by no means had his own way. On one occasion five prisoners escaped. Although it was mid-winter and snowing, R—— had the muster of half-clad wretches made in the open. The number could never be made right, and count after count was made, during a space of three days. The whole affair was a cleverly concocted device to gain for the escaped men time to get safely away. A master-carpenter among the prisoners had cut a means of communication between two of the batteries, through which, unseen by the authorities, men could slip from one to the other, get on deck, and so swell or diminish the muster roll as arranged. The trick was not discovered, but that there was a trick was evident, and R—— was determined to be revenged. He summoned the floating fire-engines in harbour, and, although it was mid-winter, actually pumped icy water into the lower deck and batteries until they were drenched, as well as the prisoners, their hammocks, and their clothes.

THE CROWN HULK, SEEN FROM THE STERN.

(*After Louis Garneray.*)

On another occasion when for counting purposes those on the *Crown* were transferred *en masse* on board the *San Antonio*, they returned to find that during their temporary absence R—— had actually, 'as a measure of precaution,' he said, destroyed all the tools and implements and books which the prisoners used in their poor little occupations and trades, and among them Garneray's canvases, easels, brushes, and colours. The immediate result was a stupor of impotent rage; this gave way to open insubordination, insult, and such a universal paroxysm of indignation that even R—— was cowed, and actually made a show of leniency, offering terms of mediation which were scornfully rejected.

Garneray relates another boxing episode with great gusto. A certain Colonel S——, belonging to a well-known English family, came to visit Captain R—— accompanied by a colossal negro, gorgeously arrayed, called Little White, and a splendid Danish hound. His purpose was to match Little White against a French boxer for the entertainment of his fashionable friends ashore. At first sight there would seem to be very poor sport in the pitting of a well-fed, well-trained giant against even the fittest champion of a crowd of half-clad, half-starved, wholly untrained prisoners of war. Although the real object of the gallant Colonel was to show off his black pet, and to charm the beauty and fashion of Portsmouth with an exhibition of prowess, to prove that he was simply animated by a love of sport, he had the consent of R—— that the prisoner champion should be prepared in some way for the contest by extra feeding and so forth.

Robert Lange, a quiet, inoffensive Breton with a quenchless hatred of the English, and a reputed athlete, at once accepted the challenge, especially as the (to him) enormous prize of twenty guineas was being offered.

The day appointed for the contest came. Great preparations had been made on the poop of the *Crown* for the reception of the fashionable company invited to assist at the spectacle of Colonel S——'s black knocking out in the first round, and probably killing, a Frenchman.

Colonel S—— arrived, and with him Little White and the big dog, and flotillas of boats brought out the company, largely consisting of ladies, 'parées avec ce luxe éclatant et de mauvais goût si essentiellement britannique,' who settled themselves on the stand rigged up for the occasion, in laughing and chattering anticipation of something funny.

Robert Lange was playing cards below when he was told that the entertainment was only wanting him. Very coolly he sent word back that he would come as soon as he had finished his hand, and nothing would induce him to hurry. Captain R—— wanted to put Lange into the *cachot* at once for this impertinence, but Colonel S—— calmed him by assuring him that it was the custom in England to grant any indulgence to a man condemned to die.

Meanwhile Little White divested himself of his gorgeous flunkey dress, and the appearance of his magnificent physique caused a chorus of admiration for him, and of pity for the presumptuous Frenchman, to burst from the company.

In due course Robert Lange slouched up, his hands in his pockets, a pipe in his mouth, and his cotton cap on the back of his head. His appearance brought out a murmur of disappointment from the visitors, who considered they were being made the victims of one of Colonel S———'s famous hoaxes. The murmurs turned to smiles when Robert confessed ignorance about seconds, and asked what a watch was wanted for. However, these things being explained to him, he chose Garneray and a fellow Breton as seconds, told Garneray to pocket the magnificent watch which the Colonel offered him, said he was ready for the dance to begin, and placed himself in a fighting position which occasioned roars of laughter from the polite crowd.

'I'm beginning to lose my temper at the mockery of these fools,' said Lange to Garneray; 'what are they waiting for?'

'Colonel,' said Garneray, 'my man is ready. May we begin?'

'There is just one formality customary on these occasions,' replied the Colonel. 'The combatants ought to shake hands to show there is no ill-feeling between them.'

The big black thrust forward his hand saying, 'Shake my hand with respect. It has bowled over many a Frenchman.'

At this gratuitous insult, which the English applauded, a thrill of indignation agitated the crowd of French prisoners.

'What does this chap say?' asked Lange of Garneray.

Garneray told him. Instantly there sprang into his face and into his eyes a light of anger very unusual to him, and what Garneray feared was that the furious Breton would violate the laws of combat and spring upon the negro before the latter had taken up his fighting position. But it was not so. Let me translate Garneray's description of what followed: 'At length Robert Lange seized the negro's hand. Their hands entwined, their gaze fixed, their inflamed faces close together, the two combatants motionless, resembled a marble group. By degrees, it seemed to me that on the face of Little White there was a look of pain. I was not wrong. Suddenly with a cry of pain which he had been suppressing the negro bit his lip with passion, half closed his eyes, threw his head back as he raised his shoulder convulsively, and seemed to lose consciousness. All this time the Breton was as calm and motionless as a statue. What was going on was something so unforeseen, so extraordinary that we did not know what to think of it. Robert Lange solved the riddle.

"'Wretch!" he cried with a resounding voice. "This hand which has done for so many Bretons shall not henceforth frighten a child!"

'In fact, the hand of the Breton had gripped the negro's with such force that the blood sprang from its fingers.

"'Stop! stop!" cried the black in his agony. But Robert was pitiless, and did not loosen his grasp until the giant was on his knees before him.'

An enthusiastic burst of cheering rose from the French prisoner spectators, and, to cut the story short, the Colonel handed Robert Lange the twenty guineas, and was obliged to apologize to the gay company assembled to see the triumph of the negro, for the unexpected and brief character of the entertainment.

Then he called his big Danish hound and prepared to embark. But the dog did not appear and could not be found. Somebody said he had last been seen going into the battery. Captain R—— started, and his face reddened deeply. 'Then—then,' he stammered. 'If your dog has got into the battery, you will never see him again!'

'Never see him again! What do you mean?' roared the Colonel.

'I mean that by this time he represents two legs of mutton, several dishes of "ratatouille", and any number of *beeftaks*! In other words, the prisoners have eaten him!'

It was even so. The vision of a large plump dog had been too much for the Raffalés, and as the irate Colonel was rowed shorewards from the ship, he saw the skin of his pet nailed on to the outer side of it.

Captain R—— revenged himself for the double fiasco by a series of brutal persecutions and punishments which culminated in open rebellion, severe fighting, much bloodshed, and at last in a proclamation by the Captain that unless the ringleaders were delivered up to him, imploring pardon for what had happened, he would have every man shot.

In the meanwhile the long duration and intensity of Captain R———'s persecution had reached the ears of the authorities, and just at the expiration of the hour which he had given the prisoners for decision, the great folk of the Admiralty arrived, and the result of a court of inquiry which lasted the whole day, and which even Garneray admits was conducted with impartiality, was that he was removed.

A few weeks later Garneray observed two of the worst of the Raffalés seated on a bench playing ecarté very seriously, and surrounded by a silent and equally serious crowd. Suspecting that this was no ordinary gambling bout, he inquired, and was told that by a drawing of lots these two men had been left to decide who should kill the ship's master, one Linch, the worst type of hulk tyrant. In vain Garneray exerted himself to prevent the committal of so terrible a crime. The game was played out, and five minutes later the master was stabbed to the heart as he stood on the upper deck.

Towards the end of 1811 the *Vengeance*, to which hulk Garneray had been shifted from the *Crown*, received her quota of the unfortunate Frenchmen who, after the capitulation of Baylen in 1808, had been imprisoned by the Spaniards on the island of Cabrera, where they had been submitted to the most terrible sufferings and hardships, and had died like flies. Garneray describes the appearance of thirty of these poor creatures who had been apportioned to the *Vengeance*, as they came alongside.

'The poor wretches, lying at the bottom of the boat, cried aloud in their agony and tossed in the delirium of fever; thin as skeletons, pale as corpses, scarcely covered, although the cold was intense, by their miserable rags.... Of these thirty only about ten had strength enough to get on board.'

The doctor of the *Vengeance* refused to receive them on board, saying that by their infection they would in a fortnight's time turn the ship into one great tomb, and they were ordered to be put on board the *Pegasus* hospital ship. While the arrangements for their reception were being made, the unfortunates were kept in their agony in the boat alongside, for the captain of the *Vengeance* said it was not worth while to disarrange his ship for such men, for so short a time.

EXTERIOR VIEW OF A HULK.

(*After Louis Garneray.*)

More brutality followed. The captain of the *Pegasus* sent word that the poor wretches should be bathed before being sent to him, saying that his hospital was so full that he had no accommodation of this sort. And this was actually done; they were plunged into icy cold water, and then packed off to the *Pegasus*, the result being that many of them were hauled on board dying.

As the doctor of the *Vengeance* predicted, the infection brought by the survivors of Cabrera spread through the ship with terrible severity, and Garneray himself was seized with fever, and was sent on board the *Pegasus*. He tells how by the intervention of a fellow-countryman who was a hospital assistant, he contrived to avoid the horrors of the compulsory cold bath on entrance, and proceeds to relate a circumstance which, horrible as it is, I give for what it is worth.

A neighbour invalid had a diamond ring on his finger. He was a soldier of Spain, and the ring no doubt had been obtained, as Garneray says, 'by the luck of war'. He was very far gone; indeed his death could only be a matter of a few hours. Garneray, rapidly becoming convalescent, heard two English attendants conspire to take the dying man away at once to the mortuary and there to relieve him of his ring. They carried him away; Garneray called for his French friend, and bid him go at once and prevent the brutal deed. He did so, and the man actually recovered, but he told Garneray that it was quite the rule in this crowded hospital ship for patients to be hurried away before they were dead into the mortuary in order to make room for others!

Garneray says:

'It is difficult to give the reader an idea of the barbarous manner in which the French were treated on this hospital ship. I will only give one more instance, for my aim is not to horrify, and there were acts of cruelty which the pen hesitates to describe. One day the English doctor was asked to authorize wine to be given to a young officer, grievously ill, in order to strengthen him. "Are you mad?" replied the doctor. "To dare to ask me to give strength to an enemy? Get out! You must be a fool!"'

When Garneray returned to the *Vengeance* he had news of the Baron de Bonnefoux—extracts from whose life upon the Chatham hulks have already been given,—and speaks of him as bent upon escaping, and fears he would be shot one of these days.

Garneray later is allowed to go on parole to Bishop's Waltham, about his sojourn at which place something will be said when the story of the Prisoners on Parole comes to be told. Suffice it therefore to say that Garneray got away from Bishop's Waltham to Portsmouth, and well across the Channel on a smuggling vessel, when he was recaptured by a British cruiser, and once again found himself a prisoner on the *Vengeance*. After more sufferings, brutal treatment, and illness, Garneray was at length made free by the Treaty of Paris in 1814.

THE VENGEANCE.

(*After Louis Garneray.*)

CHAPTER V
LIFE ON THE HULKS—(*continued*)

I next give the remarks of Colonel Lebertre, who, having broken his parole by escaping from Alresford, was captured, and put on the *Canada* hulk at Chatham. This was in 1811. He complains bitterly that officers in the hulks were placed on a level with common prisoners, and even with negroes, and says that even the *Brunswick*, which was considered a better hulk than the others, swarmed with vermin, and that although cleanliness was strongly enjoined by the authorities, no allowance for soap was made, no leave given to bathe even in summer, and that fresh clothing was very rarely issued.

But most strongly does he condemn the conduct of the idle curious who would come off from the shore to see the prisoners on the hulks.

'Les femmes même ont montré une indifférence vraiment choquante. On en a vu rester des heures entières les yeux fixés sur le Parc où se tiennent les prisonniers, sans que e spectacle de misère qui affecterait si vivement une Française ait fait couler une seule larme; le rire insultant était, au contraire, sur leurs lèvres. Les prisonniers n'ont connu qu'un seul exemple d'une femme qui s'évanouît à la vue du Parc.'

In the House of Commons on December 26, 1812, during a debate upon the condition of the foreign prisoners of war in England, Croker, Secretary to the Admiralty, declared that he had inspected the hulks at Portsmouth, and had found the prisoners thereon 'comfortable and happy and well provided with amusement', and Sir George Warrender said much the same about Chatham.

Colonel Lebertre remarks on this:

'Men sensual and hardened by pleasures! You who in full Parliament outrage your victims and declare that the prisoners are happy! Would you know the full horror of their condition, come without giving notice beforehand; dare to descend before daylight into the tombs in which you bury living creatures who are human beings like yourselves; try to breathe for one minute the sepulchral vapour which these unfortunates breathe for many years, and which sometimes suffocates them; see them tossing in their hammocks, assailed by thousands of insects, and wooing in vain the sleep which could soften for one moment their sufferings!'

He describes, as did the Baron de Bonnefoux, the Raffalés who sold all their clothes, and went naked in obedience to one of the laws of their *camaraderie*, who slept huddled together for warmth in ranks which changed position by words of command. He says that some of the prisoners were so utterly miserable that they accepted pay from the authorities to act as spies upon their fellows. He describes the rude courts of justice held, and instances how one man who stole five louis received thirty blows with a rope's end; he refers to the terrible vice prevalent upon the prison ships, and remarks that 'life on them is the touchstone of a man's character'.

When he arrived on the *Canada* there was no vacant sleeping place, but for 120 francs he bought a spot in the middle of the battery, not near a port, 'just big enough to hold his dead body'. Still, he admits that the officers treated him with as much consideration as their orders would allow.

On August 11, 1812, in response to many urgent remonstrances from influential prisoners against the custom of herding officers and men together, all the officers on the hulks at Chatham were transferred to the lower or thirty-six gun battery of the *Brunswick*, in number 460. Here they had to submit to the same tyranny as on the other ships, except that they were allowed to have wine if they could afford to pay six francs a bottle for it, which few of them could do. Later, General Pillet and other 'broke paroles', on account of the insulting letters they wrote on the subject of being allowed rum or other spirits, were confined to the regulation small beer. The Transport Office wrote: 'Indeed, when the former unprincipled conduct of these officers is considered, with their present combination to break through the rules, obviously tending to insurrection and a consequent renewal of bloodshed, we think it proper that they should immediately be removed to separate prison ships.'

We now come to the most rabid of the Frenchmen, General Pillet. Pillet was severely wounded and taken prisoner at Vimiero in 1808, and—in violation, he says, of the second article of the Convention of Cintra, which provided that no French should be considered prisoners of war, but should be taken out of Portugal with arms, &c., by British ships—was brought to

England, with many other officers. He was at once allowed to be on parole at Alresford, but, not considering himself bound by any parole terms, attempted to escape with Paolucci, Captain of the *Friedland* captured in 1808 by the *Standard* and *Active*, but was recaptured and sent to the dépôt at Norman Cross. Here his conduct was so reprehensible that he was sent to the *Brunswick* at Chatham. From the *Brunswick* he tried to escape in a vegetable boat, but this attempt failed, and it is to the subsequent rigour of his treatment that must be attributed his vitriolic hatred of Britain.

General Pillet is of opinion that the particular branch of the Navy told off for duty on the prison ships was composed of the most miserable scum of English society; of men who have either been accomplices in or guilty of great crimes, and who had been given by the magistrates the alternative of being marines or of being hanged!

He speaks of the Chatham hulks as abominably situated near foul marshes—which is undeniably true. The quarters of the prisoners were in no place high enough for a man to stand upright; fourteen little ports, unglazed but barred, of seventeen inches square, on each side of the deck, gave all the light and air obtainable. When they were shut they were fast shut, so that during the winter months the prisoners breathed foul air for sixteen hours a day. Hence they went naked, and so, when the cold air was admitted the results were fatal. The overcrowding of the hulks, says Pillet, was part of the great Government design of killing the prisoners, and asserts that even a London newspaper, quoting the opinion of a medical board in London, said that the strongest of men, after six years' life on the hulks, must be physically wrecked for life.

The hammock space allowed was six feet in length, but swinging reduced them to four and a half. Newcomers were often obliged to sleep on the bare deck, as there was no other vacant space, and there was no distinction of ranks. However, officers were generally able to buy spaces, upon which practice Pillet remarks:

'C'est une misérable spéculation pour un pauvre prisonnier affamé; il consent à vendre sa place afin de se procurer un peu plus de vivre pendant quelques jours, et afin de ne pas mourir de faim il accélère la destruction de sa santé, et se réduit dans cette horrible situation à coucher sur un plancher ruisselant d'eau, l'évaporation des transpirations forcées qui a lieu dans ce séjour d'angoisses et de la mort.'

He declares that the air is so foul when the decks are shut up that the candles will not burn, and he has heard even the guards call for help when they have opened the hatches and the air has escaped. The food he describes as execrable, so that the two boats which had the monopoly of coming alongside to sell butter, tea, coffee, sugar, potatoes, candles, and tobacco at a price one-third above that on land, did a roaring trade. The general reply to complaints was that any food was good enough for French dogs.

If they were badly fed, says Pillet, they were worse clothed. Nominally they received every eighteen months a coat, waistcoat, breeches, two pairs of stockings, two shirts, a pair of shoes, and a cap. He declares he can prove that the prisoners did not receive this complete rig-out once in four years, and that if a prisoner had any rags of his own, or received any money, he got no clothes! What clothes they did get were so badly made that they generally had to be re-made. He says that at Portsmouth, where the hulk agent Woodriff was at any rate conscientious enough to issue the clothes on the due dates, his secretary would buy back the shirts at one shilling each, and so, as Government paid three shillings each for them, and there were at Portsmouth, Forton, and Portchester some twelve thousand prisoners on the average, his 'pickings' must have been considerable!

In a note he gives the instance of the reply of Commander Mansell, who commanded the prison-ship police at Chatham in 1813, when the fact that not one quarter of the clothing due to the prisoners had been delivered to them, was proved clearly: 'I am afraid it is too true, but I have nothing to do with it. I cannot help it.'

From the *Carnet d'Étapes du Sergt.-Maj. Beaudouin, 31ᵉ demi-brigade de ligne*, I take the following account of life on the hulks.

'On October 31st, 1809, Beaudouin left Valleyfield where he had been confined since June 10th, 1804, and came on board the *Bristol* hulk at Chatham. At this time the hulks were the *Glory*, three decker, *Bristol, Crown Prince, Buckingham, Sampson (mauvais sujets), Rochester, Southwick, Irresistible, Bahama* (Danes), and *Trusty*, hospital ship, holding in all 6,550 prisoners.'

Beaudouin says:

'The difference between the land prisons and the hulks is very marked. There is no space for exercise, prisoners are crowded together, no visitors come to see them, and we are like forsaken people. There is no work but the *corvées* to get our water, and to scrape in winter and wash in summer our sleeping place. In a word, only to see them is to be horrified. The anchorage at Chatham is bounded by low and ill-cultured shores; the town is two miles away—a royal dockyard where there is much ship-building. At the side of it is a fine, new, well-armed fort, and adjoining it a little town named Rochester, where there are two windmills, and two more in Chatham. By the London road, three miles off, there are four windmills. The people of this country are not so pleasant and kind as in Scotland, in fact I believe "the sex" is not so beautiful.'

Very soon the *Bristol* was condemned and its prisoners transferred to the *Fyen*, and at the same time the *Rochester* and *Southwick* were replaced by the *Canada* and *Nassau*. On the *Fyen* were 850 prisoners, but during 1810 and 1811 a great many Chatham prisoners were sent to Norman Cross and Scotland.

Beaudouin comments thus bitterly:

'It is unfortunate for me that my circle of acquaintances is so limited, and that I cannot therefore make sufficiently known the crimes of a nation which aims at the supremacy in Europe. It poses as an example among nations, but there are no brigands or savages as well versed in wickedness as it is. Day by day they practise their cruelties upon us, unhappy prisoners. That is where they are cowardly fighters! against defenceless men! Half the time they give us provisions which the very dogs refuse. Half the time the bread is not baked, and is only good to bang against a wall; the meat looks as if it had been dragged in the mud for miles. Twice a week we get putrid salt food, that is to say, herrings on Wednesday, cod-fish on Saturday. We have several times refused to eat it, and as a result got nothing in its place, and at the same time are told that anything is good enough for a Frenchman. Therein lies the motive of their barbarity.'

A short description of the terrible *Sampson* affair is given elsewhere (p. 93), but as Beaudouin was evidently close by at the time, his more detailed account is perhaps worth quoting.

'On the *Sampson* the prisoners refused to eat the food. The English allowed them to exist two days without food. The prisoners resolved to force the English to supply them with eatable provisions. Rather than die of hunger they all went on deck and requested the captain either to give them food or to summon the Commandant of the anchorage. The brute replied that he would not summon the Commandant, and that they should have no other provisions than those which had been served out to them two days previously. The prisoners refused to touch them. The "brigand" then said: "As you refuse to have this food, I command you to return below immediately or I will fire upon you." The prisoners could not believe that he really meant what he said and refused to go below.

'Hardly had they made this declaration, when the Captain gave the word to the guard to fire, which was at once done, the crowd being fired upon. The poor wretches, seeing that they were being fired upon without any means of defence, crowded hastily down, leaving behind only the killed and wounded—fifteen killed and some twenty wounded! Then the Captain hoisted the mutiny signal which brought reinforcements from the other ships, and all were as jubilant as if a great victory had been won.

'I do not believe that any Frenchman lives who hates this nation more than I do; and all I pray for is that I may be able to revenge myself on it before I die.'

Beaudouin wrote a poem of 514 alexandrines, entitled:

Les Prisons d'Albion.

Ou la malheureuse situation des prisonniers en Angleterre.

Bellum nobis haec mala fecit.

I give in the original the first and last 'chants' of this embittered production.

I

'Tu veux, mon cher ami, que ranimant ma verve

Je te peigne sans fard, sans crainte, et sans réserve,

Le Tableau des tourmens et de l'affliction

Sous lesquels sont plongés les captifs d'Albion.

J'obéis à la voix, et ma muse craintive,

Entonnant à regret la trompette plaintive,

Va chanter sur des tons, hélas! bien douloureux,

Les maux, les maux cuisans de bien des malheureux.'

LXIV

'Je t'ai dépeint sans fard l'exacte vérité,

Tels sont les maux cruels de la captivité.

O vous qui de bonheur goûtez en paix les charmes,

Si vous lisez mes vers, donnez-nous quelques larmes;

S'ils n'impriment chez vous une tendre affection,

Vous êtes, plus que nous, dignes de compassion!'

Speaking of the horrible moral effects of the bad treatment he says:

'The ruin of their comrades and the depravities which were daily committed in public, impressed right thinking men with so frightful force that this place means a double suffering to them.'

In 1812 it was reported that a batch of incurables would be sent home to France, and Beaudouin resolved to get off with them by making himself ill. He starved himself into such a condition that he was sent into hospital, but the doctor would not pass him as an incurable. He swallowed tobacco juice, and at last, in a miserable state, turned up with the candidates. Then it was announced that no privateersmen, but only regular seamen, would be sent. Beaudouin, being a soldier, and being among the privateersmen, was in despair. However, a kindly English doctor pitied him, cured him of his self-inflicted illness, and got him leave to go.

On June 2, 1812, he was ready to sail, but was searched first for letters. Luckily none were discovered, although he had sixty sewn between the soles of his shoes, and 200 in a box with a double bottom. He sailed on June 4, the king's birthday—that day eight years previously he had arrived at Greenock amidst the Royal salutes—arrived at Morlaix, and so home to Boiscommun (Loiret), canton of Beaune-la-Rolande, arrondissement of Pithiviers.

The following experiences of an American prisoner of war are from *The Journal of a Young Man of Massachusetts*, (1816), who was a surgeon, by name Benjamin Waterhouse, captured at sea in May 1813, and confined on Melville Island, Halifax, whence he was transported to Chatham, and then to Dartmoor. The account is interesting as showing the very marked difference between the American and the French prisoners of war, and is otherwise remarkable for the hatred and contempt of the writer for Britons in general and for Scotsmen in particular, entire pages being devoted to their vilification. Waterhouse, with a hundred of his countrymen, was shipped to England on the *Regulus*, and his complaints are bitter about the shameful treatment on board—the filth, the semi-starvation, the vermin, the sleeping on stone ballast, the lack of air owing to the only opening to the lower deck being a hatchway two feet square, the brutal rule of allowing only two prisoners to go on deck at a time, and the presence in their midst of the only latrine. The captain, a Scotsman, would only yield to constant petitions and remonstrances so far as to sanction the substitution of iron bars for the hatchway.

After a miserable voyage the prisoners reached Portsmouth, and, starved, vermin-eaten, and in rags, were shipped off to the *Crown Prince*, Captain Hutchison, at Chatham, where were thirteen other prison ships and some 1,200 Americans. On this hulk, Waterhouse says, they fared 'as well as could be expected ... not that we fared so well as British prisoners fare in America', the daily allowance being half a pound of beef, one gill of barley, one and a half pounds of bread, on five days of the week, and on the others one pound cod fish, and one pound potatoes, or one pound smoked herring, porter and beer being purchasable. He dilates bitterly on the extraordinary lack of humanity in John Bull, as evidenced by the hard fare of soldiers and sailors, the scoundrelism of some officers, especially those of the provisioning departments, and, above all, the shockingly cruel punishments in the Army and Navy. During the daytime, he says, life on a prison ship was not so unpleasant, but at night the conditions were very bad—especially as American prisoners were more closely watched and guarded than were men of other nationalities. 'The French were always busy in some little mechanical employ, or in gaming, or in playing the fool, but the Americans seemed to be on the rack of invention to escape.'

Amongst themselves, the Americans elected by voting, every four weeks, a President, and twelve Committee men, whose functions were to make wholesome laws, to define crimes and award punishments, and particularly to insist upon personal cleanliness. The punishments were fines, whippings, and in very extreme cases the Black Hole. The volubility and the eloquence of the orators at these Committee Meetings very much impressed the British officers. The Frenchmen, Waterhouse says, were almost to a man gamblers:

'Their skill and address at these games of apparent hazard were far superior to the Americans. They seemed calculated for gamesters; their vivacity, their readiness, and their everlasting professions of friendship were nicely adapted to inspire confidence in the unsuspecting American Jack Tar, who has no legerdemain about him. Most of the prisoners were in the way of earning a little money; but almost all of them were deprived of it by the French gamesters. Our people stood no chance with them, but were commonly stripped of every cent, whenever they set out seriously to play with them. How often have I seen a Frenchman capering, singing, and grinning in consequence of his stripping one of our sailors of all his money; ... the officers among them are the most adroit gamesters. We have all tried hard to respect them; but there is something in their conduct so much like swindling, that I hardly know what to say of them. When they knew that we had received money for the work we had been allowed to perform, they were very attentive, and complaisant and flattering.... They would come round and say: "Ah! Boston fine town, very pretty—Cape Cod fine town, very fine! Town of Rhode Island superb! Bristol Ferry very pretty! General Washington *très grand homme*, General Madison *brave homme*!" With these expressions and broken English, they would accompany, with their monkey tricks, capering and grinning and patting us on the shoulder, with: "The Americans are brave men—fight like Frenchmen;" and by their insinuating manners allure our men once more to their wheels of fortune and billiard-tables, and as sure as they did, so sure did they strip them of all their money.'

Waterhouse adds that 'if an American, having lost all his money, wanted to borrow of a Frenchman under promise of repayment, the latter would say: "Ah mon ami! I am sorry, very sorry, indeed; it is *la fortune de guerre*. If you have lost your money you must win it back again; that is the fashion in my country—we no lend, that is not the fashion!"...

'There were here some Danes as well as Dutchmen. It is curious to observe their different looks and manners.... Here we see the thick-skulled plodding Dane, making a wooden dish; or else some of the most ingenious making a clumsy ship; while others submitted to the dirtiest drudgery of the hulk, for money; and there we see a Dutchman, picking to pieces tarred ropes ... or else you see him lazily stowed away in some corner, with his pipe ... while here and there and every where, you find a lively singing Frenchman, working in hair, or carving out of a bone, a lady, a monkey, or the central figure of the crucifixion! Among the specimens of American ingenuity I most admired their ships, which they built from three to five feet long.... Had not the French proved themselves to be a very brave people, I should have doubted it by what I have observed of them on board the prison-ship. They would scold, quarrel and fight, by slapping each other's chops with the flat hand, and cry like so many girls.... Perhaps such a man as Napoleon Bonaparte could make any nation courageous.'

Very bitter were the complaints of the Americans about the supine and indifferent attitude towards them of Beasley, their agent, who was supposed to keep constant watch and ward over the interests of his unfortunate countrymen. He lived in London, thirty-two miles away, paid no attention to complaints forwarded to him, and was heartily hated and despised. Once he paid a visit to the hulks in Gillingham Creek, but seemed anxious to avoid all interviews and questionings, and left amidst a storm of hisses and jeers.

Waterhouse dwells severely on the fact that the majority of the Americans on the *Crown Prince* and the other hulks were not men who had been fairly taken in open combat on the high seas, but men who had been impressed into the British Navy from American merchant ships previous to the war between the two countries and who, upon the Declaration of War, had given themselves up as prisoners of war, being naturally unwilling to fight against their own country, but who had been kept prisoners instead of being exchanged. This had been the British practice since 1755, but after the War of Independence it had ceased. All the same the British authorities had insisted upon the right of search for British subjects on American ships, and to the arbitrary and forcible exercise of this 'right' was very largely owing the War of 1812.

Waterhouse admits that on the whole he was treated as well on the *Crown Prince* as were the British prisoners at Salem or Boston. Recruiting sergeants for the British service came on board and tried to tempt Americans with a bounty of sixteen guineas, but they were only chaffed and sent off.

Later on, 500 more prisoners arrived from America in a pitiable condition, mostly Maryland and Pennsylvania men—'Colonel Boerstler's men who had been deceived, decoyed and captured near Beaver Dams on January 23rd, 1813'. With their cruel treatment on board the *Nemesis* on their trans-Atlantic voyage, Waterhouse contrasts favourably the kind treatment of the prisoners brought by the *Poictiers 74*, Captain Beresford, after his capture of the American *Wasp* and her prize the *Frolic*.

The author gives a glaring instance of provision cheating. By the terms of his contract, if the bread purveyor failed to send off to the hulks fresh bread when the weather was favourable, he forfeited half a pound of bread to each man. For a long time the prisoners were kept in ignorance of this agreement, but they found it out, and on the next occasion when the forfeit was due, claimed it. Commodore Osmore refused it, and issued hard ship's bread. The prisoners refused to take it. Osmore was furious, and ordered his marines to drive the prisoners, now in open mutiny, below. A disturbance was imminent, but the Americans remained firm, and the commodore gave way.

The American prisoners took in newspapers, as they were mostly intelligent and well-educated men, but paid dearly for them.

The papers were the *Statesman, Star, Bell's Weekly Messenger*, and *Whig*. The *Statesman* cost 28*s*. a month, plus 16*s*. a month for conveyance on board.

As the weather grew milder, matters were more comfortable on board until small-pox broke out. Vaccination was extensively employed, but many prisoners refused to submit to it, not from unbelief in its efficacy, but from misery and unwillingness to live! Then came typhus, in April 1814. There were 800 prisoners and 100 British on the ship. The hospital ship being crowded, part of the *Crown Prince* was set apart for patients, with the result that the mortality was very high. Still Beasley, the American agent, never came near the ship to inquire into affairs.

The gambling evil had now assumed such proportions that the Americans determined to put it down. In spite of the vigorous opposition of the Frenchmen, the 'wheels of fortune' were abolished, but the billiard-tables remained, it being urged by the Frenchmen that the rate of a halfpenny per game was not gambling, and that the game afforded a certain amount of exercise. There remained, however, a strong pro-gambling party among the Americans, and these men insisted upon continuing, and the committee sent one of them to the Black Hole without a trial. This angered his mates; a meeting was held, violent speeches were made in which the names of Hampden, Sidney, and Wilkes were introduced, and he was brought out. He was no ordinary rough tar, but a respectable well-educated New England yeoman, with the 'gift of the gab'; and the results of his harangue were that the committee admitted their error, and he was released.

Finally the billiard-tables were abolished; a great improvement was soon manifest among the captives, education was fostered, and classes formed, although a few rough characters still held aloof, and preferred skylarking, and the slanging and chaffing of passers-by in boats on the river.

In May 1814 four men went on deck and offered themselves for British service. Two got away, but two were caught by their mates, tried, and sentenced to be marked with indian ink on their foreheads with the letter T (= Traitor). The Frenchmen were now being shipped home. Some of them had been prisoners since 1803. Waterhouse comments upon the appalling ignorance among English people in the educated class of all matters American, and quotes the instance of the lady who, wishing to buy some of the articles made by the American prisoners, was confronted by the difficulty of 'not knowing their language'!

Waterhouse describes the surroundings of the *Crown Prince* thus:

'The Medway is a very pleasant river ... its banks are rich and beautiful.... The picture from the banks of the river to the top of the landscape is truly delightful, and beyond any thing I ever saw in my own country, and this is owing to the hedges.... Nearly opposite our doleful prison stands the village of Gillingham, adorned with a handsome church; on the side next Chatham stands the castle, defended by more than an hundred cannon.... This place is noted for making sulphate of iron.... Near to this village of Gillingham is a neat house with a good garden, and surrounded by trees, which was bequeathed by a lady to the oldest boatswain in the Royal Navy.'

Waterhouse complains strongly of the immorality on board: 'Such a sink of vice, I never saw, or ever dreamt of, as I have seen here,' He relates a daring escape. A hole was cut through the ship's side near the stern, the copper being removed all round except on one side so as to lap over and be opened or closed at will. Sixteen men escaped through this, and swam ashore one dark night, the sentry on duty close by being allured away by the singing of droll songs and the passing of a can of grog. At the numbering of the prisoners next morning, the correct tale was made up by the passing through a hole cut in the bulk-head of sixteen men who had been already counted. At another attempt two men slipped into the water; one of them got tired and benumbed with cold, and turned back. The sentry heard him breathing and said: 'Ah! Here is a porpoise, and I'll stick him with my bayonet,' and only the crying out of the poor would-be refugee saved him. The ship's officers on examining the hole were amazed, and one of them remarked that he did not believe that the Devil himself could keep these fellows in hell if they made up their minds to get out. The next day the other poor chap was seen lying dead on the beach, and to the disgust of the prisoners was allowed to remain there two days before he was buried.

Commodore Osmore was always the butt of the American prisoners. A yarn got about that he had procured a sheep from a farmer ashore without paying for it. Thereupon his appearance was the signal for a chorus of 'Baa! Baa!' He was mad with rage, and ordered the port through which the insulting chorus had been made to be closed. The Americans forced it open. The marines drove the prisoners from the fo'c'sle into the 'Pound'. As more 'Baa!'s resounded, they were driven below decks, and all market boats were stopped from approaching the ship, so that for two days the prisoners were without extra food. However, Captain Hutchison instituted an inquiry, and peace was arranged.

In June 1814 three men escaped in a water tank. Others would have followed, but one of the former party had stupidly written an ironical letter of thanks to Captain Hutchison, in which he described the method of escape.

A daring escape was made from the *Irresistible* in broad daylight. Four Americans saw a jolly-boat made fast to the accommodation-ladder under the charge of a sentry. One of them was a big, strong Indian of the Narragansett tribe from Rhode Island. The four men dashed down, seized the sentry, disarmed him, threw him into the boat, and pulled off. They were fired at from all sides, and boats put off from all the ships to chase them, but only one man was wounded. They reached shore and struck across the fields, which were soon covered by people in chase from the farms and brickfields, who soon ran all the prisoners down except the Indian, who out-distanced the prisoners, and would have got away had he not sprained his ankle in getting over a fence, and even then, as he was sitting down, none of the country folk would approach him, until the marines came up. The chase had been closely followed with great excitement on the ship, and on the arrival of the captured men alongside, they were loudly cheered, their healths drunk, and the Indian at once dubbed 'Baron Trenck'. Said the boys: 'If it took 350 British seamen and marines to capture four Yankees, how many British sailors and marines would it take to catch ten thousand of us?'

Two Scotsmen Waterhouse excepted from his condemnation of their nation: Galbraith, the master-at-arms, and Barnes, the sailing-master, who was wont to reprove them for misdeeds, saying: 'I expect better things of you as Americans, I consider you all in a different light from that of a d——d set of French monkeys.'

The British officers were clearly uneasy about their custody of the Americans, and felt it to be an ignoble business. Said they: 'The Yankees seemed to take a pleasure in making us uneasy, and in exciting our apprehensions of their escape, and then they laugh and make themselves merry at our anxiety. In fact, they have systematized the art of tormenting.'

The Government, too, appreciated 'the difficult task which the miserable officers of this miserable Medway fleet had to perform'. It did not wish them to be more rigorous, yet knew that more rigour was necessary. Rumours got about that in desperation the Government was about to transfer all the Americans from the prison ships to Dartmoor—the place which, *it was said*, had been lost by the Duchess of Devonshire at a game of hazard to the Prince of Wales, who determined to utilize it profitably by making a prison there.

The national festival on July 4 was duly celebrated on board the two prison ships *Crown Prince* and *Nassau*. An additional allowance of drink was sanctioned, but the American flag was only allowed to be flown as high as the 'railings'. There were drums and pipes which played Yankee Doodle on the fo'c'sle: cheers were exchanged between the ships, and the toast of the day was drunk in English porter. There was, of course, much speechifying, especially on the *Nassau*, where one orator declaimed for half an hour, and another recited a poem, 'The Impressment of an American Sailor Boy', which is too long to be quoted, but which, says our author, brought tears into many eyes. All passed off quietly, and acknowledgement is made of the 'extraordinary good behaviour of all the British officers and men on board the *Crown Prince*'.

Although Commodore Osmore was unpopular with the Americans, his charming wife exercised a good influence in the ship by her amiability and appreciation of the fact that American prisoners were not all a gang of vagabonds; and gradually a better feeling developed between captors and captured.

In August 1814 the news of the transfer to Dartmoor was confirmed, and, says Waterhouse, was received with regret on the *Crown Prince*—the ship being 'actually viewed with feelings of attachment'. The last scene, however, was marked by a disturbance.

Thirty prisoners had been told off to prepare for embarkation on a tender. At the appointed hour no tender appeared, and the embarkation was put off. But all hammocks had been packed, and upon application to Osmore for hammocks, the prisoners were told to shift as they could for the night, as the tender would arrive early the next morning, and it was not worth while to unpack the hammocks. Upon hearing this the prisoners resolved that if they were to be deprived of their night's rest, nobody else should have any. So they harnessed themselves to benches, and ran about the deck, shouting and singing, and bumping the benches against everything which would make a noise, jammed down the marines' crockery and brought into play every article which could add to the pandemonium. Osmore sent a marine down to quiet them. The marine returned, dishevelled, and disarmed. Osmore was furious. 'I'll be d——d if I do not fire on them!' he roared: 'Fire, and be d——d,' was the response. As it was useless to attempt to quiet them, and to fire would have been criminal, the commodore retired, and did what he could to sleep amid the infernal din of bumping benches, jangling metal, shouts and songs, which lasted throughout the night.

When the tender took the men off in the morning it was to the accompaniment of a great roar of 'Baa! Baa!' as a parting shot.

The remainder of the *Crown Prince* Americans were transferred to the *Bahama* on October 15, 1814. Here they found 300 of their countrymen of the vicious, baser sort, gamblers all, and without any men of influence to order them. Danes occupied the main deck and Americans the lower. Jail fever had played havoc among Danes and Americans—no less than 84 of the latter being buried in the marshes in three months.

Next to the *Bahama* lay the *Belliqueux* hulk, full of harmless and dull Scandinavians, so that the captain thereof, having nothing to do in his own ship, started to spy upon the doings aboard the *Bahama*, and succeeded in getting a marine punished for smuggling liquor. Next day, the rations were fish and potatoes. The Americans collected all their potatoes, and watched for the appearance of the *Belliqueux* commander for his spying promenade on his quarter deck, the result being that when he did appear, he was greeted with such a hail of potatoes that he was fain to beat an undignified retreat. Soon he came off in his boat to complain to Commander Wilson of the *Bahama* of his treatment. Wilson, a passionate, hot-tempered, but just and humane man, said he was very sorry, but could do nothing, so back the discomfited officer had to go, pelted with more potatoes and some coals. Said Wilson: 'These Americans are the sauciest dogs I ever saw; but d——n me if I can help liking them, nor can I ever hate men who are so much like ourselves.'

In October 1814 two hundred Americans were sent to Plymouth, where they were at once boarded by an army of loose women.

With Waterhouse's experiences at Dartmoor I deal in the chapter devoted to that prison.

CHAPTER VI
PRISON-SHIP SUNDRIES

Under this heading are included various reminiscences of, and particulars about, the prison ships which could not be conveniently dealt with in the foregoing chapters.

In April 1759 five French prisoners from the *Royal Oak* hulk at Plymouth were executed at Exeter for the murder of Jean Maneaux, who had informed the agent that his comrades had forged passports in order to facilitate their escape to France. Finding this out, they got Maneaux into an obscure corner of the ship, tied him to a ringbolt, and gave him sixty lashes with a rope to the end of which was fastened an iron thimble as thick as a man's wrist. He got loose, and fell back; they jumped on him till they broke his neck, then cut his body into small pieces, and conveyed them through a waste pipe overboard. The next day twenty-seven prisoners were arrested, and one of them pointed out the actual murderers.

In 1778 two prisoners escaped from the *San Rafael* at Plymouth, swam off to a lighter full of powder, overpowered the man in charge, ran down through all the ships in Hamoaze, round Drake's Island, and got safely away to France, where they sold the powder at a handsome price.

Even more daring was the deed of eleven Frenchmen who, early in the morning of April 7, 1808, made their escape from the hulk *Vigilant* at Portsmouth, by cutting a hole, and swimming to the *Amphitrite*, a ship in ordinary, fitted up as the abode of the Superintendent Master. They boarded a boat, hanging on the davits, clothed themselves in the greatcoats of the boat's crew, lowered her, and in the semi-darkness pulled away to the Master Attendant's buoy boat, one of the finest unarmed crafts in the harbour, valued at £1,000. They boarded her, immediately got under way at about five a.m., and successfully navigated her to Havre, or Cherbourg, which they reached in the evening, and sold her for £700. She was fitted out, armed with eight six-pounders, and went forth as a privateer under the name of *Le Buoy Boat de Portsmouth*. Her career, however, was short, for in November she was captured by the *Coquette*.

The above-mentioned prison ship *Vigilant* seems to have hardly deserved her name, for in the year 1810 alone no less than thirty-two prisoners escaped from her, and of these only eight were recaptured.

On another occasion three prisoners escaped from a hulk, got a small skiff, rowed to Yantlett Creek, where they boarded a fishing-smack of which the master and boy were asleep. The master made a stout resistance and called on the boy to help him, but he was too terrified to do so. The master was overpowered and severely beaten, and then managed to jump overboard. The Frenchmen got off, taking the boy with them.

The *Sampson* at Chatham was evidently an ill-omened ship. It was on board her that occurred the disastrous event of May 31, 1811, when the half-starved prisoners, upon being docked of half their rations for the misdeeds of a few of their number, broke out into open mutiny, which was only quelled at the cost of six prisoners being killed and a great many wounded. On the *Sampson*, also, was fought a particularly terrible duel in 1812. Two prisoners quarrelled and determined to settle their difference quietly. So, attended only by their seconds, they betook themselves to the ordinary ship prison, which happened to be empty, and, armed with sticks to which scissor-blades had been fastened, fought. One of them received a mortal thrust in the abdomen, but, although his bowels were protruding, he continued to parry his opponent's blows until he was exhausted. He died in spite of the surgeon's attentions.

On board the same ship in 1813, three prisoners decided to murder the master's mate and the sergeant of marines—men universally detested for their brutal behaviour—and drew lots as to who should do it. The lot fell upon Charles Manseraux. But he had 'compunction of conscience' because the sergeant was a married man with a family. However, he had to kill some one, and fixed on a private of the Marines. He took the opportunity when the unfortunate man was doing duty on the fo'c'sle and drove a knife into his back. Another prisoner saw the deed done, knocked Manseraux down and secured him. Manseraux and the others were tried at the Maidstone Assizes, found guilty, and executed.

Duelling and crimes of violence seem to have been rampant on certain ships more than on others. The *San Damaso* at Portsmouth was one of these, although on the Chatham hulks the unnatural deaths were so frequent that the Coroner of Rochester in 1812 claimed special fees from the Transport Office on account of the trebling of his duties, a claim which was not granted.

A very bold attempt at escape in broad daylight was made by some desperate prisoners of the *Canada* hulk at Chatham in 1812. Beef was being hoisted on board the prison ship from a lighter alongside, on board of which were half a dozen American prisoners who were assisting in the operation. Suddenly, they cut the painter, and, helped by a stiff breeze, actually sailed off, and, although the guards on all the prison ships fired at them, would have escaped if they had not run aground off Commodore's Hard, Gillingham. They sprang ashore here, and ran, but the mud was too much for them and they were captured.

The Americans, whether ashore or afloat, were the hardest prisoners to guard of any. They seem never to have relaxed in their plans and attempts to escape, and as they were invariably better supplied with money than Frenchmen and Spaniards, they could add the power of the bribe to the power which knowledge of their captors' language gave them. Hence no estimate can be formed of the real number of Americans who got away from the hulks, for, although a very exact system of roll call was in use, the ingenuity of the Americans, immensely backed by their purses, contrived matters so that not merely were the numbers on board always complete at each roll call, but upon more than one occasion, by some over-exercise of ingenuity, the captain of a hulk actually found himself commanding more prisoners than there were!

By way of relief to the monotony of this *guerre à outrance* between captors and captives we may quote instances when the better humanity of the hapless ones came to the fore.

In 1812 a prisoner made an attempt to set the hulk *Ganges* on fire at Plymouth, and a large hole was burned in her side. The other prisoners helped to extinguish the flames, and were so angry with the incendiary that they were with difficulty prevented from tearing him to pieces.

Three officers of the Inverness Militia were sailing in the harbour at Portsmouth in the same year, when a squall upset their boat, and they were thrown into the water. One of the officers could not swim, and seeing him struggling for life, a French prisoner on the *Crown* hulk at once sprang overboard and brought him safely to the ship. He was at once liberated and returned to France.

But even heroism became a cloak for trickery among these weary, hopeless, desperate exiles ever on the watch for a chance of escaping. In 1810 a French prisoner at Plymouth obtained his freedom by saving a British sentry from drowning, but the number of British sentries who, after this, met with accidents which tumbled them overboard, and the unfailing regularity with which heroic prisoner-rescuers appeared on the scene, awakened the suspicions of the authorities, who found out that these occurrences were purely commercial transactions. So they stopped automatically.

It is equally pleasing to come across, in this continually dreary record of crime and misery, a foreign testimony to English kindness. The following letter was kindly lent to me by Mr. J. E. Mace, of Tenterden, Kent, to whose grandfather it was addressed:

'Chatham. Le 10 janvier, 1798.

'*A Monsieur Mace, Tenterden.*

'CHER MONSIEUR:

'S'il est cruel d'être livré aux dégoûts et aux peines que cause la captivité la plus dure, il est bien doux de trouver des êtres sensibles qui, comme vous, cher Monsieur, savent plaindre le sort rigoureux des victimes de la guerre. Ce que vous avez eu la bonté de m'envoyer, plus encore, l'expression des beaux sentiments me touche, me pénètre de la plus vive reconnaissance, et me fait sentir avec une nouvelle force cette vérité constante:—L'Humanité rapproche et unit tous les cœurs faits pour elle. Comme vous, cher Monsieur, et avec vous, je désire avec ferveur que les principes de notre Divin Législateur reprennent leur Empire sur la terre, la conséquence en est si belle!

'Dieu vous garde beaucoup d'années.

'FARBOURIET, Colonel 12me Hussards.'

In 1807, as a consequence of the bombardment of Copenhagen and the subsequent surrender to England of the Danish fleet, there were 1,840 Danish prisoners in England, who received double the allowance of French prisoners, inasmuch as they were rather hostages than prisoners—hostages for the good behaviour of Denmark as regards Napoleon;—the captain of a man-of-war got four shillings per diem, a commanding officer two shillings, the captain of an Indiaman three shillings, and so on. In other respects they were treated as prisoners of war.

These Danes were largely taken from the hulks to man our merchant navy, and one Wipperman, a Danish clerk on H.M.S. *Utile*, seems to have made this transfer business a very profitable one, until the accusation brought against him by a Danish prisoner of war of having obtained a watch and some money under false pretences, brought to light the fact that his men rarely if ever joined the British merchant service except to desert at the first opportunity, and generally went at large as free men. He was severely punished, and his exposure brought to an end an extensive crimping system by which hundreds of dangerous foreigners had been let loose from the prison ships, many of them spies and escape-aiders.

Foreign writers have included among their various complaints against the British Government its reluctance to allow religious ministration among the prisoners of war. But the Transport Office, as we shall see later, had learned by experience that the garb of sanctity was by no means always the guarantee of sanctity, and so when in 1808 a Danish parson applied to be allowed on the prison ships at Chatham, he got his permission only on the condition that 'he does not repeat, the old offence of talking upon matters unconnected with his mission and so cause much incorrect inferences'—a vague expression which probably meant talking about outside affairs to prisoners, who had no other source of information.

In 1813 the Transport Office replied to the Bishop of Angoulême, who requested that a priest named Paucheron might minister on the prison ships at Chatham, that they could not accede inasmuch as Paucheron had been guilty 'of highly improper conduct in solemnizing a marriage between a prisoner of war and a woman in disguise of a man'.

In no branch of art did French prisoners show themselves more proficient than in that of forgery, and, although when we come to treat of the prisons ashore we shall find that, from the easier accessibility to implements there, the imitation of passports and bank notes was more perfectly effected than by the prisoners on the hulks, the latter were not always unsuccessful in their attempts.

In 1809 Guiller and Collas, two prisoners on *El Firme* at Plymouth, opened negotiations with the captain's clerk to get exchanged to the *Généreux*, telling him what their object was and promising a good reward. He pretended to entertain their proposals, but privately told the captain. Their exchange was effected, and their ally supplied them with paper, ink, and pencils of fine hair, with which they imitated notes of the Bank of England, the Naval and Commercial Bank, and an Okehampton Bank. Not having the official perforated stamp, they copied it to perfection by means of smooth halfpennies and sail-makers' needles. When all was ready, the clerk gave the word to the authorities, and the clever rascals got their reward on the gallows at Exeter in 1810, being among the first war prisoners to be executed for forgery.

In 1812 two French prisoners on a Portsmouth hulk, Dubois and Benry, were condemned to be hanged at Winchester for the forgery of a £1 Bank of England note. Whilst lying in the jail there they tried to take their own lives by opening veins in their arm with broken glass and enlarging the wounds with rusty nails, declaring that they would die as soldiers, not as dogs, and were only prevented by force from carrying out their resolve. They died crying 'Vive l'Empereur!'

In 1814 six officers were found to have obtained their liberty by forged passports. These men were, in their own vernacular, 'Broke-Paroles'—men who had been sent from parole places to prison ships, for the crime of forging passports. Further investigation caused suspicion to be fixed upon a woman calling herself Madame Carpenter, who was ostensibly a tea and sugar dealer at 46 Foley Street, Portland Chapel, London, but who had gained some influence at the Transport Office through having rendered services to British prisoners in France, which enabled her to have access to the prison ships in her pretended trade, although she was a Frenchwoman. I cannot discover what punishment she received. We shall hear more of her in the chapter upon Stapleton Prison.

A clever quibble saved the life of a prisoner on the *San Rafael* hulk at Plymouth. He was tried at Exeter for imitating a £2 note with indian ink, but pleaded that as he was under the protection of no laws he had not broken any, and was acquitted. This was before cases of murder and forgery were brought under the civil jurisdiction.

Well-deserved releases of prisoners in recognition of good actions done by them in the past were not rare. In 1808 a prisoner on the *Sampson* at Chatham, named Sabatier, was released without exchange on the representation of the London Missionary Society, who acted for Captain Carbonel of the famous privateer *Grand Bonaparte*, who had shown great kindness to the crew and passengers of the ship *Duff* which he had captured.

In the same year a prisoner at Plymouth, named Verdie, was released unconditionally on the petition of Lieut. Ross, R.N., for having kindly treated the Lieutenant's father when the latter was a prisoner in France.

In 1810 a Portsmouth prisoner was unconditionally liberated upon his proving satisfactorily that he had helped Midshipman Holgate of the *Shannon* to escape from imprisonment in France.

Almost to the very last the care of sick prisoners on the hulks seems to have been criminally neglected. For instance, the In-letters to the Transport Office during the year 1810 are full of vehement or pathetic complaints about the miserable state of the sick on the *Marengo* and *Princess Sophia* hospital ships at Portsmouth. Partly this may be due to an economical craze which affected the authorities at this time, but it must be chiefly attributed to medical inefficiency and neglect. Most of the chief medical officers of the prison ships had their own private practices ashore, with what results to the poor foreigners, nominally their sole care, can be imagined, and all of them resented the very necessary condition that they should sleep on the ships.

In this year 1810, Dr. Kirkwood, of the *Europe* hospital ship at Plymouth, was convicted of culpable neglect in regularly sleeping ashore, and was superseded. As a result of an inquiry into the causes of abnormal sickness on the *Vigilant* and at Forton Prison, Portsmouth, the surgeons were all superseded, and the order was issued that all prison-ship surgeons should daily examine the healthy prisoners so as to check incipient sickness. I append the States of the *Renown* hospital ship at Plymouth for February 1814:

'Staff:

2 surgeons, 1 assistant surgeon, 1 matron, 1 interpreter, 1 cook, 1 barber, 1 mattress maker, 1 tailor, 1 washerwoman, and 10 nurses.

Received 141. Discharged 69. Died 19. Remaining 53.

'Fever and dysentery have been the prevalent complaints among the prisoners from Pampelune, whose deplorable state the Board of Inspection are in full possession of. (Among these were some forty women "in so wretched a state that they were wholly destitute of the appropriate dress of their sex". Two of the British officers' wives collected money for the poor creatures and clothed them.) Pneumonia has recently attacked many of these ill-conditioned men termed *Romans*, many of whom were sent here literally in a state of nudity, an old hammock in the boat to cover them being excepted.'

(The *Romans* above mentioned were the most degraded and reckless of the Dartmoor prisoners, who had been sent to the hulks partly because there was no power in the prison that could keep them in order, and partly because their filthy and vicious habits were revolting to the other and more decent prisoners.)

The horrors of the English prison ships were constantly quoted by French commanders as spurs to the exertions of their men. Bonaparte more than once dwelt on them. Phillipon, the gallant defender of Badajos, afterwards a prisoner on parole in England, reminded his men of them as they crowded to hurl our regiments from the breaches. 'An appeal', says Napier, 'deeply felt, for the annals of civilized nations furnish nothing more inhuman towards captives of war than the prison ships of England.'

The accompanying drawing from Colonel Lebertre's book may give some idea of the packing process practised on the hulks. It represents a view from above of the orlop deck of the *Brunswick* prison ship at Chatham—a ship which was regarded as rather a good one to be sent to. The length of this deck was 125 feet, its breadth 40 feet in the widest part, and its height 4 feet 10 inches, so that only boys could pass along it without stooping. Within this space 460 persons slept, and as there was only space to swing 431 hammocks, 29 men had to sleep as best they could beneath the others.

Something with an element of fun in it may serve as a relief to the prevalent gloom of this chapter. It has been shown how largely gambling entered into the daily life of the poor wretches on the hulks, and how every device and excuse for it were invented and employed, but the instance given by Captain Harris in his book upon Dartmoor is one of the oddest.

'When the lights were extinguished', he says, 'and the ship's lantern alone cast a dim glimmer through the long room, the rats were accustomed to show themselves in search of the rare crumbs to be found below the hammocks. A specially tempting morsel having been placed on an open space, the arrival of the performers was anxiously looked for. They were all known by name, and thus each player was able to select his champion for the evening. As soon as a certain number had gained the open space, a sudden whistle, given by a disinterested spectator, sent them back to their holes, and the first to reach his hole was declared the winner. An old grey rat called "Père Ratapon" was a great favourite with the gamblers, for, though not so active as his younger brethren, he was always on the alert to secure a good start when disturbed.'

In justice to our ancient foe I give here a couple of extracts, for which I have to thank Mr. Gates of Portsmouth, from the *Hampshire Telegraph*, illustrative of generous behaviour towards Englishmen who had been forced to aid prisoners to escape.

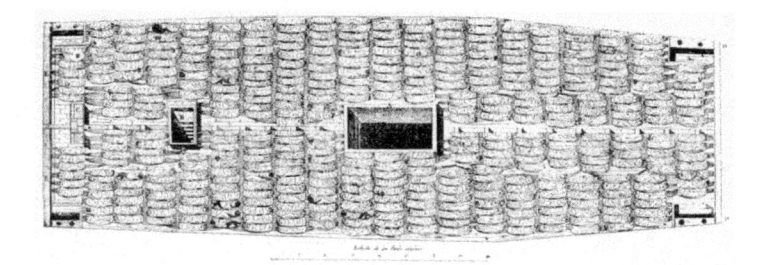

ORLOP DECK OF *BRUNSWICK* PRISON SHIP, CHATHAM.

(*After Colonel Lebertre.*)

Length, 125 feet. Breadth in widest part, 40 feet. Height, 4 feet 10 inches. Number of prisoners, 460.

'July 20th, 1801. In a cartel vessel which arrived last week from France, came over one Stephen Buckle, a waterman of this town. Three gentlemen had hired this waterman to take them to the Isle of Wight, and they had not proceeded farther than Calshot Castle when they rose upon him, gagged him, tied him hand and foot, and threatened him with instant death if he made the slightest noise or resistance. The boatman begged for mercy, and promised his assistance in any undertaking if they would spare his life; on which he was released, and was told they were French prisoners, and ordered to make for the nearest port in France, at his peril. The darkness of the night, and the calmness of the wind, favoured their intentions, for after rowing two days and nights in a small, open skiff, without having the least sustenance, they arrived safe at Cherbourg. The waterman was interrogated at the Custom House as to the prisoners' escape; when, after giving the particulars and identifying the persons, saying they threatened to murder him, the officers took the three Frenchmen into custody, to take their respective trials. The poor man's case being made known to the Government, he was ordered to be liberated, and his boat restored.'

'September 21st, 1807. Between 9 and 10 o'clock on the evening of last Sunday three weeks, two men engaged Thomas Hart, a ferryman, to take them from Gosport beach to Spithead, to go on board a ship there, as they said. When the boat reached Spithead they pretended the ship had gone to St. Helens, and requested the waterman to go out after her. Having reached that place, one of them, who could speak English, took a dagger from under his coat, and swore he would take the life of the waterman if he did not land them in France.

'Under this threat the man consented to follow their directions, and landed them at Fécamp. The men appeared to be in the uniform of officers of the British Navy. The waterman was lodged in prison at Havre de Grâce, and kept there for ten days. He was then released on representing himself to be a fisherman, his boat was returned to him, and the Frenchmen gave him six or seven pounds of bread, some cyder, and a pocket compass, and a pass to prevent his being interrupted by any French vessel he might meet with. In this state they set him adrift; he brought several letters from English prisoners in France, and from French persons to their friends in prison in this country.'

CHAPTER VII
TOM SOUVILLE
A FAMOUS PRISON-SHIP ESCAPER

In old Calais there is or was a *Rue Tom Souville*. No foreigners and not many Calaisiens know who Tom Souville was, or what he had done to deserve to have a street named after him. The answer to these questions is so interesting that I do not hesitate to allow it a chapter.

About the year 1785, Tom Souville, aged nine, was, in accordance with a frequent custom of that day, sent to England for the purpose of learning English in exchange for a little English boy who came over to France. He was quartered in the house of the Rev. Mr. Wood, of Dover, whose sailor brother took a great fancy to the little stranger, and made him his constant companion on cruises up and down the Channel, with the result that Tom Souville got to know the Channel coasts thoroughly, a stock of learning which he afterwards made use of in a fashion little dreamed of by the old salt, his mentor.

At Christmas 1786, after eighteen months' happiness at Dover, he returned to Calais, and in obedience to his irresistible bent, joined the navy. In 1795, the *Formidable*, with Tom Souville on board, was taken by H.M.S. *Queen Charlotte*, off Isle-Croix, after a fight in which she lost 320 killed and wounded out of her complement of 717, and Tom with his Captain, Linois, of whom mention will be made later in this work, were taken to Portsmouth. Tom Souville refused to sign a parole form, so was put into the *cachot* of the *Diamond* hulk; but only for a short time, as he was soon exchanged. However, in 1797 he was again captured, this time on the *Actif*, and was confined on the *Crown* hulk.

Of life on the *Crown* he gives the usual description. He speaks of the prisoner professors (who were known as the 'Académiciens') being obliged to give their lessons at night, as the noise during the daytime made teaching impossible. But as no lights were allowed 'tween decks after a certain hour, they saved up the fat of their ration meat, and put it into an oyster-shell with a wick of cotton threads, fencing it round with clothes. Sometimes the air was so foul that the light went out. If they were discovered, the guards destroyed everything, books, paper, slates, pens, &c.

Souville mentions one thing I have not noticed in any account of prison-ship life, that there were French women on board, 'de basse extraction et extrêmement grossières'.

He emphasizes the incapacity and brutality of the British doctors, and particularizes one Weiss (not a British name, one is thankful to note!) as a type. He says that the orthodox treatment of the prisoners from San Domingo, who were suffering from the *vomito negro*, was to plunge them into icy water!

A system of signalling and holding conversation between one prison ship and another was carried out by the carpenters, who had their benches on the upper deck, a regular alphabet being arranged by means of hammer knocks and shifting the position of the benches. He is the first also to mention that theatricals were performed on a prison ship; the pieces given being a two-act vaudeville, *Les Aventures d'une voyageuse sensible*, and a drama in five acts, *La Fiancée du Corsaire*. The orchestra consisted of a flute and a violin; the female dresses were lent by the ladies of Portsmouth and Gosport, who also came as spectators. But the chief amusement, he says, was to vex the authorities as much as possible, to call the captain, who had an inflated sense of his own importance, a mere turnkey, to make songs on him, and above all to play tricks at the roll call, so as to create confusion and bewilderment.

The attempts to escape were very frequent, and this in spite of a recent savage threat that for every prisoner who escaped two should be hanged. Souville describes a daring escape which inspired him to action. A cutter laden with powder was alongside one of the hulks, waiting for morning to discharge into the *Egmont* man-of-war. Lieutenant Larivière and four or five other prisoners managed to slip out of the *Crown* and board her. They found the crew fast asleep, tied and gagged them securely, and adopted their clothes. At daybreak they hoisted their sail, Larivière giving loud commands in English, and passed by the *Egmont*, waiting for her powder. She hailed them to stop, but they crowded on all sail, and although the alarm was signalled, and they were pursued, they crossed safely to Roscoff.

As Souville, when he refused to be put on parole, had openly declared that he would escape at the first opportunity, he was carefully guarded. Thanks to his excellent knowledge of English he made friends among the bluejackets of the guard, and especially with one Will, whom he had helped with money when his mother's home was threatened to be broken up for debt.

So he started the delicate and difficult operation of boring a hole in the ship's side, large enough to admit the passage of a human body, above the water line, yet not too near the grated platform running round the ship, continually patrolled by guards. He counted on Will's aid, and confided his scheme to him.

The very next morning he was conducted to the Black Hole, and was informed that his design had been betrayed, and he instantly guessed that his supposed friend Will was the betrayer, as he alone was in the secret. Whilst in the *cachot* he found a mysterious note merely saying that at a certain hour on a certain day the high tide would be over the mud-banks which had proved fatal to so many fugitives from the hulks. In the *cachot* with him were three men who had successfully shammed madness in order to get sent to France, and who were about to be liberated. One of them, whose form of assumed madness had been to crow day and night like a cock, gave Tom a clue to a hole he had commenced to bore in the event of his sham madness failing.

Souville found the hole, finished it, and on the date named in the note slipped out, and started for a three-mile swim towards a light ashore. After much labour, he negotiated the mud-banks, and landed. Exhausted, he fell asleep, and was awakened by a man. He sprang to his feet and prepared to defend himself from arrest; but the man impressed silence, and pointed to a fisher-hut whence a light shone, evidently that to which he had steered at first, but of which he had lost sight during his long struggle in the water.

He entered the hut and found Will! The whole affair, the arrest, the *cachot*, and the mysterious note turned out to be Will's plot, who explained that if he had not divulged the secret of Souville's first escape-hole when it was known that he had discovered it, he would probably have got a thousand lashes at the triangles, and that to atone for it he had conveyed to the *cachot* the note which was the means of Tom's escape.

No time was lost in completely disguising him, and he started. As he passed along the smuggler's cliff path he heard the guns which proclaimed the escape of a prisoner. At 9 a.m. he passed Kingston, and got to Farlington on the Chichester road. Here he put up at a lodging house, replying to suspicious inquiries that he was from London, bound for an American ship coming from Dover. From here he took coach to Brighton, and in two days was at Dover. At Dover he waited two more days before he could find a neutral ship to take him across, and then quietly smuggled himself on to a Danish brig bound for Calais, and hid under a coil of rope on deck. Whilst here the Admiralty people came on board to search for fugitives, and one of them actually sat on the heap of rope under which he was. The brig sailed, and then, to the astonishment of the master and crew, Tom presented himself. At first the master was disposed to put back and give Tom up, for the penalties were heavy for harbouring escaped prisoners, but the promise of a handsome reward and Tom's mention of influential friends overcame his scruples and Tom was safely landed.

He went home, got the money, of which he gave 1,000 francs to the skipper, 500 francs to the crew, and 500 to the fisherman who landed him.

Souville now started the privateering business which was to make him famous, and during the years 1806 and 1807 won for his *Glaneur* a reputation on both sides of the Channel. At Dunkirk he distinguished himself on shore by saving two lives from a runaway carriage which had been upset into the port. He then changed to the *Général Paris*, and made a number of rich captures, but on November 30, 1808, was captured off Folkestone by two corvettes and a cutter, and found himself on the *Assistance* prison ship at Portsmouth. On the *Assistance* he made so many attempts to escape that he was changed to the *Crown*. Here he met an old shipmate, Captain Havas, of the *Furet* privateer, but from policy they agreed not to let it be seen that they were friends, and they lost no time in setting to work with saws made of barrel-hoops, and bits of fencing foils for gimlets, to make a hole a square foot in size through the nine inches of the wooden ship's side, and, to avoid the noise they made being heard, they worked while the English soldiers were scrubbing the decks.

By the beginning of January 1809 the hole was ready. January 9 was a suitable day for this project, being foggy, and the only obstacle was the bitter cold of the water. They had saved up rum, and grease wherewith to rub themselves, and had a compass, a knife, a flask for the rum, and a waterproof fishing-basket to hold a change of clothes. At midnight they opened the hole; Havas slipped out, and Souville followed, but in doing so made a slight noise, but enough to attract the notice of the sentry. They swam away amidst a storm of bullets fired at random in the fog and darkness. Souville was soon caught by one of the boats which at the first alarm had put out from all the hulks. Havas hung on to the rudder of a Portuguese ship under repair, and paused to rest. When all was quiet, he climbed up, boarded the ship, crept down to the hold, got under a basket, and, utterly worn out, fell asleep.

A cabin boy coming for the basket in the morning, at the appearance of a strange man under it was terrified and cried out. Havas rushed up on deck, but at the mouth of the hatchway was met by an English soldier who promptly knocked him down, and he was secured.

The adventurers got a month's Black Hole, and when they were released found the precautions against escape were stricter than ever. In May 1809 the news came that all the prisoners taken at Guadeloupe were to be exchanged. Havas and Souville determined to profit by the opportunity, and bought two turns of exchange from soldiers, with the idea of getting away as Guadeloupe prisoners. But, in order to pass the sentry it was necessary that they should have the appearance of having served in the tropics, so they had 'to make themselves up', with false moustaches and stained faces. This was effected, and at the signal of departure the two adventurers joined the Guadeloupe contingent and were taken ashore. But on the jetty stood Captain Ross, of the *Crown*, scrutinizing the prisoners.

'You didn't expect me here, my man,' said he to Havas, at the same time taking hold of his moustache, which came off in his hand. 'Never mind; although I am in duty bound to take you before Commodore Woodriff, I'll ask him to let you off; if I don't you'll sink my ship with your eternal hole-boring through her!'

He meant what he said, for, although somewhat of a martinet (so says the biographer of Souville—Henri Chevalier), he was a good fellow at heart, but Woodriff, who had been in command at Norman Cross in 1797, was of another disposition: 'un de ces moroses Anglais dont l'air sombre cache un caractère plus dur encore que sévère.' He refused Ross's request, and even admonished him for laxity of vigilance, and so our friends were sent back to the *Crown*, and got another month's *cachot*. Then they were separated, Havas being sent to the *Suffolk* and Tom Souville to the *Vengeance*. Six uneventful months passed; then the prisoners of the *Suffolk* and *Vengeance* were transferred to the *San Antonio*, and Havas and Souville were re-united, and took into partnership Étienne Thibaut. The commander of the *San Antonio* was an affable Scot with a soft heart towards his prisoners. He took a fancy to Havas, often chatted with him, and at last engaged him as a French teacher. Captain B. had a pretty wife, 'belle en tout point, blonde, grande, svelte et gracieuse,' and a charming little girl, possessing 'de bonnes joues roses, de grands yeux bleus, et des cheveux dorés à noyer sa tête si un ruban ne les eût captivés sur son cou; enfant pétulante et gaie, fraîche comme une fleur, vive comme un oiseau'.

Havas makes friends with the child, but aims at the favour of the mother. Being a dashing, attractive, sailor-like fellow, he succeeds, and moves her sympathy for his fate. Finally Mrs. B. promises that he shall go with her to a French theatrical performance ashore, as her husband rarely quits the ship except on duty. So they go, one fine spring day, she and Havas, and a Scots Captain R. with them to save appearances, first to the hulk *Veteran* where they learn that the play, to be acted in Portchester Castle, will be Racine's *Phèdre*, and that it will commence at 4 p.m.

They attended the play. An old caulker played Theseus, Phèdre was presented by a novice, and Hippolyte by a top-man, which probably means that it was ludicrous. After the play, Captain R. went into the town, leaving Havas and Mrs. B. to enjoy a beautiful springtime walk together, winding up with refreshments in an arbour which Mrs. B. had engaged. All this time, however, Havas was not so intoxicated with the delightful novelty of a *tête-à-tête* walk with a pretty Englishwoman on a lovely day in a fair country, as not to be making mental notes of the local geography.

During the long continuance of the fine weather, which was all against their project, the three men made preparations for escape, and particularly in the manufacture of wooden skates for use over the two great mud-banks which separated the hulks from the shore, and which had always been fatal obstacles to escaping prisoners. At length the long-looked-for change in the weather came, and at 1 a.m. on a wild, stormy morning Havas and Souville got off (in the French original I find no allusion to Thibaut), well furnished with necessaries, including complete suits of stylish clothing! Once they were challenged, but the uproar of the storm saved them, and, moreover, the sea, even in the land-locked part, was so high that the sentries had been withdrawn from the external gallery. It was a hard struggle, but they reached the first mud-spit safely, got over it on their skates, swam another bit, and at the second mud-bank had to rest, as Souville was taken with a sudden vertigo. Finally, after three terrible hours of contest with wind and wave, they landed. Thence they made their way into the fields, washed and scraped the mud off, and with the stylish clothes transformed themselves, as the account says, into 'elegants'.

For four hours they walked until they struck the London road, along which they tramped for an hour, that is until about 10 a.m., and breakfasted at an inn. At 3 p.m. they reached Petersfield, went boldly to the best hotel, dined as became gentlemen of their appearance, and ordered a post-chaise to be ready to take them to Brighton at 4 a.m.

They were three days on the journey to Brighton! Souville's admirable English was their protection, and the only inconvenience they experienced was from the remarks of people who contrasted their elegant appearance with the small amount of luggage they carried, consisting of a pocket-handkerchief containing their belongings.

They arrived at Brighton at 10 a.m. on a Sunday morning. The Duke of York had arrived there to review the troops assembled at Brighton Camp on account of Bonaparte's threatened invasion, so that the town was crowded with soldiers and visitors, accommodation was not to be had, and no chance of sailing to France was likely to be offered. So they decided to walk on to Hastings, a risky proceeding, as the country swarmed with soldiers. They walked for a day and a half, and then resolved to drive. For the night they had lodged at an inn which was full of soldiers, all of whom were incited by rewards to look out for spies, so they shut themselves in their room with food and two bottles of port, and busied themselves with mending and furbishing up the elegant clothes, which were beginning to show signs of wear and tear. The next day they left by coach; their fellow passengers included a faded lady of thirty, a *comédienne*, so she said, with whom Souville soon became on such excellent terms that she gave him her address at Hastings, and on the next day he went for a pleasant walk with her, noting carefully the lie of the country and looking out for a suitable boat on the beach in which to get over to France. Boats in plenty there were; but, in accordance with the Admiralty circular, inspired by the frequent appropriations of boats by escaping foreigners, from all of them masts, oars, and sails had been removed. So our friends resolved to walk on to Folkestone. They reached the 'Bay of Rice' (Rye Bay?) and had to pass the night in the open, as there was no inn, and arrived at Folkestone at 6 p.m. the next day.

During these stirring times of war between Britain and France, the French privateers and the English smugglers found it to be to their mutual interests to be good friends, for not only were the smugglers the chief carriers of escaped French prisoners, many of whom were officers of privateers, but they were valuable sources of information concerning the movements of war-ships and likely prizes. In return the French coastal authorities allowed them free access to their ports for purposes of the contraband trade. During his career afloat Souville had done a good turn to Mr. J. P., an English smuggler captain living at Folkestone, and Mr. J. P. promised that he would requite this at the first opportunity. And so Tom determined to find him at Folkestone. His excellent English soon procured him J. P.'s address, and there the fugitives had a royal reception, dinner, bed, a bath the next morning, fresh clothes and a change of linen. At breakfast they read the news of their escape and of the big reward offered for their recapture in the local newspaper.

They spent five happy days under this hospitable roof, waiting for favourable weather, and for their host to procure them a suitable boat. This came about in due course, and after a farewell banquet, the party, consisting of Souville, arm-in-arm with Mrs. P., Havas with her sister, J. P., and three friends, proceeded to the beach, and at 9 p.m. Souville and Havas embarked for Calais, where they arrived after a good passage, and had an enthusiastic reception, for it had been reported that in escaping from the *San Antonio*, they had been engulfed in the mud-banks.

Tom Souville lost no time in resuming his privateering life, and continued to be most successful, amassing money and gaining renown at the same time, but in 1812, when on the *Renard*, having in tow a brig prize of 200 tons, he was again captured, and once more found himself on the *Crown* prison ship, in 'Southampton Lake'. The *Crown* was still commanded by Ross—called in the original (which is in the form of an interview with Souville by Eugene Sue) 'Rosa', that being the sound of the name in French ears. Ross was a fine old fellow who had lost an arm at Trafalgar, but he hated the French. Ross, knowing Tom Souville's fame, ironically conducts him personally over the *Crown*, pointing out all the latest devices for the prevention of escape, and tells Tom that he will have a corporal specially told off to 'attend to him'. He offers to allow Tom to go ashore every day if he will give his parole not to attempt escape, but Tom refuses.

On the *Crown* Tom finds an old friend, Tilmont, a privateer captain, and they at once set to work on a plan for escape. One morning Captain Ross sends for Tom and quietly informs him that one Jolivet had sold him the secret of the hole then in the process of being cut by Tom and Tilmont, and as he tells him this they walk up and down the lower deck together. Whilst they are walking there is a great noise of tramping overhead. Ross asks what it is, and Tom replies that the prisoners are dancing. The captain calls an orderly and tells him to stop the dancing, 'the noise is distressing to Monsieur here,' he adds sarcastically. Tom is annoyed and begs he will allow the poor men to amuse themselves, but the captain is obdurate. Presently the noise ceases, and to Tom's horror he hears in the ensuing silence the sound of Tilmont working away at the hole. However, it did not attract the captain's attention. The truth was that the whole affair, the betrayal of the hole, the dancing on deck, and the interview with Captain Ross, was of Souville's arranging. Jolivet got £10 10s. for betraying the secret, which he at once paid into the ship's 'Escape Fund'; he had made it a condition that Souville and Tilmont should not be punished; the dancing on deck was arranged to be at the time of the interview between the captain and Tom, so that the noise of Tilmont's final touches to the work of boring the hole should be drowned.

A few days before this, one Dubreuil had attempted to escape, but had been suffocated in the mud-bank. On the morning after the interview above described, the bugle sounded for all the prisoners to be paraded on the upper deck. Here they found the captain and officers, all in full uniform, the guard drawn up with fixed bayonets, and on the deck in front of them a long object covered with a black cloth. The cloth was removed, and the wasted body of Dubreuil, with his eyes picked out, was exposed.

Souville was called forward.

'Do you recognize the body?' asked the captain.

'Yes,' replied Tom, 'but it does not matter much. He was a bad fellow who struck his mother.'

The horrible exhibition had been intended as a deterrent lesson to the prisoners in general and to Souville in particular, especially as it was known that he and Dubreuil had been lifelong acquaintances in Calais, but, as far as Tom was concerned, his reply sufficiently proved that it was thrown away on him, whilst among the other prisoners it excited only disgust and indignation.

Tom Souville's escape was arranged for that same night.

It was quite favourable for his enterprise, dark and so stormy that the hulk rolled heavily. Tilmont made Tom take a good drink of sugar, rum, and coffee; the two men greased themselves all over thoroughly; round Tom's neck was an eelskin full of guineas, in his hat a map of the Channel, in a 'boussole' tinder and steel, a knife in the cord of his hat, and a change of clothes in a little leather bag on his back.

Overboard he slipped (Tilmont's name is not again mentioned, although he greased himself, so I presume he did not start. There are many instances of poor fellows, after much elaborate preparation, being deterred at the last moment by the darkness, the black depths below, the long swim, and the extreme uncertainty of the result). It was a hard, long struggle in the wild night, and throughout appeared the face of Dubreuil with its empty orbits before the swimmer. However, in two hours and a half he reached land. He rested for a while, cleaned the mud off, changed his clothes and started to walk.

In nine days he reached Winchelsea, walking by night and hiding by day, for this time his clothes were not of the 'elegant' style, and the land was full of spy-hunters. He went on to Folkestone, and rested by the garden wall of a villa in the outskirts. As he rested he heard the voice of a woman singing in the garden. At once he recognized it as the voice of a captain's wife who had been of the merry party at J. P.'s house on the occasion of his last visit to Folkestone, called her by name, and announced his own. He was warmly welcomed, there was a repetition of the old festivities, and in due course he was found a passage for Calais, where he arrived safely. Once more he trod the deck of the famous *Renard*, and was so successful that he saved money enough to buy a cutter on his own account. He soon became one of the most famous Channel *corsaires*; and in addition a popular hero, by his saving many lives at sea, not only of his own countrymen, but of English fishermen, and in one case, of the crew of a British ship of war which had been disabled by foul weather.

Then came the Peace of 1814; and when, after Waterloo, friendly relationship was solidly established between the two countries, Tom Souville, only at home on the ocean, obtained command of the cross-channel packet *Iris*, which he retained almost up to the day of his death in 1840, at the age of sixty-four.

CHAPTER VIII
THE PRISON SYSTEM
The Prisoners Ashore. General

During the progress of the Seven Years' War, from 1756 to 1763, it became absolutely necessary, from the large annual increase in the number of prisoners of war brought to England, that some systematic accommodation for prisoners on land should be provided. Some idea of the increase may be formed when we find that the number of prisoners of war in England at the end of 1756 was 7,261, and that in 1763, the last year of the war, it was 40,000.

The poor wretches for whom there was no room in the already overcrowded hulks were herded together wherever space could be found or made for them.

They were in borough jails—veritable hells on earth even when filled with native debtors and felons: they were in common prisons such as the Savoy and Wellclose Square in London: they were in hired and adapted strong houses such as the Wool House at Southampton, and the old pottery works in Liverpool, or in adapted country houses such as Sissinghurst in Kent, or in adapted farms like Roscrow and Kergilliack in Cornwall; or in barracks as at Winchester, Tynemouth and Edinburgh. Portchester Castle was but an adaptation, so was Forton, near Gosport, and the only place of confinement built as a prison, and kept exclusively for prisoners of war, was for a long time the Millbay prison at Plymouth.

In 1760 public attention was drawn to the 'dangerous spirit' among the French prisoners in England. Escapes were frequent, were carried out by large bodies of men, and in many cases were characterized by open acts of defiance and violence. Inquiries were made about places which could be prepared to accommodate, between them, from fifteen to twenty thousand prisoners of war. No place was too sacred for the prison-hunters. A report upon the suitability of Kenilworth Castle was drawn up by a Dr. Palmer, who concluded, 'If the buildings are completed, some thousands of prisoners will be so accommodated as I flatter myself will reflect Honour on the British Nation.'

General Simon, we shall see later, was confined in Dumbarton Castle. The Royal Palace at Linlithgow only escaped conversion into a war prison by the exertions of Viscount Dundas, Lord of the Admiralty—a fact to which Sir Walter Scott thus alludes in *Waverley*:

'They halted at Linlithgow, distinguished by its ancient palace, which, Sixty Years since, was entire and habitable, and whose venerable ruins, *not quite Sixty Years since*, very narrowly escaped the unworthy fate of being converted into a barrack for French prisoners. May repose and blessings attend the ashes of the patriotic statesman, who, amongst his last services to Scotland, interposed to prevent this profanation!'

So the business of searching for suitable places and of adaptation of unsuitable went on, the prisoners being of course the chief sufferers, which in that hard, merciless age was not a matter of much concern, and it was not until 1782 that a move in the right direction seemed to be made by the abandonment of the old evil place of confinement at Knowle, near Bristol (visited and commented on by Wesley in 1759 and 1760, and by Howard in 1779), and the transfer of the prisoners to the 'Fish Ponds' prison, better known later as Stapleton.

In 1779 Howard says, in his General Report upon the prisons on land, 'The French Government made an allowance of 3*d.* per diem to Captains, Mates, sailing masters and surgeons; 2*d.* per diem to boatswains, carpenters, and petty officers generally, and 1*d.* per diem to all below these ratings (which is almost exactly the same as the allowances made by the British Government to its prisoners abroad). There is, besides, a supply from the same Court of clothes, linen, and shoes to those who are destitute of these articles; a noble and exemplary provision much to the honour of those who at present conduct public affairs in France.'

Howard found the American prisoners, except at Pembroke, clean and well clothed, thanks to liberal supplies from their own country as well as from England. He noted the care and assiduity of the 'Sick and Hurt' Office in London, and decided that England and France treated foreign prisoners very much alike on the whole.

In 1794 Charles Townshend wrote to the Earl of Ailesbury: 'The French prisoners have their quarters in Hillsea Barracks (Portsmouth), find our biscuit and beef much better than their own, and are astonished at the good treatment they meet with. Most of them are very young, and were driven on board by the bayonet.'

I quote this as I am only too glad when I come across any record or evidence which can serve to brighten the dark dreary record of these chapters in our national history.

In 1795 there were 13,666 prisoners of war in Britain, of whom 1,357 were officers on parole; of the remainder the largest number, 4,769, were at Portchester Castle.

In 1796–7 the great dépôt at Norman Cross near Peterborough, to contain 7,000 prisoners, was built and occupied. In 1798, further inquiries were made by the Government for prison accommodation, as the inflow of prisoners was unceasing and ever increasing, the total for this year being 35,000. The advertised specifications give us an idea of the space then considered sufficient for prisoners. Besides accommodation for a garrison calculated at the proportion of one guard for every twenty prisoners, cells were required measuring eight feet by seven, and eleven feet high, for four or five prisoners, or rooms twenty-four feet by twenty-two to be divided into nine cells, and replies were received from Coldbath Fields, London, Liverpool, Manchester, Preston, Lancaster Castle, Shrewsbury, and Dorchester.

In 1799 Stapleton Prison, near Bristol, was to be enlarged so as to be ready in June 1800, for twice its then complement of prisoners.

In 1803 a very general impression was prevalent in high places that an invasion of England was imminent from Ireland with which the prisoners of war all over the country, but especially the Western counties, were to be associated, and so, at the request of Sir Rupert George of the Transport Office, a detailed report was drawn up by Mr. Yorke of the best means to be taken to guard against this. To this was appended a memorandum of the capacity and condition of various inland prisons, such as Manchester, Stafford, Shrewsbury, Dorchester, Gloucester, Coldbath Fields in London, and Liverpool.

In 1806 the great prison at Dartmoor, built to hold 6,000 prisoners, and thus relieve the dangerous congestion at Plymouth, was founded, but the first prisoners did not enter it until 1809. In 1811 a large dépôt was formed at Valleyfield near Penicuik on the Esk, about nine miles south of Edinburgh, which was gradually enlarged until at the Peace of 1814 it contained 10,000 prisoners.

So by this time, 1814, there were nine large prisons at Dartmoor, Norman Cross, Millbay, Stapleton, Valleyfield, Forton, Portchester, Chatham (where the present St. Mary's Barracks were first used as a war-prison), and Perth, holding about 45,000 prisoners; there were about 2,000 officers on parole; the hulks at Portsmouth, Plymouth, and Chatham—about fifty ships—would hold nearly 35,000 prisoners, and the grand total would be well in excess of the largest number of war prisoners in Britain in one year, that is, 72,000 in 1814.

In 1812 the following notification was sent to the Admiralty, who evidently treated it seriously, as a copy of it was sent to the agents of all the war prisons in the country:

'Extra Secret Intelligence.

'The large fleet here (Boulogne) remain perfectly inactive, but the Flotilla are only waiting for orders. I was yesterday told by one of the Captains that 6,000 men would soon be embarked, that the place of landing was to be as near as possible to Stilton Prison (Norman Cross) and that every man was to carry two complete sets of arms, &c., in order to equip the prisoners they may release.'

Three men, named La Ferre, Denisham, and De Mussy, were to land as American gentlemen, and to take charge quietly and unobtrusively. The head-quarters were to be near Liverpool, Hull, and between Portsmouth and Plymouth, whence these emissaries were to gain access to all the prisons, and prepare the minds of the inmates for the Great Event.

Nothing came of this, but the correspondence of the Transport Office reveals the fact that by one means or another a more or less regular correspondence was kept up between France and the prisons, and that there were concerned in it some very well known officers on parole, and even some Englishmen.

The captaincy of a war prison was no sinecure, and if history shows that one or two of the officers occupying the position were ill-fitted for it, assuredly they had no reason to complain of a lack of rules, regulations, and instructions from head-quarters, and they were called to order in no measured terms.

The care of the prisoners themselves, desperate, restless, cunning rascals as many of them were, seems to have bothered the agent much less than the care of those who were in any way associated with the working of the prison—the big and little officials, the officers and soldiers of the garrison, the contractors, the tradesmen, the workmen, the servants, the innkeepers, farmers, post-office officials, even the stage coachmen and guards, not to mention the neighbouring gentry, parsons and old ladies who, of course, knew very much better how to run a war-prison than did Captain Pressland, or Captain Cotgrave, or Captain Draper, or any other selected man.

Another fact which contributed to the irksomeness of the post was that although a naval captain was always the head of a war prison, and his turnkeys were generally of the same service, and he was the responsible head of the establishment, the guardianship of the prisoners was absolutely in the hands of the military authorities, who were therefore responsible for the safe-keeping of the prisoners. Any difference therefore between the naval captain and the military colonel as to the arrangement and disposal of the guards—and such differences were frequent—was sure to betray itself in the condition of the prison.

It may be easily understood that although it was the naval captain in charge of a prison who was held responsible for every escape of a prisoner, he would be pretty sure to put the *onus* of it on to the military commander, who, in turn, would be ready to attribute the mishap to anything but deficiency in the arrangement of sentries or to any slackness on the part of his men.

Take again the position of the war prisoner agent, as he was called, with regard to the numberless appeals to his humanity with which he was assailed. The period of the Great Wars was not characterized by hyper-sensitiveness on the score of human suffering and want, although I thoroughly believe that the men selected for the position of war prisoner agents were generally as kindly disposed and as sympathetic, as refined and well-bred Englishmen as could be in an age not remarkable for gentleness.

It must be remembered that they had ever to be on their guard against ruse and stratagem.

A forcible illustration is afforded by the much vexed question of the religious condition of the prisoners. In 1798 the Bishop of Léon asked that French priests should be allowed to minister to the prisoners at Portchester and Stapleton, and, although it was notorious that by far the greater number of Frenchmen were not merely indifferent to religion, but avowed preachers of atheism, the permission was given, and the Abbés De La Marc and Pasquier were told off for duty. Later on, however, it would seem that the privilege thus accorded had been grossly abused, and the permission cancelled, for the Transport Office writes:

'The T. O. regrets that it is not in their power to permit the *émigré* priests to visit War Prisons. We feel it our duty, however, to say that in the present difficult times when pretended Friends are not always distinguishable from real Foes, we feel it our Duty to be on our guard respecting Intercourse with all Prisoners of war under our charge, and though we have a sincere desire to promote the interests of the Christian Religion under any Denomination, yet where it has been, and is uniformly, if not universally, insulted by the Republicans of your Nation who constitute the bulk of our captives, we must be cautious of every species of Introduction to men so generally unprincipled, and who are at best the Dupes of an ignorant and insidious Philosophy. We allow much when we grant permission to your Priests upon the express desire of the Parties, and we appeal to you whether it be not an indulgence which would not be conceded to Protestant Divines under similar circumstances in any Roman Catholic Country, and particularly in France itself under its ancient Government.'

The bishop also applies to have a priest at Deal. The Transport Office refuses, saying that Deal is not a dépôt for prisoners, but only a receiving place, and there are no turnkeys and clerks, such 'as the admission of an Ecclesiastic might render necessary'.

In 1801, the same Bishop of Léon had the assurance to request the release of a French priest taken under arms. To this the Transport Office replied:

'The Board is rather surprised that you should apply to them on behalf of such a person, as they conceive it to be against the spirit of all Religion that men in Holy Orders should be found in Military Array, and they are more convinced that they should not comply with such a request, as no assurance can be given or be relied on that so unprincipled a man may not put off his Function for his own purposes a second time and repeat his enormity.'

In 1808, the Bishop of Moulins was chaplain to the prisoners at Norman Cross, and, according to the Rev. Arthur Brown, author of a little book about this prison, devoted his life to the spiritual regeneration of the poor fellows in captivity, although Dr. Walker, of Peterborough, estimates the bishop somewhat differently.

At any rate, his boy attendant, a prisoner, was found guilty of breaking one of the prison rules by selling straw hats clandestinely made by the prisoners, and was ordered back into confinement. The bishop, who did not live in the prison, but was staying at the *Bell*, in Stilton, applied for another prisoner attendant, but was refused.

Again, in 1814, the British and Foreign Bible Society asked that the Transport Office agents should be allowed to distribute New Testaments among the prisoners at Stapleton and Norman Cross. The Office replied:

'We cannot impress such a duty on our agents, as they consider it an impossibility to prevent the prisoners from selling them, as all the Vigilance exercised by the officers of the Department is insufficient to prevent the prisoners from making away with the most necessary articles of clothing and bedding.'

That the Transport Office were justified in their refusal is confirmed by an incident at the final embarkation of the French prisoners from the Perth dépôt in July of the same year, 1814. A considerable number of French Testaments were sent from Edinburgh to be distributed among the prisoners leaving for France. The distribution was duly made, but by the time the prisoners had reached the waterside, almost every man had sold his Testament for a trifling sum.

It cannot be doubted, I think, that the hardships endured by the prisoners in the war prisons were very much exaggerated, and also that to a very large extent the prisoners brought them upon themselves. Especially was this the case in the matter of insufficient food and clothing. Gambling was the besetting sin of the prisons, and to get the wherewithal to gamble the prisoners sold clothing, bedding, and not only their rations for the day, but for days to come. At Dartmoor the evil occasioned by the existence of the sale of rations by prisoners to 'brokers', who resold them at a profit, was so great that Captain Cotgrave, the Governor, in February 1813, sent a number of the 'brokers' to the *cachot*. To their remonstrance he replied, in writing, much as a sailor man he would have spoken:

'To the Prisoners in the Cachot for purchasing Provisions. The Orders to put you on short allowance (2/3rds) from the Commissioners of His Majesty's Transport Board is for purchasing the provisions of your fellow prisoners, by which means numbers have died from want of food, and the hospital is filled with sick not likely to recover. The number of deaths occasioned by this inhuman practise occasions considerable expense to the Government, not only in coffins, but the hospital is filled with these poor, unhappy wretches so far reduced from want of food that they linger a considerable time in the hospital at the Government's expense, and then fall a victim to the cruelty of those who have purchased their provisions, to the disgrace of Christians and whatever nation they belong to.

'The testimony of the surgeons and your countrymen prove the fact.'

The appeal was useless, and he issued a proclamation a month later, threatening to stop the markets if the practice was persisted in. This was equally fruitless. Charitable people pitied the poor half-naked prisoners in winter, and supplied them abundantly with clothing; but when the same men were pointed out to them a few days later as naked as before, and it was represented to them that by their well-meant benevolence they were actually encouraging that which it was most desirable to check, they refused to believe it. Hence it became necessary to punish severely. The most efficacious form of punishment was to put an offender's name at the bottom of the list for being exchanged against British prisoners to be sent from France or whatever country we happened to be at war with. But even this had no deterrent effect upon some, and the frenzy for gain was so remarkable that in all the prisons there was a regular market for the purchase and sale of places on the Exchange List, until the Government stopped the practice. The most common form of punishment was putting offenders on short allowance. For making away with hammock, bed, or blanket, the prisoner was put on short allowance for ten days; for making away with any two of these articles he was docked for fourteen days; for cutting or damaging bedding or clothes, he had half rations for five days and had to make the damage good.

Acts of violence brought confinement in the *cachot* or Black Hole. A prisoner who wounded a turnkey was to be kept handcuffed, with his hands behind him, for not less than twelve hours, and for not more than twenty-four!

For murder and forgery the prisoners came under the civil law; death was the penalty for both, but until 1810 no prisoner-forgers, although convicted, had been punished with death in England, owing to a doubt in the minds of judges whether prisoners of war were answerable to municipal tribunals for this sort of offence, which is not against the law of nations.

Prisoners who were not mentally or physically gifted enough to earn money by the exercise of their talents or employment in handicraft, had other opportunities of doing so. For working about the prisons as carpenters, gardeners, washermen, they were paid threepence a day. As helpers in the infirmaries—one to every ten patients—they received sixpence a day. Officers recaptured after breaking their parole or sent to prison for serious offences were glad, if they had means, to pay prisoners threepence a day to act as their servants, and do their dirty work generally. At the same rate sweepers were engaged at the ratio of one to every hundred men; cooks, in the proportion of one for every 400 men, received 4½*d.* a day, and barbers earned 3*d.* a day. At Dartmoor some five hundred prisoners were employed in these and other ways, each man wearing on his cap a tin plate with the nature of his calling thereon inscribed. A necessarily rough estimate showed that nearly half of the inmates of the war prisons made honest money in one way or another; the remainder were gamblers and nothing else. Still, a very large number of the wage-earners were gamblers also. Of these various professions and trades much will be said in the accounts of the prison life which follow, and when comparisons are instituted between the versatility, the deftness, the ingenuity, the artistic feeling, and the industry of the French prisoners in Britain, and the helpless indolence of the British prisoners abroad, testimony is unconsciously given in favour of that national system by which men of all social grades, of all professions, and of all trades, are compelled to serve in the defence of their country, as contrasted with that which, until late years, deemed only the scum of the population as properly liable to military service.

CHAPTER IX
THE PRISONS ASHORE
1. Sissinghurst Castle

About the Sissinghurst one looks on to-day there is little indeed to remind us that here stood, one hundred and fifty years ago, a famous war prison, and it is hard to realize that in this tranquil, picturesque, out-of-the-way nook of Kent, for seven long years, more than three thousand captive fighting men dragged out a weary existence.

Originally the splendid seat of the Baker family, and in the heyday of its grandeur one of the Kentish halting-places of Queen Elizabeth during her famous progress in 1571, it had far fallen from its high estate when, in 1756, Government, hard pressed to find accommodation for the annually increasing numbers of prisoners of war, leased it.

Of the 'Castle', as it came to be called, of this period, the gate-house, a line of outbuildings which were partially used as barracks for the troops on guard, and a few memories, alone survive. The great quadrangle has disappeared, but the line of the ancient moat, in parts still filled with water, in part incorporated with garden ground, still enables the visitor to trace the original extent of the buildings. Part of the line of ivy-clad buildings which face the approach are said to have been used as a small-pox hospital, and the name François may still be seen carved on the brick; the field known as the 'Horse Race' was the prison cemetery, and human remains have sometimes within living memory been disturbed therein.

Otherwise, legends of the prison linger but faintly in the neighbourhood; but from some of these it would seem that officer-prisoners at Sissinghurst were allowed out on parole. The place-name 'Three Chimneys', at a point where three roads meet, exactly one mile from Sissinghurst, is said to be a corruption of 'Trois Chemins', so called by the French prisoners whose limit it marked.

Wilsley House, just out of Cranbrook, a fine old residence, formerly belonging to a merchant prince of the Kentish cloth trade, now occupied by Colonel Alexander, is said to have been tenanted by French officers on parole, and some panel paintings in one of the rooms are said to have been their work, but I think they are of earlier date. The neighbouring Barrack Farm is said to have been the prison garrison officers' quarters, and the house next to the Sissinghurst Post Office is by tradition the old garrison canteen.

The only individual from whom I could gather any recollections of the French prisoner days was an old farm labourer named Gurr, living at Goford. He told me that his great-grandfather, ploughing one day near the prison, suddenly saw three men creeping along a hedgerow close to him. Recognizing them to be Sissinghurst prisoners, he armed himself with the coulter of his plough and went up to them. The poor fellows seemed exhausted and bewildered, and went with him back to the Castle without offering any resistance, telling him on the way that they had got out by tunnelling under the moat with small mattocks. Gurr said that he had often dug up human bones in the meadow opposite the Castle entrance.

The following letter, I think, was written from Sissinghurst, but it may be from Portchester. I insert it here as in all contemporary correspondence 'le château' means Sissinghurst.

'Le Château, 30me mai, 1756.

'MONSIEUR:

'La présente est pour vous prier de nous donner de délargissement, attendu que nous ne sommes point obligés pour une personne de nous voir detenus commes nous sommes. Nous vous avertisons que si nous n'avons pas l'élargissement nous minerons le Château, et nous sommes résolus de nous battre contre nos ennemis. Nous ne sommes point obligés de souffrir par raport d'un joli qui ne nous veu que de la peine. Nous avons des armes, de la Poudre blanche et des Bales (Balles?) pour nous défendre. Nous vous prions de nous donner la liberté le plus tôt possible, attendu que nous sommes tout prêst a suivre notre dessein. On nous a déjà tué un homme dans le prison, et nous aurons la vengeance.

'Nous avons été tranquille jusqu'aujourdui, mais présentement nous allons jouer à la Françoise des rigodons sans violons attendu que nous sommes tous d'un accord.

'Jugez de Reste,

'Votre très affectionné et

'François en général.'

SISSINGHURST CASTLE

From an old print

On June 24, 1758, the following complaint was sent up:

'NOSSEIGNEURS:

'Nous avons eu l'honneur de vous envoyer un placet en date du 17me de ce mois, et nous là vous tenus [sic] entre les mains de Mr. Paxton, Secretaire de Mr. Cook [Cooke] le 18me nous y faisions de justes plaintes touchant le Gouvernement de Mr. Cook qui n'est rien moins que tyrannique et capricieuse, et nous vous le posions tout au long sa dernière injustice. Craignans qu'on ne vous ait pas mis celuy la, nous avons pris la liberté de vous faire cette lettre pour vous prier de nous rendre justice. Si Mr. Cook n'avoit rien à se reprocher il ne retiendrait pas les lettres que nous vous addressons. Tout le monde scait ce que mérite celuy qui détourne des oreilles de justice, les cris de ceux qui la réclame et qui n'ont d'autre crime que d'être infortunés, nous espérons nosseigneurs que vous y aurez egarder que vous nous ferez justice, nous vous aurons à jamais l'obligation.

'Vos humbles et très obeisans serviteurs

'Pour tous les prisonniers en général.'

At about the same date twenty-seven paroled naval officers at Cranbrook signed a complaint that they were not allowed by the one-mile limit of their parole to visit their crews, prisoners at Sissinghurst, two miles away, to help them in their distress and to prevent them being robbed by the English who have the monopoly of getting things for sale into the prison, notably the jailers and the canteen man, not to mention others. Also that the prisoners at Sissinghurst had no chance of ventilating their grievances, which were heavy and many:

'De remédier à une injustice, ou plutôt à une cruauté que les nations les plus barbares n'exercisions. En effet c'est une tiranie audieuse que de vouloir forcer des pauvres prisonniers à n'acheter d'autre marchandises que celles venant des mains de leurs Gardiens, et d'empécher leurs parens et amis de leur envoyer à beaucoup meilleur marché aussy bien.'

Many of the letters from relations in France to prisoners at Sissinghurst are preserved at the Record Office. It is only from acquaintance with these poor tattered, blotted ebullitions of affection and despair that the modern Englishman can glean a notion of what confinement in an English prison of husbands, fathers, brothers, and lovers meant to hundreds of poor, simple peasant and fisher women of France. The breath of most of them is religious resignation: in a few, a very few, a spirit of resentment and antagonism to Britain is prominent; most of them are humble domestic chronicles blended with prayers for a speedy liberation and for courage in the meanwhile. There is nothing quite like these mid-eighteenth century letters in the correspondence of the succeeding great struggle, when the principles of the Revolution had penetrated to the homes of the lowliest. One sees reflected in it the simplicity, the childish confidence in the rightness and fitness of all in authority, and, above all, the deep sense of religion, which invested the peasantry of France with a great and peculiar charm.

During this year, 1758, the letters of complaint are many and pitiful, the chief subject being the non-delivery to prisoners of their letters, and the undue surveillance exercised over correspondence of the tenderest private nature. In 1760 the occupants of Sissinghurst received their share of the clothes provided by English compassion. Many of them were accused of selling these clothes, to which they replied that it was to buy necessaries or tobacco, or for postage, and added that they had been for a long time on half-rations.

On October 14 a desperate attempt to escape was made, and frustrated in an unnecessarily brutal manner. A prisoner named Artus, his brother, and other prisoners discovered a disused latrine. Into this they crept, broke through a brick wall by a drain, and reached the edge of the moat, and crossed it to the opposite bank close to the first of the three sentries on duty along it. This was at ten o'clock on a moonlight night. Two of the prisoners passed the first and second sentries and got some way into the fields. Artus and his brother were to follow, and were crawling on hands and knees to avoid being seen. The first sentry, who was close by, did nothing, having probably been bribed; but the other two sentries, being alarmed by a fourth sentry, who was on the right hand of the first, ran up and challenged Artus, who cried: 'Don't fire! Surrender!' But the sentry disregarded this, wounded him in two places on the arm, tearing his waistcoat, and then fired at him point blank, blowing off half his head. Artus's brother, three yards behind, was secured by a drummer who was armed with nothing but a drumstick, thus proving the utterly unnecessary killing of Artus. Two other prisoners were captured later in the drain, ready to come out.

In the *Annual Register* we read that on Saturday, July 16, 1760, the alarm was given that a thousand prisoners had broken out of the Castle and were abroad in the country. 'To arms' was beaten immediately. 'You would have been pleased to see with what readiness and alacrity the Surrey Militia here, universally, officers and men, advanced towards the place of danger', says the correspondent, 'I say, "towards," because when they got as far as Milkhouse Street, the alarm was discovered to be a mistake. Many of the townspeople and countrymen joined them.'

On one Sunday morning in 1761 the good people of Cranbrook were sent flying out of church by the news that the Sissinghurst prisoners had broken out and were scouring the country fully armed, but this also was a false alarm.

It was from the top of the still standing gatehouse-tower that the deed was perpetrated which caused the following entry in the Cranbrook Register:

'1761. William Bassuck: killed by a French prisoner.' Bassuck was on sentry-go below, and the Frenchman dropped a pail on him.

In 1762 the misery of the prisoners at Sissinghurst culminated in a Petition to the Admiralty, signed by almost all of them, of so forcible and circumstantial a character, that in common justice it could not be overlooked, and so Dr. Maxwell was sent down to examine the charges against Cooke, the agent.

The Complaints and their replies were as follows:

(1) That the provisions were bad in quality, of short measure and badly served.

Reply: Not proved.

(2) That cheese had been stopped four 'maigre' days in succession to make good damage done by prisoners.

Reply: Only upon two days.

(3) That prisoners had been put upon half allowance in the *cachot* or Black Hole for staying in the wards on account of not having sufficient clothing to leave them.

Reply: They were not put in the *cachot*, but upon half allowance for remaining in the wards during the day contrary to the Regulations. There was no need for them to lack 'cloaths'.

(4) That they were put upon half allowance for appearing at a sudden muster without clothes.

Reply: This muster was ordered by the agent, Cooke, because he suspected the prisoners of embezzling clothes and of gambling them away.

(5) That the prisoners had been threatened with being deprived of their turn of Exchange for signing this Petition to the Board of Admiralty.

Reply: There was no foundation for this statement.

(6) That Cooke had refused to pay them for more than eighteen days' work in carrying coals, although they were twenty-eight days.

Reply: In reality they had only worked for parts of these days, and had been paid for the work actually done.

(7) That Cooke showed no zeal for the welfare of the prisoners.

Reply: That there is no foundation for this statement.

(8) That they were ill-treated by the Militia guards.

This last complaint was the most serious of all, and the examination into it revealed a state of affairs by no means creditable to the authorities. Here it should be stated that on account of the great and constant demand made by the war upon the regular troops, the task of guarding the prisons was universally performed by the Militia—undesirable men from more than one point of view, especially from their lack of self-restraint and their accessibility to bribery. The following cases were cited. On November 28, 1757, Ferdinand Brehost, or Gratez, was shot dead by a sentry of General Amherst's regiment. The sentry in defence said that he had had orders to fire upon any prisoners who did not take down the clothes they hung upon the palisades when ordered to.

It was adjudged that the sentry fired too precipitately.

On the night of October 29, 1759, the prisoner Jacobus Loffe was shot dead in his hammock by a sentry.

In defence the sentry said that he called out several times for the prisoners to put out their lights. They refused and bid him fire and be damned. The evidence showed that all the prisoners were asleep, and that the light seen by the sentry was the reflection on the window of a lamp outside the building.

The same judgement as in the other case was given.

On July 11, 1760, two prisoners were shot by a sentry. John Bramston, the sentry, said in defence that a prisoner came too near the forbidden barrier, refused to keep off when ordered to, with the result that Bramston fired, killed him, and another prisoner further away.

Bramston was tried at Maidstone and acquitted, the jury finding that he did no more than his duty in accordance with the general orders at the Castle. Still, it came out in evidence that orders had been issued that sentries were not to fire if the object could be secured by the turnkey. Colonel Fairfax indeed ordered that sentries were not to fire at all. He had found out that Bramston was sometimes out of his senses, and he had discharged him from the service, but he was actually on duty after this affair, was found to have loaded his piece with two balls, and after the murder on the 11th had threatened to kill more prisoners.

On the same day two other prisoners were stabbed by sentries. In one case, however, a prisoner gave evidence in favour of the sentry, saying that he did not believe there was any intention to kill, but that the sentry being surrounded by a crowd of prisoners, pushed his bayonet to keep them at a distance for fear that they intended mischief.

It also came out that the soldiers were allowed to strike the prisoners with the flats of their sabres. This was now forbidden. Also that the soldiers abused the power they had of taking away the prisoners' knives when they made improper use of them, and actually sold the knives thus confiscated to other prisoners. Also that the soldiers wilfully damaged forms and tables so that the prisoners should be punished.

The Commissioners of the 'Sick and Hurt' Office, in their summing up of Dr. Maxwell's evidence, said that, while there was no doubt much exaggeration by the petitioners, there was too much reason for complaint, and found that the person in charge was not so much to blame, but the 'common centinels', whose understanding did not enable them to distinguish between the letter and the meaning of their orders, and that this arose from the lack of printed standing orders. The officers of the guard had arbitrary powers independent of the agent, and the latter said when asked why he did not complain to the Board, that he did not care to dispute with the officers.

It will be noted that this inquiry was not held until 1762, that is to say, until seven years of tyranny had been practised upon these unfortunate foreigners, and seven years of nameless horrors suffered in forced silence. Small wonder that throughout the correspondence of this period Sissinghurst is spoken of with disgust and loathing.

The record of only one Sissinghurst prisoner marrying an Englishwoman exists—that, in 1762, of Laurence Calberte, 'a prisoner among the French at Sissinghurst House', to Mary Pepper.

I have to thank Mr. Neve of the Castle House, Sissinghurst, for his kindness in allowing me to have the photograph taken of some exquisite little articles made in wood by Sissinghurst prisoners, and also to reproduce a picture of the 'Castle', as it was when used as a prison.

After its evacuation at the Peace of Paris, in 1763, Sissinghurst Castle became a workhouse, and when it ceased to be used for this purpose gradually fell into ruin and was pulled down.

Articles in Wood made by the Prisoners at Sissinghurst Castle, 1763

CHAPTER X
THE PRISONS ASHORE
2. NORMAN CROSS

It is just as hard for the visitor to-day to the site of Norman Cross, to realize that here stood, until almost within living memory, a huge war-prison, as it is at Sissinghurst. Whether one approaches it from Peterborough, six miles away, through the semi-rural village of Yaxley, by which name the prison was often called, or by the Great North Road from Stilton—famous for the sale, not the manufacture, of the famous cheese, and for the wreck of one of the stateliest coaching inns of England, the *Bell*—we see but a large, ordinary-looking meadow, dotted with trees, with three or four houses on its borders, and except for its size, which is nearly forty acres, differing in no way from the fields around.

An examination of the space, however, under the guidance of Dr. Walker, does reveal remains. We can trace the great ditch which passed round the prison inside the outer wall; some of the twenty-one wells which were sunk still remain, and about thirty feet of the original red brick wall, built in the old 'English bond' style, is still above ground. As, with the exceptions presently to be noted, the prisons proper, with the offices pertaining thereto, were built entirely of wood, and were sold and removed when the prison ceased to be, nothing of it remains here, although some of the buildings were re-erected in Peterborough and the neighbouring villages, and may still be seen. The only war-time buildings remaining are the Prison Superintendent's house, now occupied by Alderman Herbert, and the agent's house, now belonging to Mr. Franey, both, of course, much altered and beautified, and one which has been variously described to me as the officers' quarters and the Barrack Master's residence. In the Musée Historique Militaire at the Invalides, in Paris, there is a most minutely and beautifully executed model of the Norman Cross Prison, the work of one Foulley, who was a prisoner here for five years and three months. Not only are the buildings, wells, palisades, pumps, troughs, and other details represented, but tiny models of prisoners at work and at play are dotted about, and in front of the chief, the eastern gate, a battalion of Militia is drawn up, complete to the smallest particulars of arms and equipment.

Not the least interesting relic of the prison days is the prisoners' burial-ground at the lower end of a field sloping down from the west side of the Great North Road.

On July 28 of the present year (1914) a memorial to the prisoners of war who died at Norman Cross was unveiled by Lord Weardale. The idea originated with Dr. T. J. Walker and Mr. W. H. Sands, and was developed by the Entente Cordiale Society. The memorial is in the form of a stone pillar, surmounted by an eagle with outstretched wings, standing upon a square pedestal approached by steps, the lowermost of which is shaped like the palisading of the old prison, and faces the Great North Road, the burial ground being at the bottom of the field behind it. Upon the monument is inscribed:

'In Memoriam. This column was erected A.D. 1914 to the memory of 1,770 soldiers and sailors, natives or allies of France, taken prisoners of war during the Republican and Napoleonic wars with Great Britain, A.D. 1793–1814, who died in the military dépôt at Norman Cross, which formerly stood near this spot, 1797–1814.

Dulce et decorum est pro patriâ mori.

Erected by

The Entente Cordiale Society and friends on the initiative of the late W. H. Sands, Esq., Honorary Secretary of the Society.'

One might expect to find at Yaxley Church, as in so many other places in England associated with the sojourn of war prisoners, epitaphs or registry entries of officers who died on parole, but there are none. All that Yaxley preserves of its old connexion with the war prison are the stone caps of the prison east gate piers, which now surmount the piers of the west churchyard entrance, and the tablet in the church to the memory of Captain Draper, R.N., an agent of the prison, which is thus lettered:

'Inscribed at the desire and the sole Expence of the French Prisoners of War at Norman Cross, to the memory of Captain John Draper, R.N., who for the last 18 months of his life was Agent to the Depôt; in testimony of their esteem and gratitude for his humane attention to their comforts during that too short period. He died February 23rd, 1813, aged 53 years.'

MEMORIAL TO FRENCH PRISONERS OF WAR WHO DIED AT NORMAN CROSS

Unveiled July 28, 1914

The Rev. Arthur Brown, in his little book *The French Prisoners of Norman Cross*, says that the prisoners asked to be represented at his funeral, and that their petition concluded with the assurance that, *mauvais sujets* as some of them were, not one would take advantage of the liberty accorded them to attempt to escape. It is gratifying to know that their request was granted.

Other relics of the prisoners, in the shape of articles made by them for sale with the rudest of tools and the commonest of materials, are tolerably abundant, although the choicest are to be seen in museums and private collections, notably those in the Peterborough Museum and in the possession of Mr. Dack, the curator. Probably no more varied and beautiful specimens of French prisoner work in wood, bone, straw, and grass, than these just mentioned, are to be found in Britain.

The market at which these articles were sold was held daily from 10 a.m. till noon, according to some accounts, twice a week according to others. It was important enough, it is said, to have dwarfed that at Peterborough: as much as £200 was known to have been taken during a week, and at one time the concourse of strangers at it was so great that an order was issued that in future nobody was to be admitted unless accompanied by a commissioned officer. Visitors were searched, and severe penalties were imposed upon any one dealing in Government stores, a Yaxley tradesman in whose possession were found palliasses and other articles marked with the broad arrow being fined heavily, condemned to stand in the pillory at Norman Cross, and imprisoned for two years.

In the year 1796 it became absolutely necessary that special accommodation should be provided for the ever-increasing number of prisoners of war brought to Britain. The hulks were full to congestion, the other regular prisons,—such as they were,—the improvised prisons, and the hired houses, were crowded; disease was rife among the captives on account of the impossibility of maintaining proper sanitation, and the spirit of revolt was showing itself among men just then in the full flush of the influences of the French Revolution. Norman Cross was selected as the site of a prison which should hold 7,000 men, and it was well chosen, being a tract of land forty acres in extent, healthily situated on high ground, connected with the sea by water-ways via Lynn and Peterborough; and with London, seventy-eight miles distant, by the Great North Road. Time pressed; buildings of stone or brick were not to be thought of, so it was planned that all should be of wood, surrounded by a brick wall, but this last was not completed for some time after the opening of the prison. The skeletons of the prison blocks were framed and shaped in London, sent down, and in four months, that is to say in March 1797, the labour of 500 carpenters, working Sundays and week-days, rendered some of the blocks ready for habitation.

The first agent appointed was Mr. Delafons, but he only acted for a few days previous to the arrival of Mr. James Perrot from Portchester, on April 1, 1797. The superintendent of the transport of the prisoners was Captain Daniel Woodriff, R.N.

On March 23, 1797, Woodriff received notice and instructions about the first arrival of prisoners. On March 26 they came—934 in number—in barges from Lynn to Yaxley, at the rate of 1s. 10d. per man, and victualling at 7d. per man per day, the sustenance being one pound of bread or biscuit, and three quarters of a pound of beef.

The arrivals came in fast, so that between April 7 and May 18, 1797, 3,383 prisoners (exclusive of seven dead and three who escaped), passed under the care of the ten turnkeys and the eighty men of the Caithness Legion who guarded Norman Cross.

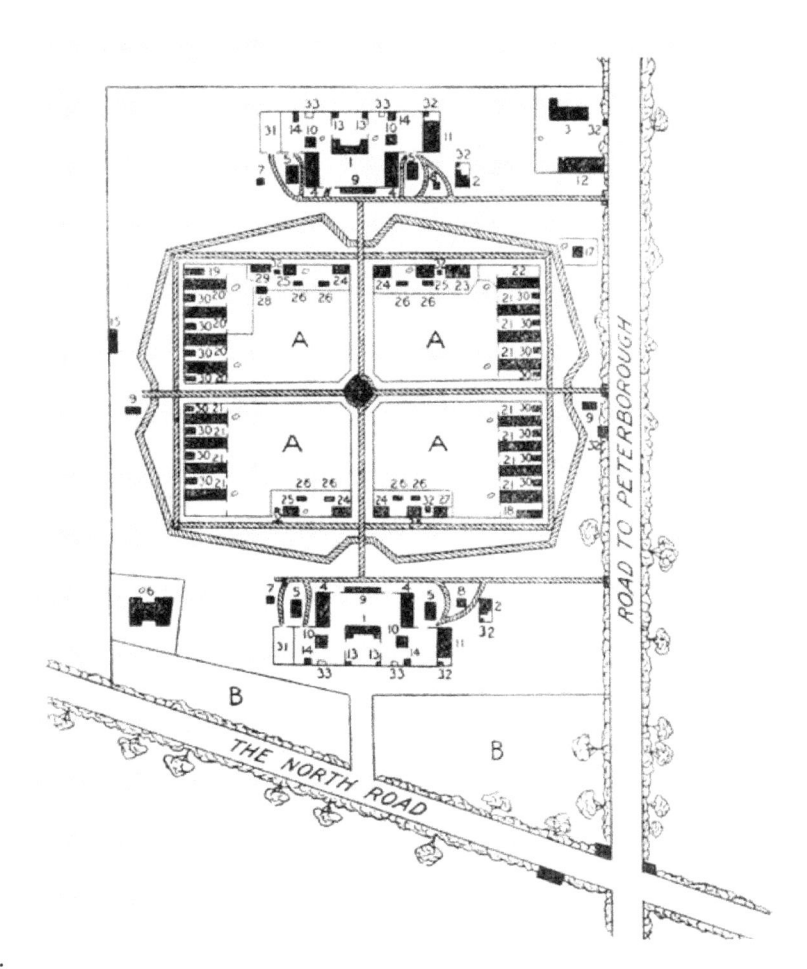

1.

Officers' Barracks.

2.

Field Officers' Barracks.

3.

Barrack Master's House.

4.

Soldiers' Barracks.

5.

Non-Commissioned Officers.

6.

Military Hospital.

7.

Magazines.

8.

Engine-house.

9.

Guard Rooms.

10.

Soldiers' Cooking-houses,

11.

Canteens.

12.

Military Straw Barn.

13.

Officers' Privies.

14.

Soldiers' Privies.

15.

Shed for spare soil carts.

16.

Block House.

17.

Agent and Superintendent's House.

18.

Prisoners' Straw Barn.

19.

Dead House.

20.

Prisoners' Hospitals.

21.

Barracks for Prisoners of War.

22.

Apartments for Clerks and Assistant Surgeons.

23.

Agent's Office.

24.

Store House.

25.

Prisoners' Cooking-houses.

26.

Turnkeys' Lodges.

27.

Prisoners' Black Hole.

28.

Wash-house to Prisoners' Hospital.

29.

Building for Medical Stores.

30.

Prisoners' Privies.

31.

Coal Yards.

32.

Privies.

33.

Ash Pits.

Wells marked thus o.

A.

Airing Grounds.

B.

Lord Carysfort's Grounds.

NORMAN CROSS PRISON. (*Hill's Plan*, 1797–1803.)

Complaints and troubles soon came to light. A prisoner in 1797, 'who appeared above the common class of men', complained that the bread and beef were so bad that they were not fit for a prisoner's dog to eat, that the British Government was not acquainted with the treatment of the prisoners, and that this was the agent's fault for not keeping a sufficiently strict eye upon his subordinates. This was confirmed, not only by inquiry among the prisoners, but by the evidence of the petty officers and soldiers of the garrison, who said 'as fellow creatures they must allow that the provisions given to the prisoners were not fit for them to eat, and that the water they had was much better than the beer'. In spite of this evidence, the samples sent up by the request of the 'Sick and Hurt' Office in reply to this complaint, were pronounced good.

In July 1797 the civil officials at Norman Cross complained of annoyances, interferences, and insults from the military. Major-General Bowyer, in command, in his reply stated: 'I cannot conceive the civil officers have a right to take prisoners out of their prisons to the canteens and other places, which this day has been mentioned to me.'

By July 18 such parts of the prison as were completed were very full, and in November the buildings were finished, and the sixteen blocks, each holding 400 prisoners, were crowded. The packing of the hammocks in these blocks was close, but not closer than in the men-of-war of the period, and not very much closer than in the machinery-crowded big ships of to-day. The blocks, or *casernes* as they were called, measured 100 feet long by twenty-four feet broad, and were two stories high. On the ground floor the hammocks were slung from posts three abreast, and there were three tiers. In the upper story were only two tiers. As to the life at Norman Cross, it appears to me from the documentary evidence available to have been more tolerable than at any of the other great prisons, if only from the fact that the place had been specially built for its purpose, and was not, as in most other places, adapted. The food allowance was the same as elsewhere; viz., on five days of the week each prisoner had one and a half pounds of bread, half a pound of beef, greens or pease or oatmeal, and salt. On Wednesday and Friday one pound of herrings or cod-fish was substituted for the beef, and beer could be bought at the canteen. The description by George Borrow in *Lavengro*—'rations of carrion meat and bread from which I have seen the very hounds occasionally turn away', is now generally admitted to be as inaccurate as his other remarks concerning the Norman Cross which he could only remember as a very small boy.

The outfit was the same as in other prisons, but I note that in the year 1797 the store-keeper at Norman Cross was instructed to supply each prisoner *as often as was necessary*, and not, as elsewhere, at stated intervals, with one jacket, one pair of trousers, two pairs of stockings, two shirts, one pair of shoes, one cap, and one hammock. By the way, the prisoners' shoes are ordered 'not to have long straps for buckles, but short ears for strings'.

On August 8, 1798, Perrot writes from Stilton to Woodriff:

'If you remember, on returning from the barracks on Sunday, Captain Llewellin informed us that a report had been propagated that seven prisoners intended to escape that day, which we both looked upon as a mere report; they were counted both that night, but with little effect from the additions made to their numbers by the men you brought from Lynn, and yesterday morning and afternoon, but in such confusion from the prisoners refusing to answer, from others giving in fictitious names, and others answering for two or three. In consequence of all these irregularities I made all my clerks, a turnkey, and a file of soldiers, go into the south east quadrangle this morning at five o'clock, and muster each prison separately, and found that six prisoners from the Officers' Prison have escaped, but can obtain none of their names except Captain Dorfe, who some time ago applied to me for to obtain liberty for him to reside with his family at Ipswich where he had married an English wife. The officers remaining have separately and conjunctively refused to give the names of the other five, for which I have ordered the whole to be put on half allowance to-morrow. After the most diligent search we could only find one probable place where they had escaped, by the end next the South Gate, by breaking one of the rails of the picket, but how they passed afterwards is a mystery still unravelled.'

During the years 1797–8 there were many Dutch prisoners here, chiefly taken at Camperdown.

William Prickard, of the Leicester Militia, was condemned to receive 500 lashes for talking of escape with a prisoner.

On February 21, 1798, Mr. James Stewart of Peterborough thus wrote to Captain Woodriff:

'I have received a heavy complaint from the prisoners of war of being beat and otherwise ill-treated by the officials at the Prison. I can have no doubt but that they exaggerate these complaints, for what they describe as a dungeon I have examined myself and find it to be a proper place to confine unruly prisoners in, being above ground, and appears perfectly dry. How far you are authorized to chastise the prisoners of war I cannot take upon me to determine, but I presume to think it should be done sparingly and with temper. I was in hopes the new system adopted, with the additional allowance of provisions would have made the prisoners more easy and contented under their confinement, but it would appear it caused more turbulence and uneasiness.... That liquor is conveyed to the prisoners I have no doubt, you know some of the turnkeys have been suspected.'

Two turnkeys were shortly afterwards dismissed for having conveyed large quantities of ale into the prison.

Rendered necessary by complaints from the neighbourhood, the following order was issued by the London authorities in 1798.

'Obscene figures and indecent toys and all such indecent representations tending to disseminate Lewdness and Immorality exposed for sale or prepared for that purpose are to be instantly destroyed.'

Constant escapes made the separation of officers from men and the suspension of all intercourse between them to be strictly enforced.

Perrot died towards the end of 1798, and Woodriff was made agent in January 1799. Soon after Woodriff's assuming office the Mayor of Lynn complained of the number of prisoners at large in the town, and unguarded, waiting with Norman Cross passports for cartel ships to take them to France. To appreciate this complaint we must remember that the rank and file, and not a few of the officers, of the French Revolutionary Army and Navy, who were prisoners of war in Britain, were of the lowest classes of society, desperate, lawless, religionless, unprincipled men who in confinement were a constant source of anxiety and watchfulness, and at large were positively dangers to society. If a body of men like this got loose, as did fifteen on the night of April 5, 1799, from Norman Cross, the fact was enough to carry terror throughout a countryside.

Yet there was a request made this year from the Norman Cross prisoners that they might have priests sent to them. At first the order was that none should be admitted except to men dangerously ill, but later, Ruello and Vexier were permitted to reside in Number 8 Caserne, under the rule 'that your officers do strictly watch over their communication and conduct, lest, under pretence of religion, any stratagems or devices be carried out to the public prejudice by people of whose disposition to abuse indulgence there have already existed but too many examples'.

That Captain Woodriff's position was rendered one of grave anxiety and responsibility by the bad character of many of the prisoners under his charge is very clear from the continual tenor of the correspondence between him and the Transport Board. The old punishment of simple confinement in the Black Hole being apparently quite useless, it was ordered that offenders sentenced to the Black Hole should be put on half rations, and also lose their turn of exchange. This last was the punishment most dreaded by the majority of the prisoners, although there was a regular market for these turns of exchange, varying from £40 upwards, which would seem to show that to many a poor fellow, life at Norman Cross with some capital to gamble with was preferable to a return to France in exchange for a British prisoner of similar grade, only to be pressed on board a man-of-war of the period, or to become a unit of the hundreds and thousands of soldiers sent here and there to be maimed or slaughtered in a cause of which they knew little and cared less.

It is worthy of note that these increased punishments were made law with the concurrence, if not at the suggestion, of the French Agent, Niou, who remarked with respect to the system of buying and selling turns of exchange, '... une conduite aussi lâche devant être arrêtée par tous les moyens possibles. Je viens en conséquence de mettre les Vendéens (I am inclined to regard 'Vendéens' as a mistake for 'vendants') à la queue des échanges.'

The year 1799 seems to have been a disturbed one at Norman Cross. In August the prisoners showed their resentment at having detailed personal descriptions of them taken, by disorderly meetings, the result being that all trafficking between them was stopped, and the daily market at the prison-gate suspended.

Stockdale, the Lynn manager of the prison traffic between the coast and Norman Cross, writes on one occasion that of 125 prisoners who had been started for the prison, 'there were two made their escape, and one shot on their march to Lynn, and I am afraid we lost two or three last night ... there are some very artful men among them who will make their escape if possible'.

Attempts to escape during the last stages of the journey from the coast to the prison were frequent. On February 4, 1808, the crews of two privateers, under an escort of the 77th Regiment, were lodged for the night in the stable of the *Angel Inn* at Peterborough. One Simon tried to escape. The sentry challenged and fired. Simon was killed, and the coroner's jury brought in the verdict of 'Justifiable homicide'.

On another occasion a column of prisoners was crossing the Nene Bridge at Peterborough, when one of them broke from the ranks, and sprang into the river. He was shot as he rose to the surface.

On account of the proximity of Norman Cross to a countryside of which one of the staple industries was the straw manufacture, the prevention of the smuggling of straw into the prison for the purpose of being made into bonnets, baskets, plaits, &c., constantly occupied the attention of the authorities. In 1799 the following circular was sent by the Transport Board to all prisons and dépôts in the kingdom:

'Being informed that the Revenues and Manufactures of this country are considerably injured by the extensive sale of Straw Hats made by the Prisoners of War in this country, we do hereby require and direct you to permit no Hat, Cap, or Bonnet manufactured by any of the Prisoners of War in your custody, to be sold or sent out of the Prison in future, under any pretence whatever, and to seize and destroy all such articles as may be detected in violation of this order.'

This traffic, however, was continued, for in 1807 the Transport Board, in reply to a complaint by a Mr. John Poynder to Lord Liverpool, 'requests the magistrates to help in stopping the traffic with prisoners of war in prohibited articles, straw hats and straw plait especially, as it has been the means of selling obscene toys, pictures, &c., to the great injury of the morals of the rising generation'.

To continue the prison record in order of dates: in 1801 the Transport Board wrote to Otto, Commissioner in England of the French Republic,

'SIR:

'Having directed Capt. Woodriff, Superintendant at Norman Cross Prison, to report to us on the subject of some complaints made by the prisoners at that place, he has informed me of a most pernicious habit among the prisoners which he has used every possible means to prevent, but without success. Some of the men, whom he states to have been long confined without receiving any supplies from their friends, have only the prison allowance to subsist on, and this allowance he considers sufficient to nourish and keep in health if they received it daily, but he states this is not the case, although the full ration is regularly issued by the Steward to each mess of 12 men. There are in these prisons, he observes, some men—if they deserve that name—who possess money with which they purchase of some unfortunate and unthinking fellow-prisoner his ration of bread for several days together, and frequently *both bread and beef for a month*, which he, the merchant, seizes upon daily and sells it out again to some other unfortunate being on the same usurious terms, allowing the former *one half-penny worth of potatoes daily* to keep him alive. Not contented with this more than savage barbarity, he purchases next his clothes and bedding, and sees the miserable man lie naked on his plank unless he will consent to allow him one half-penny a night to lie in his own hammock, which he makes him pay by a further deprivation of his ration when his original debt is paid.... In consequence of this representation we have directed Capt. Woodriff to keep a list of every man of this description of merchants above mentioned in order they may be put at the bottom of the list of exchange.'

In this year a terrible epidemic carried off nearly 1,000 prisoners. The Transport Board's Surveyor was sent down, and he reported that the general condition of the prison was very bad, especially as regarded sanitation. The buildings were merely of fir-quartering, and weather-boarded on the outside, and without lining inside, the result being that the whole of the timbering was a network of holes bored by the prisoners in order to get light inside. In the twelve solitary cells of the Black Hole there was no convenience whatever. The wells were only in tolerable condition. The ventilation of the French officers' rooms was very bad. The hospital was better than other parts of the prison. The report notes that the carpenters, sawyers, and masons were prisoners, a fact at once constituting an element of uncertainty, if not of danger. In December 1801 Woodriff found it necessary to post up an order about shamming ill in order to be changed to better quarters:

'Ayant connaissance que nombre de prisonniers français recherchent journellement les moyens de se donner l'air aussi misérable que possible dans le dessein d'être envoyés à l'Hôpital ou au No. 13 par le chirurgien de visite, et que s'ils sont reçus, soit pour l'un ou l'autre, ils vendent de suite leurs effets (s'ils ne l'ont déjà fait pour se faire recevoir) le Gouvernement done [*sic*] avis de nouveau qu'aucun prisonnier ne sera reçu pour l'Hôpital ou pour le No. 13 s'il ne produit ses effets de Literie et les Hardes qu'il peut avoir reçu dernièrement.'

Generals Rochambeau and Boyer were paroled prisoners who seem to have studied how to give the authorities as much trouble and annoyance as possible. The Transport Board, weary of granting them indulgences which they abused, and of making them offers which they contemptuously rejected, clapped them into Norman Cross in September 1804. They were placed in the wards of the military hospital, a sentinel at their doors, and no communication allowed between them, or their servants, and the rest of the prisoners. They were not allowed newspapers, no special allowance was made them of coals, candles, and wood, they were not permitted to go beyond the hospital airing ground, and Captain Pressland, the then agent of the prison, was warned to be strictly on his guard, and to watch them closely, despite his favourable remarks upon their deportment. It was at about this time that the alarm was widespread that the prisoners of war in Britain were to co-operate with an invasion by their countrymen from without. General Boyer, at Tiverton in 1803, 'whilst attentive to the ladies, did not omit to curse, even to *them*, his fate in being deprived of his arms, and without hope of being useful to his countrymen when they arrive in England'. Rochambeau at Norman Cross was even more ridiculous, for when he heard that Bonaparte's invasion was actually about to come off, he appeared for two days in the airing ground in full uniform, booted and spurred. Later news sent him into retirement.

Extracts from contemporary newspapers show that the alarm was very general. Said *The Times*:

'The French prisoners on the prospect of an invasion of this country begin to assume their Republican *fierté*; they tell their guards—"It is your turn to guard us now, but before the winter is over it will be our turn to guard you."

'The prisoners already in our hands, and those who may be added, will occasion infinite perplexity. The known licentiousness of their principles, the utter contempt of all laws of honour which is so generally prevalent among the French Republicans, and the audacity of exertions which may arise from a desire of co-operating with an invading force, may render them extremely dangerous, especially if left in the country, where the thinness of the population prevents perpetual inspection and where alarm flies so rapidly as to double any mischief.'

A suggestion was made that the prisoners should be concentrated in the prisons of London and neighbourhood, and some newspapers even echoed Robespierre's truculent advice: 'Make no prisoners.'

In 1804, in reply to another application that priests might reside within the prison boundaries, the authorities said:

'As to the French priests and the procurement of lodgings at Stilton, we have nothing to do with them, but with respect to the proposal of their inhabitation in our Dépôts, we cannot possibly allow of such a measure at this critical time to *Foreigners of that equivocal description.*'

The ever-recurring question as to the exact lines of demarcation to be drawn between the two chief men of the prison, the Agent and the Commander of the garrison, occupies a great deal of Departmental literature. We have given one specimen already, and in 1804 Captain Pressland was thus addressed by his masters in London:

'As the interior regulation and management of the Prison is entirely under your direction, we do not see any necessity for returns being made daily to the C.O. of the Guard, and we approve of your reason for declining to make such returns; but as, on the other hand, the C.O. is answerable for the security of the Prison, it is not proper that you should interfere in that respect any further than merely to suggest what may appear to you to be necessary or proper to be done.'

In the same year a serious charge was brought against Captain Pressland by the prisoners, that he was in the habit of deducting two and a half per cent from all sums passing through his hands for payment to the prisoners. He admitted having done so, and got off with a rebuke. It may be mentioned here that the pay of a prison agent was thirty shillings per diem, the same as that of a junior post captain on sea fencible service—quarters, but no allowances except £10 10s. per annum for stationery. In 1805 the boys' building was put up. At first the suggested site was on the old burial ground; but as it was urged that such a proceeding might produce much popular clamour, as well as 'other disagreeable consequences', it was put outside the outer stockade, north of the Hospital. It is said that the boys were here brought up as musicians by the Bishop of Moulins.

At this time escapes seem to have been very frequent, and this in spite of the frequent changing of the garrison, and the rule that no soldier knowing French should be on guard duty. All implements and edged tools were taken from the prisoners, only one knife being allowed, which was to be returned every night, locked up in a box, and placed in the Guard-room until the next morning, and failure to give up knives meant the Black Hole. Any prisoner attempting to escape was to be executed immediately, but I find no record of this drastic sentence being carried into effect.

From *The Times* of October 15, 1804, I take the following:

'An alarming spirit of insubordination was on Wednesday evinced by the French prisoners, about 3,000, at Norman Cross. An incessant uproar was kept up all the morning, and at noon their intention to attempt the destruction of the barrier of the prison became so obvious that the C.O. at the Barrack, apprehensive that the force under his command, consisting only of the Shropshire Militia and one battalion of the Army of reserve, would not be sufficient in case of necessity to environ and restrain so large a body of prisoners, dispatched a messenger requiring the assistance of the Volunteer force at Peterborough. Fortunately the Yeomanry had had a field day, and one of the troops was undismissed when the messenger arrived. The troops immediately galloped into the Barracks. In the evening a tumult still continuing among the prisoners, and some of them taking advantage of the extreme darkness to attempt to escape, further reinforcements were sent for and continued on duty all night. The prisoners, having cut down a portion of the wood enclosure during the night, nine of them escaped through the aperture. In another part of the prison, as soon as daylight broke, it was found that they had undermined a distance of 34 feet towards the Great South Road, under the fosse which surrounds the prison, although it is 4 feet deep, and it is not discovered they had any tools. Five of the prisoners have been re-taken.'

A little later in the year, on a dark, stormy Saturday night, seven prisoners escaped through a hole they had cut in the wooden wall, and were away all Sunday. At 8 p.m. on that day, a sergeant and a corporal of the Durham

Militia, on their way north on furlough, heard men talking a 'foreign lingo' near Whitewater toll-bar. Suspecting them to be escaped prisoners, they attacked and secured two of them, but five got off. On Monday two of these were caught near Ryall toll-bar in a state of semi-starvation, having hidden in Uffington Thicket for twenty-four hours; the other three escaped.

One of the most difficult tasks which faced the agents of prisons in general, and of Norman Cross in particular, was the checking of contraband traffic between the prisoners and outsiders. At Norman Cross, as I have said, the chief illicit trade was in straw-plaiting work. Strange to say, although the interests of the poor country people were severely injured by this trade, the wealth and influence of the chief dealers were so great that it was difficult to get juries to convict, and when they did convict, to get judges to pass deterrent sentences. In 1807, for instance, legal opinion was actually given that a publican could not have his licence refused because he had carried on the straw-plait traffic with the prisoners, although it was an open secret that the innkeepers of Stilton, Wansford, Whittlesea, Peterborough, and even the landlord of the inn which in those days stood opposite where now is the present Norman Cross Hotel, were deeply engaged in it.

In 1808, 'from motives of humanity', the prisoners at Norman Cross were allowed to make baskets, boxes, ornaments, &c., of straw, if the straw-plaiting traffic could be effectually prevented. The manufacture of these articles, which were often works of the most refined beauty and delicacy, of course did not harm the poor, rough straw-plaiters of Bedfordshire and Northamptonshire; but the radius of its sale was limited, the straw-plaiting meant quick and good returns, and the difficulty to be faced by the authorities was to ensure the rightful use of the straw introduced. In 1808 there were many courts-martial upon soldiers of the garrison for being implicated in this traffic, and in each case the soldier was severely flogged and the straw bonnet ordered to be burned. It was no doubt one of these episodes which so aroused George Borrows ire.[4] The guard of the coach from Lincoln to Stilton was put under observation by order of the Transport Office, being suspected of assisting people to carry the straw plait made in the prison to Baldock to be made into bonnets.

In 1809 Pressland writes thus seriously to the Transport Office:

'That every step that could possibly be taken by General Williams [Commander of the Garrison] and myself to prevent this illicit Traffic [has been taken], the Board will, I trust, readily admit, and I am well convinced that without the prosecution of those dealers who are particularized in the documents forwarded by the Lincoln coach this evening, it will ever continue, to the great injury of the country in general; for already eight or nine soldiers have deserted from a dread of punishment, having been detected by those whom they knew would inform against them, and I shall leave the Board to judge how far the discipline of the Regiments has been hurt, and the Soldiers seduced from their duty by the bribes they are constantly receiving from Barnes, Lunn, and Browne. It now becomes a serious and alarming case, for if these persons can with so much facility convey into the Prison sacks of 5 and 6 feet in length, they might convey weapons of every description to annoy those whose charge they are under, to the great detriment of H.M.'s service, and the lives of His subjects most probably.'

COLOURED STRAW WORK-BOX

Made by French prisoners of war

A large bundle of documents contains the trial of Barnes, Lunn, Browne, and others, for, in conjunction with bribed soldiers of the garrison, taking straw into the prison and receiving the plaited article in exchange. The evidence of soldiers of the guard showed that James, ostler at the *Bell*, Stilton, had been seen many times at midnight throwing sacks of straw over the palisades, and receiving straw plait in return, and also bonnets, and that he was always assisted by soldiers. Barnes had said that he would get straw into the prison in spite of General Williams or anybody else, as he had bought five fields of wheat for the purpose. He was acting for his brother, a Baldock straw-dealer.

The trial came off at Huntingdon on March 20, 1811, the result being that Lunn got twelve months, and the others six months each. It may be noted here that so profitable for dealers was this contraband trade in war-prison manufactured straw articles, that a Bedfordshire man, Matthew Wingrave, found it to be worth his while to buy up wheat and barley land in the neighbourhood of the great Scottish dépôt at Valleyfield, near Penicuik, and carry on business there.

As an instance of the resentment aroused by this judgement among those interested in the illicit trade, a Sergeant Ives of the West Essex Militia, who had been especially active in the suppression of the straw-plait business, was, according to the *Taunton Courier*, stopped between Stilton and Norman Cross by a number of fellows, who, after knocking him down and robbing him of his watch and money, forced open his jaws with savage ferocity and cut off a piece of his tongue.

In November 1807 a brick wall was built round Norman Cross prison; the outer palisade which it replaced being used to repair the inner.

In 1809 Flaigneau, a prisoner, was tried at Huntingdon for murdering a turnkey. The trial lasted six hours, but in spite of the instructions of the judge, the jury brought him in *Not Guilty*.

Forgery and murder brought the prisoners under the Civil Law. Thus in 1805 Nicholas Deschamps and Jean Roubillard were tried at Huntingdon Summer Assizes for forging £1 bank notes, which they had done most skilfully. They were sentenced to death, but were respited during His Majesty's pleasure, and remained in Huntingdon gaol for nine years, until they were pardoned and sent back to France in 1814.

From the *Stamford Mercury* of September 16, 1808, I take the following:

'Early on Friday morning last Charles François Maria Boucher, a French officer, a prisoner of war in this country, was conveyed from the County Gaol at Huntingdon to Yaxley Barracks where he was hanged, agreeable to his sentence at the last assizes, for stabbing with a knife, with intent to kill Alexander Halliday, in order to effect his escape from that prison. The whole garrison was under arms and all the prisoners in the different apartments were made witnesses of the impressive scene.'

I shall deal later in detail with the subject of prisoners on parole, so that it suffices here to say that every care was taken to avoid the just reproach of the earlier years of the great wars that officer prisoners of war in England were promiscuously herded on hulks and in prisons with the rank and file, and it was an important part of Prison Agent's duties to examine each fresh arrival of prisoners with a view to selecting those of character and the required rank qualifying them for the privileges of being allowed on parole in certain towns and villages set apart for the purpose.

In 1796 about 100 Norman Cross prisoners were out on parole in Peterborough and the neighbourhood. The *Wheatsheaf* at Stibbington was a favourite house of call with the parole prisoners, says the Rev. A. Brown in the before-quoted book, and this, when afterwards a farmhouse, belonged to an old man, born before the close of the war, who told Dr. Walker that as a child he had often seen the prisoners regale themselves here with the excellent cooking of his grandmother, the milestone which was their limit from Wansford, where they lodged, being just outside the house.

The parole officers seem to have been generally received with kindness and hospitality by the neighbouring gentry, and a few marriages with English girls are recorded, although when it became known that such unions were not recognized as binding by the French Government, and that even the English wives of Frenchmen were sent back from Morlaix, the cartel port, the English girls became more careful. Some of the gentry, indeed, seem to have interested themselves too deeply in the exiles, and in 1801 the Transport Office requests the attention of its Agent 'to the practices of a person of some property near Peterborough, similar to those for which Askew was convicted at the Huntingdon Assizes'—which was for aiding prisoners to escape.

By the Treaty of Paris, May 30, 1814, Peace was declared between France and Britain, and in the same month 4,617 French prisoners at Norman Cross were sent home via Peterborough and Lynn unguarded, but the prison was not finally evacuated until August. It was never again used as a prison, but was pulled down and sold.

We have already become acquainted with General Pillet as a rabid chronicler of life on the Chatham hulks; we shall meet him again out on parole, and now let us hear what he has to say about Norman Cross in his book on England.

'I have seen at Norman Cross a plot of land where nearly four thousand men, out of seven thousand in this prison, were buried. Provisions were then dear in England, and our Government, it was said, had refused to pay the balance of an account due for prisoners. To settle this account all the prisoners were put on half-rations, and to make sure that they should die, the introduction of food for sale, according to custom, was forbidden. To reduced quantity was added inferior quality of the provisions served out. There was distributed four times a week, worm-eaten biscuit, fish and salt meat; three times a week black, half baked bread made of mouldy flour or of black wheat. Soon after eating this one was seized with a sort of drunkenness, followed by violent headache, diarrhoea, and redness of face; many died from a sort of vertigo. For vegetables, uncooked beans were served up. In fact, hundreds of men sank each day, starved to death, or poisoned by the provisions. Those who did not die immediately, became so weak that gradually they could digest nothing.' (Then follow some details, too disgusting to be given a place here, of the extremities to which prisoners at Norman Cross were driven by hunger.) 'Hunger knows no rules. The corpses of those who died were kept for five or six days without being given up by their comrades, who by this means received the dead men's rations.'

This veracious chronicler continues:

'I myself took a complaint to Captain Pressland. Next day, the officers of the two militia battalions on guard at the prison, and some civilians, arrived just at the moment for the distribution of the rations. At their head was Pressland who was damning the prisoners loudly. The rations were shown, and, as the whole thing had been rehearsed beforehand, they were good. A report was drawn up by which it was shown that the prisoners were discontented rascals who grumbled at everything, that the food was unexceptionable, and that some of the grumblers deserved to be shot, for an example. Next day the food was just as bad as ever.... Certainly the prisoners had the chance of buying provisions for themselves from the wives of the soldiers of the garrison twice a week. But these women, bribed to ruin the prisoners, rarely brought what was required, made the prisoners take what they brought, and charged exorbitant prices, and, as payment had to be made in advance, they settled things just as they chose.'

With reference to the medical attendance at Norman Cross, Pillet says:

'I have been witness and victim, as prisoner of war, of the false oath taken by the doctors at Norman Cross. They were supplied with medicines, flannel, cotton stuffs, &c., in proportion to the number of prisoners, for compresses, bandages, and so forth. When the supply was exhausted, the doctor, in order to get a fresh supply, drew up his account of usage, and swore before a jury that this account was exact. The wife of the doctor at Norman Cross, like that of the doctor of the *Crown Prince* at Chatham, wore no petticoats which were not made of cotton and flannel taken from the prison stores. So with the medicines and drugs. The contractor found the supply ample, and that there was no necessity to replace it, so he shared with the doctor and the apothecary the cost of what he had never delivered, although in the accounts it appeared that he had renewed their supplies.'

With George Borrow's description in *Lavengro* of the brutalities exercised upon the prisoners at Norman Cross by the soldiers of the garrison, many readers will be familiar. As the recollection is of his early boyhood, it may be valued accordingly.

In 1808 a tourist among the churches of this part of East Anglia remarks upon the good appearance of the Norman Cross prisoners, particularly of the boys—the drummers and the 'mousses'. He adds that many of the prisoners had learned English enough 'to chatter and to cheat', and that some of them upon release took away with them from two to three hundred pounds as the proceeds of the sale of their handiwork in drawings, wood, bone and straw work, chessmen, draughts, backgammon boards, dice, and groups in wood and bone of all descriptions.

THE BLOCK HOUSE, NORMAN CROSS, 1809

From a sketch by Captain George Lloyd

In 1814 came Peace. The following extracts from contemporary newspapers made by Mr. Charles Dack, Curator of the Peterborough Museum, refer to the process of evacuation, Norman Cross Dépôt being also known as Stilton or Yaxley Barracks.

'11th April, 1814. The joy produced amongst the prisoners of war at Norman Cross by the change of affairs in France (the abdication of Bonaparte) is quite indescribable and extravagant. A large white flag is set up in each of the quadrangles of the dépôt, under which the thousands of poor fellows, who have been for years in confinement, dance, sing, laugh, and cry for joy, with rapturous delight.

'5th May, 1814. The prisoners at Stilton Barracks are so elated at the idea of being so soon liberated, that they are all bent on selling their stock, which they do rapidly at 50 per cent advanced prices. Many of them have realized fortunes of from £500 to £1,000 each.

'June 9th, Lynn. Upwards of 1,400 French prisoners of war have arrived in this town during the last week from Stilton Barracks, to embark for the coast of France. Dunkirk, we believe, is the place of their destination. In consequence of the wind having been hitherto unfavourable, they have been prevented from sailing, and we are glad to state that their conduct in this town has hitherto been very orderly; and although they are continually perambulating the street, and some of them indulging in tolerable libations of ale, we have not heard of a single act of indecorum taking place in consequence.'

To these notes the late Rev. G. N. Godwin, to whom I am indebted for many details of life at Norman Cross, added in the columns of the *Norwich Mercury*:

'The garrison of the dépôt caught the infection of wild joy, and a party of them seized the Glasgow mail coach on its arrival at Stilton, and drew it to Norman Cross, whither the horses, coachman and guard were obliged to follow. The prisoners were so elated at the prospect of being liberated that they ceased to perform any work. Many of them had realized fortunes of £500 to £1,000 each in Bank of England notes.'

The *Cambridge Chronicle* gives a pleasant picture on May 6th: 'About 200 prisoners from Norman Cross Barracks marched into this town on Sunday last ... they walked about the town and 'Varsity and conducted themselves in an orderly manner.'

Although it was rumoured that the buildings at Norman Cross were to be utilized, after the departure of the war prisoners, as a barrack for artillery and cavalry, this did not come about. The buildings were sold in lots; in Peterborough some of them were re-erected and still exist, and a pair of slatted gates are now barn-doors at Alwalton Rectory Farm, but the very memories of this great prison are fast dying out in this age of the migration of the countryman.

On October 2, 1818, the sale of Norman Cross Barracks began, and lasted nine days, the sum realized being about £10,000. A curious comment upon the condition of the prison is presented by the fact that a house built from some of it became known as 'Bug Hall', which has a parallel in the case of Portchester Castle; some cottages built from the timber of the *casernes* there, when it ceased to be a war prison, being still known as 'Bug Row'.

In Shelley Row, Cambridge, is an ancient timbered barn which is known to have been regularly used as a night-shelter for prisoners on their way to Norman Cross.

CHAPTER XI
THE PRISONS ASHORE
3. Perth

The following particulars about the great Dépôt at Perth are largely taken from Mr. W. Sievwright's book, now out of print and obtainable with difficulty.[5] Mr. P. Baxter of Perth, however, transcribed it for me from the copy in the Perth Museum, and to him my best thanks are due.

The Dépôt at Perth was completed in 1812. It was constructed to hold about 7,000 prisoners, and consisted of five three-story buildings, each 130 feet long and 30 feet broad, with outside stairs, each with a separate iron palisaded airing-ground and all converging upon what was known as the 'Market Place'. Each of these blocks held 1,140 prisoners. South of the great square was a building for petty officers, accommodating 1,100, and north of it the hospital for 150 invalids. Both of these latter buildings are still standing, having been incorporated with the present General Prison. The sleeping quarters were very crowded; so much so, says Sievwright, that the prisoners had to sleep 'spoon fashion', (as we have seen on the prison ships), the turning-over process having to be done by whole ranks in obedience to words of command; 'Attention! Squad number so and so! Prepare to spoon! One! Two! Spoon!'

Around the entire space was a deep moat, ten feet broad; beyond this an iron palisade; beyond this a wall twelve feet six inches high, with a sentry-walk round it. Three or four regiments of Militia were always kept in Perth for guard duties, which occupied 300 men. Many acres of potatoes were planted outside the prison. When peace was finally made, and the prison was emptied, the owners of these profitable acres were in despair, until one of them discovered the London market, and this has been kept ever since.

The first prisoners came from Plymouth via Dundee in August 1812. They had been lodged the first night in the church of Inchtore.[6] 'During the night', says Penny in his *Traditions of Perth*, 'the French prisoners found means to extract the brass nails and purloin the green cloth from the pulpit and seats in the Church, with every other thing they could lay their hands on.' Penny seems to have exaggerated. One prisoner stole a couple of 'mort cloths'. This so enraged his fellows that they tried him by court martial, and sentenced him to twenty-four lashes. He got seventeen there and then, but fainted, and the remainder were given him later.

The prisoners were 400 in number, and had some women with them, and were in tolerably good condition. A great many came in after Salamanca. They had been marched through Fifeshire in very bad weather. 'The poor creatures, many of them half naked, were in a miserable plight; numbers of them gave up upon the road, and were flung into carts, one above the other, and when the carts were full, and capable of holding no more, the others were tied to the backs with ropes and dragged along.'

Kirkcaldy on the Forth was the chief port for landing the prisoners; from Kirkcaldy they were marched overland to Perth.

The first attempt at escape from the new Dépôt was made in September 1812, there being at this time about 4,000 prisoners there. A prisoner slipped past the turnkey as the latter was opening a door in the iron palisading, and got away. The alarm was given; the prisoner had got to Friarton Toll, half a mile away, but being closely pursued was captured in a wheat field.

One Petite in this year was a slippery customer. He got out of Perth but was recaptured, and lodged at Montrose on the march back to gaol. Thence he escaped by unscrewing the locks of three doors, but was again caught at Ruthven print-field, and safely lodged in his old quarters in Perth gaol. Shortly after he was ordered to be transferred to Valleyfield, and a sergeant and eight men were considered necessary to escort him. They got him safely as far as Kirkcaldy, where they halted, and M. Petite was lodged for the night in the local prison; but when they came for him in the morning, he was not to be found, and was never heard of again!

Here Sievwright introduces a story from Penny, of date previous to the Dépôt.

'On April 20th, 1811, it was reputed at the Perth Barracks that four French prisoners had passed through Perth. A detachment of soldiers who were sent in pursuit on the road to Dundee, found, not those they were seeking, but four others, whom they conveyed to Perth and lodged in gaol. On the morning of April 24th, they managed to effect their escape. By cutting some planks out of the partition of their apartment, they made their way to the Court Room, from the window of which they descended to the street. On their table was found a letter expressing their gratitude to the magistrates and inhabitants of Perth for the civilities they had received, and promising a return of the kindness to any Scotsman whom they might find among the British prisoners in France.'

As a supplement to this, it is recorded that two of the original quarry were afterwards captured, but were released unconditionally later on, when one of them proved that he had humanely treated General Walker, when the latter was lying seriously wounded at Badajos, saved him from being dispatched by a furious grenadier, and had him removed to a hospital. The General gave him his name and address, and promised to help him should occasion arise.

In January 1813 three prisoners got off in a thick fog and made their way as far as Broughty Ferry on the Forth. On their way, it came out later, they stopped in Dundee for refreshment without any apparent dread of disturbance, and were later seen on the Fort hill near Broughty Ferry. In the evening they entered a shop, bought up all the bread in it and had a leather bottle filled with spirits. At nine the same evening they boarded Mr. Grubb's ship *Nancy*, and immediately got under weigh unnoticed. The *Nancy* was of fifteen tons burden, and was known to be provisioned for ten days, as she was going to start the next morning on an excursion. The prisoners escaped, and a woman and two Renfrewshire Militiamen were detained in prison after examination upon suspicion of having concealed and aided the prisoners with information about the *Nancy* which they could hardly have obtained ordinarily.

This was on Thursday, January 21. On the night of Monday, 18th, a mason at the Dépôt, on his way from Newburgh to Perth, was stopped by three men at the Coates of Fingask on the Rhynd road, and robbed of £1 18*s.* 6*d.* The robbers had the appearance of farm servants, but it seems quite likely that they were the daring and successful abductors of the *Nancy*.

On January 21, 1813, there were 6,788 prisoners at the Dépôt. On the evening of February 22, 1813, seven prisoners bribed a sentinel to let them escape. He agreed, but at once gave information, and was instructed to keep up the deception. So, at the fixed hour the prisoners, awaiting with confident excitement the arrival of their deliverer, were, instead, found hiding with scaling-ladders, ropes, and all implements necessary for escape upon them, and a considerable sum of money for their needs. They were at once conveyed to the punishment cells under the central tower.

At Perth, as elsewhere, the prisoners were allowed to amuse themselves, and to interest themselves in the manufacture of various knick-knacks, toys, boxes, and puzzles, from wood, and the bones of their beef; of these they made a great variety, and many of them are masterpieces of cunning deftness, and wonderfully beautiful in delicacy and perfection of workmanship. They made straw plait, a manufacture then in its infancy in this country; numbers made shoes out of bits of cloth, cutting up their clothes for the purpose, and it is possible that their hammocks may have yielded the straw. It is said that after a time straw plait and shoes were prohibited as traffic. Some of the prisoners dug clay out of their court-yards and modelled figures of smugglers, soldiers, sailors, and women. The prisoners had the privilege of holding a market daily, to which the public were admitted provided they carried no contraband articles. Potatoes, vegetables, bread, soap, tobacco, and firewood, were all admitted. Large numbers of the inhabitants went daily to view the markets, and make purchases. The prisoners had stands set out all round the railing of the yards, on which their wares were placed. Many paid high prices for the articles. While some of the prisoners were busy selling, others were occupied in buying provisions, vegetables and other necessaries of food. Some of the prisoners played the flute, fiddle, and other instruments, for halfpence; Punch's opera and other puppet shows were also got up in fine style. Some were industrious and saving; others gambled and squandered the clothes from their bodies, and wandered about with only a bit of blanket tied round them.

From Penny's *Traditions of Perth* comes the following market trick:

'As much straw plait as made a bonnet was sold for four shillings, and, being exceedingly neat, it was much inquired after. In this trade many a one got a bite, for the straw was all made up in parcels, and for fear of detection smuggled into the pockets of the purchasers.

'An unsuspecting man having been induced by his wife to purchase a quantity of straw plait for a bonnet, he attended the market and soon found a seller. He paid the money, but, lest he should be observed, he turned his back on the prisoner, and got the things slipped into his hand, and thence into his pocket. Away he went with his parcel, well pleased that he had escaped detection (for outsiders found buying straw plait were severely dealt with by the law), and on his way home he thought he would examine his purchase, when, to his astonishment and no doubt to his deep mortification, he found instead of straw plait, a bundle of shavings very neatly tied up. The man instantly returned, and told of the deception, and insisted on getting back his money. But the prisoner from whom the purchase had been made could not be seen. Whilst trying to get a glimpse of his seller, he was told that if he did not go away he would be informed against, and fined for buying the supposed straw plait. He was retiring when another prisoner came forward and said he would find the other, and make him take back the shavings and return the money. Pretending deep commiseration, the second prisoner said he had no change, but if the straw plait buyer would give him sixteen shillings, he would give him a one pound note, and take his chance of the man returning the money. The dupe gave the money and took the note—which was a forgery on a Perth Bank.'

Attempts to escape were almost a weekly occurrence, and some of them exhibited very notable ingenuity, patience, and daring. On March 26, 1813, the discovery was made of a subterranean excavation from the latrine of No. 2 Prison, forty-two feet long, and so near the base of the outer wall that another hour's work would have finished it.

On April 4, 1813, was found a pit twenty feet deep in the floor of No. 2 Prison, with a lateral cut at about six feet from the bottom. The space below this cut was to receive water, and the cut was to pass obliquely upwards to allow water to run down. A prisoner in hospital was suspected by the others of giving information about this, and when he was discharged he was violently assaulted, the intention being to cut off his ears. He resisted, however, so that only one was taken off. Then a rope was fastened to him, and he was dragged through the moat while men jumped on him. He was rescued just in time by a Durham Militiaman.

On the 28th of the same month three prisoners got with false keys into an empty cellar under the central tower. They had provided themselves with ordinary civilian attire which they intended to slip over their prison clothes, and mix with the market crowd. They were discovered by a man going into the cellar to examine the water pipes. Had they succeeded a great many more would have followed.

On May 5, 1813, some prisoners promised a big bribe to a soldier of the Durham Militia if he would help them to escape. He pretended to accede, but promptly informed his superiors, who told him to keep up the delusion. So he allowed six prisoners to get over the outer wall by a rope ladder which they had made. Four were out and two were on the burial ground which was between the north boundary wall and the Cow Inch, when they were captured by a party of soldiers who had been posted there. The other two were caught in a dry ditch. They were all lodged in the *cachot*. It was well for the 'faithful Durham', for the doubloons he got were only three-shilling pieces, and the bank notes were forgeries!

In June three men escaped by breaking the bar of a window, and dropping therefrom by a rope ladder. One of them who had got on board a neutral vessel at Dundee ventured ashore and was captured; one got as far as Montrose, but was recognized; of the fate of the third we do not hear.

A duel took place between two officers with sharpened foils. The strictest punctilio was observed at the affair, and after one had badly wounded the other, hands were shaken, and honour satisfied.

About this time a clerk in the Dépôt was suspended for attempting to introduce a profligate woman into the prison.

The usual market was prohibited on Midsummer market day, 1813, and the public were excluded, as it was feared that the extraordinary concourse of people would afford opportunities for the prisoners to escape by mixing with them in disguise.

The Medical Report of July 1813 states that out of 7,000 prisoners there were only twenty-four sick, including convalescents, and of these only four were confined to their beds.

On August 15, 1813, the prisoners were not only allowed to celebrate the Emperor's birthday, but the public were apprised of the fête and invited to attend a balloon ascent. The crowd duly assembled on the South Inch, but the balloon was accidentally burst. There were illuminations of the prisons at night, and some of the transparencies, says the chronicler, showed much taste and ingenuity. Advantage was taken of the excitement of this gala day to hurry on one of the most daring and ingenious attempts to escape in the history of the prison. On the morning of August 24 it was notified that a number of prisoners had escaped through a mine dug from the latrine of No. 2 prison to the bottom of the southern outer wall. It was supposed that they must have begun to get out at 2 a.m. that day, but one of them, attempting to jump the 'lade', fell into the water with noise enough to alarm the nearest sentry, who fired in the direction of the sound. The alarm thus started was carried on by the other sentries, and it was found that no fewer than twenty-three prisoners had got away. Ten of them were soon caught. Two who had got on board a vessel on the Perth shore were turned off by the master. One climbed up a tree and was discovered. One made an attempt to swim the Tay, but had to give up from exhaustion, and others were captured near the river, which, being swollen by recent rains, they had been unable to cross; and thirteen temporarily got away.

Of these the *Caledonian Mercury* wrote:

'Four of the prisoners who lately escaped from the Perth Dépôt were discovered within a mile of Arbroath on August 28th by a seaman belonging to the Custom House yacht stationed there, who procured the assistance of some labourers, and attempted to apprehend them, upon which they drew their knives and threatened to stab any one who lay [*sic*] hold of them, but on the arrival of a recruiting party and other assistance the Frenchmen submitted. They stated that on Thursday night—(they had escaped on Tuesday morning) they were on board of a vessel at Dundee, but which they were unable to carry off on account of a neap tide which prevented her floating; other three or four prisoners had been apprehended and lodged in Forfar Gaol. It has been ascertained that several others had gone Northwards by the Highland Road in the direction of Inverness.'

The four poor fellows in Forfar Jail made yet another bold bid for liberty. By breaking through the prison wall, they succeeded in making a hole to the outside nearly large enough for their egress before they were discovered. The only tool they had was a part of the fire-grate which they had wrenched in pieces. Their time was well chosen for getting out to sea, for it was nearly high water when they were discovered. Two others were captured near Blair Atholl, some thirty miles north of Perth, and were brought back to the Dépôt.

Brief allusion has been made to the remarkable healthiness of the prisoners at Perth. The London papers of 1813 lauded Portchester and Portsmouth as examples of sanitary well-being to other prisoner districts, and quoted the statistics that, out of 20,680 prisoners there, only 154 were on the sick list, but the average at Perth was still better. On August 26, 1813, there were 7,000 prisoners at Perth, of whom only fourteen were sick. On October 28, out of the same number, only ten were sick; and on February 3, 1814, when the weather was very severe, there was not one man in bed.

The forgery of bank notes and the manufacture of base coin was pursued as largely and as successfully at Perth as elsewhere. In the *Perth Courier* of September 19, 1813, we read:

'We are sorry to learn that the forgery of notes of various banks is carried on by prisoners at the Dépôt, and that they find means to throw them into circulation by the assistance of profligate people who frequent the market. The eagerness of the prisoners to obtain cash is very great, and as they retain all they procure, they have drained the place almost entirely of silver so that it has become a matter of difficulty to get change of a note.... Last week a woman coming from the Market at the Dépôt was searched by an order of Captain Moriarty, when there was found about her person pieces of base money in imitation of Bank tokens (of which the prisoners are suspected to have been the fabricators), to the amount of £5 17*s*. After undergoing examination, the woman was committed to gaol.'

It was publicly announced on September 16, 1813, that a mine had been discovered in the floor of the Officers' Prison, No. 6, at the Dépôt. This building, a two-story oblong one, now one of the hospitals, still stands to the south of the General Prison Village Square. An excavation of sufficient diameter to admit the passage of a man had been cut with iron hoops, as it was supposed, carried nineteen feet perpendicularly down-wards and thirty feet horizontally outwards.

A detachment of the guard having been marched into the prison after this discovery, the men were stoned by the prisoners, among whom the soldiers fired three shots without doing any injury. At 11 o'clock the next Sunday morning, about forty prisoners were observed by a sentry out of their prison, strolling about the airing ground of No. 3. An alarm was immediately given to the guard, who, fearing a general attempt to escape, rushed towards the place where the prisoners were assembled, and, having seized twenty-four of them, drove the rest back into the prison. In the tumult three of the prisoners were wounded and were taken to the hospital. The twenty-four who were seized were lodged in the *cachot*, where they remained for a time, together with eleven retaken fugitives.

Next morning, on counting over the prisoners in No. 3, twenty-eight were missing. As a light had been observed in the latrine about 8 o'clock the preceding evening, that place was examined and a mine was discovered communicating with the great sewer of the Dépôt. Through this outlet the absentees had escaped. Two of them were taken on the following Monday morning at Bridge of Earn, four miles distant, and three more on Thursday.

A short time previous to this escape, 800 prisoners had been transferred to Perth from the Penicuik Dépôt, and these, it was said, were of a most turbulent and ungovernable character, so that the influence of these men would necessitate a much sterner discipline, and communication between the prisoners and the public much more restricted than hitherto. In the foregoing case the punishments had been very lenient, the market being shut only for one day.

Gradually most of the escaped prisoners were retaken, all in a very exhausted state.

Not long after, heavy rains increased the waters of the canal so that, by breaking into it, they revealed an excavation being made from No. 1.

In the same month three prisoners got out, made their way to Findon, Kincardineshire, stole a fishing-boat, provisioned it by thefts from other boats, and made off successfully.

Yet another mine was discovered this month. It ran from a latrine, not to the great sewer, but in a circuitous direction to meet it. The prisoners while working at this were surrounded by other prisoners, who pretended to be amusing themselves, whilst they hid the workers from the view of the sentries. But an unknown watcher through a loophole in a turret saw the buckets of earth being taken to the well, pumped upon and washed away through the sewer to the Tay, and he gave information.

Yet again a sentry noticed that buckets of earth were being carried from No. 6 prison, and informed the officer of the guard, who found about thirty cartloads of earth heaped up at the two ends of the highest part of the prison known as the Cock Loft.

On April 11, 1814, the news of the dethronement of Bonaparte reached Perth, and was received with universal delight. The prisoners in the Dépôt asked the agent, Captain Moriarty, to be allowed to illuminate for the coming Peace and freedom, but at so short a notice little could be done, although the tower was illuminated by the agent himself. That the feeling among the prisoners was still strong for Bonaparte, however, was presently shown when half a dozen prisoners in the South Prison hoisted the white flag of French Royalty. Almost the whole of their fellow captives clambered up the walls, tore down the flag, and threatened those who hoisted it with violent treatment if they persisted.

The guard removed the Royalists to the hospital for safety, and later their opponents wrote a penitential letter to Captain Moriarty. In June 1814 the removal of the prisoners began. Those that went down the river in boats were heartily cheered by the people. Others marched to Newburgh, where, on the quay, they held a last market for the sale of their manufactures, which was thronged by buyers anxious to get mementoes and willing to pay well for them. 'All transactions were conducted honourably, while the additional graces of French politeness made a deep impression upon the natives of Fife, both male and female,' adds the chronicler. It was during this march to Newburgh that the prisoners sold the New Testaments distributed among them by a zealous missionary.

Altogether it was a pleasant wind-up to a long, sad period, especially for the Frenchmen, many of whom got on board the transports at Newburgh very much richer men than when they first entered the French dépôt, or than they would have been had they never been taken prisoners. Especially pleasant, too, is it to think that they left amidst tokens of goodwill from the people amongst whom many of them had been long captive.

The Dépôt was finally closed July 31, 1814.

During one year, that is between September 14, 1812, and September 24, 1813, there were fourteen escapes or attempted escapes of prisoners. Of these seven were frustrated and seven were more or less successful, that is to say, sixty-one prisoners managed to get out of the prison, but of these thirty-two were recaptured while twenty-nine got clean away.

From 1815 to 1833 the Dépôt was used as a military clothing store, and eventually it became the General Prison for Scotland.

CHAPTER XII
THE PRISONS ASHORE
4. PORTCHESTER

Of the thousands of holiday-makers and picnickers for whom Portchester Castle is a happy recreation ground, and of the hundreds of antiquaries who visit it as being one of the most striking relics of combined Roman and Norman military architecture in Britain, a large number, no doubt, learn that it was long used as a place of confinement for foreign prisoners of war, but are not much impressed with the fact, which is hardly to be wondered at, not only because the subject of the foreign prisoners of war in Britain has never received the attention it deserves, but because the interest of the comparatively modern must always suffer when in juxtaposition with the interest of the far-away past.

But this comparatively modern interest of Portchester is, as I hope to show, very real.

As a place of confinement Portchester could never, of course, compare with such purposely planned prisons as Dartmoor, Stapleton, Perth, or Norman Cross. Still, from its position, and its surrounding walls of almost indestructible masonry, from fifteen to forty feet high and from six to ten feet thick, it answered its purpose very well. True, its situation so near the Channel would seem to favour attempts to escape, but it must be remembered that escape from Portchester Castle by no means implied escape from England, for, ere the fugitive could gain the open sea, he had a terrible gauntlet to run of war-shipping and forts and places of watch and ward, so that although the number of attempted escapes from Portchester annually was greater than that of similar attempts from other places of confinement, the successful ones were few.

Portchester is probably the oldest regular war prison in Britain. In 1745 the *Gentleman's Magazine* records the escape of Spanish prisoners from it, taken, no doubt, during the War of the Austrian Succession, but it was during the Seven Years' War that it became eminent.

An Inside View of PORTCHESTER CASTLE *in* HAMPSHIRE. *Dedicated to the Officers of the Militia.*

Engraved from a Drawing taken on the Spot by an Officer.

In 1756 Captain Fraboulet of the French East India Company's frigate *Astrée*, who appears to have been a medical representative of the Government, reported on the provisions at Portchester as being very good on the whole, except the small beer, which he described as being very weak, and 'apt to cause a flux of blood', a very prevalent malady among the prisoners. He complained, and the deficiency was remedied. Of the hospital accommodation he spoke badly. There was no hospital in the Castle itself, so that patients had either to be sent to Fareham, two miles away, where the hospital was badly placed, being built of wood and partly on the muddy shores of the river, or to Forton, which, he says, is seven miles off. This distance, he says, could be reduced, if done by water, but it was found impossible to find boatmen to take the invalids, the result being that they were carted there, and often died on the way. He also complained that in the hospital the dying and the convalescent were in the same wards, and he begged the Government to establish a hospital at Portchester. He says that he will distribute the King's Bounty no more to invalids, as they spend it improperly, bribing sentries and attendants, and all who have free access and egress, to get them unfit food, such as raw fruit, salt herrings, &c. He will only pay healthy men. He has done his best to re-establish order in the Castle; has asked the Commissioners of the 'Sick and Hurt' Office to put down the public gaming-tables; to imprison those who gamble and sell their kits and food, and to stop the sale of raw fruit, salt fish, and all food which promotes flux of blood.

In 1766 Valérie Coffre quarrelled with a fellow prisoner, Nicholas Chartier, and killed him with a knife. He was found guilty and sentenced to death. He was attended by a Roman Catholic priest, was very earnest in his devotions, and was executed at Winchester, the whole of his fellow prisoners being marched thither under a strong guard to witness the scene. He was a handsome, well-built man of twenty-two.

In 1784 the Castle was properly fitted up as a War Prison. The ancient moat outside the walls, which during long years of neglect had become choked up with rubbish, was filled with water, and the keep was divided into five stories, connected with a wooden stairway at the side, and the entire Castle was arranged for the accommodation of about 8,000 prisoners.

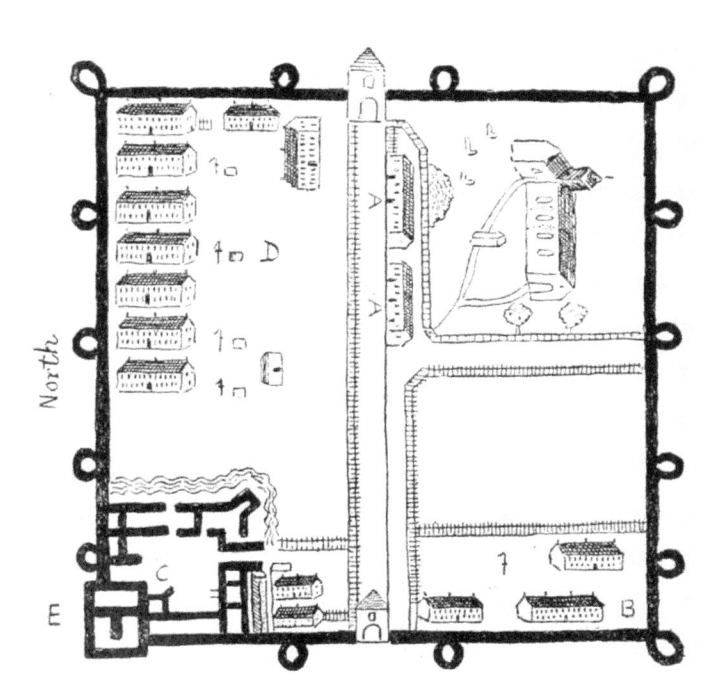

PLAN OF PORTCHESTER CASTLE, 1793.

A. Kitchens, B. Hospital. C. Black Hole. D. Caserns. E. Great Tower.

In 1794 the prisoners captured in Howe's victory of the 'Glorious First of June' were lodged in Portchester. One of the prizes taken, the *Impétueux*, took fire, and at one time there was danger that the fire would spread. The prisoners at Portchester were delighted, and danced about singing the *Ça ira* and the *Marseillaise*, but happily the ship grounded on a mud-bank, and no further damage was done.

In 1796 two prisoners quarrelled over politics, one stabbed the other to death, and was hanged at Winchester.

In 1797 the agent in charge complained that many Portsmouth people, under pretence of attending Portchester Parish Church, which stood within the Castle *enceinte*, came really to buy straw hats and other forbidden articles manufactured by the prisoners.

The inconvenience of the position of this church was further manifested by a daring escape which was made about this time. One Sunday morning, just as service had begun, the sentry on duty at the Water Gate saw three naval officers in full uniform come towards him from the churchyard. Thinking that they were British officers who had seen their men into church and were going for a walk, he presented arms and allowed them to pass. Soon after it was discovered that three smart French privateer captains had escaped, and without doubt they had contrived to get second-hand British naval uniforms smuggled in to them by *soi-disant* worshippers!

A comical incident is recorded in connexion with Portchester churchyard. A sentry was always on duty at an angle of the churchyard close to the South or Water Gate, where there was and still is a remarkable echo. Upon one wild, stormy night, this position was occupied by a soldier of the Dorset Militia, which, with the Denbighshire Militia, performed garrison duty at the Castle. Suddenly the man saw against the wall a tall, white figure with huge horns. He mastered up courage enough to challenge it, but the only reply was a distinct repetition of his words. He fired his piece, but in his agitation evidently missed his aim, for the figure bounded towards him, and he, persuaded that he had to do with the Devil, ran, and gave the alarm. Captain M., the officer of the guard, cursed the man for his fears and, drawing his sword, ran out to meet the intruder. The figure charged him, bowled him over among the gravestones, and made for the Landport Gate, the sentry at which had just opened it at the sound of the disturbance in the churchyard, to see what was going on. The figure disposed of him as he had done Captain M., and made straight away for the door of the Denbighshires' drum-major's quarters, where it proved to be the huge, white regimental goat, who, when disturbed by the sentry, had been browsing upon his hind legs, on the pellitory which grows on the Castle walls!

From the Rev. J. D. Henderson's little book on Portchester I take the following:

'One Francis Dufresne, who was confined here for more than five years, escaped again and again, despite the vigilance of his guards. He seems to have been as reckless and adventurous as any hero of romance, and the neighbourhood was full of stories of his wanderings and the tricks he resorted to to obtain food. Once, after recapture, he was confined in the Black Hole, a building still to be seen at the foot of the Great Tower, called the "Exchequer" on plans of the Castle. Outside walked a sentry day and night, but Dufresne was not to be held. He converted his hammock into what sailors call a "thumb line", and at the dead of night removed a flat stone from under his prison door, crawled out, passed with silent tread within a few inches of the sentry, gained a winding stair which led to the summit of the Castle wall, from which he descended by the cord, and, quickly gaining the open country, started for London, guiding himself by the stars. Arrived in London, he made his way to the house of M. Otto, the French Agent for arranging the exchange of prisoners. Having explained, to the amazement of Otto, that he had escaped from Portchester, he said:

'"Give me some sort of a suit of clothes, and a few sous to defray my expenses to the Castle, and I'll return and astonish the natives."

'Otto, amused at the man's cleverness and impudence, complied, and Dufresne in a few days alighted from the London coach at Fareham, walked over to Portchester, but was refused admission by the guard, until, to the amazement of the latter, he produced the passport by which he had travelled. He was soon after this exchanged.

'Sheer devilment and the enjoyment of baffling his custodians seems to have been Dufresne's sole object in escaping. For a trifling wager he would scale the walls, remain absent for a few days, living on and among the country folk, and return as he went, so that he became almost a popular character even with the garrison.'

Much romance which has been unrecorded no doubt is interwoven with the lives of the foreign prisoners of war in Britain. Two cases associated with Portchester deserve mention.

The church register of 1812 records the marriage of Patrick Bisson to Josephine Desperoux. The latter was one of a company of French ladies who, on their voyage to Mauritius, were captured by a British cruiser, and sent to Portchester. Being non-combatants, they were of course not subjected to durance vile in the Castle, but were distributed among the houses of the village, and, being young and comely, were largely entertained and fêted by the gentry of the neighbourhood, the result being that one, at least, the subject of our notice, captivated an English squire, and married him.

The second case is that of a French girl, who, distracted because her sailor lover had been captured, enlisted as a sailor on a privateer on the bare chance of being captured and meeting him. As good luck would have it, she was captured, and sent to the very prison where was her sweetheart, Portchester Castle. For some months she lived there without revealing her sex, until she was taken ill, sent to the hospital, where, of course, her secret was soon discovered. She was persuaded to return to France on the distinct promise that her lover should be speedily exchanged.

An attempt to escape which had fatal results was made in 1797. Information was given to the authorities that a long tunnel had been made from one of the prison blocks to the outside. So it was arranged that, at a certain hour after lock-up time, the guards should rush in and catch the plotters at work. They did so, and found the men in the tunnel. Shortly afterwards the alarm was given in another quarter, and prisoners were caught in the act of escaping through a large hole they had made in the Castle wall. All that night the prisoners were very riotous, keeping candles lighted, singing Republican songs, dancing and cheering, so that 'it was found necessary' to fire ball cartridges among them, by which many men were wounded. But the effect of this was only temporary. Next morning the tumult and disorder recommenced. The sentries were abused and insulted, and one prisoner, trying to get out at a ventilator in the roof of one of the barracks, was shot in the back, but not mortally. Another was shot through the heart, and the coroner's verdict at the inquest held upon him was 'Justifiable Homicide'.

On another occasion treachery revealed a plot of eighteen Spaniards, who, armed with daggers which they had made out of horseshoe files, assembled in a vault under one of the towers with the idea of sallying forth, cutting down the sentries, and making off; but the guards crawled in and disarmed them after a short struggle.

In 1798 a brewer's man, John Cassel, was sentenced to six months' imprisonment for helping two French captains to escape by carrying them away in empty beer casks.

In *The Times* of July 2, 1799, I find the following:

'Three French prisoners made their escape from Portchester to Southampton. A party of pleasure seekers had engaged Wassell's vessel to go to the Isle of Wight. At an early hour on Saturday morning on repairing to the Quay, the man could not discover his pleasure boat. Everyone was concerned for his loss, and many hours elapsed before any tidings could be heard of her, when some fishing-boats gave information that they had met her near Calshot Castle about 3 a.m., but had no suspicion she had been run away with. In the evening news came that in steering so as to keep as far from Spithead as possible, the Frenchmen were near running ashore at Ryde. This convinced the pilots that Wassell was not on board the vessel, when they went to its assistance, secured the three men and saved the vessel.'

'The bodies of six drowned Frenchmen were found in Portsmouth Harbour; their clothes were in bundles on their backs, and their swimming, no doubt, was impeded thereby.'

'1800, August: A naked French prisoner was found in a field near Portchester. He said he had lived on corn for three days, and that the body of his friend was lying on the beach close by.'

The quiet pathos of the above two bald newspaper announcements must appeal to everybody who for a moment pictures in his mind what the six poor, drowned fellows, and the two friends—one taken, the other left—must have gone through in their desperate bids for liberty. These are the little by-scenes which make up the great tragedy of the War Prisoners in England.

In December of this year there was great sickness and mortality at Portchester.

In the same year a plot to murder sentries and escape was discovered the day before the date of the arranged deed. Forty men were concerned in the plot, and upon them were found long knives, sharpened on both sides, made out of iron hoops.

In 1807 a Portchester prisoner named Cabosas was fined one shilling at Winchester for killing a fellow prisoner in a duel, and in the same year one Herquiand was hanged at Winchester for murder in the Castle.

CLOCK MADE IN PORTCHESTER CASTLE, 1809

by French prisoners of war, from bones saved from their rations

In 1810 it was reported that Portchester Castle was too crowded, and that only 5,900 prisoners could be kept in health there instead of the usual 7,000.

I will now give some accounts of life at Portchester, and I begin with one by an English officer, 'The Light Dragoon,' as a relief from the somewhat monotonous laments which characterize the average foreign chronicler, although it will be noted that our writer does not allow his patriotism to bias his judgement.

Placed on guard over the prisoners, he says:

'Whatever grounds of boasting may belong to us as a nation, I am afraid that our methods of dealing with the prisoners taken from the French during the war scarcely deserves to be classed among them. Absolute cruelties were never, I believe, perpetrated on these unfortunate beings; neither, as far as I know, were they, on any pretence whatever, stinted in the allowance of food awarded to them. But in other respects they fared hardly enough. Their sleeping apartments, for instance, were very much crowded. Few paroles were extended to them (it is past dispute that when the parole was obtained they were, without distinction of rank, apt to make a bad use of it), while their pay was calculated on a scale as near to the line of starvation as could in any measure correspond with our nation's renown for humanity. On the other hand, every possible encouragement was given to the exercise of ingenuity among the prisoners themselves by the throwing open of the Castle yard once or twice a week, when their wares were exhibited for sale, amid numerous groups of jugglers, tumblers, and musicians, all of whom followed their respective callings, if not invariably with skill, always with most praiseworthy perseverance. Moreover, the ingenuity of the captives taught them how on these occasions to set up stalls on which all manner of trinkets were set forth, as well as puppet shows and Punch's opera.... Then followed numerous purchases, particularly on the part of the country people, of bone and ivory knick-knacks, fabricated invariably with a common penknife, yet always neat, and not infrequently elegant. Nor must I forget to mention the daily market which the peasantry, particularly the women, were in the habit of attending, and which usually gave scope for the exchange of Jean Crapaud's manufacture for Nancy's eggs, or Joan's milk, or home-baked loaf....

'It happened one night that a sentry whose post lay outside the walls of the old Castle, was startled by the sound as of a hammer driven against the earth under his feet. The man stopped, listened, and was more and more convinced that neither his fears nor his imagination had misled him. So he reported the circumstance to the sergeant who next visited his post, and left him to take in the matter such steps as might be expedient. The sergeant, having first ascertained, as in duty bound, that the man spoke truly, made his report to the captain on duty, who immediately doubled the sentry at the indicated spot, and gave strict orders that should as much as one French prisoner be seen making his way beyond the Castle walls, he should be shot without mercy.

'Then was the whole of the guard got under arms: then were beacons fired in various quarters; while far and near, from Portsmouth not less than from the cantonments more close at hand, bodies of troops marched upon Portchester. Among others came the general of the district, bringing with him a detachment of sappers and miners, by whom all the floors of the several bedrooms were tried, and who soon brought the matter home to those engaged in it. Indeed one man was taken in the gallery he was seeking to enlarge, his only instrument being a spike nail wherewith to labour. The plot thus discovered was very extensive and must, if carried through, have proved a desperate one to both parties. For weeks previous to the discovery, the prisoners, it appeared, had been at work, and from not fewer than seven rooms, all of them on the ground floor, they had sunk shafts 12 feet in depth, and caused them all to meet at one common centre, whence as many chambers went off. These were driven beyond the extremity of the outer wall, and one, that of which the sentry was thus unexpectedly made aware, the ingenious miners had carried forward with such skill, that in two days more it would have been in a condition to be opened.

'The rubbish, it appeared, which from these several covered ways they scooped out, was carried about by the prisoners in their pockets till they found an opportunity of scattering it over the surface of the great square. Yet the desperate men had a great deal more to encounter than the mere obstacles which the excavation of the castle at Portchester presented.

'Their first proceeding after emerging into the upper air must needs have been to surprise and overpower the troops that occupied the barracks immediately contiguous, an operation of doubtful issue at the best, and not to be accomplished without a terrible loss of life, certainly on one side, probably on both. Moreover, when this was done, there remained for the fugitives the still more arduous task of making their way through the heart of the garrison town of Portsmouth, and seizing a flotilla of boats, should such be high and dry upon the beach. Yet worse even than this remained, for both the harbour and the roads wore crowded with men-of-war the gauntlet of whose batteries the deserters must of necessity have run....'

One wishes that the British officer could have given us some account of the inner life at Portchester, from his point of view, but the foreign narratives which follow seem to have been written in a fair and broad spirit which would certainly have not been manifest had the *genius loci* of the hulks been influencing the minds of the writers.

The two following accounts, by St. Aubin and Philippe Gille, were written by men who were probably in Portchester at the same time, as both had come to England from Cabrera—that terrible prison island south of Majorca, to which the Spaniards sent the captives of Baylen in July 1808—unfortunates whose prolonged living death there must ever remain an indelible stain upon our conduct during the Peninsular War.

St. Aubin describes the Castle as divided into two by a broad road running between palisades, on the one side of which were a large and a small tower and nine two-storied wooden buildings, and on the other a church, kitchens, storehouses, offices, and hospital. It is evident that what he calls the large tower is the castle keep, for this held from 1,200 to 1,500 prisoners, while each of the nine barracks accommodated 500.

St. Aubin gives us the most detailed account of the Portchester prisoners and their life. At 6 a.m. in summer, and 7 in winter, the bell announced the arrival of the soldiers and turnkeys, who opened the doors and counted the prisoners. At 9 o'clock the market bell rang and the distributions of bread were made. The prisoners were divided into *plats* or messes of twelve, each *plat* was again subdivided, and each had two *gamelles* or soup-pots. At midday the bell announced the closing of the market to English sellers, who were replaced by French, and also the distribution of soup and meat. At sunset the bell went again, jailers and soldiers went through the evening count, all were obliged to be within doors, and lights were put out.

Occasionally in the *grand pré*, as the enclosure within the walls was called, there was a general airing of prisons and hammocks, and the prisoners were obliged to stay out of doors till midday; during this performance the masons went round to sound walls and floors, to see that no attempts to escape were being engineered. Each story of the tower and the prisons had two prison superintendents at eight shillings per month, who were responsible for their cleanliness, and a barber. The doctor went through the rooms every day.

The prisoners prepared their own food, the wages of the master cooks being sevenpence per diem. St. Aubin complains bitterly of the quality of the provisions, especially of the bread, and says that it was quite insufficient on account of the avarice of the contractors, but at any rate, he says, it was regularly distributed.

In spite of all this, Portchester was preferred by the prisoners to other dépôts, because it was easy to get money and letters from France; and it may be noted that while we get little or no mention of recreation and amusement at Norman Cross, or Stapleton, or Perth, unless gambling comes within the category, we shall see that at Portchester the prisoners seem to have done their very best to make the long days pass as pleasantly as possible.

Portchester was a veritable hive of industry. There were manufacturers of straw hats, stockings, gloves, purses, and braces. There were cunning artificers in bone who made tobacco boxes, dominoes, chessmen, models of all kinds, especially of men-of-war, one of which latter, only one foot in length, is said to have been sold for £26, as well as of the most artistic ornaments and knick-knacks. There were tailors, goldsmiths (so says St. Aubin), shoemakers, caterers, limonadiers, and comedians of the Punch and Judy and marionette class. There were professors of mathematics, of drawing, of French, of English, of Latin, of fencing, of writing, of dancing, of the *bâton*, and of *la boxe*. St. Aubin quotes as a strange fact that most of the prisoners who, on going to Portchester, knew neither reading nor writing, 'en sont sortis la tête et la bourse passablement meublées.'

But the unique feature of Portchester industry was its thread lace manufacture.

BONE MODEL OF H.M.S. *VICTORY*

Made by prisoners of war at Portsmouth

The brilliant idea of starting this belonged to a French soldier prisoner who had been born and bred in a lace-making country, and had been accustomed to see all the women working at it. He recalled the process by memory, took pupils, and in less than a year there were 3,000 prisoners in Portchester making lace, and among these were 'capitalists' who employed each as many as from fifty to sixty workmen. So beautiful was this lace, and so largely was it bought by the surrounding families, that the English lace-makers protested, its manufacture within the prison was forbidden, and it is said that the work of suppression was carried out in the most brutal manner, the machines being broken and all lace in stock or in process of manufacture destroyed.

Gambling, says St. Aubin, was the all-pervading vice of Portchester, as in the other prisons. For 'capitalists' there was actually a roulette table, but the rank and file gambled upon the length of straws, with cards or dominoes, for their rations, their clothes, or their bedding. The authorities attempted occasionally to check the mania among the most enslaved by placing them apart from their fellows, reclothing them, and making them eat their rations, but in vain, for they pierced the walls of their places of confinement, and sold their clothes through the apertures. Duels, as a consequence, were frequent, the usual time for these being the dinner hour, because all the prisoners were then temporarily in the *salles*.

St. Aubin thus describes his fellow prisoners. Sailors, he says, were brusque but obliging; soldiers were more honest, softer and less prompt to help; maîtres d'armes were proud and despotic. The scum of the community were the Raffalés, who lived in the top story of the tower. Among the two hundred of these there were only two or three suits of clothes, which were worn in turn by those who had to go out foraging for food. These men terrorized the rest, and their captain was even held in some sort of fear, if not respect, by the authorities.

The prison amusements were various. The prisoners who had no occupations played draughts, cards, dominoes, and billiards. On Sundays the beer-man came, and much drunkenness prevailed, especially upon fête days, such as St. Martin's, Christmas, and August 15, the Emperor's birthday: the principal drinks being compounds of beer and spirits known as 'strom' and 'shum'. On St. Cecilia's Day the musicians always gave an entertainment, but the chief form of amusement was the theatre.

This was arranged in the basement of the large tower—that is, the keep, where three hundred people could be accommodated. Part of the boxes were set apart for English visitors, who appreciated the French performances so much that they even said that they were better than what they were accustomed to in Portsmouth, and flocked to them, much to the disgust of the native managers, who represented to the authorities that those untaxed aliens were taking the bread out of their mouths. The Government considered the matter, and upon the plea that the admission of the English public to the French theatre was leading to too great intimacy between the peoples, and thus would further the escapes of prisoners, took advantage of the actual escape of a prisoner in English dress to ordain that although the theatre might continue as heretofore, no English were to be admitted. The result of this was that the receipts dropped from £12 to £5 a night.

St. Aubin remarks, *en passant*, that Commander William Patterson and Major Gentz, who were chiefly responsible for the retention of the theatre, were the only Englishmen he ever met who were worthy of respect!

Of the pieces played, St. Aubin mentions *L'Heureuse Étourderie* by himself; the tragedies *Zaïre, Mahomet, Les Templiers*; the comedies *Les Deux Gendres, Les Folies amoureuses, Le Barbier de Séville, Le Tyran domestique, Défiance et Malice*; many dramas, and even vaudevilles and operas such as *Les Deux Journées, Pierre le Grand, Françoise de Foix*, of which the music was composed by prisoners and played by an orchestra of twelve.

A terrible murder is said to have been the outcome of theatricals in the prison. In describing it St. Aubin starts with the opinion that 'Les maîtres d'armes sont toujours fort vilains messieurs'. There was a quarrel between a gunner and a *maître des logis*; some said it was about a theatrical part, but others that the gunner, Tardif, had committed a crime in past days, had described it in writing, that the paper had fallen from his hammock into that of Leguay, the *maître des logis*, and that Tardif determined to get the possessor of his secret out of the way. So he attacked Leguay, who ran bleeding to his hammock, followed by Tardif, who then dispatched him, and displayed a strange, fierce joy at the deed when overpowered and tied to a pillar. He was tried, and condemned to be hanged at Portchester in the sight of all the prisoners. 'The scaffold was erected on the Portsmouth road', says St. Aubin, not within the Castle precincts, as another account states. He had previously sold his body for ten francs to a surgeon for dissection.

At the request of the prisoners the body of Leguay was buried in Portchester churchyard. All joined to raise funds for the funeral, and the proceeds of a performance of *Robert, chef de brigands*, was devoted to the relief of the widow and children of the murdered man.

At the funeral of Leguay, sous-officiers of his regiment, the 10th Dragoons, carried the coffin, which was preceded by a British military band, and followed by the sous-officiers in uniform, British officers, and inhabitants of the neighbourhood.

Tardif was conveyed from Winchester to the *King's Arms* Inn at Portchester, where Mr. White, the Roman Catholic priest, tried to get him to take the last Sacrament, but in vain: Tardif only wanted the execution to be got over as soon as possible. He was taken in a cart to the prison yard, where were assembled 7,000 prisoners. Again the priest urged him to repent, but it was useless. The cap was drawn over his face, but he tore it away, and died as he had lived. The behaviour of the spectator prisoners was exemplary.

At the Peace and Restoration of 1814, although the Portchester prisoners were Bonapartists almost to a man, quite a boyish joy was exhibited at the approaching liberation: great breakfasts were given in the village, and by the end of May the Castle was empty.

The notes on Portchester of Philippe Gille, author of *Mémoires d'un Conscrit de 1798*, are as interesting as those of St. Aubin, particularly as regards the amusements of the prisoners, and I make no apology for adding to them his immediately previous experiences, as they are not distasteful reading.

Gille was taken prisoner in Baylen, and at first was put on board No. 27 Hulk, at Cadiz, in which ship, he says, were crowded no less than 1,824 prisoners! Thence he was sent to Cabrera and relates his frightful experiences on that prison island.

After a time the prisoners were taken on board British ships, and learned that their destination was an English prison—perhaps the dreaded hulks!

Gille was on board the *Britannia*. Let me tell the effect of the change in his own words, they are so gratifying:

'Aux traitements cruels des féroces Espagnols succédaient tout à coup les soins compatissants des soldats et matelots anglais; ces braves gens nous témoignaient toutes sortes d'égards. Ils transportèrent à bras plusieurs de nos camarades malades ou amputés. Les effets qui nous appartenaient furent aussi montés par leurs soins, sans qu'ils nous laissaient prendre la peine de rien.'

On board there were cleanliness and space, good food for officers and men alike, and plenty of it, the allowance being the same for six prisoners as for four British. Rum was regularly served out, and Gille lays stress on a pudding the prisoners made, into the composition of which it entered.

They duly reached Plymouth; the beautiful scenery impressed Gille, but he was most astonished when the market-boats came alongside to see fish-women clothed in black velvet, with feathers and flowers in their hats!

Thence to Portsmouth, where they got a first sight of the hulks, which made Gille shudder, but he was relieved to learn that he and his fellows were destined for a shore prison.

On September 28, 1810, they arrived at Portchester. Here they were minutely registered, and clothed in a sleeved vest, waistcoat, and trousers of yellow cloth, and a blue and white striped cotton shirt, and provided with a hammock, a flock mattress of two pounds weight, a coverlet, and tarred cords for hammock lashings.

Gille gives much interesting detail about the theatre. The Agent, William Patterson, found it good policy to further any scheme by which the prisoners could be kept wholesomely occupied, and so provided all the wood necessary for the building of the theatre, which was in charge of an ex-chief-machinist of the Théâtre Feydau in Paris, Carré by name. He made a row of boxes and a hall capable of holding 300 people, and thoroughly transformed the base story of the keep, which was unoccupied because prisoners confined there in past times had died in great numbers, and the authorities deemed it unwholesome as a sleeping-place.

Carré's Arabian *Féerie* was a tremendous success, but it led to the Governmental interference with the theatre already mentioned. An English major who took a lively interest in the theatre (probably the Major Gentz alluded to by St. Aubin) had his whole regiment in to see it at one shilling a head, and published in the Portsmouth papers a glowing panegyric upon it, and further invited the directors of the Portsmouth Theatre to 'come to see how a theatre should be run'. They came, were very pleased and polite, but very soon after came an order from the authorities that the theatre should be shut. However, by the influence of the Agent, it was permitted to continue, on the condition that no English people were to be admitted.

Carré painted a drop-scene which was a masterpiece. It was a view of Paris from a house at the corner of the Place Dauphine on the Pont-Neuf, showing the Café Paris on the point of the island, the Bridges of the Arts, the Royal and the Concorde, and the Bains des Bons-Hommes in the distance, the Colonnade of the Louvre, the Tuileries with the national flag flying, the Hôtel de Monnaies, the Quatre Nations, and the 'théatins' of the Quai Voltaire. It may be imagined how this home-touch aroused the enthusiasm of the poor exiles!

New plays were received from Paris, amongst them *Le Petit Poucet*, *Le Diable ou la Bohémienne*, *Les Deux Journées* and *Adolphe et Clara*. The musical pieces were accompanied by an orchestra (of prisoners, of course) under Corret of the Conservatoire, who composed fresh music for such representations as *Françoise de Foix* and *Pierre le Grand*, as their original music was too expensive, and who played the cornet solos, Gourdet being first violin.

Gille's own *métier* was to make artificial flowers, and to give lessons in painting, for which he took pupils at one franc fifty centimes a month—the regulation price for all lessons. He also learned the violin, and had an instrument made by a fellow prisoner.

At Portchester, as elsewhere, a Masonic Lodge was formed among the prisoners.

In 1812 was brought to light the great plot for the 70,000 prisoners in England to rise simultaneously, to disarm their guards, who were only militia men, and to carry on a guerilla warfare, avoiding all towns. At Portchester the 7,000 prisoners were to overpower the garrison, which had two cannon and 800 muskets, and march to Forton, where were 3,000 prisoners. The success of the movement was to depend upon the co-operation of the Boulogne troops and ships, in keeping the British fleet occupied, but the breaking up of the Boulogne Camp, in order to reinforce the Grand Army for the expedition to Russia, caused the abandonment of the enterprise.

The news of the advance of the Allies in France only served to bind the Imperialists together: the tricolour cockade was universally worn, and an English captain who entered the Castle wearing a white cockade was greeted with hisses, groans, and even stone-throwing, and was only saved from further mischief by the Agent—a man much respected by the prisoners—who got him away and gave him a severe lecture on his foolishness. On Easter Day, 1814, the news of Peace, of the accession of Louis XVIII, and of freedom for the prisoners came. The Agent asked the prisoners to hoist the white flag as a greeting to the French officer who was coming to announce formally the great news, and to arrange for the departure of the prisoners. A unanimous refusal was the result, and a British soldier had to hoist the flag. Contre-amiral Troude came. There was a strong feeling against him, inasmuch as it was reported that in order to gain his present position he had probably given up his fleet to England, and a resolution was drawn up not to acclaim him. All the same, Gille says, the speech he made so impressed the prisoners that he was loudly cheered, and went away overcome with emotion.

The next day his mission took him to the prison ships. Here he did not succeed so well, for as he approached one of the hulks he had a large basket of filth thrown over him, and he had to leave without boarding her. By way of punishment, the prisoners on this ship were made the last to leave England.

On May 15, 1814, the evacuation of Portchester began. Gille left on the 20th, carrying away the best of feelings towards the Agent and the Commandant, the former showing his sympathy with the prisoners to the very last, by taking steps so that the St. Malo men, of whom there were a great many, should be sent direct to their port instead of being landed at Calais.

Gille describes a very happy homeward voyage, thanks largely to the English doctor on the ship, who, finding that Gille was a Mason, had him treated with distinction, and even offered to help him with a loan of money.

Pillet, the irrepressible, tells a yarn that 'Milor Cordower (Lord Cawdor), Colonel du régiment de Carmarthen', visiting the Castle one day, was forgetful enough to leave his horse unattended, tied up in the courtyard; when he returned there was no horse to be found, and it turned out that the prisoners, mad with hunger, had taken the horse, killed it, and eaten it raw. Pillet adds that all dogs who strayed Portchester way suffered the same fate, and that in support of his statement he can bring many naval officers of Lorient and Brest.

Pillet's story, I think, is rather better than Garneray's about the great Dane on the prison ship (see pp. 68–71).

The last French prisoners left Portchester at the end of May 1814, but American prisoners were here until January 1816. After the Peace all the wooden buildings were taken down and sold by auction (a row of cottages in Fareham, built out of the material, still enjoys the name of 'Bug Row'). Relics of this period of the Castle's history are very scanty. The old Guard House at the Land Gate, now the Castle Custodian's dwelling, remains much as it was, and a line of white stones on the opposite side of the approach marks the boundary of the old prison hospital, which is also commemorated in the name Hospital Lane.

The great tower still retains the five stories which were arranged for the prisoners, and on the transverse beams are still the hooks to which the hammocks were suspended. Some crude coloured decoration on the beams of the lowest story may have been the work of the French theatrical artists, but I doubt it.

Names of French and other prisoners are cut on many of the walls and wooden beams, notably at the very top of the great tower, which is reached by a dark, steep newel stair of Norman work, now almost closed to the public on account of the dangerous condition of many of the steps. This was the stair used by Dufresne, and the number of names cut in the topmost wall would seem to show that the lofty coign, whence might be seen a widespread panorama, stretching on three sides far away to the Channel, and to these poor fellows possible liberty, was a favourite resort. I noted some twenty decipherable names, the earliest date being 1745 and the latest 1803.

Only one death appears in the Church Register—that of 'Peter Goston, a French prisoner', under date of December 18, 1812.

There seems to have been no separate burial ground for the rank and file of the prisoners, but it is said that they were shovelled away into the tide-swept mud-flats outside the South Gate, and that, for economy, a single coffin with a sliding bottom did duty for many corpses. But human remains in groups have been unearthed all around the Castle, and, as it is known that at certain periods the mortality among the prisoners was very high, it is believed that these are to be dated from the prisoner-of-war epoch of the Castle's history.

No descendants of the prisoners are to be traced in or about Portchester; but Mrs. Durrand, who is a familiar figure to all visitors to the Castle, believes that her late husband's grandfather was a French prisoner of war here.

It may be noted that Arthur Wellesley, afterwards Duke of Wellington, was at one time an officer of the garrison at Portchester.

Note on the Portchester Theatricals

A correspondent of the French paper *L'Intermédiaire*, the equivalent of our *Notes and Queries*, gives some details. The Portchester Theatricals originated with the prisoners who came from Cabrera and the Isle de Léon. On these awful islands the prisoners played entirely as amateurs, but at Portchester the majority of the actors were salaried; indeed, only three were not.

I give a list of the actors in or about the year 1810:

1. *Sociétaires* (salaried subscribers).

Hanin, an employé in the English prison office, with the purely honorary title of Director.
Breton, Sergeant, 2nd Garde de Paris	Comique.
Reverdy, Sergeant, 2nd Garde de Paris	père noble.
Lafontaine, Sergeant, 2nd Garde de Paris	jeune premier.
Gruentgentz, Sergeant, 2nd Garde de Paris	mère et duègne.
Moreau, Captain 2nd Garde de Paris	les Colins.
Blin de Balue, Sergeant, Marine Artillery	les tyrans.
Sutat (?), Maréchal des logis	jeune première.
Wanthies, Captain, 4th Legion	soubrette et jeune première.
Defacq, fourrier, chasseurs à cheval	jeune premier en séconde.
Siutor or Pintor, marin	jouant les accessoires.
Palluel, fourrier, 2nd Garde de Paris	bas comique.
Carré, soldat, 2nd Garde de Paris	machiniste.
Montlefort, Marine	artificier.

2. *Amateurs.*

Gille, fourrier, 1st Legion	jeunes premiers.
Quantin, fourrier, 1st Legion	les ingénues.
Iwan, chasseurs à cheval	les confidents.

The orchestra consisted of four violins, two horns, three clarinets, and one 'octave'.

In the above list both Gille and Quantin wrote memoirs of their stay at Portchester. The former I have quoted.

A French writer thus sarcastically speaks of the dramatic efforts of these poor fellows:

'Those who never have seen the performances of wandering *troupes* in some obscure village of Normandy or Brittany can hardly form an idea of these prison representations wherein rough sailors with a few rags wrapped about them mouth the intrigues and sentiments of our great poets in the style of the cabaret.'

No doubt the performances on the hulks were poor enough. The wonder to us who know what life was on the hulks is, not that they were poor, but that there was any heart to give them at all. But there is plenty of evidence that the performances in such a prison as Portchester, wherein were assembled many men of education and refinement, were more than good. At any rate, we have seen that they were good enough to attract English audiences to such an extent as to interfere with the success of the local native theatres, and to bring about the exclusion from them of these English audiences.

CHAPTER XIII
THE PRISONS ASHORE
5. LIVERPOOL

Liverpool became a considerable dépôt for prisoners of war, from the force of circumstances rather than from any suitability of its own. From its proximity to Ireland, the shelter and starting and refitting point of so many French, and, later, American privateers, Liverpool shared with Bristol, and perhaps with London, the position of being the busiest privateering centre in Britain.

Hence, from very early days in its history, prisoners were continually pouring in and out; in, as the Liverpool privateers, well equipped and armed by wealthy individuals or syndicates, skilfully commanded and splendidly fought, swept the narrow seas and beyond, and brought in their prizes; out, as both sides were ready enough to exchange men in a contest of which booty was the main object, and because the guarding of hundreds of desperate seafaring men was a matter of great difficulty and expense in an open port with no other than the usual accommodation for malefactors.

Before 1756 the prisoners of war brought into Liverpool were stowed away in the common Borough Gaol and in an old powder magazine which stood on the north side of Brownlow Street, where Russell Street now is. Prisoners taken in the Seven Years' War and the American War of Independence were lodged in the Tower Prison at the lower end of Water Street, on the north side, where now Tower Buildings stand, between Tower Garden and Stringers Alley, which remained the chief jail of Liverpool until July 1811. It was a castellated building of red sandstone, consisting of a large square embattled tower, with subordinate towers and buildings, forming three sides of a quadrangle of which the fourth side was occupied by a walled garden, the whole covering an area of about 3,700 square yards.

THE OLD TOWER PRISON, LIVERPOOL.

(*From an old print.*)

In 1756 the Admiralty had bought the dancing-room and the buildings adjoining at the bottom of Water Street, and 'fitted them up for the French prisoners in a most commodious manner, there being a handsome kitchen with furnaces, &c., for cooking their provisions, and good lodging rooms both above and below stairs. Their lordships have ordered a hammock and bedding (same as used on board our men of war), for each prisoner, which it is to be hoped will be a means of procuring our countrymen who have fallen into their hands better usage than hitherto, many of them having been treated with great inhumanity.'

One of the most famous of the early French 'corsaires', Thurot—who during the Seven Years' War made Ireland his base, and, acting with the most admirable skill and audacity, caused almost as much loss and consternation on this coast as did Paul Jones later—was at last brought a prisoner into Liverpool on February 28, 1760.

The romance of Felix Durand, a Seven Years' War prisoner at the Tower, is almost as interesting as that of Louis Vanhille, to which I devote a separate chapter.

The wife of one P., an ivory carver and turner in Dale Street, and part owner of the *Mary Ellen* privateer, had a curiously made foreign box which had been broken, and which no local workman could mend. The French prisoners were famous as clever and ingenious artisans, and to one of them, Felix Durand, it was handed. He accepted the job, and wanted ample time to do it in. Just as it should have been finished, fifteen prisoners, Durand among them, escaped from the Tower, but, having neither food nor money, and, being ignorant of English and of the localities round Liverpool, all, after wandering about for some time half-starved, either returned or were captured.

Says Durand, describing his own part in the affair:

'I am a Frenchman, fond of liberty and change, and I determined to make my escape. I was acquainted with Mr. P. in Dale Street; I did work for him in the Tower, and he has a niece who is *tout à fait charmante*. She has been a constant ambassadress between us, and has taken charge of my money to deposit with her uncle on my account. She is very engaging, and when I have had conversation with her, I obtained from her the information that on the east side of our prison there were two houses which opened into a short narrow street [perhaps about Johnson Lane or Oriel Chambers]. Mademoiselle is very kind and complacent, and examined the houses and found an easy entrance into one.'

So, choosing a stormy night, the prisoners commenced by loosening the stone work in the east wall, and packing the mortar under their beds. They were safe during the day, but once when a keeper did come round, they put one of their party in bed, curtained the window grating with a blanket, and said that their compatriot was ill and could not bear the light. So the officer passed on. At last the hole was big enough, and one of them crept through. He reported an open yard, that it was raining heavily, and that the night was *affreuse*. They crept out one by one and got into the yard, whence they entered a cellar by the window, traversed a passage or two, and entered the kitchen, where they made a good supper, of bread and beef. While cutting this, one of them let fall a knife, but nobody heard it, and, says Durand, 'Truly you Englishmen sleep well!'

Finally, as a neighbouring clock struck two, they managed to get past the outer wall, and one man, sent to reconnoitre, reported: 'not a soul to be seen anywhere, the wind rushing up the main street from the sea.'

They then separated. Durand went straight ahead, 'passed the Exchange, down a narrow lane [Dale Street] facing it, in which I knew Mademoiselle dwelt, but did not know the house; therefore I pushed on till I came to the foot of a hill. I thought I would turn to the left at first, but went on to take my chance of four cross roads—' (Old Haymarket, Townsend Lane, now Byron Street, Dale Street, and Shaw's Brow, now William Brown Street).

He went on until he came to the outskirts of Liverpool by Townsend Mill (at the top of London Road), and so on the road to Prescot, ankle-deep in mud. He ascended Edge Hill, keeping always the right-hand road, lined on both sides with high trees, and at length arrived at a little village (Wavertree) as a clock struck three. Then he ate some bread and drank from a pond. Then onwards, always bearing to the right, on to 'the quaint little village of Hale,' his final objective being Dublin, where he had a friend, a French priest.

At Hale an old woman came out of a cottage and began to take down the shutters. Durand, who, not knowing English, had resolved to play the part of a deaf and dumb man, quietly took the shutters from her, and placed them in their proper position. Then he took a broom and swept away the water from the front of the door; got the kettle and filled it from the pump, the old woman being too astonished to be able to say anything, a feeling which was increased when her silent visitor raked the cinders out of the grate, and laid the fire. Then she said something in broad Lancashire, but he signified that he was deaf and dumb, and he understood her so far as to know that she expressed pity. At this point he sank on to a settle and fell fast asleep from sheer exhaustion from walking and exposure. When he awakened he found breakfast awaiting him, and made a good meal. Then he did a foolish thing. At the sound of horses' hoofs he sprang up in alarm and fled from the house—an act doubly ill-advised, inasmuch as it betrayed his affliction to be assumed, and, had his entertainer been a man instead of an old woman, would assuredly have stirred the hue and cry after him.

He now took a wrong turning, and found himself going towards Liverpool, but corrected his road, and at midday reached a barn where two men were threshing wheat. He asked leave by signs to rest, which was granted. We shall now see how the native ingenuity of the Frenchman stood him in good stead in circumstances where the average Englishman would have been a useless tramp and nothing more. Seeing some fresh straw in a corner, Durand began to weave it into a dainty basket. The threshers stayed their work to watch him, and, when the article was finished, offered to buy it. Just then the farmer entered, and from pity and admiration took him home to dinner, and Durand's first act was to present the basket to the daughter of the house. Dinner finished, the guest looked about for work to do, and in the course of the afternoon he repaired a stopped clock with an old skewer and a pair of pincers, mended a chair, repaired a china image, cleaned an old picture, repaired a lock, altered a key, and fed the pigs!

The farmer was delighted, and offered him a barn to sleep in, but the farmer's daughter injudiciously expressed her admiration of him, whereupon her sweetheart, who came in to spend the evening, signed to him the necessity of his immediate departure.

For weeks this extraordinary man, always simulating a deaf-mute, wandered about, living by the sale of baskets, and was everywhere received with the greatest kindness.

But misfortune overtook him at length, although only temporarily. He was standing by a very large tree, a local lion, when a party of visitors came up to admire it, and a young lady expressed herself in very purely pronounced French. Unable to restrain himself, Durand stepped forward, and echoed her sentiments.

'Why!' exclaimed the lady. 'This is the dumb man who was at the Hall yesterday repairing the broken vases!'

The result was that he was arrested as an escaped prisoner of war, sent first to Ormskirk, and then back to his old prison at the Liverpool Tower.

However, in a short time, through the influence of Sir Edward Cunliffe, one of the members for Liverpool, he was released, and went to reside with the P.'s in Dale Street. In the following September Mr. Durand and Miss P. became man and wife, and he remained in Liverpool many years, as partner in her uncle's business.

In 1779 Howard the philanthropist, in his tour through the prisons of Britain, visited the Liverpool Tower. He reported that there were therein 509 prisoners, of whom fifty-six were Spaniards, who were kept apart from the French prisoners, on account of racial animosities. All were crowded in five rooms, which were packed with hammocks three tiers high. The airing ground was spacious. There were thirty-six invalids in a small dirty room of a house at some distance from the prison. There were no sheets on the beds, but the surgeons were attentive, and there were no complaints.

At the prison, he remarked, the bedding required regulation. There was no table hung up of regulations or of the victualling rate, so that the prisoners had no means of checking their allowances. The meat and beer were good, but the bread was heavy. The late Agent, he was informed, had been very neglectful of his duties, but his successor bore a good character, and much was expected of him.

It has been said that most of the prisoners of war in Liverpool were privateersmen. In 1779 Paul Jones was the terror of the local waters, and as his continual successes unsettled the prisoners and incited them to continual acts of mutiny and rebellion, and escapes or attempts to escape were of daily occurrence, a general shifting of prisoners took place, many of the confined men being sent to Chester, Carlisle, and other inland towns, and the paroled men to Ormskirk and Wigan.

In 1779 Sir George Saville and the Yorkshire Militia subscribed £50 to the fund for the relief of the French and Spanish prisoners in Liverpool. The appeal for subscriptions wound up with the following complacent remark:

'And as the Town of Liverpool is already the Terror of our Foes, they will by this means (at the time they acknowledge our Spirit and Bravery) be obliged to reverence our Virtue and Humanity.'

In 1781 the Rev. Gilbert Wakefield wrote:

'The American and French Wars had now been raging for some months, and several hundred prisoners of the latter nation had been brought into Liverpool by privateers. I frequently visited them in their confinement, and was much mortified and ashamed of their uniform complaints of hard usage and a scanty allowance of unwholesome provision. What I occasionally observed in my visits gave me but too much reason to believe the representations of this pleasing people, who maintained their national sprightliness and good humour undamped even in captivity. I was happy to learn later from the prisoners themselves the good effects of my interference, and the Commissary, the author of their wrongs, was presently superseded.... When I met him in the street later there was fire in his eye, and fury in his face.'

In 1793, the New Borough Gaol in Great Howard Street, (formerly Milk House Lane), which had been built in 1786, but never used, was made ready for prisoners of war.

The following letter to the *Liverpool Courier* of January 12, 1798, was characterized by *The Times* as 'emanating from some sanguinary Jacobin in some back garret of London':

'The French prisoners in the dungeons of Liverpool are actually starving. Some time ago their usual allowance was lessened under pretence of their having bribed the sentinels with the superfluity of their provisions. Each prisoner is allowed ½ lb. of beef, 1 lb. bread, &c., and as much water as he can drink. *The meat is the offal of the Victualling Office*—the necks and shanks of the butchered; the bread is so bad and so black as to incite disgust; and the water so brackish as not to be drunken, and they are provided with straw. The officers, contrary to the rule of Nations, are imprisoned with the privates, and are destined with them to experience the dampness and filth of these dismal and unhealthy dungeons. The privileges of Felons are not allowed them. Philanthropos.'

So the Mayor and Magistrates of Liverpool made minute inspection of the prison (which had been arranged in accordance with Howard's recommendations), and published a report which absolutely contradicted the assertions of 'Philanthropos'. There were, it said, six large detached buildings, each of three stories, 106 feet long, twenty-three feet high, and forty-seven feet wide; there were two kitchens, each forty-eight feet long, twenty feet broad, and thirteen feet high. In the two upper stories the prisoners slept in cells or separate compartments, nine feet long, seven feet broad, and eleven feet high, each with a glazed window, and in each were generally three or four, never more than five, prisoners. The Hospital occupied two rooms, each thirty-three feet long, thirty feet broad, and eleven feet high. The officer-prisoners, seventy in number, occupied a separate building, and the other prisoners, 1,250 in number, were in the five buildings. The mortality here, from May 15 to December 31, 1798, among 1,332 prisoners was twenty-six.

Richard Brooke, in *Liverpool from 1775 to 1800*, says:

'Amongst the amusements some of the French prisoners during their confinement here performed plays in a small theatre contrived for that purpose within the walls, and in some instances they raised in a single night £50 for admission money. Many of my readers will recollect that with the usual ingenuity of the French the prisoners manufactured a variety of snuff-boxes, rings, trinkets, crucifixes, card-boxes, and toys which were exhibited in a stand at the entrance of the Gaol and sold for their benefit.'

One famous prisoner here was a Pole, named Charles Domery, whose voracity was extraordinary. He ate anything. After the surrender of the frigate on which he was captured he was so hungry that he was caught tearing the mangled limb of one of his fallen comrades. In one year he ate 174 cats, some of them alive, besides dogs, rats, candles, and especially raw meat. Although he was daily allowed the rations of ten men, he was never satisfied. One day the prison doctor tested his capacity, and at a sitting he ate fourteen pounds of raw meat and two pounds of candles, and washed it all down with five bottles of porter. Some of the French prisoners used to upbraid him with his Polish nationality, and accuse him of disloyalty to the Republic. Once, in a fit of anger at this, he seized a knife, cut two wide gashes on his bare arm, and with the blood wrote on the wall 'Vive la République!'

He stood six feet two inches, was well made, and rather thin, and, despite the brutality of his taste in food, was a very amiable and inoffensive man.

The following touching little letter was evidently written by a very poor prisoner whose wife shared his confinement.

'De Livrepool: Ce 21 Septanbre 1757.

'Mon cher frere je vous dis ses deux mot pour vous dire que ma tres cher femme à quitte ce monde pour aller à lotre monde; je vous prit de priyer pour elle et de la recommender a tous nos bons paran.

'Je suis en pleuran votre

'Serviteur et frere

'JOSEPH LE BLAN.'

From Brooke's *Liverpool* I also take the following:

'A considerable number of prisoners were confined in the Borough Gaol, a most ill-judged place of confinement when its contiguity to Coast and Shipping, and the facilities afforded for escape of prisoners in case of the appearance of an Enemy off the Coast are considered. In general the prisoners were ill clad and appeared dispirited and miserable, and the mortality among them was very considerable; the hearse was constantly in requisition to convey from the Gaol the corpse of some poor Frenchman to the public cemetery at St. John's Church (where they were buried unmarked in a special corner set apart for felons and paupers). Soon after the Peace of Amiens, 1802, eleven hundred were liberated, some of whom had been there for years.'

One of these men had accumulated three hundred guineas by his manufactures.

As no book alludes to Liverpool as possessing a war-prison after 1802, it may be concluded that it ceased to have one after that date. This, I think, is probable, as it was eminently unsuitable owing to its position and its proximity to disturbed Ireland.[7]

CHAPTER XIV
THE PRISONS ASHORE
6. Greenlaw—Valleyfield

About a mile and a half on the Edinburgh side of Penicuik, on the great south road leading to Peebles and Dumfries, is the military station of Glencorse, the dépôt of the Royal Scots Regiment. Until about ten years ago the place was known as Greenlaw, but the name was changed owing to postal confusion with Greenlaw in Berwickshire.

In 1804, when, for many reasons, war-prisoners were hurried away from England to Scotland, the old mansion house of Greenlaw was bought by the Government and converted into a dépôt for 200 prisoners of war. It was situated in the south-west corner of a park of sixty acres, and consisted of a great square building, which was surrounded by a high wooden palisade, outside which was an airing ground, and space for the necessary domestic offices, guard rooms, garrison quarters, and so forth, within an outer stone wall. Other buildings, chiefly in wood, were added, and until 1811 it was the only Scottish war-prison south of Edinburgh.

For a year Greenlaw depended upon regulars from Edinburgh for its garrison, but after 1805 the drain upon the army for foreign service was so great, that the Militia was again requisitioned to do duty at the war-prisons. The garrison at Greenlaw consisted of one captain, four subalterns, eight sergeants, four drummers, and 155 rank and file, the head-quarters being at the Old Foundry in Penicuik. Discipline seems to have been strict, and special attention was given to the appearance and turn-out of the men. Eleven sentries were on duty night and day, each man having six blank and six ball cartridges, the latter only to be used in case of serious need—a very necessary insistance, as the militiamen, although of a better class generally than their successors of recent years, were more apt to be carried away by impulse than seasoned regulars. A private of the Stirling Militia was condemned in 1807 to receive 800 lashes for being drunk and out of quarters after tattoo, for having struck his superior officer, and used mutinous language—and this was a sentence mitigated on account of his previous good conduct and his expression of regret.

After the Peace of 1814, Greenlaw seems to have remained untenanted until 1846, when extensive buildings were added—mostly of wood—and it was made the military prison for Scotland. This it continued to be until 1888. In 1876 still further additions were made in a more substantial fashion, as it was decided to make it also the Scottish South Eastern Military Dépôt. In 1899 the old military prisons in wood were demolished, and with them some of the original war-prison buildings, so that all at present existing of the latter are the stone octagon Guard House, in the war-times used as the place of confinement for officers, and the line of building, now the married men's quarters, then the garrison officer's quarters, and some of the original stone boundary wall.

In 1810 the Government bought the Esk Mills at Valleyfield, and on February 6, 1811, the first batch of 350 prisoners arrived. Building was rapidly pushed forward to provide accommodation for 5,000 prisoners at a cost of £73,000, the new war-prison being known as Valleyfield.

'About nine miles south of Edinburgh,' says a writer in *Chambers's Journal* for 1887, 'on the main road to Peebles, stands the village of Penicuik, for the most part built on the high road overlooking and sloping down the valley of the North Esk. Passing through the village, and down the slope leading to the bridge that spans the Esk and continues the road, we turn sharply to the left just at the bridge, and a short distance below are the extensive paper-mills of Messrs. Alexander Cowan and Sons, called the Valleyfield Paper Mills.'

I followed this direction, and under the courteous guidance of Mr. Cowan saw what little remains of one of the most famous war-prisons of Britain.

Until 1897 one of the original 'casernes' was used as a rag store. In August of that year this was pulled down. It measured 300 feet long, 'and its walls were eleven feet six inches thick.'[8] It had formed one of the first buildings at Glencorse. Valleyfield House, now the residence of Mr. Cowan, was in the days of the war-prison used as the Hospital.

In 1906, during excavations for the new enamelling house at the Mills, a dozen coffins were unearthed, all with their heads to the east. The new buildings of 1812 at Valleyfield consisted of six 'casernes', each from 80 to 100 feet long, of three stories, built of wood, with openings closed by strong wooden shutters. They were without fire-places, as it was considered that the animal heat of the closely-packed inmates would render such accessories unnecessary! The whole was surrounded by a stout wooden stockade, outside which was a carriage-road.

Notwithstanding apparent indifference to the comfort of the prisoners, the mortality at Valleyfield during three years and four months was but 309, being at the rate of 18·5 per mille, and in this is included a number of violent deaths from duels, quarrels, and the shooting of prisoners attempting to escape.

In the beautiful hillside garden of Valleyfield House is a monument, erected by Mr. Alexander Cowan, to the memory of these prisoners, inaugurated on June 26, 1830, the day on which George IV died. On it was inscribed:

'The mortal remains of 309 prisoners of war who died in this neighbourhood between 21st March, 1811, and 26th July, 1814, are interred near this spot.'

'Grata Quies Patriae: sed et Omnis Terra Sepulchrum.' 'Certain inhabitants of this parish, desiring to remember that all men are brethren, caused this monument to be erected in the year 1830.'

On the other side:

'Près de ce Lieu reposent les cendres de 309 Prisonniers de Guerre morts dans ce voisinage entre le 21 Mars 1811 et le 26 Juillet 1814. Nés pour bénir les vœux de vieillissantes mères, par le sort appelés à devenir amants, aimés époux et pères.

'Ils sont morts exilés. Plusieurs Habitants de cette Paroisse, aimant à croire que tous les Hommes sont Frères, firent élever ce monument l'an 1830.'

It may be noted that Sir Walter Scott, who showed a warm interest in the erection of the monument, suggested the Latin quotation, which is from Saumazarius, a poet of the Middle Ages. Despite the inscription, the monument was raised at the *sole expense* of Mr. Alexander Cowan.

MONUMENT AT VALLEYFIELD TO PRISONERS OF WAR.

An interesting episode is associated with this monument. In 1845, Mr. John Cowan of Beeslack, on a visit to the Paris Invalides, found an old Valleyfield prisoner named Marcher, and on his return home sent the old soldier a picture of the Valleyfield Memorial, and in the Cowan Institute at Penicuik, amongst other relics of the war-prison days, is an appreciative letter from Marcher, dated from the Invalides, December 1846.

Marcher, when asked his experience of Valleyfield, said that it was terribly cold, that there were no windows, no warmth, no fruit, but that the cabbages were very large. He lost an arm at Waterloo.

The guard consisted of infantry of the Ayr and Kircudbright militia and artillery, who had their camp on the high ground west of Kirkhill Village. On one occasion an alarm that prisoners were escaping was given: the troops hurried to the scene of action, the artillery with such precipitancy that horses, guns, and men were rolled down the steep hill into the river, luckily without injuries.

The attempts to escape were as numerous here as elsewhere, and the Black Hole, made of hewn ashlar work, never lacked occupants. One man, a sailor, it was impossible to keep within, and, like his fellow countryman, Dufresne, at Portchester, was used to getting in and out when he liked, and might have got away altogether, but for his raids upon farm-houses and cottages around, which caused the natives to give him up. On one occasion three prisoners rigged a false bottom to the prison dust-cart, hid themselves therein, and were conveyed out of the prison. When the cart stopped, the prisoners got out, and were entering a wood, when a soldier met them. Him they cut at, and he, being unarmed, let them go. They were, however, recaptured. On December 18, 1811, fourteen prisoners got out, but were all recaptured. One memorable attempt to get out by a tunnel from one of the original buildings, to another in course of erection, and thence to the outer side of the stockade, was made in the same year. The tunnel was one hundred yards long, and the enormous quantity of earth excavated was carried out in the men's pockets, dropped about on the airing ground, and trodden down. The venture only failed owing to the first man mistaking the hour of day, and emerging before sunset, whereupon he was seen by a sentry and fired on.

It was at the daily market when the country people were brought into acquaintance with the prisoners, that many attempts to escape were made, despite the doubling of the guards. One prisoner had arranged with the carter who came every morning to take away the manure that he would conceal himself in the cart, keep himself covered up with the filth, and thus pass the sentries. The field where the rubbish was emptied was just outside the village, and the prisoner would know that it was time for him to crawl out and run away when the cart halted. All started well; the cart passed through the gate, and passed the first, second, and third sentries, and was close to where the Free Church manse now stands, when a friend of the carter hailed him in a loud voice. The cart pulled up, and the poor prisoner, thinking that this was the signal, jumped out, and was shot down before he had gone many yards.

Another prisoner, by name Pirion, broke his parole, and was making his way to London by the coach road, and took shelter from the rain when he had got as far south as Norman Cross, not knowing where he was. He was recognized as an old Norman Cross prisoner, and was arrested and brought back.

In 1812 the report upon the condition of Valleyfield was very bad, and in particular it was recommended that a special stockade should be built to hide the half-naked prisoners from public view at the market.

In 1813 a Valleyfield prisoner was released in order that he might help a Mr. Ferguson in the cod and herring fishery: almost as easy a release as that of the Norman Cross prisoner who was freed because he had instructed the Earl of Winchester's labourers at Burleigh, by Stamford, in the use of the Hainault scythe!

At one time very few of the prisoners at Valleyfield were Frenchmen. About twenty of them were allowed to live on parole outside the prison, and some of them enjoyed the friendship of the Cowan family; one in particular, Ancamp, a Nantes merchant, had been a prisoner nine and a half years, and had had a son born to him since his capture, whom he had never seen.

In 1814, Valleyfield was evacuated, and remained unoccupied until 1820, when, after having been advertised for sale and put up to auction several times without success, it was purchased by Cowan for £2,200.

In Penicuik many relics of the prisoners' manufactures may still be seen, and what is now the public park was formerly the vegetable garden of the prison.

An elderly lady at Lasswade told Mr. Bresnil of Loanhead that she remembered in her childhood an old farmer who was pointed out as having made his fortune by providing oatmeal to the prisoners at Valleyfield of an inferior quality to that for which he had contracted.

I shall now give two accounts of life at these prisons. The first is by Sergeant-Major Beaudouin, of the 31st Line Regiment, whom we have met before in this book on the hulks at Chatham. He was captured off Havana, 26th Germinal, An XII, that is, on April 16, 1804, on board one of the squadrons from St. Nicholas Mole, San Domingo, and brought via Belfast to Greenock, at which port he happened to arrive on June 4, in the midst of the celebrations of the King's birthday. (It may be mentioned that he quitted England finally, eight years later, on the same day.) Bonaparte in effigy, on a donkey, was being paraded through the street preparatory to being burned, and the natives told him that they hoped some fine day to catch and burn Bonaparte himself, which upset Beaudouin and made him retort that despite all England's strength France would never be conquered, and that 100,000 Frenchmen landed in England would be sufficient to conquer it, whereupon a disturbance ensued.

Beaudouin landed at Port Glasgow, and thence to Renfrew and Glasgow, of which city he remarks:

'Cette ville paraît très grande et belle; costume très brillant. Ce qu'il y a de remarquable c'est que les paysans sont aussi bien mis comme ceux de la ville; on ne peut en faire la différence que par le genre. Ce qui *jure* beaucoup dans leur costume, c'est que les femmes marchent presque toujours nu-pieds. La quantité de belles femmes n'est pas grande, comme on dit; en outre, en général elles out les bouches commes des fours.'

From Glasgow the prisoners marched to Airdrie, ten miles, where the people were affable. For the six prisoners there was an escort of a sergeant, a corporal, and eight men.

From Airdrie they proceeded to Bathgate, fourteen miles, thence to Edinburgh, twenty-two miles, where they were lodged for the night in the guard-house of the Castle. From Edinburgh they came to Greenlaw, ten miles, June 10, 1804.

Beaudouin thus describes Greenlaw:

'Cette prison est une maison de campagne. À deux milles où loge le détachement qui nous garde est Penicuik. Cette maison est entourée de deux rangs de palissades avec des factionnaires tout autour; à côté est situé un petit bois qui favorise quelquefois des désertions.'

At first they were quartered with Dutch prisoners, but when peace was made between Britain and Holland, these latter left.

At Greenlaw there were 106 French and 40 Spanish prisoners. The Spaniards were very antagonistic to the French, and also among themselves, quarrelling freely and being very handy with their knives. Beaudouin gives many instances of their brutality. At call-over a Spaniard waited for another to come through the door, and stabbed him in the face. An Italian and a Spaniard fought with knives until both were helpless. Two Spaniards quarrelled about their soup, and fought in public in the airing ground. The guard did not attempt to interfere—and wisely.

'Les Espagnols,' says Beaudouin, 'possèdent toutes les bonnes qualités. Premièrement ils sont paresseux à l'excès, sales, traîtres, joueurs, et voleurs comme des pies.'

He describes Valleyfield as cold, with very little fine weather, but healthy. At the end of a week or so the newly arrived prisoners settled to work of different kinds. Some plaited straw for bonnets, some made *tresse cornue* for baskets and hats; some carved boxes, games, &c.; some worked hair watch-chains; some made coloured straw books and other knick-knacks, all of which they sold at the barriers.

Beaudouin learned to plait straw, and at first found it difficult as his fingers were so big. The *armateur*, the employer, gave out the straw, and paid for the worked article three sous per 'brasse', a little under six feet. Some men could make twelve 'brasses' a day. Beaudouin set to work at it, and in the course of a couple of months became an adept. After four years came the remonstrance of the country people that this underpaid labour by untaxed men was doing infinite injury to them; the Government prohibited the manufactures, and much misery among the prisoners resulted. From this prohibition resulted the outside practice of smuggling straw into the prison, and selling it later as the manufactured article, and a very profitable industry it must have been, for we find that, during the trial of Matthew Wingrave in 1813, for engaging in the straw-plait trade with the prisons at Valleyfield, it came out that Wingrave, who was an extensive dealer in the article, had actually moved up there from Bedfordshire on purpose to carry on the trade, and had bought cornfields for the purpose. The evidence showed that he was in the habit of bribing the soldiers to keep their eyes shut, and that not a few people of character and position were associated with him in the business.

Beaudouin then learned to make horsehair rings with names worked into them: these fetched sixpence each: rings in human hair were worth a shilling. For five years and a half he worked at this, and in so doing injured his eyesight. 'However,' he said, 'it kept me alive, which the rations would never have done.'

Nominally the clothing was renewed every year, but Beaudouin declares that he had only one change in five and a half years. To prevent the clothes from being sold, they were of a sulphur-yellow colour.

'En un mot, les Anglais sont tous des brigands,' he says, and continues:

'I have described many English atrocities committed in the Colonies; they are no better here. In the prison they have practised upon us all possible cruelties. For instance, drum-beat was the signal for all lights to be put out, and if by chance the drum is not heard and the lights remain, the prisoners are fired upon without warning, and several have been shot.'

The prisoners signed a petition about their miserable condition generally, and this outrage in particular, and sent it up to the Transport Board. Fifteen days later the Agent entered the prison furious: 'I must know who wrote that letter to the Government,' he roared, 'and I will put him into the *blokhall* (Black Hole) until he says who put it in the post.'

It ended in his being dismissed and severely punished. Ensign Maxwell of the Lanark Militia, who had ordered the sentry to fire into the prison because a light was burning there after drum-beat, whereby a prisoner, Cotier, was killed, was condemned to nine months' imprisonment in the Tolbooth. This was in 1807.[9] Many of the prisoners went to Edinburgh as witnesses in this case, and thereafter an order was posted up forbidding any firing upon the prisoners. If lights remained, the guard was to enter the prison, and, if necessary, put the offenders into the Black Hole, but no violence was to be used.

On March 30, 1809, all the French prisoners at Greenlaw were ordered to Chatham, of which place very bad reports were heard from men who had been on the hulks there.

'Ils disent qu'ils sont plus mal qu'à Greenlaw. Premièrement, les vivres sont plus mauvais, excepté le pain qui est un peu meilleur: en outre, aucun ouvrage ne se fait, et aucun bourgeois vient les voir. Je crains d'y aller. Dieu merci! Jusqu'à ce moment-ci je me suis monté un peu en linge, car, quand je suis arrivé au prison mon sac ne me gênait point, les Anglais, en le prenant, ne m'ont laissé que ce que j'avais sur le dos. Quand je fus arrivé au prison ma chemise était pourrie sur mon dos et point d'autre pour changer.'

On October 31, 1809, Beaudouin left Greenlaw, where he had been since June 10, 1804, for Sheerness, Chatham, and the *Bristol* prison-ship.

The next reference to Greenlaw is from James Anton's *A Military Life*. He thus describes the prison at which he was on guard:

'The prison was fenced round with a double row of stockades; a considerable space was appropriated as a promenade, where the prisoners had freedom to walk about, cook provisions, make their markets and exercise themselves at their own pleasure, but under the superintendence of a turnkey and in the charge of several sentries.... The prisoners were far from being severely treated: no work was required at their hands, yet few of them were idle. Some of them were occupied in culinary avocations, and as the guard had no regular mess, the men on duty became ready purchasers of their *labscuse*, salt-fish, potatoes, and coffee. Others were employed in preparing straw for plaiting; some were manufacturing the cast-away bones into dice, dominoes, paper-cutters, and a hundred articles of toy-work ... and realized considerable sums of money.... Those prisoners were well provided for in every respect, and treated with the greatest humanity, yet to the eye of a stranger they presented a miserable picture of distress, while some of them were actually hoarding up money ... others were actually naked, with the exception of a dirty rag as an apron.... And strangers who visited the prison commiserated the apparent distress of this miserable class, and charity was frequently bestowed on purpose to clothe their nakedness; but no sooner would this set of despicables obtain such relief, than they took to the cards, dice, or dominoes, and in a few hours were as poor and naked as ever.... When they were indulged with permission to remain in their hammocks, when the weather was cold, they drew the worsted out of the rags that covered them, wound it up in balls, and sold it to the industrious knitters of *mitts*, and left themselves without a covering by night. The inhabitants of Penicuik and its neighbourhood, previous to the establishment of this dépôt of prisoners, were as comfortable and contented a class of people as in any district in Britain. The steep woody banks of the Esk were lined with prospering manufactories.... When the militiamen were first quartered here, they met with a welcome reception; ... in the course of a few years, those kindly people began to consider the quartering of soldiers upon them more oppressive than they at first anticipated. Trade declined as prisoners increased.... One of the principal factories, Valleyfield, was afterwards converted into another dépôt for prisoners, and Esk Mills into a barrack for the military; this gave a decisive blow to trade.'

To Mr. Robert Black, and indirectly to Mr. Howden, I am much indebted for information about Greenlaw. To Mr. Cowan for helping me at Valleyfield I have already expressed my obligation, but I must not omit to say that much of the foregoing information about Valleyfield and the Esk Mills has been taken from *The Reminiscences of Charles Cowan of Logan House, Midlothian*, printed for private circulation in 1878.

CHAPTER XV
THE PRISONS ASHORE
7. STAPLETON, NEAR BRISTOL

Bristol, as being for so many centuries the chief port of western England, always had her full quota of prisoners of war, who, in the absence of a single great place of confinement, were crowded away anywhere that room could be made for them. Tradition says that the crypt of the church of St. Mary Redcliff was used for this purpose, but it is known that they filled the caverns under the cliff itself, and that until the great Fishponds prison at Stapleton, now the workhouse, was built in 1782, they were quartered in old pottery works at Knowle, near Totterdown and Pile Hill, on the right-hand side of the road from Bristol, on the south of Firfield House.

In volume XI of Wesley's *Journal* we read:

'Monday, October 15, 1759, I walked up to Knowle, a mile from Bristol, to see the French prisoners. About eleven hundred of them, we were informed, were confined in that little place, without anything to lie on but a little dirty straw, or anything to cover them but a few foul thin rags, either by day or night, so that they died like rotten sheep. I was much affected, and preached in the evening, Exodus 23, verse 9. £18 was contributed immediately, which was made up to £24 the next day. With this we bought linen and woollen cloth, which was made up into shirts, waistcoats, and breeches. Some dozens of stockings were added, all of which were carefully distributed where there was the greatest want. Presently after, the Corporation of Bristol sent a large quantity of mattresses and blankets, and it was not long before contributions were set on foot in London and in various parts of the Kingdom.'

But it was to be the same story here as elsewhere of gambling being the cause of much of the nakedness and want, for he writes:

'October 24, 1760. I visited the French prisoners at Knowle, and found many of them almost naked again. In hopes of provoking others to jealousy I made another collection for them.'

In 1779 John Howard visited Knowle on his tour of inspection of the prisoners of England. He reported that there were 151 prisoners there, 'in a place which had been a pottery', that the wards were more spacious and less crowded than at the Mill Prison at Plymouth, and that in two of the day rooms the prisoners were at work—from which remark we may infer that at this date the industry which later became so notable a characteristic of the inmates of our war-prisons was not general. The bread, he says, was good, but there was no hospital, the sick being in a small house near the prison, where he found five men together in a dirty and offensive room.

In 1782 the prison at Fishponds, Stapleton, was built. Howard visited it in that year, and reported that there were 774 Spaniards and thirteen Dutchmen in it, that there were no chimneys to the wards, which were very dirty, as they were never washed, and that an open market was held daily from 10 to 3. In 1794 there were 1,031 French prisoners at Stapleton, of whom seventy-five were in hospital.

In 1797 the ferment among the prisoners caused by reports of the success of Tate's 'invasion' at Fishguard, developed into an open riot, during which a sentry fired and accidentally killed one of his comrades. Tradition says that when the Bristol Volunteers were summoned to take the place of the Militia, who had been hurried away to Fishguard, as there could be found no arms for them, all the mop-sticks in Bristol were bought up and furnished with iron heads, which converted them into very respectable pikes. It was on this occasion that, in view of the desperate feeling among the prisoners and the comparative inefficiency of their guards, it was suggested that all the prisoners should be lowered into the Kingswood coal-pits!

In 1799 the prison was enlarged at the contract price of £475; the work was to be done by June 1800, and no Sunday labour was to be employed, although Sanders, of Pedlar's Acre, Lambeth, the contractor, pleaded for it, as a ship, laden with timber for the prison, had sunk, and so delayed the work.

In 1800 the following report upon the state of Stapleton Prison was drawn up and published by two well-known citizens of Bristol, Thomas Batchelor, deputy-governor of St. Peter's Hospital, and Thomas Andrews, a poor-law guardian:

'On our entrance we were much struck with the pale, emaciated appearance of almost every one we met. They were in general nearly naked, many of them without shoes and stockings, walking in the Courtyard, which was some inches deep in mud, unpaved and covered with loose stones like the public roads in their worst state. Their provisions were wretched indeed; the bread fusty and disagreeable, leaving a hot, pungent taste in the mouth; the meat, which was beef, of the very worst quality. The quantity allowed to each prisoner was one pound of this infamous bread, and ½ lb. of the carrion beef weighed with its bone before dressing, for their subsistence for 24 hours. No vegetables are allowed except to the sick in the hospital. We fear there is good reason for believing that the prices given to the butcher and baker are quite sufficient for procuring provisions of a far better kind. On returning to the outer court we were shocked to see two poor creatures on the ground leading to the Hospital Court; the one lying at length, apparently dying, the other with a horse-cloth or rug close to his expiring fellow prisoner as if to catch a little warmth from his companion in misery. They appeared to be dying of famine. The majority of the poor wretches seemed to have lost the appearance of human beings, to such skeletons were they reduced. The numbers that die are great, generally 6 to 8 a day; 250 have died within the last six weeks.'

After so serious a statement made publicly by two men of position an inquiry was imperative, and 'all the accusations were [it was said] shown to be unfounded'. It was stated that the deaths during the whole year 1800 were 141 out of 2,900 prisoners, being a percentage of $4\frac{3}{4}$; but it was known that the deaths in November were forty-four, and in December thirty-seven, which, assuming other months to have been healthier would be about 16 per cent., or nearly seven times the mortality even of the prison ships. The chief cause of disease and death was said to be want of clothing, owing to the decision of the French Government of December 22, 1799, not to clothe French prisoners in England; but the gambling propensities of the prisoners had even more to do with it. 'It was true,' said the Report of the Commission of Inquiry, 'that gambling was universal, and that it was not to be checked. It was well known that here, as at Norman Cross, some of the worst gamblers frequently did not touch their provisions for several days. The chief forms of gambling were tossing, and deciding by the length of straws if the rations were to be kept or lost even for weeks ahead. This is the cause of all the ills, starvation, robbery, suicide, and murder.' But it was admitted that the chief medical officer gave very little personal attention to his duties, but left them to subordinates.

It was found that there was much exaggeration in the statements of Messrs. Batchelor and Andrews, but from a modern standard the evidence of this was by no means satisfactory. All the witnesses seem to have been more or less interested from a mercantile point of view in the administration of the prison, and Mr. Alderman Noble, of Bristol, was not ashamed to state that he acted as agent on commission for the provision contractor, Grant of London.

Messrs. Batchelor and Andrews afterwards publicly retracted their accusations, but the whole business leaves an unpleasant taste in the mouth, and one may make bold to say that, making due allowance for the embellishment and exaggeration not unnaturally consequent upon deeply-moved sympathies and highly-stirred feelings, there was much ground for the volunteered remarks of these two highly respectable gentlemen.

In 1801, Lieutenant Ormsby, commander of the prison, wrote to the Transport Board:

'Numbers of prisoners are as naked as they were previous to the clothing being issued. At first the superintendants were attentive and denounced many of the purchasers of the clothing, but they gradually got careless. We are still losing as many weekly as in the depth of winter. The hospital is crowded, and many are forced to remain outside who ought to be in.'

This evidence, added to that of commissioners who reported that generally the distribution of provisions was unattended by any one of responsible position, and only by turnkeys—men who were notoriously in league with the contractors—would seem to afford some foundation for the above-quoted report. About this time Dr. Weir, the medical inspection officer of the Transport Board, tabulated a series of grave charges against Surgeon

Jeffcott, of Stapleton, for neglect, for wrong treatment of cases, and for taking bribes from the prison contractors and from the prisoners. Jeffcott, in a long letter, denies these accusations, and declares that the only 'presents' he had received were 'three sets of dominoes, a small dressing box, four small straw boxes, and a line of battle ship made of wood,' for which he paid. The result of the inquiry, however, was that he was removed from his post; the contractor was severely punished for such malpractices as the using of false measures of the beer quart, milk quart, and tea pint, and with him was implicated Lemoine, the French cook.

That the peculation at Stapleton was notorious seems to be the case, for in 1812 Mr. Whitbread in Parliament 'heartily wished the French prisoners out of the country, since, under pretence of watching them, so many abuses had been engendered at Bristol, and an enormous annual expense was incurred.'

In 1804 a great gale blew down part of the prison wall, and an agitation among the prisoners to escape was at once noticeable. A Bristol Light Horseman was at once sent into the city for reinforcements, and in less than four hours fifty men arrived—evidently a feat in rapid locomotion in those days!

From the Commissioners' Reports of these times it appears that the law prohibiting straw plaiting by the prisoners was much neglected at Stapleton, that a large commerce was carried on in this article with outside, chiefly through the bribery of the soldiers of the guard, who did pretty much as they liked, which, says the report, was not to be wondered at when the officers of the garrison made no scruple of buying straw-plaited articles for the use of their families.

As to the frequent escapes of prisoners, one potent cause of this, it was asserted, was that in wet weather the sentries were in the habit of closing the shutters of their boxes so that they could only see straight ahead, and it was suggested that panes of glass be let in at the sides of the boxes.

The provisions for the prisoners are characterized as being 'in general' very good, although deep complaints about the quality of the meat and bread are made.

'The huts where the provisions are cooked have fanciful inscriptions over their entrances, which produce a little variety and contribute to amuse these unfortunate men.'

All gaming tables in the prison were ordered to be destroyed, because one man who had lost heavily threw himself off a building and was killed; but billiard tables were allowed to remain, only to be used by the better class of prisoners. The hammocks were condemned as very bad, and the issue of the fish ration was stopped, as the prisoners seemed to dislike it, and sold it.

In 1805 the new prison at Stapleton was completed, and accommodation for 3,000 additional prisoners afforded, making a total of 5,000. Stapleton was this year reported as being the most convenient prison in England, and was the equivalent of eight prison-ships.

In 1807 the complaints about the straw-plaiting industry clandestinely carried on by the Stapleton prisoners were frequent, and also that the prison market for articles manufactured by the prisoners was prejudicial to local trade.

Duelling was very frequent among the prisoners. On March 25, 1808, a double duel took place, and two of the fighters were mortally wounded. A verdict of manslaughter was returned against the two survivors by the coroner's jury, but at the Gloucester assizes the usual verdict of 'self-defence' was brought in. In July 1809 a naval and a military officer quarrelled over a game of marbles; a duel was the result, which was fought with sticks to which sharpened pieces of iron had been fixed, and which proved effective enough to cause the death of one of the combatants. A local newspaper stated that during the past three years no less than 150 duels had been fought among the prisoners at Stapleton, the number of whom averaged 5,500, and that the coroner, like his *confrères* at Dartmoor and Rochester, was complaining of the extra work caused by the violence of the foreigners.

In 1809 a warder at Stapleton Prison was dismissed from his post for having connived at the conveyance of letters to Colonel Chalot, who was in prison for having violated his parole at Wantage by going beyond the mile limit to meet an English girl, Laetitia Barrett. Laetitia's letters to him, in French, are at the Record Office, and show that the Colonel was betrayed by a fellow prisoner, a rival for her hand.

In 1813 the Bristol shoemakers protested against the manufacture of list shoes by the Stapleton prisoners, but the Government refused to issue prohibiting orders.

STAPLETON PRISON

From the Gentleman's Magazine, 1814

Forgery was largely practised at Stapleton as in other prisons, and in spite of warnings posted up, the country people who came to the prison market were largely victimized, but Stapleton is particularly associated with the wholesale forgery of passports in the year 1814, by means of which so many officer prisoners were enabled to get to France on the plea of fidelity to the restored Government. In this year a Mr. Edward Prothero of 39, Harley Street, Bristol, sent to the Transport Office information concerning the wholesale forgery of passports, in the sale of which to French officers a Madame Carpenter, of London (already mentioned in Chapter VI), was concerned.

The signing of the Treaty of Paris, on May 30, 1814, stopped whatever proceedings might have been taken by the Government with regard to Madame Carpenter, but it appears that some sort of inquiry had been instituted, and that Madame Carpenter, although denying all traffic in forged passports, admitted that she was on such terms with the Transport

Board on account of services rendered by her in the past when residing in France to British prisoners there, as to be able to ask favours of it. The fact is, people of position and influence trafficked in passports and privileges, just as people in humbler walks of life trafficked in contracts for prisons and in the escape of prisoners, and Madame Carpenter was probably the worker, the business transactor, for one or more persons in high place who, even in that not particularly shamefaced age, did not care that their names should be openly associated with what was just as much a business as the selling of legs of mutton or pounds of tea.

In spite of what we have read about the misery of life at Stapleton, it seems to have been regarded by prisoners elsewhere as rather a superior sort of place. At Dartmoor, in 1814, the Americans hailed with delight the rumour of their removal to Stapleton, well and healthily situated in a fertile country, and, being near Bristol, with a good market for manufactures, not to speak of its being in the world, instead of out of it, as were Dartmoor and Norman Cross; and the countermanding order almost produced a mutiny.

It appears that dogs were largely kept at Stapleton by the prisoners, for after one had been thrown into a well it was ordered that all should be destroyed, the result being 710 victims! They were classed as 'pet' dogs, but one can hardly help suspecting that men in a chronic state of hunger would be far more inclined to make the dogs feed them than to feed dogs as fancy articles.

It is surprising to read that, notwithstanding the utter irreligion of so many French prisoners in Britain, in more than one prison, at Millbay and Stapleton for instance, Mass was never forgotten among them. At Stapleton an officer of the fleet, captured at San Domingo, read the prayers of the Mass usually read by the priest; an altar was painted on the wall, two or three cabin-boys served as acolytes, as they would have done had a priest been present, and there was no ridicule or laughter at the celebrations.

After the declaration of peace in 1815, the *raison d'être* of Stapleton as a war-prison of course ceased. In 1833 it was bought by the Bristol Poor-Board and turned into a workhouse.

CHAPTER XVI
THE PRISONS ASHORE
8. FORTON, NEAR PORTSMOUTH

Although the Fortune Prison, as it seems to have been very generally called, had been used for war-prisoners during the Seven Years' War, its regular adaptation to that purpose was probably not before 1761, in which year 2,000 prisoners were removed thither from Portchester 'guarded by the Old Buffs'. During the War of American Independence many prisoners of that nationality were at Forton, and appear to have been ceaselessly engaged in trying to escape. In 1777 thirty broke out, of whom nineteen were recaptured and were so harshly punished that they complained in a letter which somehow found its way into the London papers. The next year, the Westminster Militia, encamped on Weovil Common, attracted by alarm guns at Forton, marched thither, and found American and French prisoners escaping through a hole in the outer wall, but were too late to prevent five-and-twenty from getting away altogether. The attempt was supposed to be the sequel of a plot by which, a fortnight previously, eleven Americans had escaped. On the same day there was a mutiny in the prison hospital, provoked, it was alleged, by the neglect and the callous treatment of patients by the doctors and their subordinates.

In the same year, 1778, another batch of no less than fifty-seven Americans made a desperate attempt to get out. The Black Hole at Forton was underneath part of the prisoners' sleeping quarters. A hole large enough for the passage of a man was made in the floor of a sleeping room, being covered by a bed—that is, a mattress—and through this the earth from a tunnel which led from the Black Hole to beyond the prison walls, was brought and hidden in the chimney and in hammocks until opportunities came for its removal elsewhere. As no report was published of the recapture of these men, we may presume that they got away.

In 1779 Howard made his report upon Forton. He found there 251 Americans and 177 Frenchmen. The condition of the former, he says, was satisfactory—probably a result of the generous public subscription of the previous year in aid of them.

Of the French part of the prison he speaks badly. The meat was bad, the bread loaves were of short weight, the straw in the mattresses had been reduced to dust by long use, and many of them had been emptied to clear them of vermin. The floors of the hospital and the sleeping quarters, which were laid rough, were dirty and offensive.

The prisoners complained to Howard, who told them to write to the Commissioners of the 'Sick and Hurt' Office. They replied that, as every letter had to be examined by the Agent, this would be of no good.

Howard emphasizes severely the evident roguery of the contractors employed in the furnishing of provisions and clothing.

The year 1793 was marked at Forton, as elsewhere, by a general insubordinate feeling among the Frenchmen, of whom there were 850 in the prison. In April, a sentry on guard outside the palisade heard a mysterious scraping sound beneath his feet, and gave the alarm. Examination revealed two loose planks in one of the sleeping-rooms, which, being taken up, exposed the entrance to a tunnel, afterwards found to run twenty-seven feet to the outer side of the palisade. One of the prisoners confessed that a plot had been made to kill the Agent and his officers.

In July the following report was made upon Forton:

'The French at Forton continue extremely restless and turbulent, and cannot bear their captivity with moderation and temper though they are exceedingly well supplied with provisions and every necessity their situation requires. A sailor made a desperate attempt to disarm a sentinel through the bar of the compartment where he was confined. The sentry with great exertion disengaged himself, and fired at the offender, but wounded unfortunately another prisoner, not the aggressor. Friday se'nnight, the guard discovered a plot by which several prisoners had planned an escape over the wall by tying together their hammocks and blankets. The sentry on duty fired in at the windows, and hit one of the rioters, who is since dead.

'Three French prisoners were dangerously wounded while endeavouring to escape from Forton. One of them with a drawn knife rushed upon the guard, a private of the Anglesea Militia, who fired at him. The Frenchman seized him by the coat, whereupon the guard ran the offender through the body.'

General Hyde, the Commandant at Portsmouth, ordered, in consequence of the insubordination fomented by the French political excitement of the time, that no prisoners should be allowed to wear the national cockade, or to scribble seditious statements on the prison walls, or to play any national music, under penalty of the *cachot*. It is almost unnecessary to say that the enforcement of these orders was physically impossible.

In 1794 an epidemic at Forton caused the deaths of 200 prisoners in one month.

In 1806 the great amount of sickness at Forton brought about an official inquiry, the result of which was the superseding of the head surgeon.

In 1807, a fire broke out one day in the prison at 2 p.m., which continued until 9 a.m. The prisoners behaved very well, helping to put the fire out, and not attempting to escape.

In November, 1810, no less than 800 prisoners were on the sick list.

In 1811, Sous-lieutenant Doisy de Villargennes, of the 26th French line regiment, arrived at Portsmouth, a prisoner of war, taken after Fuentes d'Oñoro, and was allowed to be on parole ashore pending his dispatch to an inland parole town. He knew that his foster-brother was in prison at Forton, and got leave to visit him. I am particularly glad to give the testimony of a French prisoner of war to the improved state of affairs—at Forton, at any rate. He says:

'Il y régnait l'ordre le plus parfait, sous un règlement sévère mais humain. Nous n'entendîmes pas de sanglots de désespoir, nous ne vîmes point la tristesse dans les yeux des habitants, mais de tous côtés, au contraire, c'étaient des éclats de rire ou des chansons patriotiques qui résonnaient. . . . Mon frère de lait me conduisit vers un petit coin confortable qu'il occupait en compagnie d'un camarade. J'y remarquai un lit de bonne apparence, ainsi que d'autres meubles modestes qu'ils avaient pu acheter avec leur propre argent. La cuisine occupait le compartiment voisin; elle servait à 200 hommes, et l'odeur qu'elle répandait ne faisait nullement présumer que les habitants pussent être affamés. Je restai à dîner. Je ne dirai pas que le repas était somptueux, mais les mets étaient suffisants et de bonne qualité, et bien que servis dans des plats et assiettes d'étain, avec des couteaux et des fourchettes du même métal, ils étaient accompagnés d'une si cordiale réception que le souvenir de ce dîner m'a toujours laissé sous une agréable impression.'

There were no wines or liqueurs, but abundance of 'the excellent ale which England alone produces'. Doisy asked whence came the money to pay for all this abundance. His host told him that, being a basket-maker's son, and knowing the trade, he got permission to work at it and to sell his goods. For a time this was very successful, but the large output of cheap, untaxed work from the prison brought remonstrance from the straw-workers of Portsmouth, Barnstaple, and other places, with the result that Government prohibited it. But the ingenious Frenchman soon found another string for his bow, and he became, with many others, a manufacturer of ornaments and knick-knacks, boxes, combs, toys, and especially ship models, from the bones of his food. These beef and mutton bones were carefully saved on all sides, and those who could not work them, sold them at good prices to those who could. Germain Lamy, his foster-brother, told Doisy that he and his comrade worked at the bone model of a seventy-four, with rigging made of hair, for six months, and sold it for £40.

Lamy was released at the peace of 1814. He took back to France 16,500 francs; bought a little farm, married, and settled down, but died of cholera in 1832.

In 1813 took place the 'Brothers murder,' a crime which made a very great and lasting sensation.

Three Frenchmen—François Relif, Jean Marie Dauze, and Daniel du Verge, escaped from Forton, and engaged George Brothers, a pilot and boatman, to take them, they said, from the Point to one of the ships at Spithead. Off the Block-House they told him that they intended to escape, and proposed that he should take them over to France. He refused: they threatened, but he persisted and tried to signal the shipping. Whereupon they attacked him, stabbed him in sixteen places, threw his body overboard, and set their course seaward. This was seen from the shore, a fleet of boats set off in pursuit, and, after a smart chase—one account says of fifteen miles—the fugitives were captured, although it was thought that they would have escaped had they known how to manage a sailing boat. They were taken on board H.M.S. *Centaur*, searched, and upon them were found three knives and a large sum of money. They were taken then to jail ashore. One of the prisoners was found to have thirty crown pieces concealed about him, and confessed that having saved up this money, which he had made by the sale of lace, toys, and other manufactures, he had bought a suit of decent clothes, and, mixing with visitors to the dépôt, thus disguised had got off. In the meanwhile the body of Brothers had been recovered, placed first in one of the casemates of Point Battery, and then taken amidst an enormous crowd to his house in Surrey Street, Landport.

The three murderers were executed at Winchester. The funeral of Brothers in Kingston churchyard was the occasion of a large public demonstration, and, be it recorded, the prisoners at Forton expressed their abhorrence of the crime by getting up a subscription for the murdered man's widow and children, to which it is said one of the murderers contributed £7.

CHAPTER XVII
THE PRISONS ASHORE
9. Millbay, near Plymouth

Saxon prisoners taken at Leuthen were at the 'New Prison,' Plymouth, in 1758. In this year they addressed a complaint to the authorities, praying to be sent elsewhere, as they were ostracized, and even reviled, by the French captives, and a round-robin to the officer of the guard, reminding him that humanity should rule his actions rather than a mere delight in exercising authority, and hinting that officers who had made war the trade of their lives probably knew more about its laws than Mr. Tonkin, the Commissioner in charge of them, appeared to know.

In 1760 no less than 150 prisoners contrived to tunnel their way out of the prison, but all except sixteen were recaptured.

Of the life at the old Mill Prison, as it was then called, during the War of American Independence, a detailed account is given by Charles Herbert of Newburyport, Massachusetts, captured in the *Dolton*, in December 1776, by H.M.S. *Reasonable*, 64.

With his sufferings during the voyage to England we have nothing to do, except that he was landed at Plymouth so afflicted with 'itch', which developed into small-pox, that he was at once taken to the Royal Hospital. It is pleasing to note that he speaks in the highest terms of the care and kindness of the doctor and nurses of this institution.

When cured he was sent to Mill Prison, and here made money by carving in wood of boxes, spoons and punch ladles, which he sold at the Sunday market.

Very soon the Americans started the system of tunnelling out of the prison, and attempting to escape, which only ceased with their final discharge. Herbert was engaged in the scheme of an eighteen feet long excavation to a field outside, the earth from which, they rammed into their sea-chests. By this, thirty-two men got out, but eleven were captured, he being one.

Men who could make no articles for sale in the market sold their clothes and all their belongings.

Theft among the prisoners was punished by the offenders being made to run the gauntlet of their comrades, who were armed with nettles for the occasion.

Herbert complains bitterly of the scarcity and quality of the provisions, particularly of the bread, which he says was full of straw-ends. 'Many are tempted to pick up the grass in the yard and eat it; and some pick up old bones that have been laying in the dirt a week or ten days and pound them to pieces and suck them. Some will pick snails out of holes in the wall and from among the grass and weeds in the yard, boil them, eat them, and drink the broth. Men run after the stumps of cabbages thrown out by the cooks into the yard, and trample over each other in the scuffle to get them.'

Christmas and New Year were, however, duly celebrated, thanks to the generosity of the prison authorities, who provided the materials for two huge plum-puddings, served out white bread instead of the regulation 'Brown George', mutton instead of beef, turnips instead of cabbage, and oatmeal.

Then came a time of plenty. In London £2,276 was subscribed for the prisoners, and £200 in Bristol. Tobacco, soap, blankets, and extra bread for each mess were forthcoming, although the price of tobacco rose to five shillings a pound. Candles were expensive, so marrow-bones were used instead, one bone lasting half as long as a candle.

On February 1, 1778, five officers—Captains Henry and Eleazar Johnston, Offin Boardman, Samuel Treadwell, and Deal, got off with two sentries who were clothed in mufti, supplied by Henry Johnston. On February 17, the two soldiers were taken, and were sentenced, one to be shot and the other to 700 lashes, which punishment was duly carried out. Of the officers, Treadwell was recaptured, and suffered the usual penalty of forty days Black Hole, and put on half allowance. Continued attempts to escape were made, and as they almost always failed it was suspected that there were traitors in the camp. A black man and boy were discovered: they were whipped, and soon after, in reply to a petition from the whites, all the black prisoners were confined in a separate building, known as the 'itchy yard.'

Still the attempts continued. On one occasion two men who had been told off for the duty of emptying the prison offal tubs into the river, made a run for it. They were captured, and among the pursuers was the prison head-cook, whose wife held the monopoly of selling beer at the prison gate, the result being that she was boycotted.

Much complaint was made of the treatment of the sick, extra necessaries being only procurable by private subscription, and when in June 1778, the chief doctor died, Herbert writes: 'I believe there are not many in the prison who would mourn, as there is no reason to expect that we can get a worse one.'

On Independence Day, July 4, all the Americans provided themselves with crescent-shaped paper cockades, painted with the thirteen stars and thirteen stripes of the Union, and inscribed at the top 'Independence', and at the bottom 'Liberty or Death'. At one o'clock they paraded in thirteen divisions. Each in turn gave three cheers, until at the thirteenth all cheered in unison.

The behaviour of a section of blackguards in the community gave rise to fears that it would lead to the withdrawal of charitable donations. So articles were drawn up forbidding, under severe penalties, gambling, 'blackguarding', and bad language. This produced violent opposition, but gradually the law-abiders won the day.

An ingenious attempt to escape is mentioned by Herbert. Part of the prison was being repaired by workmen from outside. An American saw the coat and tool-basket of one of these men hanging up, so he appropriated them, and quietly sauntered out into the town unchallenged. Later in the day, however, the workman recognized his coat on the American in the streets of Plymouth, and at once had him arrested and brought back.

On December 28, 1778, Herbert was concerned in a great attempt to escape. A hole nine feet deep was dug by the side of the inner wall of the prison, thence for fifteen feet until it came out in a garden on the other side of the road which bounded the outer wall. The difficulty of getting rid of the excavated dirt was great, and, moreover, excavation could only be proceeded with when the guard duty was performed by the Militia regiment, which was on every alternate day, the sentries of the 13th Regular regiment being far too wideawake and up to escape-tricks. Half the American prisoners—some two hundred in number—had decided to go. All was arranged methodically and without favour, by drawing lots, the operation being conducted by two chief men who did not intend to go.

Herbert went with the first batch. There were four walls, each eight feet high, to be scaled. With five companions Herbert managed these, and got out, their aim being to make for Teignmouth, whence they would take boat for France. Somehow, as they avoided high roads, and struck across fields, they lost their bearings, and after covering, he thinks, at least twenty miles, sat down chilled and exhausted, under a haystack until daybreak. They then restarted, and coming on to a high road, learned from a milestone that, after all, they were only three miles from Plymouth!

Day came, and with it the stirring of the country people. To avoid observation, the fugitives quitted the road, and crept away to the shelter of a hedge, to wait, hungry, wet, and exhausted, during nine hours, for darkness. The end soon came.

In rising, Herbert snapped a bone in his leg. As it was being set by a comrade, a party of rustics with a soldier came up, the former armed with clubs and flails. The prisoners were taken to a village, where they had brandy and a halfpenny cake each, and taken back to Plymouth.

At the prison they learned that 109 men had got out, of whom thirty had been recaptured. All had gone well until a boy, having stuck on one of the walls, had called for help, and so had given the alarm. Altogether only twenty-two men escaped. Great misery now existed in the prison, partly because the charitable fund had been exhausted which had hitherto so much alleviated their lot, and partly on account of the number of men put on half allowance as a result of their late escape failure, and so scanty was food that a dog belonging to one of the garrison officers was killed and eaten.

Herbert speaks in glowing terms of the efforts of two American 'Fathers', Heath and Sorry, who were allowed to visit the prison, to soften the lot of the captives.

Finally, on March 15, 1779, Herbert was exchanged after two years and four months' captivity.

In a table at the end of his account, he states that between June 1777, and March 1779, there were 734 Americans in Mill Prison, of whom thirty-six died, 102 escaped, and 114 joined the British service. Of these last, however, the majority were British subjects.

In 1779 Howard reported that there were 392 French and 298 American prisoners in Millbay. He noted that neither the wards nor the court-yards apportioned to the Frenchmen were so spacious and convenient as were those in the American part of the prison, nor were the provisions so good. In the hospital there were fifty patients; it was dirty and offensive, and Howard found only three pairs of sheets in use.

(Herbert, above quoted, said that the hospital was not worthy of the name, that when it rained the wet beat upon the patients as they lay in their beds.)

A new hospital was building, Howard continues, but he considered the wards were being made too low and too close, being seventeen feet ten inches wide, and ten feet high. In the American blocks the regulations were hung up according to rule, and he notes Article 5 of these to the effect that: 'As water and tubs for washing their linen and clothes will be allowed, the prisoners are advised to keep their persons as clean as possible, it being conducive to health.'

I now make an extract from *The Memoirs of Commodore Barney*, published in Boston, 1832, chiefly on account of his stirring escape from Millbay, therein described.

Barney was captured in December 1780 by H.M.S. *Intrepid*, Captain Malloy, whom he stigmatizes as the embodiment of all that is brutal in man. He was carried to England on the *Yarmouth, 74*, with seventy other American officers. They were confined, he says, in the hold, under three decks, twelve feet by twenty feet, and three feet high, without light and almost without air. The result was that during the fifty-three days' passage in the depths of winter, from New York to Plymouth, eleven of them died, and that when they arrived at Plymouth, few of them were able to stand, and all were temporarily blinded by the daylight.

It sounds incredible, but Mrs. Barney, the editress of the volume, says: 'What is here detailed is given without adornment or exaggeration, almost in the very words of one who saw and suffered just as he has described.'

Barney was sent first to a hulk, which he describes as a Paradise when compared with the *Yarmouth*, and as soon as they could walk, he and his companions went to Mill Prison, 'as rebels.'

He lost no time in conspiring to escape. With infinite pains he and others forced their way through the stone walls and iron gratings of the common sewer, only to find, after wading through several hundred feet of filth, their exit blocked by a double iron grating. He then resolved to act independently, and was suddenly afflicted by a sprain which put him on crutches. He found a sympathetic friend in a sentry who, for some reason or other, had often manifested friendship for the American prisoners. This man contrived to obtain for him a British officer's undress uniform. One day Barney said to him, 'To-day?' to which the laconic reply was 'Dinner', by which Barney understood that his hours on duty would be from twelve till two.

Barney threw his old great coat over the uniform; arranged with his friends to occupy the other sentries' attention by chaff and chat; engaged a slender youth at roll-call time to carry out the old trick of creeping through a hole in the wall and answer to Barney's name as well as his own; and then jumped quickly on to the shoulders of a tall friend and over the wall.

Throwing away his great-coat, he slipped four guineas into the accomplice sentry's hand, and walked quietly off into Plymouth to the house of a well-known friend to the American cause. No little alarm was caused here by the sudden appearance of a visitor in British uniform, but Barney soon explained the situation, and remained concealed until night, when he was taken to the house of a clergyman. Here he found two Americans, not prisoners, desirous of returning to America, and they agreed to buy a fishing boat and risk the crossing to France.

So the British uniform was exchanged for fisher garb, the boat purchased, and the three started. As his companions were soon prostrate from sea-sickness, Barney had to manage the craft himself; passed through the British war-ships safely, and seemed to be safe now from all interference, when a schooner rapidly approached, showing British colours, and presently lowered a boat which was pulled towards them.

Instantly, Barney resolved to play a game of bluff. Luckily, in changing his attire he had not left the British uniform behind. The boat came alongside and a privateer officer came aboard and asked Barney his business.

'Government business to France,' replied Barney with dignity—and displayed the British uniform.

The officer was not satisfied, and said that he must report to his captain. This he did; the privateer captain was no more satisfied than his lieutenant, and politely but firmly declared his intention of carrying Barney back to Plymouth, adding that it must be funny business to take a British officer in uniform over to France in a fishing boat.

'Very well,' said Barney, calm and dignified to the end; 'then I hold you responsible, for the interruption of my errand, to Admiral Digby, to whose flag-ship I will trouble you to take me.'

All the same Barney saw that the game was up, and back towards Plymouth he had to turn. Barney's story is not very clear as to how he managed to escape the notice of the crew of the privateer, on board which he now was, but he slipped into a boat alongside, cut her adrift, and made for 'Cawsen'. Landing here, and striking away inland, he thought it best to leave the high road, and so, climbing over a hedge, he found himself in Edgcumbe Park. Presently he came upon an old gardener at work. Barney accosted him, but all the reply he got was: 'It's a fine of half a guinea for crossing a hedge.' Barney had no money, but plenty of pleasant talk, the result of which was that the old man passed him out by a side gate and showed him a by-way towards the river. Barney, for obvious reasons, wished to avoid the public ferry, so crossed over in a butcher's boat, and passing under the very wall of Mill Prison, was soon in Plymouth and at the clergyman's house.

He had had a narrow escape, for in less than an hour after Admiral Digby had received the privateer captain's report, a guard had been sent off from Mill Prison to Cawsand, and had he kept to the high road he would assuredly have been captured. Whilst at the clergyman's house, the Town Crier passed under the window, proclaiming the reward of five guineas for the apprehension of 'Joshua Barney, a Rebel Deserter from Mill Prison'.

Barney remained here three days. Then, with a fresh outfit, he took a post chaise for Exeter. At midnight the Town Gate was reached, and a soldier closely examined Barney and compared him with his description on the Apprehension bill. Again his *sang-froid* came to the rescue, and he so contorted his face and eyes that he was allowed to proceed, and his escape was accomplished.

In 1783 Barney was at Plymouth again; this time as a representative of the Republic in a time of peace, and although an individual of importance, entertaining all the great officials of the port on the *George Washington*, and being entertained by them in return, he found time not only to visit the kindly clergyman who had befriended him, but to look up the old gardener at Mount Edgcumbe, amply pay the fine so long due, and discover that the old man was the father of the sentry who had enabled him to escape from Mill Prison!

An account by another American, Andrew Sherburne, published at Utica, in 1825, of a sojourn in Mill Prison in 1781, is quoted only for his remarks on the hospital system, which do not accord with those of other writers. He says:

'However inhuman and tyrannical the British Government was in other respects, they were to be praised and respected for the suitable provision they made for the sick in the hospitals at Mill Prison.'

In 1798 Vochez, the official sent to England by the French Directory to inquire into the true state of French prisoners under our care, brought an action against certain provision contractors for astounding breaches of their engagements, in the shape of a system of short weightage carried on for years, and of supplying provisions of an inferior character. In this he was supported by Captain Lane, a travelling inspector of prisons, and an honest official, and this, wrote Vochez, 'despite the contradiction by a number of base and interested prisoners brought to London for that express purpose to attack the unblemished character of that officer.'

Captain Lane insisted that the Governor of the Prison should give certificates as to the badness of the provisions supplied; this was done, and Vochez's case was established. The Admiralty entirely endorsed Captain Lane's recommendation that in every case the Governors of Prisons should certify as to the character of provisions supplied by contractors, highly complimented him on his action, and very heavily mulcted the rascally contractors. Unhappily, the vile system was far from being abolished. The interests of too many influential people were linked with those of the contractors for a case such as the above to be more than a flash in the pan, and the prison contractors continued to flourish until the very end of the Great War period.

In 1799 Mill Prison was practically rebuilt, and became known as Millbay. The condition of it at this time seems to have been very bad. It was said that some of the poor inmates were so weak for lack of proper food that they fell from their hammocks and broke their necks, that supplies of bedding and clothing were only to be had from 'capitalists' among the prisoners, who had bought them from the distribution officers and sold them at exorbitant rates.

In 1806, at the instance of some Spanish prisoners in Millbay, a firm of provision contractors was heavily mulcted upon proof that for a long time past they had systematically sent in stores of deficient quality.

In 1807 the Commissioners of the Transport Office refused an application that French prisoners at Millbay should be allowed to manufacture worsted gloves for H.M.'s 87th Regiment, on the grounds that, if allowed, it would seriously interfere with our own manufacturing industry, and further, would lead to the destruction by the prisoners of their blankets and other woollen articles in order to provide materials for the work.

I now proceed to give a very interesting account of prisoner life in Millbay Prison from Édouard Corbière's book, *Le Négrier*.

When a lad of fifteen, Corbière was captured on the *Val de Grâce* privateer by H.M.S. *Gibraltar*, in 1807. The *Val de Grâce* must have been a very small craft, for not only did she not show fight, but the *Gibraltar* simply sent off a boat's crew, made fast hawsers and tackles, and hoisted the Frenchman bodily on board. Corbière and his fellows were sent to Millbay. Before describing his particular experiences, he gives a page or so to a scathing picture of our shore prisons, but he impressively accentuates the frightful depravity brought about by the sufferings endured, and says that nobody who had not lived in an English war-prison could realize the utter depths of wickedness to which men could fall. At Millbay, he says, the *forts à bras* ruled all by mere brute strength. Victories at fights or wrestling matches were celebrated by procession round the airing grounds, and the successful men formed the 'Government' of the *Pré*, as the airing ground was called, regulating the gambling, deciding disputes, officiating at duels—of which there were many, the weapons being razors or compass points fixed on the ends of sticks—and generally exercising despotic sway. They were usually topsmen and sailors. The *Romains* were the pariahs at Millbay, and the *Rafalés* the lowest of all, naked rascals who slept in ranks, spoon fashion, as described elsewhere.

The usual industries were carried on at Millbay. Much money was made by the straw plaiters and workers, some of the latter earning 18 sous a day. But the straw 'capitalists', the men who bought straw wholesale through the soldiers of the guard, and who either employed workers themselves, or sold the straw to other employers, accumulated fortunes, says Corbière, of from 30,000 to 40,000 francs. There were teachers of sciences, languages, music, dancing and fencing. There were eating-cabins where a 'beef steak' could be got for four sous. There were theatrical performances, but not of the same character or quality as, for instance, at Portchester.

On Sundays, as at Stapleton, the prayers of the Mass were read. Each province was particular in observing its own festivals—Basques and Bretons notably.

A great many 'broke-paroles' were here, and, Corbière remarks, the common sailors took advantage of their fallen position and ostentatiously treated them as equals, and even as inferiors. Not so the soldiers, who punctiliously observed the distinctions of rank; and there were even instances of private soldiers helping officers not used to manual labour to supplement their daily rations.

Corbière also emphasizes the fact that, notwithstanding the depth of degradation to which the prisoners sank among themselves, they always preserved a proud attitude towards strangers, and never begged of visitors and sight-seers.

In the prison, regular Courts of Justice were held, the chief *maître d'armes* being generally elected President *if he could read*. The Court was held within the space of twelve hammocks, shut in by hangings of old cloth. The only ordinary punishment was flogging, but a very terrible exception was made in the following case. One of the grandest and boldest projects for escape from a war-prison which had ever been conceived had been secretly proceeded with at Millbay for some time. It consisted of a tunnel no less than 532 yards long (Corbière's words are 'half a quarter league', and the French league of this time measured 2 miles 743 yards) coming out in a field, by which the whole of the 5,000 prisoners were to get away after overcoming and disarming the guard. The enormous quantity of earth excavated was carried by the workers in their pockets and emptied into the latrines, and although I give the account as written, I cannot repress a doubt that Corbière, who was then but a boy, may have been mistaken in his figures, for this process alone of emptying a tunnel, big enough to allow the passage of a man, in continual fear of detection, must have been very long and laborious.

At any rate one Jean Caffé sold the secret to the authorities, the result being that on the appointed night, when the tunnel was full of escaping prisoners, the first man to emerge at the outlet was greeted by Scots soldiers, and the despairing cry arose, *Le trou est vendu*!

Drums beat, the alarm brought more soldiers from Plymouth, and the would-be escapers were put back into prison, but, so maddened were they at the failure at the eleventh hour of their cherished plot, that they refused to put out the lights, sang songs of defiance, and broke out into such a riot that the guard fired into them, with what result Corbière does not state.

The next morning, search was made for Caffé, who no doubt had been hidden by the authorities, and the miserable man was found with some guineas in his pocket. The rage of his countrymen was the deeper because Caffé had always been regarded as a poor, witless sort of fellow, for whom everybody had pity, and who existed upon the charity of others, and the cry arose that he should be at once put to death. But the chief of the *Pré*, who happened to be Corbière's captain on the *Val de Grâce*, and of whom more anon, said 'Non! Il faut auparavant le flétrir!'

So Caffé was dragged before the entire assembly of prisoners. A professional tattooer then shaved his head, laid him on a table, and held him down whilst on his forehead was pricked: 'Flétri pour avoir VENDU 5000 de ses camarades dans la nuit du 4 Septembre 1807.'

This accomplished, he was taken to a well, thrown down it, and stones hurled on him until he was hidden from sight, and his cries could be heard no more. Corbière adds that, so far from the authorities trying to stop this summary execution, the British commander said that it served him right, and that he would have done the same.

Ivan, the privateer captain who had been chief official at the foregoing execution, had won his position as a *Chef de Pré* in the following way. He was dancing at a ball in Calais when the news was brought him that a rich British prize had been sighted, and without stopping to change his costume, he had hurried on board the *Val de Grâce*, so that the prize should not escape him. Hence, when captured by the *Gibraltar*, he was in full dancing kit,—laced coat, ruffles, silk stockings and all—and in the same garb had been introduced into Millbay Prison, much to the amusement of his fellow countrymen. Particularly did he attract the attention of the chief *fort à bras*, who had a good deal to say about carpet knight and armchair sailor, which was so distasteful to Ivan that he challenged him, fought him, and half-killed him. The result of which was that the same night he was elected a *Chef de Pré* with much pomp and circumstance. Furthermore, discovering among the prisoners old comrades of the *Sans Façon* privateer, they elected him head cook, a position in the prison of no small consideration.

Now Mr. Milliken, purser of the prison, had a pretty wife who took such a fancy to the handsome, dashing young French privateer captain that she made him a present of a New Testament, although it was well she did not hear his description of it as 'le beau fichu cadeau'. At the same time Milliken, socially superior, Corbière remarks, to his wife, pitying the boy (Corbière himself) thus thrust by fate at the very threshold of his life into the wild, wicked world of a war-prison, offered him employment in his office, which he gladly accepted, going there every day, but returning every night to the prison. Milliken's office was on the ground floor of his dwelling-house, and Mrs. Milliken with her servant Sarah were constantly in and out, the result being that the boy became very friendly with them, and their chief object seemed to be to make his life as happy as possible, the only cloud upon it being his separation every day from Ivan, for whom he had an affection bordering upon idolatry. For weeks Corbière had the happiest of lives, indulged in every way by Mrs. Milliken, and made much of by her visitors, to most of whom a lively, intelligent, French lad was a refreshing novelty. To dress him up in feminine attire was a favourite amusement of the ladies, 'and', says Corbière, 'they were good enough to say that, except for my rolling gait, begot of a lifetime spent afloat, I should pass well for a distinguished-looking girl.'

One morning Mrs. Milliken gave him bad news. Ivan had escaped from the prison. He says: 'Whatever feeling I had of gladness that my dear friend was out of prison, was smothered not merely by the sense of my own desolate position, but by surprise that he should have left me.'

A day or two later a young woman appeared at the back door of the Millikens' house, which gave on to the street, looked around cautiously for a few moments, and then rapidly passed down the street. It was Corbière. It was a daring move, and it was not long before he wished he had not made it, for Plymouth streets in these piping war-times were no place for a respectable girl, and no doubt his flurried, anxious look, and palpable air of being a stranger, commanded unusual attention. Whither he was going he had no idea, and for an hour he went through what he confesses to have been one of the severest trials of a life full of adventure and ordeal. He was on the point of trying to find his way back to the Millikens' house, when an old Jew man, with a bag over his shoulder, brushed against him, and at the same time whispered his name. It was Ivan. The boy could have shouted for joy, but Ivan impressed silence, and motioned him to follow. Arrived at Stonehouse, Ivan paused at a house, whispered to Corbière to walk on, return, and enter, and went in himself. This was done, and Corbière describes how, when at last together in the house, they unrestrainedly indulged their joy at being again together, and Ivan explained how both of their escapes had been arranged by Mrs. Milliken. Then Ivan detailed his plan for getting out of England. He had thirty false one-pound notes, manufactured in Millbay Prison, which he had bought for a guinea, and the next day they would start off on foot for Bigbury, about fifteen miles distant, on the coast, near which they would charter a smuggler to take them across.

That evening they went into the town to make a few necessary purchases, and in his delight at being free again, Ivan proposed that they should go to the theatre at Plymouth Dock. They did, and it nearly proved the undoing of them, for some American sailors were there who naturally regarded as fair game a nice-looking, attractively dressed girl in the company of a bearded old Jew, and paid Corbière attentions which became so marked as to provoke Ivan, the result being a row, in the course of which Ivan's false beard was torn off, and Corbière's dress much deranged, and the cry of 'Runaway prisoners!' beginning to be heard, the two rushed out of the theatre, and through the streets, until they were in the open country.

They spent the night, which luckily was warm and fine, in a ditch, and the next morning saw an anchored boat riding close in shore. They swam out and boarded her, and found that there were rudder and oars chained, but no sails or mast. Ivan broke the chain, and rigged up some of Corbière's female clothes on an oar, for sail and mast. Some days ensued of much suffering from hunger and thirst, as, being without bearings, they simply steered by the sun, south-east, and at last they were sighted and picked up by the *Gazelle*, French 'aventurier', of St. Malo, and in her went to Martinique.

In 1809 the Transport Office, in reply to French prisoners at Millbay asking leave to give fencing lessons outside the prison, refused, adding that only officers of the guard were allowed to take fencing lessons from prisoners, and those in the prison.

In 1811 a dozen prisoners daubed themselves all over with mortar, and walked out unchallenged as masons. Five were retaken. Another man painted his clothes like a British military uniform, and got away, as he deserved to.

In 1812 additional buildings to hold 2,000 persons were erected at Millbay.

In 1813 a notable scene, indicative of the prevalence occasionally of a nice feeling between foes, was witnessed at Millbay, at the funeral of Captain Allen of the United States ship *Argus*, who had died of wounds received in the action with the *Pelican*. Allen had been first lieutenant of the *United States* in her victorious action with the British *Macedonian*, and had received his promotion for his bravery in that encounter. Moreover, all the British prisoners taken by him testified to his humanity and kindness. A contemporary newspaper says:

'The Funeral Procession as it moved from the Mill Prison to the Old Church, afforded a scene singularly impressive to the prisoners, who beheld with admiration the respect paid by a gallant, conquering enemy to the fallen hero. 500 British Marines first marched in slow time, with arms reversed; the band of the Plymouth Division of Marines followed, playing the most solemn tunes. An officer of Marines in military mourning came after these. Two interesting black boys, the servants of the deceased, then preceded the hearse. One of these bore his master's sword, and the other his hat. Eight American officers followed the hearse, and the procession was closed with a number of British Naval officers.

'On the arrival of the body at the Old Church, it was met by the officiating Minister, and three volleys over the grave closed the scene.'

CHAPTER XVIII
THE PRISONS ASHORE
10. DARTMOOR

In July 1805, the Transport Office, impressed by the serious crowding of war-prisoners on the hulks at Plymouth and in the Millbay Prison, requested their representative, Mr. Daniel Alexander, to meet the Hon. E. Bouverie, at the house of Sir Thomas Tyrwhitt, warden of the Stannaries, at Tor Royal, with the view of choosing a site for a great war-prison to hold 5,000 men.

Mr. Baring-Gould more than hints that the particular spot chosen owed its distinction entirely to the personal interests of Sir Thomas. Says he:

'It is on the most inclement site that could have been selected, catching the clouds from the South West, and condensing fog about it when everything else is clear. It is exposed equally to the North and East winds. It stands over 1,400 feet above the sea, above the sources of the Meavy, in the highest as well as least suitable situation that could have been selected; the site determined by Sir Thomas, so as to be near his granite quarries.'

On March 20, 1806, the first stone was laid; on May 24, 1809, the first prisoners came to it; in July the first two prisoners got out of it by bribing the sentries, men of the Notts Militia. The Frenchmen were recaptured, one at a place called 'The Jumps', the other at Kingsbridge. The soldiers, four in number, confessed they had received eight guineas each for their help, and two of them were condemned to be shot.

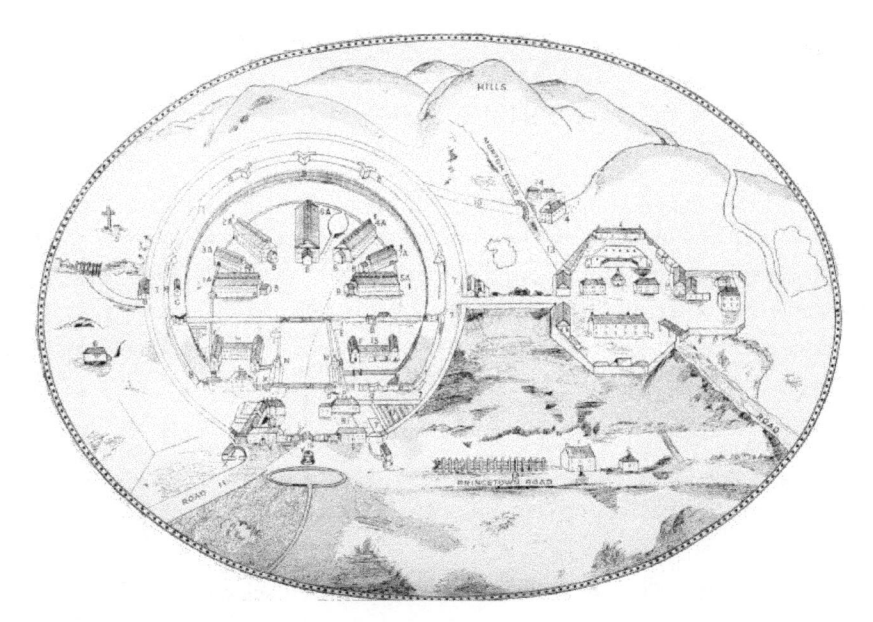

DARTMOOR WAR-PRISON, IN 1812.

From a Sketch signed 'John Wethems' in the Public Record Office.

(*Reproduced by kind permission of Mr. Basil Thomson and Col. Winn.*)

Key to the Plan.

1A

Prison.

2A

Prison.

3A

Prison.

4A

Prison.

5A

Prison.

6A

Prison. (New Building).

7A

Prison. (New Building).

B

Cookeries.

C

Cachot or Dungeon.

D

Watch-houses.

E

Basins.

F

Petty Officers' Prison.

G

Market-place.

H

Hospital.

I

Receiving-house.

J

Pharmacy.

K

Bathing-place.

L

Matron's House.

M

Washing-house.

N

Storage.

N

Store-houses.

O

Storage.

P

Jailor's Lodgings

Q

Jailor's Lodge.

R1

Mr. Holmden's (Clerk) House.

R2

Mr. Bennet's House.

R3

Mr. Winkworth's House.

S

Captain Cotgrave's House.

T

Agent's Office.

U

Agent's Garden.

V

Doctor's House.

W

Doctor's Garden.

X

Stables.

Y

Reservoir.

Z

Barracks.

1

Mr. Carpenter's House.

2

Bakehouse.

3

Bell.

4

Miller's House.

5

Burial-ground.

6

Dead-house.

7

Military Walk.

8

Ramparts.

9

Iron Rails, inside of which prisoners are confined.

10

Streams of water running from the reservoir.

11

Tavistock Road.

12

Princetown Road.

13

Morton Road.

14

Prison where Mr. V. made his first entry on December 12, 1811, with the track.

15

Prison where Mr. V. lives now, and track of walk allowed.

16

Mr. V. has liberty to go as far as 5th *Gate.*

17

New latter wall, is a mile in circumference.

Thirty acres were enclosed by stone walls, the outer of which was sixteen feet high,[10] and was separated by a broad military way from the inner wall, which was hung with bells on wires connected with all the sentry boxes dotted along it. One half of the circle thus enclosed was occupied by five huge barracks, each capable of holding more than 1,000 men, with their airing grounds and shelters for bad weather, their inner ends converging on a large open space, where was held the market. Each barrack consisted of two floors, and above the top floor ran, the length of the building, a roof room, designed for use when the weather was too bad even for the outdoor shelters, but, as we shall see, appropriated for other purposes. On each floor, a treble tier of hammocks was slung upon cast-iron pillars. Each barrack had its own airing ground, supply of running water, and Black Hole. The other half-circle was occupied by two spacious blocks, one the hospital, the other the petty officers' prison, by the officials' quarters, the kitchen, washing-houses, and other domestic offices, and outside the main, the Western Gate, the barrack for 400 soldiers and the officers' quarters. The cost of the prison was £135,000.

By the foreign prisoners of war Dartmoor was regarded, and not without reason, as the most hateful of all the British prisons. At Norman Cross, at Stapleton, at Perth, at Valleyfield, at Forton, at Millbay, they were at any rate within sight and hearing of the outer world. Escape from any one of these places was, of course, made as difficult as possible, but when once an exit was effected, the rest was comparatively easy. But escape from Dartmoor meant very much more than the mere evading of sentries, the breaching and scaling of walls, or the patient labour of underground burrowing. When all this was accomplished the fugitive found himself not in a crowded city, where he could be lost to sight among the multitude, nor in the open country where starvation was at any rate impossible, nor by a water highway to freedom, nor, in short, in a world wherein he could exercise his five senses with at least a chance of success; but in the wildest, most solitary, most shelterless, most pathless, and, above all, most weather-tormented region of Britain. Any one who has tried to take his bearings in a Dartmoor fog, or who has been caught by a Dartmoor snowstorm at the fall of day can realize this; those who have not had one or other of these experiences, cannot do better than read *The American Prisoner*, by Mr. Eden Phillpotts.

More than this: at the other prisons a more or less sympathetic public was near at hand which kept the prisoners in touch with the free life without, even if many of its members were merely curious gapers and gazers, or purchasers of manufactures. At Dartmoor the natives who came to the prison gates, came only to sell their produce. Being natives of a remote district, they were generally prejudiced against the prisoners, and Farmer Newcombe's speech in Mr. Phillpotts' *Farm of the Dagger*, accurately reproduces the sentiments prevalent among them:

'Dartymoor's bettern they deserve anyway. I should like to know what's too bad for them as makes war on us. 'Tis only naked savages, I should have thought, as would dare to fight against the most civilized and God-fearing nation in the world.'

Finally, it is much to be feared that the jacks-in-office and petty officials at Dartmoor, secure in their seclusion as they thought, were exacting and tyrannical to a degree not ventured upon in other places of confinement more easily accessible to the light of inspection, and unsurrounded by a desert air into which the cries of anguish and distress would rise in vain.

All the same, it was not long before the condition of prison life in Dartmoor became known, even in high places.

In July 1811, the *Independent Whig* published revelations of the state of Dartmoor which caused Lord Cochrane, member for Westminster, to bring the facts before the notice of the House of Commons, but he expressed his disappointment that his exposure had been without result, asserting that the Government was afraid of losing what little character it had. He declared that the soil of Dartmoor was one vast marsh, and was most pestilential. Captivity, said he, was irksome enough without the addition of disease and torture. He asserted that the prison had been built for the convenience of the town, and not the town for the convenience of the prison, inasmuch as the town was a speculative project which had failed. 'Its inhabitants had no market, were solitary, insulated, absorbed, and buried in their own fogs.' To remedy this it was necessary to do something, and so came about the building of the prison.

The article in the *Independent Whig* which attracted Lord Cochrane's attention was as follows:

'To foreigners, bred for the most part in a region the temperature of which is so comparatively pure to the air of our climate at the best of times, a transition so dreadful must necessarily have fatal consequences, and indeed it is related that the prisoners commonly take to their beds at the first arrival, which nothing afterwards can induce them to quit.... Can it bear reflection, much less inspection? Six or seven thousand human beings, deprived of liberty by the chance of war ... consigned to linger out probably many tedious years in misery and disease!

'While we declaim against the injustice and tyranny of our neighbours, shall we neglect the common duties of humanity? If we submit to crowd our dungeons with the virtuous and the just of our country, confounding moral guilt with unintentional error, and subjecting them to indiscriminate punishment and the most inhuman privations, though we submit to this among ourselves, do not let us pursue the same system towards individuals thrown on our compassion by the casualties of war, lest we provoke a general spirit of retaliation, and plunge again the civilized world into the vortex of Barbarism. Let us not forget that the prisoner is a living trust in our hands, not to be subject to the wayward fancy of caprice, but a deposit placed at our disposal to be required at a future hour. It is a solemn charge, involving the care of life and the principle of humanity.'

'Humanitas' wrote in the *Examiner*, commenting upon Whitbread's defence and laudation of Dartmoor as a residence, and amazed at the selection of such a place as the site for a prison:

'The most inclement climate in England; for nine months there is no sun, and four and a half times as much rain as in Middlesex. The regiments on duty there have to be changed every two months. Were not the deaths during the first three years 1,000 a year, and 3,000 sick? Did not from 500 to 600 die in the winter of 1809? Is it not true that since some gentlemen visited the prison and published their terrible experiences, nobody has been allowed inside?'

The writer goes on, not so much to condemn the treatment of the prisoners as to blame the Government for spending so much money on such a site.

The Transport Office took counsel's opinion about prosecuting these two newspapers for libel. It was as follows:

'In my opinion both these papers are libellous. The first is the strongest, but if the statement of deaths in the other is, as I conceive it is, wholly unsupported by the fact, this is equally mischievous. It is not, however, by any means clear to me that a jury will take the same view of the subject, ... but unless some serious consequences are to be apprehended from suffering these publications to go unnoticed, I should not be inclined to institute prosecutions upon them.

V. GIBBS.'

Later on, Vicary Gibbs thinks that they should be prosecuted, but wants information about the heavy mortality of November 1809 to April 1810, and also tables of comparison between the deaths in our own barracks and those in French prisons.

I cannot trace the sequel of this, but, reading by the light of the times, it is probable that the matter was hushed up in the same way as were the exposures of Messrs. Batchelor and Andrews at Stapleton a few years previously. The heavy mortality of the six months of 1809–10 was due to an epidemic of measles, which carried off no less than 419 persons in the four months of 1810 alone.

Violent deaths among Dartmoor prisoners, whether from suicide or duel or murder, were so frequent, even in the earliest years of the prison, that in 1810 the coroner of this division of the county complained, praying that on account of the large numbers of inquests held—greater, he said, since the opening of the prison than during the preceding fourteen years—the ordinary allowance to jurors of 8*d*. per man be increased to 1*s*. He emphasized the difficulty of collecting jurors, these being principally small farmers and artificers, who had in most cases to travel long distances. The Parish of Lydford paid the fees, and the coroner's request was granted.

From the *Story of Dartmoor Prison* by Mr. Basil Thomson, I have, with the kind permission of the author, taken many of the following facts, and with these I have associated some from the pen of the French writer, Catel.

In the preface to the latter's book we read:

'About six leagues to the North of Plymouth, under a dark and melancholy sky, in a cold and foggy atmosphere, a rocky, dry and almost naked soil, covered eight months of the year with a mantle of snow, shuts in a space of some square leagues. This appearance strikes the view, and communicates a sort of bitterness to the soul. Nature, more than indifferent in complete stagnation, seems to have treated with avaricious parsimony this corner of land, without doubt the ugliest in England. It is in this place, where no human thought dare hope for the smallest betterment, that British philanthropy conceived and executed the double project of building a prison in time of war for French prisoners, in time of Peace for her own criminals condemned to penal servitude. Comment is needless. The reader will appreciate the double humanitarian thought which is apparent in its conception.'

Mr. Thomson informs us that the present Infirmary was the old petty officers' prison. Here were confined officers who had broken their parole and who had been recaptured. Some of Rochambeau's San Domingo officers were here, and the building was known as the 'Petit Cautionnement'. As most of the officers here had private means, they formed a refined little society, dressed and lived well, and had servants to attend on them, taken from the ordinary prisoners, who were paid 3*d.* a day. Duels were frequent. In 1809, on the occasion of some national or provincial festival, there was a procession with band and banners. One Souville, a *maître d'armes*, felt himself slighted because he had not been chosen to carry the national flag, and snatched it from a youth of eighteen, to whom it had been entrusted. The youth attacked him with his fists and gave him a thrashing, which so enraged the other, whose *métier* was that of arms, that he challenged him. The youth could not fence, but as the weapons were sticks with razor-blades affixed, this was not of serious moment. Souville, however, cut one of the youth's fingers off.

In 1812 two prisoners fought with improvised daggers with such ferocity that both died before they could be carried to the hospital. In 1814, two fencing masters, hitherto great friends, quarrelled over the merits of their respective pupils, and fought with fists. The beaten man, Jean Vignon, challenged the other to a more real trial by combat, and they fought in the 'cock-loft' of No. 4 Prison—where are now the kitchen and chapel. Vignon killed his opponent while the latter was stooping to pick up his foil, was brought up before the civil court, and condemned to six months for manslaughter.

Every day, except Sunday, a market was held from nine to twelve. Here, in exchange for money and produce, the prisoners sold the multifarious articles of their manufacture, excepting woollen mittens and gloves, straw hats or bonnets, shoes, plaited straw, obscene toys and pictures, or articles made out of prison stores.

The chief punishment was relegation to the *cachot* or Black Hole. At first this was a small building in the Infirmary Yard of such poor construction that it was frequent for the inmates to break out of it and mix with the other prisoners. But in 1811 the French prisoners built a new one, twenty feet square, arch-roofed, and with a floor of granite blocks weighing a ton each.

Some escapes from Dartmoor were notable, one, indeed, so much so that I have given the hero of it, Louis Vanhille, a chapter to himself. Sevegran, a naval surgeon, and Aunay, a naval officer, observing that fifty men were marched into the prison every evening to help the turnkeys to get the prisoners into their respective *casernes*, made unto themselves Glengarry caps and overcoats out of odds and ends of cloth and blanket and, with strips of tin to look like bayonets, calmly fell in at the rear of the guard as they left the prison, and, favoured by rain and darkness, followed out of the prison, and, as the troops marched into barracks, got away. They had money, so from Plymouth—whither they tramped that night—they took coach to London. In order that they should have time to get well away, their accomplices in the prison at the call-over the next morning got up a disturbance which put the turnkey out of his reckoning, and so they were not at once missed.

Next evening, three other prisoners, Keronel, Vasselin, and Cherabeau, tried the same trick. All went well. At the third gate, the keeper asked if the locking-up was finished, and as there was no reply he said: 'All these lobsters are deaf with their caps over their ears.' The men escaped.

Dr. Walker quotes an attempt of a similar character from Norman Cross:

'A French prisoner made himself a complete uniform of the Hertfordshire Militia, and a wooden gun, stained, surmounted by a tin bayonet. Thus equipped, he mixed with the guard, and when they were ordered to march out, having been relieved, Monsieur fell in and marched out too. Thus far he was fortunate, but when arrived at the guard room, lo! what befell him.

'His new comrades ranged their muskets on the rack, and he endeavoured to follow their example; but, as his wooden piece was unfortunately a few inches too long, he was unable to place it properly. This was observed, so of course his attempt to get away was frustrated.'

The bribing of sentries was a very necessary condition of escape. One or two pounds would generally do it, and it was through the sky-light of the 'cock-lofts' that the prisoners usually got out of the locked-up barracks.

In February 1811, four privates of the Notts Militia were heavily bribed for the escape of two French officers. One of them, thinking he was unfairly treated in the division of the money, gave information, and a picket was in waiting for the escaping Frenchmen. The three men were sentenced to 900 lashes each. Two were pardoned, but one, who had given the prisoners firearms, got 450.

In March, 1812, Edward Palmer, a 'moorman,' was fined £5 and got twelve months' imprisonment for procuring a disguise for a French prisoner named Bellaird.

Early in the same year three prisoners escaped with the connivance of a Roscommon Militiaman. The sequel moves one's pity. Pat was paid in bank-notes. He offered them for exchange, and, to his amazement, was informed not only that he could receive nothing for them, but that he must consider himself under arrest for uttering forged notes. It was too true. The three Frenchmen had paid him handsomely in notes fabricated by one Lustique. The Irishman would not say where he got the notes, and it really did not matter, for if he had admitted that he received them as the price of allowing French prisoners to escape, he would have been flogged to death: as it was, he and Lustique were hanged.

Forgery was a prominent Dartmoor industry. Bank of England notes were forged to some extent, but local banks such as Grant, Burbey and Co. of Portsmouth, Harris, Langholme, and Harris of Plymouth, the Plymouth Commercial Bank, the Tamar Bank, the Launceston and Totnes Bank, were largely victimized. To such an extent were these frauds carried out that it was ordered that an official should attend at the prison market to write his name on all notes offered by prisoners in payment for goods received.

It was no doubt with reference to the local knowledge of soldiers on guard being valuable to intending escapes from the prison that the authorities refused the application of the 1st Devon Militia to be on guard at Dartmoor, as there were 'several strong objections to the men of that regiment being employed'.

There were distinct grades among the Dartmoor prisoners. First came 'Les Lords'—'broke parole' officers, and people with money. Next came 'Les Laboureurs', the clever, industrious men who not only lived comfortably by the sale of the articles they manufactured, but saved money so that some of them left the prison at the Declaration of Peace financially very much better off than when they came. These were the 'respectable prisoners'.

After the labourers came the 'Indifférents'—loafers and idlers, but not mischief-makers or harm-workers; the 'Misérables', mischievous rascals for ever plotting and planning; and finally, the most famous of all, the 'Romans', so called because they existed in the cock-loft, the 'Capitole', of one of the barracks. These men, almost entirely privateersmen, the scum and sweepings of sea-port towns, or land rascals with nothing to lose and all to gain in this world, formed a veritable power in the prison. Gamblers to a man, they were mostly naked, and held so faithfully to the theory of Communism, that when it was necessary that someone should descend from the cock-loft eyrie in order to beg, borrow, or, what was more usual, to steal food or rags, the one pair of breeches was lent to him for the occasion. The only hammock among them belonged to the 'General' or, to be more correct, was his temporarily, for not even in Hayti were generals made and unmade with such dispatch. The sleeping arrangement was that, mention of which has already been made, known as the 'spoon' system, by which the naked men lay so close together for warmth that the turn-over of the ranks had to be made at certain intervals by word of command. Catel tells an excellent story of the 'Romans'. These gentry held a parade on one of the anniversaries, and were drawn up in order when a fine plump rat appeared on the airing ground—a new arrival, clearly, or he would have kept carefully away. This was too much for half-famished men; the ranks were instantly broken and the chase began. As luck would have it, the rat ran into the garrison kitchens, where the day's rations were being prepared, and in a very few minutes the pots and pans were cleared of their contents. Soldiers were at once hurried to the scene, but being few in number they were actually overpowered and disarmed by the 'Romans', who marched them to the Governor's house. Here the 'General', with a profound salute, spoke as follows:

'Sir, we have come here to deliver over to you our prisoners and their arms. It is a happy little occurrence this, as regards your soldiers, quiet now as sheep. We beg, you, therefore, to grant them as reward double rations, and to make up the loss we have caused in the provisions of our honoured visitors.'

Catel adds that the rat was caught and eaten raw!

Gradually, their violence and their thieving propensities made them a terror to the other prisoners; the Americans, in particular, objected to their filthy habits, and at length their conduct became so intolerable that they were marched off to the Plymouth hulks, on which they were kept until the Peace of 1814.

It is an interesting fact that when an epidemic swept the prisons and carried off the decent and cleanly by hundreds, the impregnable dirt-armour of the 'Romans' kept them unscathed. This epidemic was the terrible visitation of malignant measles which from November 1809 to April 1810 inclusive, claimed about 400 victims out of 5,000 prisoners. The burial-ground was in the present gas-house field; the mortuary, where the bodies were collected for burial, was near the present General Hospital. No funeral rites were observed, and not more than a foot of earth heaped over the bodies.

Catel also relates a very clever and humorous escape. Theatricals were largely patronized at Dartmoor, as in the other prisons. A piece entitled *Le Capitaine Calonne et sa dame* was written in eulogy of a certain British garrison officer and his lady, and, being shown to them in manuscript, so flattered and delighted them, that, in order that the piece should not lack local colour at the opening performance, the Captain offered to lend a British suit of regimentals, and his lady to provide a complete toilette, for the occasion.

These, of course, were gladly accepted. The theatre was crowded, and the new piece was most successful, until the opening of the third act, when the manager stepped forward, and, amidst whistles and catcalls, said: 'Messieurs, the play is finished. The English Captain and his lady are out of the prison.' This was true. During the second act the prisoner-Captain and his lady quietly passed out of the prison, being saluted by guards and sentries, and got away to Tavistock. Catel relates with gusto the adventure of the real captain and his wife with the said guards and sentinels, who swore that they had left the prison some time before.

The delight of the prisoners can be pictured, and especially when it was rumoured two days later that the real Captain received his uniform, and his lady her dress, in a box with a polite letter of thanks from the escaped prisoners.

An escape of a similar character to the foregoing was effected from one of the Portsmouth hulks. On one occasion a prisoner acted the part of a female so naturally, that an English naval Captain was deceived completely. He proposed to the supposed girl to elope. The pseudo-maiden was nothing loth, and (said the late Rev. G. N. Godwin in a lecture from which I take this) there is an amusing sketch showing the Captain in full uniform passing the gangway with the lady on his arm, the sentry presenting arms meanwhile. Of course, when the gallant officer discovered his mistake, there was nothing for it but to assist in the escape of the astute prisoner.

In 1812, Hageman, the bread contractor, was brought up for fraudulent dealing, and was mulcted in £3,000, others concerned in the transactions being imprisoned for long terms.

I am glad to be able to ring a change in the somewhat monotonous tone of the prisoners' complaints, inasmuch as American prisoners have placed on record their experiences: one of them, Andrews, in a very comprehensive and detailed form.

From the autumn of 1812 to April of 1813, there were 900 American prisoners at Chatham, 100 at Portsmouth, 700 at Plymouth, 'most of them destitute of clothes and swarming with vermin.' On April 2, 1813, the Transport Board ordered them all to Dartmoor, no doubt because of their ceaseless attempts to escape from the hulks. They were horrified, for they knew it to have the reputation of being the worst prison in England.

From the Plymouth hulks *Hector* and *Le Brave*, 250 were landed at New Passage, and marched the seventeen miles to Dartmoor, where were already 5,000 French prisoners. On May 1, 1813, Cotgrave, the Governor, ordered all the American prisoners to be transferred to No. 4 *caserne*, where were already 900 French 'Romans'.

DARTMOOR. THE ORIGINAL MAIN ENTRANCE.

(*From a sketch by the Author.*)

The garrison at Dartmoor consisted of from 1,200 to 1,500 men, who, says Andrews, without the smallest foundation of fact, had been told off for this duty as punishment for offences. The truth is, that as our small regular army was on duty in many places elsewhere, the Militia had to be drawn upon for the garrisoning of war-prisons, and that on account of the many 'pickings' to be had, war-prison duty was rather sought than shunned. The garrison was frequently changed at all the war-prisons for no other reason than that between guards and guarded an undesirable intimacy usually developed.

The American prisoners, who, throughout the war, were generally of a superior type to the Frenchmen, very much resented this association of them with the low-class ruffians in No. 4. I may here quote Mr. Eden Phillpotts's remarks in his *Farm of the Dagger*.

'There is not much doubt that these earlier prisoners of war suffered very terribly. Their guards feared them more than the French. From the hulks came warnings of their skill and ingenuity, their courage, and their frantic endeavours to regain liberty. The American Agent for Prisoners of War at Plymouth, one Reuben Beasley, was either a knave or a fool, and never have unhappy sufferers in this sort endured more from a callous, cruel, or utterly inefficient and imbecile representative. With sleepless rigour and severity were the Americans treated in that stern time; certain advantages and privileges permitted to the French at Princetown were at first denied them, and to all their petitions, reasonable complaints, and remonstrances, the egregious Beasley turned a deaf ear, while the very medical officer at the gaol at that season lacked both knowledge of medicine and humanity, and justified his conduct with falsehood before he was removed from office.'

Theirs was indeed a hard lot. This last-mentioned brute, Dyer, took note of no sickness until it was too far gone to be treated, and refused patients admission to the hospital until the last moment: for fear, he said, of spreading the disease. They were, as Mr. Phillpotts says, denied many privileges and advantages allowed to Frenchmen of the lowest class; they were shut out from the usual markets, and had to buy through the French prisoners, at 25 per cent. above market prices.

On May 18, 1813, 250 more Americans came from the *Hector* hulk, and on July 1, 100 more.

July 4, 1813, was a dark day in the history of the prison. The Americans, with the idea of getting up an Independence Day celebration, got two flags and asked permission to hold a quiet festival. Captain Cotgrave, the Governor, refused, and sent the guard to confiscate the flags. Resistance was offered; there was a struggle and one of the flags was captured. In the evening the disturbance was renewed, an attempt was made to recapture the flag, the guard fired upon the prisoners and wounded two. The feeling thus fostered burst out into a flame on July 10, when the 'Romans' in the two upper stories of No. 4 Prison collected weapons of all sorts, and attacked the Americans unexpectedly, with the avowed purpose of killing them all. A terrible encounter was the result, in the midst of which the guards charged in and separated the two parties, but not until forty on both sides had been badly wounded. After this a wall fifteen feet high was built to divide the airing ground of No. 4.

Andrews describes the clothing of the prisoners as consisting of a cap of wool, one inch thick and coarser than rope yarn, a yellow jacket—not large enough to meet round the smallest man, although most of the prisoners were reduced by low living to skeletons—with the sleeves half-way up the arms, a short waistcoat, pants tight to the middle of the shin, shoes of list with wooden soles one and a half inches thick.

An epidemic of small-pox broke out; complaints poured in to Beasley about the slack attention paid to it, about the overcrowding, the consequent vermin, and the frauds of the food contractors, but without results. Then came remonstrances about the partiality shown in giving all lucrative offices to French prisoners, that is to say, positions such as one sweeper to every 100 men at threepence a day, one cook to every 200 at fourpence halfpenny; barber at threepence; nurses in the hospital at sixpence—all without avail. As a rule the Americans were glad to sell their ration of bad beef to Frenchmen, who could juggle it into fancy dishes, and with the money they bought soap and chewing-tobacco.

At length Beasley came to see for himself, but although he expressed surprise at the crowding of so many prisoners, and said he was glad he had not to be in Dartmoor, he could promise no redress.

Andrews alludes to the proficiency of the French prisoners in the science of forging not only bank-notes, but shillings out of Spanish dollars which they collected from the outside of the market, making eight full-weight shillings out of every four dollars. The performers were chiefly officers who had broken parole. The ordinary run of Dartmoor prisoners, he says, somewhat surprisingly, so far from being the miserable suffering wretches we are accustomed to picture them, were light-hearted, singing, dancing, drinking men who in many cases were saving money.

WOODEN WORKING MODEL OF A FRENCH TRIAL SCENE

Made by prisoners of war at Dartmoor

Isaac Cotgrave he describes as a brutal Governor, who seemed to enjoy making the lot of the prisoners in his charge as hard as possible, and he emphasizes the cruelty of the morning out-of-door roll-call parade in the depth of winter; but he speaks highly of the kindness and consideration of the guards of a Scottish Militia regiment which took over the duty.

Hitherto the negroes, who formed no inconsiderable part of American crews, were mixed with the white men in the prisons. A petition from the American white prisoners that the blacks should be confined by themselves, as they were dirty by habit and thieves by nature, was acceded to.

Gradually the official dread of American determination to obtain liberty was modified, and a general freedom of intercourse was instituted which had not been enjoyed before. A coffee-house was established, trades sprang up, markets for tobacco, potatoes, and butter were carried on, the old French monopoly of trade was broken down, and the American prisoners imitated their French companions in manufacturing all sorts of objects of use and ornament for sale. The French prisoners by this time were quite well off, the different professors of sciences and arts having plenty of pupils, straw-plaiting for hats bringing in threepence a day, although it was a forbidden trade, and plenty of money being found for theatrical performances and amusements generally.

The condition of the Americans, too, kept pace, for Beasley presently announced further money allowances, so that each prisoner now received 6s. 8d. per month, the result being a general improvement in outward appearance.

On May 20, 1814, peace with France was announced amidst the frenzied rejoicings of the French prisoners. All Frenchmen had to produce their bedding before being allowed to go. One poor fellow failed to comply, and was so frantic at being turned back, that he cut his throat at the prison gate. 500 men were released, and with them some French-speaking American officers got away, and when this was followed by a rumour that all the Americans were to be removed to Stapleton, where there was a better market for manufactures, and which was far healthier than Dartmoor, the tone of the prison was quite lively and hopeful. This rumour, however, proved to be unfounded, but it was announced that henceforth the prisoners would be occupied in work outside the prison walls, such as the building of the new church, repairing roads, and in certain trades.

On July 3, 1814, two *Argus* men fought. One killed the other and was committed to Exeter for manslaughter.

On July 4, Independence Day celebrations were allowed, and money being comparatively abundant, a most successful banquet on soup and beef was held.

On July 8, a prisoner, James Hart, died, and over his burial-place the following epitaph was raised:

'Your country mourns your hapless fate,

So mourn we prisoners all;

You've paid the debt we all must pay,

Each sailor great and small.

Your body on this barren moor,

Your soul in Heaven doth rest;

Where Yankee sailors one and all,

Hereafter will be blest.'

The prison was much crowded in this year, 1814; in No. 4 barrack alone there were 1,500 prisoners, and yet the new doctor, Magrath, who is described by Andrews as being both skilful and humane, gave very strong testimony to its healthiness.

In reply to a general petition from the prisoners for examination into their grievances, a Commission was sent to Dartmoor in 1813, and the next year reported that the only complaints partially justifiable were that of overcrowding, which was largely due to the preference of the prisoners for the new buildings with wooden floors, which were finished in the summer of 1812; and that of the 'Partial Exchange', which meant that whereas French privateers when they captured a British ship, landed or put the crew in a neutral ship and kept the officers, British captors kept all.

Two desperate and elaborate attempts at escape by tunnelling were made by American prisoners in 1814. Digging was done in three barracks simultaneously—from No. 4, in which there were 1,200 men, from No. 5, which was empty, and from No. 6, lately opened and now holding 800 men—down in each case twenty feet, and then 250 feet of tunnel in an easterly direction towards the road outside the boundary wall. On September 2 Captain Shortland, the new Agent, discovered it; some say it was betrayed to him, but the prisoners themselves attributed it to indiscreet talking. The enormous amount of soil taken out was either thrown into the stream running through the prison, or was used for plastering walls which were under repair, coating it with whitewash.

When the excitement attendant on this discovery had subsided, the indefatigable Americans got to work again. The discovered shafts having been partially blocked by the authorities with large stones, the plotters started another tunnel from the vacant No. 5 prison, to connect with the old one beyond the point of stoppage. Mr. Basil Thomson has kindly allowed me to publish an interesting discovery relative to this, made in December, 1911:

'While excavating for the foundations of the new hall at Dartmoor, which is being built on the site of IV. A and B Prison, the excavators broke into what proved to be one of the subterranean passages which were secretly dug by the American prisoners in 1814 with a view to escape. Number IV Prison, then known as Number V, was at that time empty, and, as Charles Andrews tells us, the plan was to tunnel under the boundary walls and then, armed with daggers forged at the blacksmith's shop, to emerge on a stormy night and make for Torbay, where there were believed to be fishing boats sufficient to take them to the French coast. No one was to be taken alive. The scheme was betrayed by a prisoner named Bagley (of Portsmouth, New Hampshire), who, to save him from the fury of the prisoners, was liberated and sent home.... One of these tunnels was disclosed when the foundation of IV. C Hall were dug in 1881. The tunnel found last month may have been the excavation made after the first shaft had been filled up. It was 14 feet below the floor of the prison, 3 feet in height, and 4 feet wide. More than one person explored it on hands and knees as far as it went, which was about 20 feet in the direction of the boundary wall. A marlin spike and a ship's scraper of ancient pattern were found among the débris, and are now in the Prison Museum.'

At this time (Sept. 1814) there were 3,500 American prisoners at Dartmoor, and so constant were they in their petty annoyance, almost persecution, of their guardians; so independent were they of rules and regulations; so constant with their petitions, remonstrances, and complaints; so untiring in their efforts to escape; so averse to anything like settling down and making the best of things, as did the French, that the authorities declared they would rather be in charge of 20,000 Frenchmen than of 2,000 Americans.

After the above-related attempts to escape, the prisoners were confined to Nos. 2 and 3 barracks, and put on two-thirds ration allowance to pay for damage done.

In October, 1814, eight escaped by bribing the sentries to procure them military coats and caps, and so getting off at night. Much amusement, too, was caused one evening by the jangling of the alarm bells, the hurrying of soldiers to quarters, and subsequent firing at a 'prisoner' escaping over the inner wall—the 'prisoner' being a dummy dressed up.

In November, 5,000 more prisoners came into the prison. There was much suffering this winter from the cold and scanty clothing. A petition to have fires in the barracks was refused. A man named John Taylor, a native citizen of New York City, hanged himself in No. 5 prison on the evening of December 1.

Peace, which had been signed at Ghent on December 24, 1814, was declared at Dartmoor, and occasioned general jubilation. Flags with 'Free Trade and Sailors' Rights' thereon paraded with music and cheering, and Shortland politely requested that they should be withdrawn, but met with a flat refusal. Unfortunately much of unhappy moment was to happen between the date of the ratification of the Treaty of Ghent in March, 1815, and the final departure of the prisoners. Beasley was unaccountably negligent and tardy in his arrangements for the reception and disposal of the prisoners, so that although *de jure* they were free men, *de facto* they were still detained and treated as prisoners. Small-pox broke out, and it was only by the unwearying devotion and activity of Dr. Magrath, the prison surgeon, that the epidemic was checked, and that the prisoners were dissuaded from going further than giving Beasley a mock trial and burning him in effigy.

On April 20, 1815, 263 ragged and shoeless Americans quitted Dartmoor, leaving 5,193 behind. The remainder followed in a few days, marching to Plymouth, carrying a huge white flag on which was represented the goddess of Liberty, sorrowing over the tomb of the killed Americans, with the legend: 'Columbia weeps and will remember!' Before the prisoners left, they testified their gratitude to Dr. Magrath for his unvarying kindness to them, by an address.

'Greenhorn,' another American, gives little details about prison life at Dartmoor, which are interesting as supplementary to the fuller book of Andrews.

'Greenhorn' landed at Plymouth on January 30, 1815, after the Treaty of Ghent had been signed, but before its ratification, and was marched via Mannamead, Yelverton, and the Dursland Inn to Dartmoor.

He describes the inmates of the American 'Rough Alleys' as corresponding in a minor degree to the French 'Romans', the principal source of their poverty being a gambling game known as 'Keno'.

He says—and it may be noted—that he found the food at Dartmoor good, and more abundant than on board ship. The American prisoners kept Sunday strictly, all buying, selling, and gambling was suspended by public opinion, and every man dressed in his cleanest and best, and spent the day quietly. He speaks of the great popularity of Dr. Magrath, although he made vaccination compulsory. Ship-model making was a chief industry. The Americans settled their differences in Anglo-Saxon fashion, the chief fighting-ground being in Bath Alley. Announcements of these and of all public meetings and entertainments were made by a well-known character, 'Old Davis,' in improvised rhyme. Another character was the pedlar Frank Dolphin.

In dress, it was the aim of every one to disguise the hideous prison-garb as much as possible, the results often being ludicrous in the extreme.

Everybody was more or less busy. There were schoolmasters and music teachers, a band, a boxing academy, a dancing school, a glee-club, and a theatre. There were straw-basket making, imitation Chinese wood-carving, and much false coining, the lead of No. 6 roof coming in very handy for this trade. Washermen charged a halfpenny a piece, or one penny including soap and starch.

No. 4 was the bad prison—the Ball Alley of the roughs. Each prison, except No. 4, was managed by a committee of twelve, elected by the inmates. From their decisions there was no appeal. Gambling was universal, ranging from the penny 'sweet-cloth' to *Vingt-et-un*. Some of the play was high, and money was abundant, as many of the privateersmen had their prize-money. One man possessed £1,100 on Monday, and on Thursday he could not buy a cup of coffee. The rule which precluded from the privilege of parole all but the masters and first mates of privateers of fourteen guns and upwards brought a number of well-to-do men into the prison, and, moreover, the American Government allowance of 2½d. a day for soap, coffee, and tobacco, circulated money.

The following notes from the *Journal of a Young Man of Massachusetts*, Benjamin Waterhouse by name, whom we have already met on the Chatham hulks, are included, as they add a few details of life at Dartmoor to those already given.

Waterhouse says:

'I shall only say that I found it, take it all in all, a less disagreeable prison than the ships; the life of a prudent, industrious, well-behaved man might here be rendered pretty easy, for a prison life, as was the case with some of our own countrymen and some Frenchmen; but the young, the idle, the giddy, fun-making youth generally reaped such fruit as he sowed. Gambling was the wide inlet to vice and disorder, and in this Frenchmen took the lead. These men would play away everything they possessed beyond the clothes to keep them decent. They have been known to game away a month's provision, and when they had lost it, would shirk and steal for a month after for their subsistence. A man with some money in his pocket might live pretty well through the day in Dartmoor Prison, there being shops and stalls where every little article could be obtained; but added to this we had a good and constant market, and the bread and meat supplied by Government were not bad; and as good I presume as that given to British prisoners by our own Government.'

BONE MODEL OF GUILLOTINE

Made by prisoners of war at Dartmoor

He speaks very highly of the tall, thin, one-eyed Dr. Magrath, the prison doctor, but of his Scots assistant, McFarlane, as a rough, inhuman brute. Shortland, the governor, he describes as one who apparently revelled in the misery and discomfort of the prisoners under his charge, although in another place he defines him as a man, not so much bad-hearted, as an ill-educated, tactless boor.

Waterhouse describes the peculiarly harsh proceeding of Shortland after the discovery of the tunnel dug from under No. 6 caserne. All the prisoners with their baggage were driven into the yard of No. 1: thence in a few days to another yard, and so on from yard to yard, so that they could not get time to dig tunnels; at the same time they were subjected to all kinds of petty bullyings, such as being kept waiting upon numbering days in the open, in inclement weather, until Shortland should choose to put in an appearance. On one of these occasions the Americans refused to wait, and went back to their prisons, for which offence the market was stopped for two days.

At the end of 1814 there were at Dartmoor 2,350 Americans. There seemed to be much prosperity in the prison: the market was crowded with food, and hats and boots and clothes; Jew traders did a roaring trade in watches, seals, trinkets, and bad books; sharp women also were about, selling well-watered milk at 4$d.$ a gallon; the 'Rough Alleys' were in great strength, and kept matters lively all over the prison.

Number 4 caserne was inhabited by black prisoners, whose ruler was 'King Dick,' a giant six feet five inches in height, who, with a huge bearskin hat on head, and a thick club in hand, exercised regal sway, dispensing justice, and, strange to say, paying strict attention to the cleanliness of his subjects' berths. Nor was religion neglected in No. 4, for every Sunday 'Priest Simon' preached, assisted by 'Deacon John', who had been a servant in the Duke of Kent's household, and who at first urged that Divine Service should be modelled on that customary on British men-of-war and in distinguished English families, but was overruled by the decision of a Methodist preacher from outside. 'King Dick' always attended service in full state. He also kept a boxing school, and in No. 4 were also professors of dancing and music and fencing, who had many white pupils, besides theatricals twice a week, performed with ludicrous solemnity by the black men, whose penchant was for serious and tragical dramas. Other dramatic performances were given by an Irish Regular regiment from Spain, which relieved the Derby Militia garrison, in the cock-loft of No. 6 caserne, the admission thereto being 6$d.$

Still, there was much hunger, and when it was rumoured that Jew clothes-merchants in the market were dealing with undue sharpness with unfortunate venders, a raid was made by the Americans upon their stalls and booths which wrought their destruction.

Beasley was still a *bête noire*. His studied neglect of the interests of those whose interests were in his charge, his failure to acquaint himself by personal attention with their complaints, made him hated far more than were the British officials, excepting Shortland. One day he was tried in effigy, and sentenced to be hung and burnt. A pole was rigged from the roof of No. 7 caserne, Beasley's effigy was hung therefrom, was cut down by a negro, taken away by the 'Rough Alleys', and burnt. On the same day, 'Be you also ready' was found painted on the wall of Shortland's house. He said to a friend:

'I never saw or ever read or heard of such a set of Devil-daring, God-provoking fellows, as these same Yankees. I had rather have the charge of 5,000 Frenchmen, than 500 of these sons of liberty; and yet I love the dogs better than I do the d——d frog-eaters.'

On March 20, 1815, came the Ratification of Peace, but, although this made the Americans virtually free men, much of a lamentable nature was to happen ere they practically became so.

As is so often the case in tragedy, a comparatively trifling incident brought it about.

On April 4, 1815, the provision contractors thought to get rid of their stock of hard bread (biscuit) which they held in reserve by serving it out to the prisoners instead of the fresh bread which was their due. The Americans refused to have it, swarmed round the bakeries on mischief intent, and refused to disperse when ordered to. Shortland was away in Plymouth at the time, and the officer in charge, seeing that it was useless to attempt to force them with only 300 Militia at his command, yielded, and the prisoners got their bread. When Shortland returned, he was very angry at what he deemed the pusillanimous action of his subordinate, swore that if he had been there the Yankees should have been brought to order at the point of the bayonet, and determined to create an opportunity for revenge.

This came on April 6. According to the sworn testimony of witnesses at the subsequent inquiry, some boys playing at ball in the yard of No. 7 caserne, knocked a ball over into the neighbouring barrack yard, and, upon the sentry on duty there refusing to throw it back, made a hole in the wall, crept through it, and got the ball. Shortland pretended to see in this hole-making a project to escape, and made his arrangements to attract all the prisoners out of their quarters by ringing the alarm bell, and, in order to prevent their escape back into them, had ordered that one of the two doors in each caserne should be closed, although it was fifteen minutes before the regulation lock-up time at 6 o'clock. It was sworn that he had said: 'I'll fire the d——d rascals presently.'

At 6 p.m. the alarm bell brought the prisoners out of all the casernes—wherein they were quietly settled—to see what was the cause. In the market square were 'several hundred' soldiers, with Shortland at their head, and at the same time many soldiers were being posted in the inner wall commanding the prison yards. One of these, according to a witness, called out to the crowd of prisoners to go indoors as they would be charged on very soon. This occasioned confusion and alarm and some running about. What immediately followed is not very clear, but it was sworn that Shortland ordered the soldiers to charge the prisoners huddled in the market square; that the soldiers—men of the Somerset Militia—hesitated; that the order was repeated, and the soldiers charged the prisoners, who retreated into the prison gates; that Shortland ordered the gates to be opened, and that the consequent confusion among hundreds of men vainly trying to get into the casernes by the one door of each left open, and being pushed back by others coming out to see what was the matter, was wilfully magnified by Shortland into a concerted attempt to break out, and he gave the word to fire.

It was said that, seeing a hesitation among his officers to repeat the command, Shortland himself seized a musket from a soldier and fired the first shot. Be that as it may, the firing became general from the walls as well as from the square; soldiers came to the doors of two of the casernes and fired through them, with the result, according to American accounts, that seven men were killed, thirty were dangerously wounded, and thirty slightly wounded; but according to the Return signed by Shortland and Dr. Magrath, five were killed and twenty-eight wounded.

A report was drawn up, after the inquiry instituted directly following the event, by Admiral Duckworth and Major-General Brown, and signed by the Assistant Commissioners at the Inquiry, King for the United States, and Larpent for Great Britain, which came to no satisfactory conclusion. It was evident, it said, that the prisoners were in an excited state about the non-arrival of ships to take them home, and that Shortland was irritated about the bread affair; that there was much unauthorized firing, but that it was difficult exactly to apportion blame. This report was utterly condemned by the committee of prisoners, who resented the tragedy being styled 'this unfortunate affair', reproached King for his lack of energy and unwarrantable self-restraint, and complained of the hurried and imperfect way in which the inquiry was conducted and the evidence taken. At this distance of time an Englishman may ask: 'If it was known that peace between the two countries had been ratified on March 20, how came it that Americans were still kept in confinement and treated as prisoners of war on April 6?' On the other hand, it is hardly possible to accept the American view that the tragedy was the deliberate work of an officer of His Majesty's service in revenge for a slight.

By July, 1815, all the Americans but 450 had left, and the last Dartmoor war-prisoners, 4,000 Frenchmen, taken at Ligny, came in. These poor fellows were easy to manage after the Americans; 2,500 of them came from Plymouth with only 300 Militiamen as guard, whilst for Americans the rule was man for man.

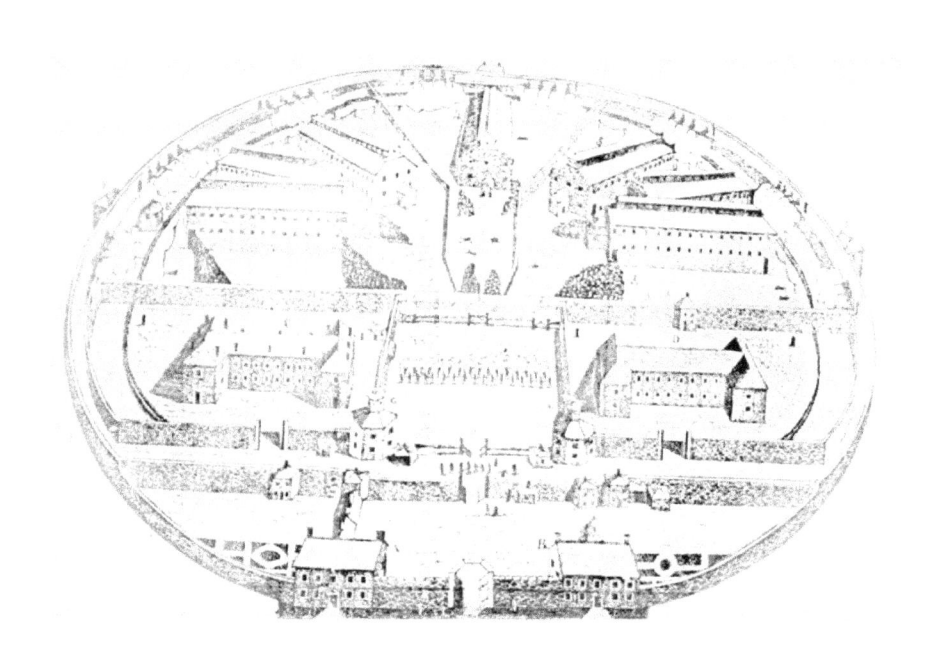

Dartmoor Prison

Illustrating the 'Massacre' of 1815

A. Surgeon's House. B. Captain Shortland's House. C. Hospital. D. Barracks. E. *Cachot*, or Black Hole. F. Guard Houses. G. Store Houses.

The last war-prisoners left Dartmoor in December, 1815, and from this time until 1850 it was unoccupied, which partially accounts for the utter desecration of the burial-ground, until, under Captain Stopforth, it was tidied up in garden fashion, divided into two plots, one for Americans, the other for Frenchmen, in the centre of each of which was placed a memorial obelisk in 1865.

The present church at Princetown was built by war-prisoners, the stone-work being done by the French, the wood-work by the Americans. The East Window bears the following inscription:

'To the Glory of God and in memory of the American Prisoners of War who were detained in the Dartmoor War Prison between the years 1809 and 1815, and who helped to build this Church, especially of the 218 brave men who died here on behalf of their country. This Window is presented by the National Society of United States Daughters of 1812. Dulce est pro patria mori.'

CHAPTER XIX
SOME MINOR PRISONS

As has been already stated, before the establishment of regular prisons became a necessity by the increasing flow of prisoners of war into Britain, accommodation for these men had to be found or made wherever it was possible. With some of these minor prisons I shall deal in this chapter.

WINCHESTER

Measured by the number of prisoners of war confined here, Winchester assuredly should rank as a major establishment, but it seems to have been regarded by the authorities rather as a receiving-house or a transfer office than as a real prisoner settlement, possibly because the building utilized—a pile of barracks which was originally intended by Charles the Second to be a palace on the plan of Versailles, but which was never finished, and which was known as the King's House Prison—was not secure enough to be a House of Detention. It was burned down in 1890.

In 1756 there were no less than 5,000 prisoners at Winchester. In 1761 the order for the withdrawal of the military from the city because of the approaching elections occasioned much alarm, and brought vigorous protests from leading inhabitants on account of the 4,000 prisoners of war who would be left practically unguarded, especially as these men happened to be just then in a ferment of excitement, and a general outbreak among them was feared. Should this take place, it was represented that nothing could prevent them from communicating with the shipping in Southampton River, and setting free their countrymen prisoners at Portchester and Forton Hospital, Gosport.

In 1779 Howard visited Winchester. This was the year when the patients and crew of a captured French hospital ship, the *Ste. Julie*, brought fever into the prison, causing a heavy mortality.

Howard reported that 1,062 prisoners were confined here, that the wards were lofty and spacious, the airing yards large, that the meat and beer were good, but that the bread, being made with leaven, and mixed with rye, was not so good as that served out to British prisoners. He recommended that to prevent the prisoners from passing their days lying indolently in their hammocks, work-rooms should be provided. Several prisoners, at the time of his visit, were in the Dark Hole for attempting to escape, and he observed that to be condemned to forty days' confinement on half-rations in order to pay the ten shillings reward to the men who apprehended them seemed too severe. The hospital ward was lofty and twenty feet wide. Each patient had a cradle, bedding, and sheets, and the attendance of the doctor was very good. He spoke highly of Smith, the Agent, but recommended a more regular system of War-Prison inspection.

Forgery was a prevalent crime among the Winchester prisoners. In 1780 two prisoners gave information about a systematic manufacture of false passports in the prison, and described the process. They also revealed the existence of a false key by which prisoners could escape into the fields, the maker of which had disappeared. They dared not say more, as they were suspected by their fellow-prisoners of being informers, and prayed for release as reward.

To the letter conveying this information the Agent appended a note:

'I have been obliged this afternoon to take Honoré Martin and Apert out of the prison that they may go away with the division of prisoners who are to be discharged to-morrow, several prisoners having this morning entered the chamber in which they sleep, with naked knives, declaring most resolutely they were determined to murder them if they could find them, to prevent which their liberty was granted.'

In 1810 two prisoners were brought to Winchester to be hanged for forging seven-shilling pieces. I think this must be the first instance of prisoners of war being hanged for forgery.

ROSCROW AND KERGILLIACK, NEAR PENRYN, CORNWALL

In spite of the great pains I have taken to get information about these two neighbouring prisons, the results are most meagre. Considering that there were war-prisoners there continuously from the beginning of the Seven Years' War in 1756 until the end of the century, that there were 900 prisoners at Roscrow, and 600 at Kergilliack, it is surprising how absolutely the memory of their sojourn has faded away locally, and how little information I have been able to elicit concerning them from such authorities on matters Cornish as Mr. Thurstan Peter, Sir Arthur Quiller-Couch, Mr. Otho Peter, and Mr. Vawdrey of St. Budock. The earliest document referring to these prisoners which I have found is a letter of thanks from the prisoners at Kergilliack in 1757, for the badly needed reform of the hospital, but I do not think that the two places ranked amongst the regular war-prisons until twenty years later. At no time were they much more than adapted farms. Roscrow consisted of a mansion, in a corner of which was a public-house, to which a series of substantial farm-buildings was attached, which, when surrounded by a wall, constituted the prison. Kergilliack, or Regilliack, as I have seen it written, was of much the same character.[11]

In 1797 the Roscrow prisoners, according to documents I found at the Archives Nationales in Paris, were nearly all privateersmen. Officers and men were herded together, which the former deeply resented; as they did much else, such as being bullied by a low class of jailers, the badness of the supplies, the rottenness of the shoes served out to them, the crowded sleeping accommodation, the dirt, and lastly the fact that pilchards formed a chief part of their diet.

In this year a Guernsey boy named Hamond revealed to the authorities a mine under the foundation of the house, five feet below the ground and four feet in diameter, going out twenty yards towards the inside fence. He had found the excavated earth distributed among the prisoners' hammocks, and told the turnkey. He was instantly removed, as he would certainly have been murdered by the other prisoners.

The tunnel was a wonder of skill and perseverance. It was said that the excavators had largely worked with nothing but their hands, and that their labour had been many times increased by the fact that in order to avoid the constant occurrence of rock they had been obliged to make a winding course.

Complaints increased: the bad bread was often not delivered till 5 p.m. instead of 8 a.m., the beer was undrinkable, and the proportion of bone to meat in the weighed allowance ridiculous. The Agent paying no attention to reiterated complaints, the following petition, signed at Kergilliack as well as at Roscrow, was sent to the Transport Office Commissioners for 'that redress which we have a right to expect from Mr. Bannick's [the Agent] exertions on our behalf; but, unfortunately for us, after making repeated applications to him whenever chance threw him in our way, as he seldom visited the prison, we have the mortification of finding that our reasonable and just remonstrances have been treated with the most forbidding frowns and the distant arrogance of the most arbitrary Despot when he has been presented with a sample of bread delivered to us, or rather, rye, flour, and water cemented together, and at different times, and as black as our shoes.

(Signed)

'THE GENERAL BODY OF FRENCH OFFICERS

CONFINED IN ROSCROW PRISON.'

A further remonstrance was set forth that the Agent and his son, who was associated with him, were bullies; that the surgeon neglected his duties; and that the living and sleeping quarters were bad and damp.

The only result I can find of these petitions, is a further exasperation of the prisoners by the stopping of all exchange privileges of those who had signed them.

The following complaints about the hospital at Falmouth in the year 1757 I have placed at the end of this notice, as I cannot be sure that they were formulated by, or had anything to do with, foreign prisoners of war. From the fact that they are included among a batch of documents at the Record Office dealing with prisoners of war, I think it is quite possible that they may be associated with them, inasmuch as Falmouth, like Dover, Deal, and other coast ports, was a sort of receiving office for prisoners captured on privateers, previous to their disposal elsewhere.

It was complained that:

1.

No bouillon was served if no basin was brought: the allowance being one small basin in 24 hours.

2.

Half the beds had no sheets, and what sheets there were had not been changed for six months.

3.

Beds were so scarce that new arrivals were kept waiting in the open yards.

4.

The attendants were underpaid, and therefore useless.

5.

No bandages were supplied, so that the patients' own shirts had to be torn up to make them.

6.

Stimulants and meat were insufficient, and the best of what there was the attendants secured beforehand.

7.

Half-cured patients were often discharged to make room for others.

From what Mr. Vawdrey, the Vicar of St. Budock, Falmouth, has written to me, it is certain that French officers were on parole in different places of this neighbourhood. Tradition says that those who died were buried beneath a large tree on the right hand of the north entrance of the church. There are entries in the registers of the deaths of French prisoners, and, if there is no evidence of marriages, there is that 'some St. Budock girls appear to have made captivity more blessed for some of them'. Some people at Meudon in Mawnan, named Courage, farmers, trace their descent from a French lieutenant of that name. Mawnan registers show French names. Pendennis Castle was used as a war-prison, both for French from the Peninsula, and for Americans during the war of 1812.

SHREWSBURY

I am indebted to Mr. J. E. Anden, M.A., F.R. Hist. S., of Tong, Shifnal, for the following extracts from the diary of John Tarbuck, a shoemaker, of Shrewsbury:

'September, 1783. Six hundred hammocks were slung in the Orphan Hospital, from which all the windows were removed, to convert it into a

Dutch prison, and as many captive sailors marched in. Many of the townspeople go out to meet them, and amongst the rest Mr. Roger Yeomans, the most corpulent man in the country, to the no small mirth of the prisoners, who, on seeing him, gave a great shout: "Huzza les Anglais! Roast beef for ever!" This exclamation was soon verified to their satisfaction, as the Salop gentry made a subscription to buy them some in addition to that allowed by their victors, together with shoes, jackets, and other necessaries. 'Twas pleasing to see the poor creatures' gratitude, for they'd sing you their songs, tho' in a foreign land, and some companies of their youth would dance with amazing dexterity in figures totally unlike the English dances with a kind of regular confusion, yet with grace, ease, and truth to the music. I remember there was one black boy of such surprising agility that, had the person seen him, who, speaking against the Abolition of the slave-trade, said there was only a link between the human and the brute creation, it would have strengthened his favourite hypothesis, for he leaped about with more of the swiftness of the monkey than the man.

'I went one Sunday to Church with them, and I came away much more edified than from some sermons where I could tell all that was spoken. The venerable appearance and the devotion evident in every look and gesture of the preacher, joined to the grave and decent deportment of his hearers ... had a wonderful effect on my feelings and tended very much to solemnize my affections.

'May, 1785. Four of the Dutch prisoners escape by means of the privy and were never retaken. Many others enlist in the English service, and are hissed and shouted at by their fellows, and deservedly so. The Swedes and Norwegians among them are marched away (being of neutral nations) to be exchanged.'

A newspaper of July 1784 (?) says:

'On Thursday last an unfortunate affair happened at the Dutch Prison, Shrewsbury. A prisoner, behaving irregular, was desired by a guard to desist, which was returned by the prisoner with abusive language and blows, and the prisoner, laying hold of the Centinel's Firelock, forced off the bayonet, and broke the belt. Remonstrance proving fruitless, and some more of the Prisoners joining their stubborn countryman, the Centinel was obliged to draw back and fire among them, which killed one on the spot. The Ball went through his Body and wounded one more. The man that began the disturbance escaped unhurt.'

The prisoners left Shrewsbury about November 1785.

A correspondent of a Shrewsbury newspaper in 1911 writes:

'A generation ago there were people living who remembered the rebuilding of Montford Bridge by prisoners of war. They went out each Monday, tradition says, in carts and wagons, and were quartered there during the week in farm-houses and cottages near their work, being taken back to Shrewsbury at the end of each week.'

The correspondence evoked by this letter, however, sufficiently proved that this was nothing more than tradition.

YARMOUTH

Prisoners were confined here during the Seven Years' War, although no special buildings were set apart for their reception, and, as elsewhere, they were simply herded with the common prisoners in the ordinary lock-up. In 1758 numerous complaints came to the 'Sick and Hurt' Office from the prisoners here, about their bad treatment, the greed of the jailer, the bad food, the lack of medical attendance and necessaries, and the misery of being lodged with the lowest class of criminals. Prisoners who were seriously ill were placed in the prison hospital; the jailer used to intercept money contributed by the charitable for the benefit of the prisoners, and only paid it over after the deduction of a large commission. The straw bedding was dirty, scanty, and rarely changed; water had to be paid for, and there was hardly any airing ground.

After the building of Norman Cross Prison, Yarmouth became, like Deal and Falmouth, a mere receiving port, but an exceedingly busy one, the prisoners being landed there direct from capture, and generally taken on by water to Lynn, whence they were conveyed by canal to Peterborough.

From the *Norwich Mercury* of 1905 I take the following notes on Yarmouth by the late Rev. G. N. Godwin:

'Columns of prisoners, often 1,000 strong, were marched from Yarmouth to Norwich, and were there lodged in the Castle. They frequently expressed their gratitude for the kindness shown them by the Mayor and citizens. One smart privateer captain coolly walked out of the Castle in the company of some visitors, and, needless to say, did not return.

'From Yarmouth they were marched to King's Lynn, halting at Costessy, Swanton Mosley (where their "barracks" are still pointed out), East Dereham, where some were lodged in the detached church tower, and thence to Lynn. Here they were lodged in a large building, afterwards used as a warehouse, now pulled down. [For a further reference to East Dereham and its church tower, see p. 453.]

'At Lynn they took water, and were conveyed in barges and lighters through the Forty Foot, the Hundred Foot, the Paupers' Cut, and the Nene to Peterborough, whence they marched to Norman Cross.

'In 1797, 28 prisoners escaped from the gaol at Yarmouth by undermining the wall and the row adjoining. All but five of them were retaken. In the same year 4 prisoners broke out of the gaol, made their way to Lowestoft, where they stole a boat from the beach, and got on board a small vessel, the crew of which they put under the hatches, cut the cable, and put out to sea. Seven hours later the crew managed to regain the deck, a rough and tumble fight ensued, one of the Frenchmen was knocked overboard, and the others were ultimately lodged in Yarmouth gaol.'

Edinburgh

For the following details about a prison which, although of importance, cannot from its size be fairly classed among the chief Prisoners of War dépôts of Britain, I am largely indebted to the late Mr. Macbeth Forbes, who most generously gave me permission to use freely his article in the *Bankers' Magazine* of March 1899. I emphasize his liberality inasmuch as a great deal of the information in this article is of a nature only procurable by one with particular and peculiar facilities for so doing. I allude to the system of bank-note forgery pursued by the prisoners.

Edinburgh Castle was first used as a place of confinement for prisoners of war during the Seven Years' War, and, like Liverpool, this use was made of it chiefly on account of its convenient proximity to the waters haunted by privateers. The very first prisoners brought in belonged to the *Chevalier Bart* privateer, captured off Tynemouth by H.M.S. *Solebay*, in April 1757, the number of them being 28, and in July of the same year a further 108 were added.

'In the autumn of 1759 a piteous appeal was addressed to the publishers of the *Edinburgh Evening Courant* on behalf of the French prisoners of war in Edinburgh Castle by one who "lately beheld some hundreds of French prisoners, many of them about naked (some without any other clothing but shirts and breeches and even these in rags), conducted along the High Street to the Castle." The writer says that many who saw the spectacle were moved to tears, and he asked that relief might be given by contributing clothing to these destitute men. This letter met with a favourable response from the citizens, and a book of subscriptions was opened forthwith. The prisoners were visited and found to number 362. They were reported to be "in a miserable condition, many almost naked," and winter approaching. There were, however, revilers of this charitable movement, who said that the public were being imposed upon; that the badly clothed were idle fellows who disposed of their belongings; that they had been detected in the Castle cutting their shoes, stockings, and hammocks into pieces, in the prospect of getting these articles renewed. "One fellow, yesterday, got twenty bottles of ale for a suit of clothes given him by the good people of the town in charity, and this he boasted of to one of the servants in the sutlery."

'The promoters of the movement expressed their "surprise at the endeavours used to divert the public from pursuing so humane a design.".... They also pointed out that the prisoners only received an allowance of 6*d*. a day, from which the contractor's profit was taken, so that little remained for providing clothes. An estimate was obtained of the needs of the prisoners, and a list drawn up of articles wanted. Of the 362 persons confined 8 were officers, whose subsistence money was 1s. a day, and they asked no charity of the others; no fewer than 238 had no shirt, and 108 possessed only one. Their other needs were equally great. The "City Hospitals for Young Maidens" offered to make shirts for twopence each, and sundry tailors to make a certain number of jackets and breeches for nothing. The prisoners had an airing ground, but as it was necessary to obtain permission before visiting them, the chance they had of disposing of any of their work was very slight indeed.'

William Fergusson, clerk to Dr. James Walker, the Agent for the prisoners of war in the Castle, described as a man of fine instincts, seems to have been one of the few officials who, brought into daily contact with the prisoners, learned to sympathize with them, and to do what lay in their power to mitigate the prisoners' hard lot.

Early in May 1763, the French prisoners in the Castle, numbering 500, were embarked from Leith to France, the Peace of Paris having been concluded.

During the Revolutionary War with France, Edinburgh Castle again received French prisoners, mostly, as before, privateersmen, the number between 1796 and 1801 being 1,104. In the later Napoleonic wars the Castle was the head-quarters of Scotland for distributing the prisoners, the commissioned officers to the various parole towns of which notice will be taken in the chapters treating of the paroled prisoners in Scotland, and the others to the great dépôts at Perth and Valleyfield. We shall see when we come to deal with the paroled foreign officers in Scotland in what pleasant places, as a rule, their lines were cast, and how effectively they contrived to make the best of things, but it was very much otherwise with the rank and file in confinement.

'An onlooker', says Mr. Forbes, 'has described the appearance of the prisoners at Edinburgh Castle. He says:—These poor men were allowed to work at their tasteful handicrafts in small sheds or temporary workshops at the Castle, behind the palisades which separated them from their free customers outside. There was just room between the bars of the palisade for them to hand through their exquisite work, and to receive in return the modest prices which they charged. As they sallied forth from their dungeons, so they returned to them at night. The dungeons, partly rock and partly masonry, of Edinburgh Castle, are historic spots which appeal alike to the sentiment and the imagination. They are situate in the south and east of the Castle, and the date of them goes far back.' It is unnecessary to describe what may still be seen, practically unchanged since the great war-times, by every visitor to Edinburgh.

In 1779 Howard visited Edinburgh during his tour round the prisons of Britain. His report is by no means bad. He found sixty-four prisoners in two rooms formerly used as barracks; in one room they lay in couples in straw-lined boxes against the wall, with two coverlets to each box. In the other room they had hammocks duly fitted with mattresses. The regulations were hung up according to law—an important fact, inasmuch as in other prisons, such as Pembroke, where the prison agents purposely omitted to hang them up, the prisoners remained in utter ignorance of their rights and their allowances. Howard reported the provisions to be all good, and noted that at the hospital house some way off, where were fourteen sick prisoners, the bedding and sheets were clean and sufficient, and the medical attention good.

This satisfactory state of matters seems to have lasted, for in 1795 the following letter was written by the French prisoners in the Castle to General Dundas:

'Les prisonniers de guerre français détenus au château d'Edinburgh ne peuvent que se louer de l'attention et du bon traitement qu'ils ont reçu de Com.-Gén. Dundas et officiers des brigades Écossoises, en foi de quoi nous livrons le présent.

'FR. LEROY.'

Possibly the ancient *camaraderie* of the Scots and French nations may have had something to do with this pleasant condition of things, for in 1797 Dutch prisoners confined in the Castle complained about ill treatment and the lack of clothing, and the authorities consented to their being removed to 'a more airy and comfortable situation at Fountainbridge'.

In 1799 the Rev. Mr. FitzSimmons, of the Episcopal Chapel, an Englishman, was arraigned before the High Court of Justiciary for aiding in the escape of four French prisoners from the Castle, by concealing them in his house, and taking them to a Newhaven fishing boat belonging to one Neil Drysdale, which carried them to the Isle of Inchkeith, whence they escaped to France. Two of them had sawn through the dungeon bars with a sword-blade which they had contrived to smuggle in. The other two were parole prisoners. He was sentenced to three months' imprisonment in the Tolbooth.

A French prisoner in 1799, having learned at what hour the dung which had been collected in the prison would be thrown over the wall, got himself put into the hand-barrow used for its conveyance, was covered over with litter, and was thrown down several feet; but, being discovered by the sentinels in his fall, they presented their pieces while he was endeavouring to conceal himself. The poor bruised and affrighted fellow supplicated for mercy, and waited on his knees until his jailers came up to take him back to prison.

In 1811 forty-nine prisoners contrived to get out of the Castle at one time. They cut a hole through the bottom of the parapet wall at the south-west corner, below the 'Devil's Elbow,' and let themselves down by a rope which they had been smuggling in by small sections for weeks previously. One man lost his hold, and fell, and was mortally injured. Five were retaken the next day, and fourteen got away along the Glasgow road. Some were retaken later near Linlithgow in the Polmount plantations, exhausted with hunger. They had planned to get to Grangemouth, where they hoped to get on board a smuggler. They confessed that the plot was of long planning. Later still, six more were recaptured. They had made for Cramond, where they had stolen a boat, sailed up the Firth, and landed near Hopetoun House, intending to go to Port Glasgow by land. These poor fellows said that they had lived for three days on raw turnips. Not one of the forty-nine got away.

I now come to the science of forgery as practised by the foreign prisoners of war in Scotland, and I shall be entirely dependent upon Mr. Macbeth Forbes for my information.

The Edinburgh prisoners were busy at this work between 1811 and the year of their departure, 1814.

The first reputed case was that of a Bank of Scotland one-guinea note, discovered in 1811. It was not a very skilful performance, for the forged note was three-fourths of an inch longer than the genuine, and the lettering on it was not engraved, but done with pen and printing ink. But this defect was remedied, for, three weeks after the discovery, the plate of a guinea note was found by the miller in the mill lade at Stockbridge (the north side of Edinburgh), in cleaning out the lade.

In 1812 a man was tried for the possession of six one-pound forged notes which had been found concealed between the sole of his foot and his stocking. His story as to how he came into possession of them seems to have satisfied the judge, and he was set free; but he afterwards confessed that he had received them from a soldier of the Cambridge Militia under the name of 'pictures' in the house of a grocer at Penicuik, near the Valleyfield Dépôt, and that the soldier had, at his, the accused man's, desire, purchased them for 2s. each from the prisoners.

In July 1812 seven French prisoners of war escaped from Edinburgh Tolbooth, whither they had been transferred from the Castle to take their trial for the forgery of bank-notes. 'They were confined', says a contemporary newspaper, 'in the north-west room on the third story, and they had penetrated the wall, though very thick, till they got into the chimney of Mr. Gilmour's shop (on the ground floor), into which they descended by means of ropes. As they could not force their way out of the shop, they ascended a small stair to the room above, from which they took out half the window and descended one by one into the street, and got clear off. In the course of the morning one of them was retaken in the Grass Market, being traced by the sooty marks of his feet. We understand that, except one, they all speak broken English. They left a note on the table of the shop saying that they had taken nothing away.'

Afterwards three of the prisoners were taken at Glasgow, and another in Dublin.

From the first discoveries of forgeries by prisoners of war, the Scottish banks chiefly affected by them had in a more or less satisfactory way combined to take steps to prevent and to punish forgeries, but it was not until they offered a reward of £100 for information leading to the discovery of persons forging or issuing their notes that a perceptible check to the practice was made. This advertisement was printed and put outside the dépôt walls for the militia on guard, a French translation was posted up inside for the prisoners, and copies of it were sent to the Agents at all parole towns. With reference to this last, let it be said to the credit of the foreign officers on parole, both in England and Scotland, that, although a Frenchman has written to the contrary, there are no more than two recorded instances of officers on parole being prosecuted or suspected of the forgery of bank-notes. (See pp. 320 and 439.) Of passport forgeries there are a few cases, and the forgery mentioned on p. 439 may have been of passports and not of bank-notes.

In addition, says Mr. Macbeth Forbes, the military authorities were continually on the *qui vive* for forgers. The governors of the different dépôts ordered the turnkeys to examine narrowly notes coming in and out of prison. The militiamen had also to be watched, as they acted so frequently as intermediaries, as for instance:

'In November 1813 Mr. Aitken, the keeper of the Canongate Tolbooth, detected and took from the person of a private soldier in a militia regiment stationed over the French prisoners in Penicuik, and who had come into the Canongate Prison to see a friend, forged guineas and twenty-shilling notes on two different banks in this city, and two of them in the country, amounting to nearly £70. The soldier was immediately given over to the civil power, and from thence to the regiment to which he belonged, until the matter was further investigated.'

In July 1813 the clerk of the Valleyfield Dépôt sent to the banks twenty-six forged guinea notes which were about to be sold, but were detected by the turnkey.

The Frenchmen seem to have chiefly selected for imitation the notes of the Bank of Scotland, and the Commercial Banking Company of Scotland, as these had little or no pictorial delineation, and consisted almost entirely of engraved penmanship. The forgers had to get suitable paper, and, as there were no steel pens in those days, a few crow quills served their purpose. They had confederates who watched the ins and outs of the turnkey; and, in addition to imitating the lettering on the face of the note, they had to forge the watermark, the seals of the bank, and the Government stamp. The bones of their ration food formed, literally, the groundwork of the forger's productions, and as these had to be properly scraped and smoothed into condition before being in a state to be worked upon with ordinary pocket-knives, if the result was often so crude as to deceive only the veriest yokel, the Scottish banks might be thankful that engraving apparatus was unprocurable.

The following advertisement of the Bank of Scotland emphasizes this crudity of execution:

'Several forged notes, in imitation of the notes of the governor and company of the Bank of Scotland, having appeared, chiefly in the neighbourhood of the dépôts of French prisoners of war, a caution is hereby, on the part of the said governors and company, given against receiving such forged notes in payment. And whoever shall, within three months from the date hereof, give such information as shall be found sufficient, on lawful trial, to convict any one concerned in forging or feloniously uttering any of the said notes, shall receive a reward of a hundred pounds sterling. These forged notes are executed by the hand with a pen or pencil, without any engraving. In most of them the body of the note has the appearance of foreign handwriting. The names of the bank officers are mostly illegible or ill-spelled. The ornamental characters of the figures generally ill-executed. The seals are very ill-imitated. To this mark particular attention is requested.'

The seals, bearing the arms of the Bank of Scotland, are of sheep's bone, and were impressed upon the note with a hammer, also probably of bone, since all metal tools were prohibited. The partially executed forgery of a Bank of Scotland guinea note shows the process of imitating the lettering on the note in dotted outline, for which the forgers had doubtless some good reason, which is not at once patent to us.

Until 1810 the punishment for forgery was the hulks. During that year the law in England took a less merciful view of the crime, and offenders were sentenced to death; and until 1829, when the last man was hanged for forgery, this remained the law.

As to Scotland Mr. Forbes says: 'The administration was probably not so severe as in England ... no French prisoner suffered anything more than a slight incarceration, and a subsequent relegation to the prison ships, where some thousands of his countrymen already were.'

Armed with a Home Office permit I visited the prisons in the rock of Edinburgh Castle. Owing to the facts that most of them have been converted into military storerooms and that their substance does not lend itself readily to destruction, they remain probably very much as when they were filled with the war-prisoners, and, with their heavily built doors and their strongly barred apertures, which cannot be called windows, their darkness and cold, the silence of their position high above even the roar of a great city, convey still to the minds of the visitors of to-day a more real impression of the meaning of the word 'imprisonment' than does any other war-prison, either extant or pictured. At Norman Cross, at Portchester, at Stapleton, at Dartmoor, at Perth, there were at any rate open spaces for airing grounds, but at Edinburgh there could have been none, unless the narrow footway, outside the line of caverns, from the wall of which the precipice falls sheer down, was so utilized.

Near the entrance to the French prisons the following names are visible on the wall:

Charles Jobien, Calais, 1780.

Morel de Calais, 1780.

1780. Proyol prisonnier nee natif de bourbonnais (?).

With the Peace of 1814 came the jail-delivery, and it caused one of the weirdest scenes known in that old High Street so inured to weird scenes. The French prisoners were marched down by torchlight to the transport at Leith, and thousands of citizens lined the streets. Down the highway went the liberated ones, singing the war-songs of the Revolution—the *Marseillaise* and the *Ça ira*. Wildly enthusiastic were the pale, haggard-looking prisoners of war, but the enthusiasm was not exhausted with them, for they had a great send-off from the populace.

In Sir T. E. Colebrooke's *Life of Mountstuart Elphinstone*, Mr. John Russell of Edinburgh writes that when he first knew Mountstuart, his father, Lord Elphinstone, was Governor of Edinburgh Castle, in which were confined a great number of French prisoners of war. With these prisoners the boy Mountstuart loved to converse, and, learning from them their revolutionary songs, he used to walk about singing the *Marseillaise*, *Ça ira*, and *Les Aristocrates à la Lanterne*, much to the disgust of the British officers, who, however, dared not check such a proceeding on the part of the son of the Governor. Mountstuart also wore his hair long in accordance with the revolutionary fashion.

CHAPTER XX
LOUIS VANHILLE: A FAMOUS ESCAPER

I devoted Chapter VII to the record of Tom Souville, a famous ship-prison-breaker, and in this I hope to give quite as interesting and romantic an account of the career of Louis Vanhille, who was remarkable in his method in that he seemed never to be in a hurry to get out of England, but actually to enjoy the power he possessed of keeping himself uninterfered with for a whole year in a country where the hue and cry after him was ceaseless.

At the outset I must make my acknowledgement to M. Pariset of the University of Nancy, for permission to use his monograph upon this really remarkable man.

Louis Vanhille, purser of the *Pandour* privateer, was sent to Launceston on parole May 12, 1806. He is described as a small man of thirty-two, of agreeable face and figure, although small-pox marked, fair as befitted his Flemish origin, and speaking English almost perfectly. He was socially gifted, he painted and caricatured, could dress hair, and could make mats, and weave bracelets in seventeen patterns. He was well-off to boot, as the *Pandour* had been a successful ship, and he had plenty of prize money.

In Launceston he lodged with John Tyeth, a pious Baptist brewer. Tyeth had three married daughters and two unmarried, Fanny and a younger, who kept the Post Office at Launceston. Although Tyeth was a Baptist, one of his daughters was married to Bunsell, the Rector of Launceston, so that decorum and preciseness prevailed in the local atmosphere, to which Vanhille politically adapted himself so readily as to become a convert to Tyeth's creed. In addition he paid marked attention to Miss Fanny, who was plain-looking but kept the Post Office; an action which occasioned watchfulness on the part of Tyeth *père*, who, in common with most Englishmen of his day, regarded all Frenchmen as atheists and revolutionaries. Vanhille's manner and accomplishments won him friends all round. Miss Johanna Colwell, an old maid, a sentimental worker of straw hats, who lived opposite the brewery, pitied him. Further on, at Mr. Pearson's, lodged Vanhille's great friend, Dr. Derouge, an army surgeon, who cured Vanhille of small-pox. Then there was Dr. Mabyn of Camelford, Dr. Frankland, R.N., John Rowe the tailor, Dale the ironmonger, who, although tradesmen, were of that well-to-do, highly respectable calibre which in old-time country towns like Launceston placed them on a footing of friendliness with the 'quality'. Vanhille seems to have settled himself down to become quite Anglicized, and to forget that he was a prisoner on parole, and that any such individual existed as Mr. Spettigue, the Agent. He went over to Camelford to dine with Dr. Mabyn; he rode to Tavistock on the Tyeth's pony to visit the Pearces, ironmongers of repute, and particularly to see the Misses Annie and Elizabeth Penwarden, gay young milliners who spoke French. He was also much in the society of Fanny Tyeth, made expeditions with her to see 'Aunt Tyeth' at Tavistock, and was regarded as her *fiancé*.

Dr. Derouge began to weary of captivity, and tried without success to get exchanged. The reason given for his non-success was that he had got a girl with child. Launceston was scandalized; only a Frenchman could do such a thing. The authorities had to find some one to pay for the child's subsistence as the mother could not afford to, and so Proctor, Guardian of the Poor, and Spettigue, the Agent, fastened it on Dr. Derouge, and he was ordered to pay £25. But he could not; so Vanhille, who had come into some money upon the death of his mother, paid it. What followed is not quite clear. In a letter dated December 5, 1811, Spettigue, in a letter to the Admiralty, says that Derouge and Vanhille tried to escape, but were prevented by information given by one Burlangier, 'garde-magasin des services réunis de l'armée de Portugal.' He reported their absences at Camelford, and finally they were ordered to Dartmoor on December 12, 1811. The Transport Office instructed Spettigue to keep a watch on Tyeth and others. Launceston was angry at this; it missed Derouge and Vanhille, and went so far as to get the Member of Parliament, Giddy, to address the Transport Office on the matter, and request their reinstatement on parole, but the reply was unsatisfactory.

At Dartmoor, Vanhille and Derouge were sent to the subalterns' quarters. Very soon the attractive personality of Vanhille led him to an influential position among the prisoners, and he was elected their representative in all matters of difference between them and the authorities, although Cotgrave, the Governor, refused to acknowledge him as such, saying that he preferred a prisoner of longer standing, and one whom he knew better.

Vanhille now determined to get out of Dartmoor. To reach France direct was difficult, but it was feasible by America, as he had a sister well married in New Orleans who could help him.

At the daily market held at the prison gate Vanhille became acquainted with Mary Ellis. Piece by piece she brought him from Tavistock a disguise—an old broad-brimmed hat, big boots, and brown stockings, and by August 21, 1812, he was ready. On that day he received from his comrades a sort of testimonial or letter of recommendation for use after his escape at any place where there might be Frenchmen:

'Le comité représentant les officiers militaires et marchands détenus dans la prison Royale de Dartmoor certifient que Louis Vanhille est un digne et loyal Français, et un compagnon d'infortune digne de tous les égards de ses compatriotes... pour lui servir et valoir ce que de raison en cas de mutation de prison.'

The next day he put on his disguise, mixed with the market folk, crossed the court of his quarter, and the market place, passed two sentries who took him for a potato merchant, got to the square in the middle of which were the Agent's house and offices, passed another gate, the sentry at which took no notice of him, turned sharp to the right by the stables and the water reservoir, and got on to the main road. He walked rapidly on towards Tavistock, and that night slept under the Tyeth roof at Launceston—a bold policy and only to be adopted by one who knew his ground thoroughly well, and who felt sure that he was safer, known in Launceston, than he would be as a stranger in Plymouth or other ports.

Next day he went to Camelford, and called on Dr. Mabyn, who said: 'Monsieur Vanhille, comme ami je suis heureux de vous voir, mais à présent je ne puis vous donner asile sous mon toit,' Thence he went to Padstow, but no boatman would take him to Bristol or Cork, so he returned to Launceston and remained there two days. Here he bought a map, changed his disguise, and became Mr. Williams, a pedlar of odds and ends. Thence he went on to Bideford, Appledore, and by boat to Newport, thence to Abergavenny, a parole town, where he met Palierne, an old Launceston comrade; thence back to Launceston, where he rested a couple of days. Then, always on foot, he went to Exeter, Okehampton, and Tawton, took wagon to London, where he only stayed a night, then on to Chatham—a dangerous neighbourhood on account of the hulks, and back to Abergavenny via Guildford, Petersfield, Alresford, Winchester, Salisbury, Warminster, Bath, and Bristol, arriving at Abergavenny on September 21, 1812.[12]

From Abergavenny Vanhille went by Usk to Bristol, but could find no suitable ship to take him to America, so he took coach back to Launceston, and spent two weeks there with the Tyeths, which would seem to show that Spettigue was either purposely blind or very stupid. Vanhille then crossed Cornwall rapidly to Falmouth—always, be it remembered, as a pedlar. Falmouth was a dangerous place, being the chief port for the Cartel service with Morlaix, and a strict look-out was kept there for passengers intending to cross the Channel. Vanhille went to the *Blue Anchor* Inn, and here he met the famous escape agent, Thomas Feast Moore, *alias* Captain Harman, &c., who at once recognized what he was, and proffered his services, stating that he had carried many French officers over safely. This was true, but what he omitted to state was that he was at present in the Government service, having been pardoned for his misdeeds as an escape agent on condition that he made use of his experience by giving the Government information about intending escapers.[13]

Vanhille wanted no aid to escape, but he cleared out from Falmouth at once, was that evening at Wadebridge, the next day at Saltash, then, avoiding Launceston, went by Okehampton, Moreton-Hampstead, and Exeter to Cullompton, and thence by coach to Bristol, where he arrived on October 15, 1812.

After his escape from Dartmoor, this extraordinary man had been fifty-five days travelling on foot, in carriage, and by boat, and had covered 1,238 miles, by far the greater number of which he tramped, and this with the hue and cry after him and offers of reward for his arrest posted up everywhere.

He now dropped the pedlar pretence and became an ordinary Briton. At Bristol he learned that the *Jane*, Captain Robert Andrews, would leave for Jamaica next month. He corresponded with his Launceston friends, who throughout had been true to him, and, in replying, the Tyeths had to be most careful, assuming signatures and disguising handwriting, and Miss Fanny at the Post Office would with her own hands obliterate the postmark. Old Tyeth sent him kind and pious messages. On November 10 the

Jane left Bristol, but was detained at Cork a month, waiting for a convoy, and did not reach Montego Bay, Jamaica, until January 2, 1813. From Jamaica there were frequent opportunities of getting to America, and Vanhille had every reason to congratulate himself at last on being a free man.

Unfortunately the Customs people in Jamaica were particularly on the alert for spies and runaways, especially as we were at war with the United States. Vanhille was suspected of being what he was, and the examination of his papers not being satisfactory, he was arrested and sent home, and on May 20, 1813, found himself a prisoner at Forton. He was sent up to London and examined by Jones, of Knight and Jones, solicitors to the Admiralty, with a view of extracting from him information concerning his accomplices in Launceston, a town notorious for its French proclivities.

Jones writes under date of June 14, 1813, to Bicknell, solicitor to the Transport Office, that he has examined Vanhille, who peremptorily refuses to make any disclosures which may implicate the persons concerned in harbouring him after he had escaped from Dartmoor, and who ultimately got him out of the kingdom. He hopes, however, to reach them by other means.

Harsh treatment was now tried upon him, he was half starved, and as he was now penniless could not remedy matters by purchase. In three weeks he was sent on board the *Crown Prince* hulk at Chatham, and later to the *Glory*. Correspondence between him and Dr. Derouge at Launceston was discovered, and Derouge was sent to a Plymouth hulk. Dale, the Launceston ironmonger, who had been one of the little friendly circle in that town, had fallen into evil ways, and was now starving in Plymouth. Jones, the Admiralty lawyer, received a communication from him saying that for a consideration he would denounce all Vanhille's friends. He was brought up to London, and he told all their names, with the result that they were summoned. But nothing could be got out of them. Mrs. Wilkins at the inn, who for some reason disliked Vanhille, would have given information, but she had none to give.

Dale was sent back to Plymouth, saying that if he could see Dr. Derouge, who would not suspect him, he would get the wanted information. So the two men met in a special cabin, and rum was brought. Derouge, unsuspecting, tells all the story of the escape from Dartmoor, and brings in the name of Mary Ellis, who had provided Vanhille with his disguise. Then he begins to suspect Dale's object, and will not utter another word.

Dale is sent to Launceston to get more information, but fails; resolves to find out Mary Ellis at Tavistock, but five weeks elapse, and no more is heard of him, except that he arrived there half dead with wet and fatigue.

The Peace of 1814 brought release to Vanhille, and on April 19 he reached Calais.

M. Pariset concludes his story with the following remark: 'Vanhille avait senti battre le cœur anglais qui est, comme chacun sait, bienveillant et fidèle, après qu'il s'est donné.'

I should here say that M. Pariset's story does not go further than the capture of Vanhille in Jamaica. The sequel I have taken from the correspondence at the Record Office. I have been told that the name of Vanhille is by no means forgotten in Launceston.

CHAPTER XXI
THE PRISON SYSTEM
PRISONERS ON PAROLE

When we come to the consideration of the parole system, we reach what is for many reasons the most interesting chapter in a dark history. Life on the hulks and in the prisons was largely a sealed book to the outside public, and, brutal in many respects as was the age covered by our story, there can be little question that if the British public had been made more aware of what went on behind the wooden walls of the prison ships and the stone walls of the prisons, its opinion would have demanded reforms and remedies which would have spared our country from a deep, ineffaceable, and, it must be added, a just reproach.

But the prisoners on parole played a large part in the everyday social life of many parts of England, Wales, and Scotland, for at least sixty years—a period long enough to leave a clear impression behind of their lives, their romances, their virtues, their vices, of all, in fact, which makes interesting history—and, although in one essential particular they seem to have fallen very far short of the traditional standard of honour, the memory of them is still that of a polished, refined, and gallant race of gentlemen.

The parole system, by which officers of certain ratings were permitted, under strict conditions to which they subscribed on their honour, to reside in certain places, was in practice at any rate at the beginning of the Seven Years' War, and in 1757 the following were the parole towns:

In the West: Redruth, Launceston, Callington, Falmouth, Tavistock, Torrington, Exeter, Crediton, Ashburton, Bideford, Okehampton, Helston, Alresford, Basingstoke, Chippenham, Bristol, Sodbury (Gloucestershire), and Bishop's Waltham. In the South: Guernsey, Ashford, Tenterden, Tonbridge, Wye (Kent), Goudhurst, Sevenoaks, Petersfield, and Romsey. In the North: Dundee and Newcastle-on-Tyne. Kinsale in Ireland, Beccles in Suffolk, and Whitchurch in Shropshire. At first I had doubts if prisoners on parole were at open ports like Falmouth, Bristol, and Newcastle-on-Tyne, but an examination of the documents at the Record Office in London and the Archives Nationales in Paris established the fact, although they ceased to be there after a short time. Not only does it seem that parole rules were more strictly enforced at this time than they were later, but that violation of them was regarded as a crime by the Governments of the offenders. Also, there was an arrangement, or at any rate an understanding, between England and France that officers who had broken their parole by escaping, should, if discovered in their own country, either be sent back to the country of their imprisonment, or be imprisoned in their own country. Thus, we read under date 1757:

'René Brisson de Dunkerque, second capitaine et pilote du navire *Le Prince de Soubise*, du dit port, qui étoit détenu prisonnier à Waltham en Angleterre, d'où il s'est évadé, et qui, étant de retour à Dunkerque le 16ème Oct. 1757, y a été mis en prison par ordre du Roy.'

During 1778, 1779, and six months of 1780, two hundred and ninety-five French prisoners alone had successfully escaped from parole places, the greatest number being, from Alresford forty-five, Chippenham thirty-three, Tenterden thirty-two, Bandon twenty-two, Okehampton nineteen, and Ashburton eighteen.

In 1796 the following ratings were allowed to be on parole: 1. Taken on men-of-war: Captain, lieutenant, ensign, surgeon, purser, chaplain, master, pilot, midshipman, surgeon's mate, boatswain, gunner, carpenter, master-caulker, master-sail-maker, coasting pilot, and gentleman volunteer.

2. Taken on board a privateer or merchantman: Captain, passenger of rank, second captain, chief of prizes, two lieutenants for every hundred men, pilot, surgeon, and chaplain.

No parole was to be granted to officers of any privateer under eighty tons burthen, or having less than fourteen carriage guns, which were not to be less than four-pounders.

In 1804 parole was granted as follows:

1. All commissioned officers of the Army down to sous-lieutenant.

2. All commissioned officers of the Navy down to gardes-marine (midshipmen).

3. Three officers of privateers of a hundred men, but not under fourteen guns.

4. Captains and next officers of merchant ships above fifty tons.

The parole form in 1797 was as follows:

'By the Commissioners for conducting H.M's. Transport Service, and for the care and custody of Prisoners of War.

'These are to certify to all H.M's. officers, civil and military, and to whom else it may concern, that the bearer ... as described on the back hereof is a detained (French, American, Spanish or Dutch) prisoner of war at ... and that he has liberty to walk on the great turnpike road within the distance of one mile from the extremities of the town, but that he must not go into any field or cross road, nor be absent from his lodging after 5 o'clock in the afternoon during the six winter months, viz. from October 1st to March 31st, nor after 8 o'clock during the summer months. Wherefore you and everyone of you [*sic*] are hereby desired and required to suffer him, the said ... to pass and repass accordingly without any hindrance or molestation whatever, he keeping within the said limits and behaving according to law.'

The form of parole to be signed by the prisoner was this:

'Whereas the Commissioners for conducting H.M's. Transport service and for the care and custody of French officers and sailors detained in England have been pleased to grant ... leave to reside in ... upon condition that he gives his parole of honour not to withdraw one mile from the boundaries prescribed there without leave for that purpose from the said Commissioners, that he will behave himself decently and with due regard to the laws of the kingdom, and also that he will not directly or indirectly hold any correspondence with France during his continuance in England, but by such letter or letters as shall be shown to the Agent of the said Commissioners under whose care he is or may be in order to their being read and approved by the Superiors, he does hereby declare that having given his parole he will keep it inviolably.'

In all parole towns and villages the following notice was posted up in prominent positions:

'Notice is hereby given,

'That all such prisoners are permitted to walk or ride on the great turnpike road within the distance of one mile from the extreme parts of the town (not beyond the bounds of the Parish) and that if they shall exceed such limits or go into any field or cross-road they may be taken up and sent to prison, and a reward of Ten Shillings will be paid by the Agent for apprehending them. And further, that such prisoners are to be in their lodgings by 5 o'clock in the winter, and 8 in the summer months, and if they stay out later they are liable to be taken up and sent to the Agent for such misconduct. And to prevent the prisoners from behaving in an improper manner to the inhabitants of the town, or creating any riots or disturbances either with them or among themselves, notice is also given that the Commissioners will cause, upon information being given to their Agents, any prisoners who shall so misbehave to be committed to prison. And such of the inhabitants who shall insult or abuse any of the Prisoners of War on parole, or shall be found in any respect aiding or assisting in the escape of such prisoners shall be punished according to law.'

The rewards offered for the conviction of prisoners for the violation of any of the conditions of their parole, and particularly for recapturing escaped prisoners and for the conviction of aiders in escape, were liberal enough to tempt the ragamuffins of the parole places to do their utmost to get the prisoners to break the law, and we shall see how this led to a system of persecution which possibly provoked many a foreign officer, perfectly honourable in other respects, to break his parole. I do not attempt to defend the far too general laxity of principle which made some of the most distinguished of our prisoners break their solemnly pledged words by escaping or trying to escape, but I do believe that the continual dangling before unlettered clowns and idle town loafers rewards varying from ten guineas for recapturing an escaped prisoner to ten shillings for arresting an officer out of his lodging a few minutes after bell ringing, or straying a few yards off the great turnpike, was putting a premium upon a despicable system of spying and trapping which could not have given a pleasurable zest to a life of exile.

Naturally, the rules about the correspondence of prisoners on parole were strict, and no other rules seem to have been more irksome to prisoners, or more frequently violated by them. All letters for prisoners on parole had to pass through the Transport Office. Remittances had to be made through the local agent, if for an even sum in the Bank of England notes, if for odd shillings and pence by postal orders. It is, however, very certain that a vast amount of correspondence passed to and from the prisoners independently of the Transport Office, and that the conveyance and receipt of such correspondence became as distinctly a surreptitious trade called into existence by circumstances as that of aiding prisoners to escape.

Previous to 1813 the money allowance to officers on parole above and including the rank of captain was ten shillings and sixpence per week per man, and below that rank eight shillings and ninepence. In that year, complaints were made to the British Government by M. Rivière, that as it could be shown that living in England was very much more expensive than in France, this allowance should be increased. Our Government admitted the justice of the claim, and the allowances were accordingly increased to fourteen shillings, and eleven shillings and eightpence. It may be noted, by the way, that this was the same Rivière who in 1804 had denied our right to inquire into the condition of British prisoners in France, curtly saying: 'It is the will of the Emperor!'

The cost of burying the poor fellows who died in captivity, although borne by the State, was kept down to the most economical limits, for we find two orders, dated respectively 1805 and 1812, that the cost was not to exceed £2 2*s.*, that plain elm coffins were to be used, and that the expense of gloves and hat-bands must be borne by the prisoners. Mr. Farnell, the Agent at Ashby-de-la-Zouch, was called sharply to order for a charge in his accounts of fourteen shillings for a hat-band!

In 1814 funerals at Portsmouth were cut down to half a guinea, but I presume this was for ordinary prisoners. The allowances for surgeons in parole places in 1806 were:

For cures when the attendance was for more than five days, six shillings and eightpence, when for less, half that sum. Bleeding was to be charged sixpence, and for drawing a tooth, one shilling. Serious sick cases were to be sent to a prison hospital, and no allowance for medicines or extra subsistence was to be made.

We must not allow sentimental sympathy with officers and gentlemen on parole to blind our eyes to the fact constantly proved that it was necessary to keep the strictest surveillance over them. Although, if we except their propensity to regard lightly their parole obligations, their conduct generally may be called good, among so many men there were necessarily some very black sheep. At one time their behaviour in the parole towns was often so abominable as to render it necessary to place them in smaller towns and villages.

In 1793 the Marquis of Buckingham wrote thus to Lord Grenville from Winchester (*Dropmore MSS.*):

'I have for the last week been much annoyed by a constant inundation of French prisoners who have been on their route from Portsmouth to Bristol, and my officers who, during the long marches have had much of their conversation, all report that the language of the common men was, with very few exceptions, equally insolent, especially upon the subject of monarchy. The orders which we received with them were so perfectly proper that we were enabled to maintain strict discipline among them, but I am very anxious that you should come to some decisions about your *parole prisoners* who are now nearly doubled at Alresford and (Bishop's) Waltham, and are hourly more exceptionable in their language and in their communication with the country people. I am persuaded that some very unpleasant consequences will arise if this practice is not checked, and I do not know how it is to be done. Your own good heart will make you feel for the French priests now at Winchester to whom these people (230 at Alresford, 160 at Waltham) have openly avowed massacre whenever the troops are removed.... Pray think over some arrangement for sending your parole prisoners out of England, for they certainly serve their country here better than they could do at sea or in France (so they say openly).'

The authorities had to be constantly on their guard against deceptions of all kinds practised by the paroled prisoners, in addition to the frequent breaches of parole by escape. Thus applications were made almost daily by prisoners to be allowed either to exchange their places of residence for London, or to come to London temporarily 'upon urgent private affairs'. At first these permissions were given when the applicants were men whose positions or reputations were deemed sufficient guarantees for honourable behaviour, but experience soon taught the Transport Office that nobody was to be trusted, and so these applications, even when endorsed by Englishmen of position, were invariably refused.

For instance, in 1809, the Office received a letter from one Brossage, an officer on parole at Launceston, asking that he might be removed to Reading, as he was suffering from lung disease. The reply was that as a rule people suffering from lung disease in England were only too glad to be able to go to Cornwall for alleviation or cure. The truth was that M. Brossage wanted to exchange the dullness of a Cornish town for the life and gaiety of Reading, which was a special parole town reserved for officers of distinction.

Another trick which the authorities characterized as 'an unjustifiable means of gaining liberty', was to bribe an invalid on the roster for France to be allowed to personate him. Poor officers were as glad to sell their chance in this way, as were poor prisoners on hulks or in prisons.

In 1811 some officers at Lichfield obtained their release because of 'their humane conduct at the late fire at Mr. Lee's house'. But so many applications for release on account of similar services at fires came in that the Transport Office was suspicious, and refused them, 'especially as the French Government does not reward British officers for similar services.'

In the same year one Andoit got sent to Andover on parole in the name of another man, whom no doubt he impersonated, although he had no right to be paroled, and at once made use of the opportunity and escaped.

Most touching were some of the letters from paroled officers praying to have their places of parole changed, but when the Transport Office found out that these changes were almost invariably made so that old comrades and friends could meet together to plan and arrange escapes, rejection became the invariable fate of them. For some time many French officers on parole had been permitted to add to their incomes by giving lessons in dancing, drawing, fencing, and singing in English families, and for these purposes had special permits to go beyond the usual one mile limit. But when in 1811, M. Faure applied to go some distance out of Redruth to teach French, and M. Ulliac asked to be allowed to exceed limits at Ashby-de-la-Zouch to teach drawing, the authorities refused, and this despite the backing up of these requests by local gentry, giving as their reason: 'If complied with generally the prisoners would become dispersed over all parts of the country without any regular control over their conduct.' Prisoners were not even allowed to give lessons away from their lodgings out of parole hours.

Very rarely, except in the cases of officers of more than ordinarily distinguished position, were relaxations of parole rules permitted. General Pillet at Bishop's Waltham in 1808, had leave to go two miles beyond the usual one mile limit two or three times a week, 'to take the air.' General Pageot at Ashbourne was given eight days' leave to visit Wooton Lodge in 1804, with the result related elsewhere (p. 414).

In 1808 General Brenier, on parole at Wantage, was allowed 3s. a day 'on account of the wound in his thigh', so unusual a concession as to cause the Transport Office to describe it as 'the greatest rate of allowance granted to any prisoner of war in this country under any circumstances'. Later, however, some prisoners at Bath were made the same allowance.

At first sight it seems harsh on the part of the Transport Office to refuse permission for a prisoner at Welshpool to lodge with the postmistress of that place, but without doubt it had excellent reason to think that for purposes of escape as well as for carrying on an unsuspected correspondence, the post-office would be the very place for a prisoner to live at. Again, the forgery of documents was very extensively carried on by the prisoners, and in 1803 the parole agents were advised:

'With respect to admitting prisoners of war at Parole we beg to observe that we think it proper to adhere to a regulation which from frequent abuses we found it absolutely necessary to adopt last war; namely, that no blank form of parole certificates be sent to the agents at the depots, but to transmit them to the Agents, properly filled up whenever their ranks shall have been ascertained at this office, from lists sent by the agents and from extracts from the *Rôle d'Équipage* of each vessel captured.'

Of course, the reason for this was that blank parole forms had been obtained by bribery, had been filled up, and that all sorts of undesirable and dangerous rascals got scattered among the parole places.

So long back as 1763 a complaint came from Dover that the Duc de Nivernois was in the habit of issuing passes to prisoners of war on parole in England to pass over to Calais and Boulogne as ordinary civilians, and further inquiry brought out the fact that he was not the only owner of a noble name who trafficked in documents which, if they do not come under the category of forgeries, were at any rate false.

In 1804 a letter from France addressed to a prisoner on parole at Tiverton was intercepted. It was found to contain a blank printed certificate, sealed and signed by the Danish vice-consul at Plymouth. Orders were at once issued that no more certificates from him were to be honoured, and he was accused of the act. He protested innocence, and requested that the matter should be examined, the results being that the documents were found to be forgeries.

Of course, the parole agents, that is to say, the men chosen to guard and minister to the wants of the prisoners in the parole towns, occupied important and responsible positions. At first the only qualifications required were that they should not be shopkeepers, but men fitted by their position and their personality to deal with prisoners who were officers, and therefore *ipso facto*, gentlemen. But during the later years of the great wars they were chosen exclusively from naval lieutenants of not less than ten years' standing, a change brought about by complaints from many towns and from many prisoners that the agents were palpably underbred and tactless, and particularly perhaps by the representation of Captain Moriarty, the agent at Valleyfield near Edinburgh, and later at Perth, that 'the men chosen were attorneys and shopkeepers for whom the French officers have no respect, so that the latter do just what they like', urging that only Service men should occupy these posts.

The duties of the parole agent were to see that the prisoners under his charge fulfilled all the obligations of their parole, to muster them twice a week, to minister to their wants, to pay them their allowances, to act as their financial agents, to hear and adjust their complaints, to be, in fact, quite as much their guide, philosopher, and friend as their custodian. He had to keep a strict account of all receipts and payments, which he forwarded once a month to the Transport Office: he had to keep a constant watch on the correspondence of the prisoners, not merely seeing that they held and received none clandestinely, but that every letter was to pass the examination of the Transport Office; and his own correspondence was voluminous, for in the smallest parole places there were at least eighty prisoners, whilst in the larger, the numbers were close upon four hundred.

For all this the remuneration was 5 per cent. upon all disbursements for the subsistence of the prisoners with allowances for stationery and affidavits, and it may be very naturally asked how men could be found willing to do all this, in addition to their own callings, for such pay. The only answer is that men were not only willing but anxious to become parole agents because of the 'pickings' derivable from the office, especially in connexion with the collection and payment of remittances to prisoners. That these 'pickings' were considerable there can be no doubt, particularly as they were available from so many sources, and as the temptations were so many and so strong to accept presents for services rendered, or, what was more frequent, for duty left undone.

On the whole, and making allowance for the character of the age and the numberless temptations to which they were exposed, the agents of the parole towns seem to have done their hard and delicate work very fairly. No doubt in the process of gathering in their 'pickings' there was some sharp practice by them, and a few instances are recorded of criminal transactions, but a comparison between the treatment of French prisoners on parole in England and the English *détenus* in France certainly is not to our discredit.

The Transport Office seems to have been unremitting in its watchfulness on its agents, if we are to judge by the mass of correspondence which passed between the one and the others, and which deals so largely with minutiae and details that its consideration must have been by no means the least heavy of the duties expected from these gentlemen.

Mr. Tribe, Parole Agent at Hambledon, seems to have irritated his superiors much by the character of his letters, for in 1804 he is told:

'As the person who writes your letters does not seem to know how to write English you must therefore in future write your own letters or employ another to write them who can write intelligibly.'

And again:

'If you cannot really write more intelligibly you must employ a person to manage your correspondence in future, but you are not to suppose that he will be paid by us for his trouble.'

Spettigue, Parole Agent at Launceston, got into serious trouble in 1807 for having charged commissions to prisoners upon moneys paid to them, and was ordered to refund them. He was the only parole agent who was proved to have so offended.

Smith, Parole Agent at Thame, was rebuked in February, 1809, for having described aloud a prisoner about to be conveyed from Thame to Portsmouth under escort as a man of good character and a gentleman, the result being that the escort were put off their guard, and the prisoner escaped, Smith knowing all the time that the prisoner was the very reverse of his description, and that it was in consequence of his having obtained his parole by a 'gross deception', that he was being conveyed to the hulks at Portsmouth. However, Kermel, the prisoner, was recaptured.

Enchmarsh, Parole Agent at Tiverton, was reprimanded in July 1809 for having been concerned in the sale, by a prisoner, of a contraband article, and was reminded that it was against rules for an agent to have any mercantile transactions with prisoners.

Lewis, Parole Agent at Reading, was removed in June 1812, because when the dépôt doctor made his periodical round in order to select invalids to be sent to France, he tried to bribe Dr. Weir to pass General Joyeux, a perfectly sound man, as an invalid and so procure his liberation.

Powis, Parole Agent at Leek in Staffordshire, son of a neighbouring parson, was removed in the same year, having been accused of withholding moneys due to prisoners, and continually failing to send in his accounts.

On the other hand, Smith, the Agent at Thame, was blamed for having shown excessive zeal in his office by hiring people to hide and lie in wait to catch prisoners committing breaches of parole. Perhaps the Transport Office did not so much disapprove of his methods as un-English and mean, but they knew very well that the consequent fines and stoppages meant his emolument.

That parole agents found it as impossible to give satisfaction to everybody as do most people in authority is very clear from the following episodes in the official life of Mr. Crapper, the Parole Agent at Wantage in 1809, who was a chemist by trade, and who seems to have been in ill odour all round. The episodes also illustrate the keen sympathy with which in some districts the French officers on parole were regarded.

On behalf of the prisoners at Wantage, one Price, J.P., wrote of Crapper, that 'being a low man himself, he assumes a power which I am sure is not to your wish, and which he is too ignorant to exercise'. It appears that two French officers, the generals Maurin and Lefebvre, had gone ten miles from Wantage—that is, nine miles beyond the parole limit—to dine with Sir John Throckmorton. Crapper did his duty and arrested the generals; they were leniently punished, as, instead of being sent to a prison or a hulk, they were simply marched off to Wincanton. The magistrates refused to support Crapper, but, despite another letter in favour of the generals by another J.P., Goodlake, who had driven them in his carriage to Throckmorton's house, and who declared that Crapper had a hatred for him on account of some disagreement on the bench, the Transport Office defended their agent, and confirmed his action.

From J. E. Lutwyche, Surveyor of Taxes, in whose house the French generals lodged, the Transport Office received the following:

'GENTLEMEN,

'I beg leave to offer a few remarks respecting the French generals lately removed from Wantage. Generals Lefebvre and Maurin both lodged at my house. The latter always conducted himself with the greatest Politeness and Propriety, nor ever exceeded the limits or time prescribed by his parole until the arrival of General Lefebvre. Indeed he was not noticed or invited anywhere till then, nor did he at all seem to wish it, his time being occupied in endeavouring to perfect himself in the English language. When General Lefebvre arrived, he, being an object of curiosity and a man of considerable rank, was invited out, and of course General Maurin (who paid him great attention) with him, which certainly otherwise would never have been the case. General Lefebvre has certainly expressed himself as greatly dissatisfied with the way in which he had been taken, making use of the childish phrase of his being entrapped, and by his sullen manner and general conduct appeared as if he was not much inclined to observe the terms of his parole.'

Another anti-Crapperist writes:

'Gentlemen,

'I take this liberty in informing you that in case that the Prisoners of War residing here on Parole be not kept to stricter orders, that they will have the command of this Parish. They are out all hours of the night, they do almost as they have a mind to do: if a man is loaded ever so hard, he must turn out of the road for them, and if any person says anything he is reprimanded for it.

'They have too much liberty a great deal.

'I am, Gentlemen,

'With a good wish to my King and Country,

'A True Englishman.'

Another correspondent asserted that although Mr. Crapper complained of the generals' breach of parole, he had the next week allowed thirty of the French prisoners to give a ball and supper to the little tradesmen of the town, which had been kept up till 3 a.m.

Crapper denied this, and said he had refused the application of the prisoners for a dance until 10 p.m., given at an inn to the 'ladies of the town—the checked apron Ladies of Wantage'.

Yet another writer declared that Crapper was a drunkard, and drank with the prisoners. To this, Crapper replied that if they called on him as gentlemen, he was surely entitled to offer them hospitality. The same writer spoke of the French prisoners being often drunk in the streets, of Crapper fighting with them at the inns, and accused him of withholding money from them. Crapper, however, appears as Parole Agent for Wantage, with 340 prisoners in his charge, some time after all this.

I have given Crapper's case at some length merely as an instance of what parole agents had to put up with, not as being unusual. Ponsford at Moreton-Hampstead, Smith at Thame, and Eborall at Lichfield, seem to have been provoked in much the same way by turbulent and defiant prisoners.

For very palpable reasons the authorities did not encourage close *rapprochements* between parole agents and the prisoners under their charge. At Tavistock in 1779, something wrong in the intercourse between Ford, the Agent, and his flock, had led to an order that not only should Ford be removed, but that certain prisoners should be sent to Launceston. Whereupon the said prisoners petitioned to be allowed to remain at Tavistock under Ford:

'A qui nous sommes très sincèrement attachés, tant par les doux façons qu'il a scu toujours avoir pour nous, même en exécutant ses ordres, que par son honnêteté particulière et la bonne intelligence qu'il a soin de faire raigner autant qu'il est possible entre les différentes claces de personnes qui habitent cette ville et les prisonniers qu'y sont;—point sy essentiel et sy particulièrement bien ménagé jusqu'à ce jour.'

On the other hand, one Tarade, a prisoner, writes describing Ford as a 'petit tyran d'Afrique', and complains of him, evidently because he had refused Tarade a passport for France. Tarade alludes to the petition above quoted, and says that the subscribers to it belong to a class of prisoners who are better away. Another much-signed petition comes from dislikers of Ford who beg to be sent to Launceston, so we may presume from the action of the authorities in ordering Ford's removal, that he was not a disinterested dispenser and withholder of favours.

In Scotland the agents seem generally to have been on very excellent terms with the prisoners in their charge, and some friendships were formed between captors and captives which did not cease with the release of the latter. Mr. Macbeth Forbes relates the following anecdote by way of illustration:

'The late Mr. Romanes of Harryburn (whose father had been Agent at Lauder) says about M. Espinasse, for long a distinguished French teacher in Edinburgh, who was for some time a parole prisoner at Lauder: "When I was enrolled as a pupil with M. Espinasse some fifty years ago, he said: 'Ah! your fader had *me*!' supplying the rest of the sentence by planting the flat part of his right thumb into the palm of his left hand—'Now I have *you*!' repeating the operation. And when my father called to see M. Espinasse, he was quite put out by M. Espinasse seizing and hugging and embracing him, shouting excitedly: 'Ah, mon Agent! mon Agent!'"

Smith at Kelso, Nixon at Hawick, Romanes at Lauder, and Bell at Jedburgh, were all held in the highest esteem by the prisoners under them, and received many testimonials of it.

The following were the Parole Towns between 1803 and 1813:

Abergavenny.

Alresford.

Andover.

Ashbourne.

Ashburton.

Ashby-de-la-Zouch.

Biggar.

Bishop's Castle.

Bishop's Waltham.

Brecon.

Bridgnorth.

Chesterfield.

Chippenham.

Crediton.

Cupar.

Dumfries.

Hambledon.

Hawick.

Jedburgh.

Kelso.

Lanark.

Lauder.

Launceston.

Leek.

Lichfield.

Llanfyllin.

Lochmaben.

Lockerbie.

Melrose.

Montgomery.

Moreton-Hampstead.

Newtown.

Northampton.

North Tawton.

Odiham.

Okehampton.

Oswestry.

Peebles.

Peterborough.

Reading.

Sanquhar.

Selkirk.

South Molton.

Tavistock.

Thame.

Tiverton.

Wantage.

Welshpool.

Whitchurch.

Wincanton.

CHAPTER XXII
PAROLE LIFE

The following descriptions of life in parole towns by French writers may not be entirely satisfactory to the reader who naturally wishes to get as correct an impression of it as possible, inasmuch as they are from the pens of men smarting under restrictions and perhaps a sense of injustice, irritated by ennui, by the irksomeness of confinement in places which as a rule do not seem to have been selected because of their fitness to administer to the joys of life, and by the occasional evidences of being among unfriendly people. But I hope to balance this in later chapters by the story of the paroled officers as seen by the captors.

The original French I have translated literally, except when it has seemed to me that translation would involve a sacrifice of terseness or force.

Listen to Lieutenant Gicquel des Touches, at Tiverton, after Trafalgar:

'A pleasant little town, but which struck me as particularly monotonous after the exciting life to which I was accustomed. My pay, reduced by one-half, amounted to fifty francs a month, which had to satisfy all my needs at a time when the continental blockade had caused a very sensible rise in the price of all commodities.... I took advantage of my leisure hours to overhaul and complete my education. Some of my comrades of more literary bringing-up gave me lessons in literature and history, in return for which I taught them fencing, for which I always had much aptitude, and which I had always practised a good deal. The population was generally kindly disposed towards us; some of the inhabitants urging their interest in us so far as to propose to help me to escape, and among them a young and pretty *Miss* who only made one condition—that I should take her with me in my flight, and should marry her when we reached the Continent. It was not much trouble for me to resist these temptations, but it was harder to tear myself away from the importunities of some of my companions, who, not having the same ideas as I had about the sacredness of one's word, would have forced me to escape with them.

'Several succeeded: I say nothing about them, but I have often been astonished later at the ill-will they have borne me for not having done as they did.'

Gicquel was at Tiverton six years and was then exchanged.

A Freemasons' Lodge, *Enfants de Mars*, was opened and worked at Tiverton about 1810, of which the first and only master was Alexander de la Motte, afterwards Languages Master at Blundell's School. The Masons met in a room in Frog Street, now Castle Street, until, two of the officers on parole in the town escaping, the authorities prohibited the meetings. The Tyler of the Lodge, Rivron by name, remained in Tiverton after peace was made, and for many years worked as a slipper-maker. He had been an officer's servant.

The next writer, the Baron de Bonnefoux, we have already met in the hulks. His reminiscences of parole life are among the most interesting I have come across, and are perhaps the more so because he has a good deal of what is nice and kind to say of us.

On his arrival in England in 1806, Bonnefoux was sent on parole to Thame in Oxfordshire. Here he occupied himself in learning English, Latin, and drawing, and in practising fencing. In the Mauritius, Bonnefoux and his shipmates had become friendly with a wealthy Englishman settled there under its French Government at l'Île de France. This gentleman came to Thame, rented the best house there for a summer, and continually entertained the French officer prisoners. The Lupton family, of one son and two daughters, the two Stratford ladies, and others, were also kind to them, whilst a metropolitan spirit was infused into the little society by the visits of a Miss Sophia Bode from London, so that with all these pretty, amiable girls the Baron managed to pass his unlimited leisure very pleasantly. On the other hand, there was an element of the population of Thame which bore a traditional antipathy to Frenchmen which it lost no opportunity of exhibiting. It was a manufacturing section, composed of outsiders, between whom and the natives an ill-feeling had long existed, and it was not long before our Baron came to an issue with them. One of these men pushed against Bonnefoux as he was walking in the town, and the Frenchman retaliated. Whereupon the Englishman called on his friends, who responded. Bonnefoux, on his side, called up his comrades, and a regular *mêlée*, in which sticks, stones, and fists were freely used, ensued, the immediate issue of which is not reported. Bonnefoux brought his assailant up before Smith, the Agent, who shuffled about the matter, and recommended the Baron to take it to Oxford, he in reality being in fear of the roughs. Bonnefoux expressed his disgust, Smith lost his temper, and raised his cane, in reply to which the Baron seized a poker. Bonnefoux complained to the Transport Office, the result of which was that he was removed to Odiham in Hampshire, after quite a touching farewell to his English friends and his own countrymen, receiving a souvenir of a lock of hair from 'la jeune Miss Harriet Stratford aux beaux yeux bleus, au teint éblouissant, à la physionomie animée, à la taille divine'.

The populace of Odiham he found much pleasanter than that of Thame, and as the report of the part he had taken in the disturbance at Thame had preceded him, he was enthusiastically greeted. The French officers at Odiham did their best to pass the time pleasantly. They had a Philharmonic Society, a Freemasons' Lodge, and especially a theatre to which the local gentry resorted in great numbers, Shebbeare, the Agent, being a good fellow who did all in his power to soften the lot of those in his charge, and was not too strict a construer of the laws and regulations by which they were bound.

Bonnefoux made friends everywhere; he seems to have been a light-hearted genial soul, and did not spare the ample private means he had in helping less fortunate fellow prisoners. For instance, a naval officer named Le Forsiney became the father of an illegitimate child. By English law he had to pay six hundred francs for the support of the child, or be imprisoned. Bonnefoux paid it for him.

In June 1807, an English friend, Danley, offered to take him to Windsor, quietly of course, as this meant a serious violation of parole rules. They had a delightful trip: Bonnefoux saw the king, and generally enjoyed himself, and got back to Odiham safely. He said nothing about this escapade until September, when he was talking of it to friends, and was overheard by a certain widow, who, having been brought up in France, understood the language, as she sat at her window above. Now this widow had a pretty nurse, Mary, to whom Bonnefoux was 'attracted', and happening to find an unsigned letter addressed to Mary, in which was: 'To-morrow, I shall have the grief of not seeing you, but I shall see your king,' she resolved upon revenge. A short time after, there appeared in a newspaper a paragraph to the effect that a foreigner with sinister projects had dared to approach the king at Windsor. The widow denounced Bonnefoux as the man alluded to: the Agent was obliged to examine the matter, the whole business of the trip to Windsor came out, and although Danley took all the blame on himself, and tried to shield Bonnefoux, the order came that the latter was at once to be removed to the hulks at Chatham.

In the meanwhile a somewhat romantic little episode had happened at Odiham. Among the paroled prisoners there was a lieutenant (*Aspirant de première classe*) named Rousseau, who had been taken in the fight between Admiral Duckworth and Admiral Leissegnes off San Domingo in February, 1806. His mother, a widow, was dying of grief for him, and Rousseau resolved to get to her, but would not break his parole by escaping from Odiham. So he wrote to the Transport Office that if he was not arrested and put on board a prison ship within eight days, he would consider his parole as cancelled, and would act accordingly, his resolution being to escape from any prison ship on which he was confined, which he felt sure he could do, and so save his parole. Accordingly, he was arrested and sent to Portsmouth.

Bonnefoux, pending his removal to Chatham, was kept under guard at the *George* in Odiham, but he managed to get out, hid for the night in a new ditch, and early the next morning went to a prisoner's lodging-house in the outskirts of Odiham, and remained there three days. Hither came Sarah Cooper, daughter of a local pastry-cook, no doubt one of the dashing young sailor's many *chères amies*. She had been informed of his whereabouts by his friends, and told him she would conduct him to Guildford.

The weather was very wet, and Sarah was in her Sunday best, but said that she did not mind the rain so long as she could see Bonnefoux. Says the latter:

'Je dis alors à Sara que je pensais qu'il pleuvrait pendant la nuit. Elle répliqua que peu lui importait; enfin j'objectai cette longue course à pied, sa toilette et ses capotes blanches, car c'était un dimanche, et elle leva encore cette difficulté en prétendant qu'elle avait du courage et que dès qu'elle avait appris qu'elle pouvait me sauver elle n'avait voulu ni perdre une minute pour venir me chercher.... Je n'avais plus un mot à dire, car pendant qu'elle m'entraînait d'une de ses petites mains elle me fermait gracieusement la bouche.'

They reached Guildford at daybreak, and two carriages were hired, one to take Bonnefoux to London, the other to take Sarah back to Odiham. They parted with a tender farewell, Bonnefoux started, reached London safely, and put up at the Hôtel du Café de St. Paul.

In London he met a Dutchman named Vink, bound for Hamburg by the first vessel leaving, and bought his berth on the ship, but had to wait a month before anything sailed for Hamburg. He sailed, a fellow passenger being young Lord Onslow. At Gravesend, officers came on board on the search for Vink. Evidently Vink had betrayed him, for he could not satisfactorily account for his presence on the ship in accordance with the strict laws then in force about the embarkation of passengers for foreign ports; Bonnefoux was arrested, for two days was shut down in the awful hold of a police vessel, and was finally taken on board the *Bahama* at Chatham, and there met Rousseau, who had escaped from the Portsmouth hulk but had been recaptured in mid-Channel.

Bonnefoux remained on the Chatham hulk until June 1809, when he was allowed to go on parole to Lichfield. With him went Dubreuil, the rough privateer skipper whose acquaintance he made on the *Bahama*, and who was released from the prison ship because he had treated Colonel and Mrs. Campbell with kindness when he made them prisoners.

Dubreuil was so delighted with the change from the *Bahama* to Lichfield, that he celebrated it in a typical sailor fashion, giving a banquet which lasted three days at the best hotel in Lichfield, and roared forth the praises of his friend Bonnefoux:

De Bonnefoux nous sommes enchantés,

Nous allons boire à sa santé!

Parole life at Lichfield he describes as charming. There was a nice, refined local society, pleasant walks, cafés, concerts, réunions, and billiards. Bonnefoux preferred to mix with the artisan class of Lichfield society, admiring it the most in England, and regarding the middle class as too prejudiced and narrow, the upper class as too luxurious and proud. He says:

'Il est difficile de voir rien de plus agréable à l'œil que les réunions des jeunes gens des deux sexes lois [*sic*] des foires et des marchés.'

Eborall, the Agent at Lichfield, the Baron calls a splendid chap: so far from binding them closely to their distance limit, he allowed the French officers to go to Ashby-de-la-Zouch, to the races at Lichfield, and even to Birmingham. Catalini came to sing at Lichfield, and Bonnefoux went to hear her with Mary Aldrith, his landlord's daughter, and pretty Nancy Fairbrother.

And yet Bonnefoux resolved to escape. There came on 'business' to Lichfield, Robinson and Stevenson, two well-known smuggler escape-agents, and they made the Baron an offer which he accepted. He wrote, however, to the Transport Office, saying that his health demanded his return to France, and engaging not to serve against England.

With another naval officer, Colles, he got away successfully by the aid of the smugglers and their agents, and reached Rye in Sussex. Between them they paid the smugglers one hundred and fifty guineas. At Rye they found another escaped prisoner in hiding, the Captain of the *Diomède*, and he added another fifty guineas. The latter was almost off his head, and nearly got them caught through his extraordinary behaviour. However, on November 28, 1809, they reached Boulogne after a bad passage.

Robinson with his two hundred guineas bought contraband goods in France and ran them over to England. Stevenson was not so lucky, for a little later he was caught at Deal with an escaped prisoner, was fined five hundred guineas, and in default of payment was sent to Botany Bay.

General d'Henin was one of the French generals who were taken at San Domingo in 1803. He was sent on parole to Chesterfield in Derbyshire, and, unlike several other officers who shared his fate, was most popular with the inhabitants through his pleasing address and manner. He married whilst in Chesterfield a Scots lady of fortune, and for some years resided with her at Spital Lodge, the house of the Agent, Mr. Bower. He and Madame d'Henin returned to Paris in 1814, and he fought at Waterloo, where his leg was torn off by a cannon shot.

His residence in England seems to have made him somewhat of an Anglophile, for in Horne's *History of Napoleon* he is accused of favouring the

British at Waterloo, and it was actually reported to Napoleon by a dragoon that he 'harangued the men to go over to the enemy'. This, it was stated, was just before the cannon shot struck him.

From Chesterfield, d'Henin wrote to his friend General Boyer at Montgomery, under date October 30, 1804. After a long semi-religious soliloquy, in which he laments his position but supposes it to be as Pangloss says, that 'all is for the best in this best of worlds', he speaks of his bad health, of his too short stay at 'Harrowgate' (from which health resort, by the way, he had been sent, for carrying on correspondence under a false name), of his religious conversion, and of his abstemious habits, and finishes:

'Rien de nouveau. Toujours la même vie, triste, maussade, ennuyeuse, déplaisante et sans fin, quand finira-t-elle? Il fait ici un temps superbe, de la pluie, depuis le matin jusqu'au soir, et toujours de la pluie, et du brouillard pour changer. Vie de soldat! Vie de chien!'

All the same, it is consoling to learn from the following letters written by French officers on parole to their friends, that compulsory exile in England was not always the intolerable punishment which so many authors of reminiscences would have us believe. Here is one, for instance, written from a prisoner on parole at Sevenoaks to a friend at Tenterden, in 1757:

'I beg you to receive my congratulations upon having been sent into a country so rich in pretty girls: you say they are unapproachable, but it must be consoling to you to know that you possess the trick of winning the most unresponsive hearts, and that one of your ordinary looks attracts the fair; and this assures me of your success in your secret affairs: it is much more difficult to conquer the middle-class sex.... Your pale beauty has been very ill for some weeks, the reason being that she has overheated herself dancing at a ball with all the Frenchmen with whom she has been friendly for a certain time, which has got her into trouble with her mother.... Roussel has been sent to the "Castle" (Sissinghurst) nine days ago, it is said for having loved too well the Sevenoaks girls, and had two in hand which cost him five guineas, which he had to pay before going. Will you let me know if the country is suitable for you, how many French there are, and if food and lodgings are dear?

'To Mr. Guerdon. A French surgeon on parole at Tenterden.'

The next is from a former prisoner, then living at Dunkirk, to Mrs. Miller at the Post Office, Leicester, dated 1757. Note the spelling and punctuation:

'MADAME,—

Vous ne scaurié croire quell plaisire j'ai de m'entretenir avec vous mon cœur ne peut s'acoutumer à vivre sans vous voire. Je nait pas encore rencontré notre chère compagnon de voyage. Ne m'oublié point, ma chère Elizabeth vous pouvé estre persuadé du plaisire que j'auré en recevant de vos nouvelles. Le gros Loys se porte bien il doit vous écrire aussi qu'à Madame Covagne. Si vous voye Mrs. Nancy donne luy un baisé pour moy'.

A prisoner writes from Alresford to a friend in France:

'I go often to the good Mrs. Smith's. Miss Anna is at present here. She sent me a valentine yesterday. I go there sometimes to take tea where Henrietta and Betsi Wynne are. We played at cards, and spent the pleasantest evening I have ever passed in England.'

A Captain Quinquet, also at Alresford, thus writes to his sister at Avranches:

'We pass the days gaily with the Johnsons, daughters and brother, and I am sure you are glad to hear that we are so happy. Come next Friday! Ah! If that were possible, what a surprise! On that day we give a grand ball to celebrate the twenty-fifth wedding anniversary of papa and mamma. There will be quite twenty people, and I flatter myself we shall enjoy ourselves thoroughly, and if by chance on that day a packet of letters should arrive from you—Mon Dieu! What joy!'

He adds, quite in the style of a settled local gossip, scraps of news, such as that Mrs. Jarvis has a daughter born; that poor Mr. Jack Smith is dead; that Colonel Lewis's wife, a most amiable woman, will be at the ball; that Miss Kimber is going to be married; that dear little Emma learns to speak French astonishingly well; that Henrietta Davis is quite cured from her illness, and so forth.

There is, in fact, plenty of evidence that the French officers found the daughters of Albion very much to their liking. Many of them married and remained in England after peace was declared, leaving descendants who may be found at this day, although in many cases the French names have become anglicized.

In Andover to-day the names of Jerome and Dugay tell of the paroled Frenchmen who were here between 1810 and 1815, whilst, also at Andover, 'Shepherd' Burton is the grandson of Aubertin, a French prisoner.

At Chesterfield (Mr. Hawkesly Edmunds informs me), the names of Jacques and Presky still remain.

Robins and Jacques and Etches are names which still existed in Ashbourne not many years ago, their bearers being known to be descended from French prisoners there.

At Odiham, Alfred Jauréguiberry, second captain of the *Austerlitz* privateer, married a Miss Chambers. His son, Admiral Jauréguiberry, described as a man admirable in private as in public life, was in command of the French Squadron which came over to Portsmouth on the occasion of Queen Victoria's Jubilee Naval Review in 1887, and he found time to call upon an English relative.

Louis Hettet, a prisoner on parole at Bishop's Castle, Montgomeryshire, in 1814, married Mary Morgan. The baptism of a son, Louis, is recorded in the Bishop's Castle register, March 6, 1815. The father left for France after the Peace of 1814; Mrs. Hettet declined to go, and died at Bishop's Castle not many years ago. The boy was sent for and went to France.

Mrs. Lucy Louisa Morris, who died at Oswestry in 1908, aged 83, was the second daughter of Lieutenant Paris, of the French Navy, a prisoner on parole at Oswestry.

In 1886 Thomas Benchin, descendant of a French prisoner at Oswestry, died at Clun, in Shropshire, where his son is, or was lately, living. Benchin was famed for his skill in making toys and chip-wood ornaments.

Robinot, a prisoner on parole at Montgomery, married, in June 1807, a Miss Andrews, of Buckingham.

At Wantage, in 1817, General de Gaja, formerly a prisoner on parole, married a grand-daughter of the first Duke of Leicester, and his daughter married, in 1868, the Rev. Mr. Atkinson, vicar of East Hendred.

At Thame, François Robert Boudin married Miss Bone, by banns, in 1813; in the same year Jacques Ferrier married Mary Green by banns; Prévost de la Croix married Elizabeth Hill by licence; and in 1816 Louis-Amédée Comte married Mary Simmons, also by licence. All the bridegrooms were or had been prisoners on parole.

In the register of Leek I find that J. B. B. Delisle, Commandant of the port of Caen, married Harriet Sheldon; François Néan married Mary Lees, daughter of the landlord of the *Duke of York*; Sergeant Paymaster Pierre Magnier married Frances Smith, who died in 1874, aged 84; Joseph Vattel, cook to General Brunet, married Sarah Pilsbury. Captains Toufflet and Chouquet left sons who were living in Leek in 1880 and 1870 respectively, and Jean Mien, servant to General Brunet, was in Leek in 1870.

Notices of other marriages—at Wincanton, for instance—will be found elsewhere.

Against those who married English girls and honourably kept to them, must, however, be placed a long list of Frenchmen who, knowing well that in France such marriages were held invalid, married English women, and basely deserted them on their own return to France, generally leaving them with children and utterly destitute. The correspondence of the Transport Office is full of warnings to girls who have meditated marriage with prisoners, but who have asked advice first. As to the subsistence of wives and children of prisoners, the law was that if the latter were not British subjects, their subsistence was paid by the British Government, otherwise they must seek Parish relief. In one of the replies the Transport Office quotes the case of Madame Berton, an Englishwoman who had married Colonel Berton, a prisoner on parole at Chesterfield, and was permitted to follow her husband after his release and departure for France, but who, with a son of nineteen months old, on arrival there, was driven back in great want and distress by the French Government.

In contrast with the practice of the British Government in paying for the subsistence of the French wives and children of prisoners of war, is that of the French Government as described in the reply of the Transport Office in 1813 to a Mrs. Cumming with a seven-year-old child, who applied to be allowed a passage to Morlaix in order to join her husband, a prisoner on parole at Longwy:

'The Transport Office is willing to grant you a passage by Cartel to Morlaix, but would call your attention to the situation you will be placed in, on your arrival in France, provided your husband has not by his means or your own the power of maintaining you in France, as the French Government make no allowance whatever to wives and children belonging to British prisoners of war, and this Government has no power to relieve their wants. Also to point out that Longwy is not an open Parole Town like the Parole Towns in England, but is walled round, and the prisoners are not allowed to proceed beyond the walls, so that any resources derivable from your own industry appears to be very uncertain.'

The Transport Office were constantly called upon to adjudicate upon such matters as this:

'In 1805, Colonel de Bercy, on parole at Thame, was "in difficulty" about a girl being with child by him. The Office declined to interfere, but said that if the Colonel could not give sufficient security that mother and child should not be a burden upon the rates, he must be imprisoned until he did.'

By a rule of the French Government, Englishwomen who had already lived in France with their husbands there as prisoners of war could not return to France if once they left it. This was brought about by some English officers' wives taking letters with them on their return from England, and, although as a matter of policy it could not be termed tyrannical, it was the cause naturally of much distress and even of calamity.

The next account of parole life in England is by Louis Garneray, the marine painter, whose description of life on the hulks may be remembered as being the most vivid and exact of any I have given.

After describing his rapture at release from the hulk at Portsmouth and his joyous anticipation of comparative liberty ashore, Garneray says:

'When I arrived in 1811 under escort at the little village (Bishop's Waltham in Hampshire) which had been assigned to me as a place of residence, I saw with some disillusion that more than 1,200 [*sic*] French of all ranks [*sic*] had for their accommodation nothing but some wretched, tumble-down houses which the English let to them at such an exorbitant price that a year's rent meant the price of the house itself. As for me, I managed to get for ten shillings a week, not a room, but the right to place my bed in a hut where already five officers were.'

The poor fellow was up at five and dressed the next morning:

'What are you going to do?' asked one of my room mates. 'I'm going to breathe the morning air and have a run in the fields,' I replied.

'Look out, or you'll be arrested.'

'Arrested! Why?'

'Because we are not allowed to leave the house before six o'clock.'

Garneray soon learned about the hours of going out and coming in, about the one-mile limit along the high road, that a native finding a prisoner beyond the limit or off the main road had not only the right to knock him down but to receive a guinea for doing so. He complained that the only recreations were walking, painting, and reading, for the Government had discovered that concerts, theatricals, and any performances which brought the prisoners and the natives together encouraged familiarity between the two peoples and corrupted morals, and so forbade them. Garneray then described how he came to break his parole and to escape from Bishop's Waltham.

He with two fellow-prisoner officers went out one hot morning with the intention of breakfasting at a farm about a mile along the high road. Intending to save a long bit they cut across by a field path. Garneray stumbled and hurt his foot and so got behind his companions. Suddenly, hearing a cry, he saw a countryman attack his friends with a bill-hook, wound one of them on the arm, and kill the other, who had begun to expostulate with him, with two terrible cuts on the head. Garneray, seizing a stick, rushed up, and the peasant ran off, leaving him with the two poor fellows, one dead and the other badly wounded. He then saw the man returning at the head of a crowd of countrymen, armed with pitchforks and guns, and made up his mind that his turn had come. However, he explained the situation, and had the satisfaction of seeing that the crowd sided with him against their brutal compatriot. They improvised a litter and carried the two victims back to the cantonment, whilst the murderer quietly returned to his work.

When the extraordinary brutality of the attack and its unprovoked nature became known, such indignation was felt among the French officers in the cantonment that they drew up a remonstrance to the British Government, with the translation of which into English Garneray was entrusted. Whilst engaged in this a rough-mannered stranger called on him and warned him that he had best have nothing to do with the remonstrance.

He took the translated document to his brother officers, and on his way back a little English girl of twelve years quietly and mysteriously signed to him to follow her. He did so to a wretched cottage, wherein lived the grandmother of the child. Garneray had been kind to the poor old woman and had painted the child's portrait for nothing, and in return she warned him that the constables were going to arrest him. Garneray determined to escape.

He got away from Bishop's Waltham and was fortunate enough to get an inside place in a night coach, the other places being occupied by an English clergyman, his wife, and daughter. Miss Flora soon recognized him as an escaped prisoner and came to his rescue when, at a halting place, the coach was searched for a runaway from Bishop's Waltham. Eventually he reached Portsmouth, where he found a good English friend of his prison-ship days, and with him he stayed in hiding for nearly a year, until April 1813.

Longing to return to France, he joined with three recently-escaped French officers in an arrangement with smugglers—the usual intermediaries in these escapes—to take them there. To cut short a long story of adventure and misadventure, such as we shall have in plenty when we come to that part of this section which deals with the escapes of paroled prisoners, Garneray and his companions at last embarked with the smugglers at an agreed price of £10 each.

The smugglers turned out to be rascals; and a dispute with them about extra charges ended in a mid-Channel fight, during which one of the smugglers was killed. Within sight of the French coast the British ship *Victory* captured them, and once more Garneray found himself in the *cachot* of the Portsmouth prison-ship *Vengeance*.

Garneray was liberated by the Treaty of Paris in 1814, after nine years' captivity. He was then appointed Court Marine Painter to Louis XVIII, and received the medal of the Legion of Honour.

The Marquis d'Hautpol was taken prisoner at Arapiles, badly wounded, in July 1812, and with some four hundred other prisoners was landed at Portsmouth on December 12, and thence sent on parole to 'Brigsnorth, petite ville de la Principauté de Galles', clearly meant for Bridgnorth in Shropshire. Here, he says, were from *eight to nine hundred* other prisoners, some of whom had been there eight or nine years, but certainly he must have been mistaken, for at no parole place were ever more than four hundred prisoners. The usual rules obtained here, and the allowance was the equivalent of one franc fifty centimes a day.

Wishing to employ his time profitably he engaged a fellow-prisoner to teach him English, to whom he promised a salary as soon as he should receive his remittances. A letter from his brother-in-law told him that his sisters, believing him dead, as they had received no news from him, had gone into mourning, and enclosed a draft for 4,000 francs, which came through the bankers Perregaux of Paris and 'Coutz' of London. He complains bitterly of the sharp practices of the local Agent, who paid him his 4,000 francs, but in paper money, which was at the time at a discount of twenty-five per cent, and who, upon his claiming the difference, 'me répondit fort insolemment que le papier anglais valait autant que l'or français, et que si je me permettais d'attaquer encore le crédit de la banque, il me ferait conduire aux pontons'. So he had to accept the situation.

The Marquis, as we shall see, was not the man to invent such an accusation, so it may be believed that the complaints so often made about the unfair practice of the British Government, in the matter of moneys due to prisoners, were not without foundation. The threat of the Agent to send the Marquis to the hulks if he persisted in claiming his dues, may have been but a threat, but it sounds as if these gentlemen were invested with very great powers. The Marquis and a fellow prisoner, Dechevrières, adjutant of the 59th, messed together, modestly, but better than the other poorer men, who clubbed together and bought an ox head, with which they made soup and ate with potatoes.

A cousin of the Marquis, the Comtesse de Béon, knew a Miss Vernon, one of the Queen's ladies of honour, and she introduced the Marquis to Lord 'Malville', whose seat was near Bridgnorth, and who invited him to the house. I give d'Hautpol's impression in his own words:

'Ce lord était poli, mais, comme tous les Anglais, ennemi mortel de la France. J'étais humilié de ses prévenances qui sentaient la protection. Je revins cependant une seconde fois chez lui; il y avait ce jour-là nombreuse compagnie; plusieurs officiers anglais s'y trouvaient. Sans égards pour ma position et avec une certaine affectation, ils se mirent à déblatérer en français contre l'Empereur et l'armée. Je me levai de table indigné, et demandai à Lord Malville la permission de me retirer; il s'efforce de me retenir en blâmant ses compatriotes, mais je persistai. Je n'acceptai plus d'invitations chez lui.'

All good news from the seat of war, says the Marquis, was carefully hidden from the prisoners, so that they heard nothing about Lützen, Bautzen, and Dresden. But the news of Leipsic was loudly proclaimed. The prisoners could not go out of doors without being insulted. One day the people dressed up a figure to represent Bonaparte, put it on a donkey, and paraded the town with it. Under the windows of the lodging of General Veiland, who had been taken at Badajos, of which place he was governor, they rigged up a gibbet, hung the figure on it, and afterwards burned it.

At one time a general uprising of the prisoners of war in England was seriously discussed. There were in Britain 5,000 officers on parole, and 60,000 men on the hulks and in prisons. The idea was to disarm the guards all at once, to join forces at a given point, to march on Plymouth, liberate the men on the hulks, and thence go to Portsmouth and do the same there. But the authorities became suspicious, the generals were separated from the other officers, and many were sent to distant cantonments. The Marquis says that there were 1,500 at Bridgnorth, and that half of these were sent to Oswestry. This was in November, 1813.

So to Oswestry d'Hautpol was sent. From Oswestry during his stay escaped three famous St. Malo privateer captains. After a terrible journey of risks and privations they reached the coast—he does not say where—and off it they saw at anchor a trading vessel of which nearly all the crew had come ashore. In the night the prisoners swam out, with knives in their mouths, and boarded the brig. They found a sailor sleeping on deck; him they stabbed, and also another who was in the cabin. They spared the cabin boy, who showed them the captain's trunks, with the contents of which they dressed themselves. Then they cut the cable, hoisted sail and made off—all within gunshot of a man-of-war. They reached Morlaix in safety, although pursued for some distance by a man-of-war. The brig was a valuable prize, for she had just come from the West Indies, and was richly laden. This the Frenchmen at Oswestry learned from the English newspapers, and they celebrated the exploit boisterously.

Just after this the Marquis received a letter from Miss Vernon, in which she said that if he chose to join the good Frenchmen who were praying for restoration of the Bourbons, she would get him a passport which would enable him to join Louis XVIII at Hartwell. To this the Marquis replied that he had been made prisoner under the tricolour, that he was still in the Emperor's service, and that for the moment he had no idea of changing his flag, adding that rather than do this he preferred to remain a prisoner. Miss Vernon did not write again on this topic until the news came of the great events of 1814—the victories of the British at San Sebastian, Pampeluna, the Bidassoa, the Adur, Orthez and Toulouse, when she wrote:

'I hope that now you have no more scruples; I send you a passport for London; come and see me, for I shall be delighted to renew our acquaintance.'

He accepted the offer, went to London, and found Miss Vernon lodged in St. James's Palace. Here she got apartments for him; he was fêted and lionized and taken to see the sights of London in a royal carriage. At Westminster Hall he was grieved to see the eagle of the 39th regiment, taken during the retreat from Portugal, and that of the 101st, taken at Arapiles. Then he returned to France.

CHAPTER XXIII
THE PRISONERS ON PAROLE IN SCOTLAND

With the great Scottish prisons at Perth, Valleyfield, and Edinburgh I have dealt elsewhere, and it is with very particular pleasure that I shall now treat of the experiences of prisoners in the parole towns of Scotland, for the reason that, almost without exception, our involuntary visitors seem to have been treated with a kindness and forbearance not generally characteristic of the reception they had south of the Tweed, although of course there were exceptions.

As we shall see, Sir Walter Scott took kindly notice of the foreigners quartered in his neighbourhood, but that he never lost sight of the fact that they were foreigners and warriors is evident from the following letter to Lady Abercorn, dated May 3, 1812:

'I am very apprehensive of the consequences of a scarcity at this moment, especially from the multitude of French prisoners who are scattered through the small towns in this country; as I think, very improvidently. As the peace of this county is intrusted to me, I thought it necessary to state to the Justice Clerk that the arms of the local militia were kept without any guard in a warehouse in Kelso; that there was nothing to prevent the prisoners there, at Selkirk, and at Jedburgh, from joining any one night, and making themselves masters of this dépôt: that the sheriffs of Roxburgh and Selkirk, in order to put down such a commotion, could only command about three troops of yeomanry to be collected from a great distance, and these were to attack about 500 disciplined men, who, in the event supposed, would be fully provided with arms and ammunition, and might, if any alarm should occasion the small number of troops now at Berwick to be withdrawn, make themselves masters of that sea-port, the fortifications of which, although ruinous, would serve to defend them until cannon was brought against them.'

The Scottish towns where prisoners of war on parole were quartered, of which I have been able to get information, are Cupar, Kelso, Selkirk, Peebles, Sanquhar, Dumfries, Melrose, Jedburgh, Hawick, and Lauder.

By the kind permission of Mrs. Keddie ('Sarah Tytler') I am able to give very interesting extracts from her book, *Three Generations: The Story of a Middle-Class Scottish Family*, referring to the residence of the prisoners at Cupar, and the friendly intercourse between them and Mrs. Keddie's grandfather, Mr. Henry Gibb, of Balass, Cupar.

'Certainly the foreign officers were made curiously welcome in the country town, which their presence seemed to enliven rather than to offend. The strangers' courageous endurance, their perennial cheerfulness, their ingenious devices to occupy their time and improve the situation, aroused much friendly interest and amusement. The position must have been rendered more bearable to the sufferers, and perhaps more respectable in the eyes of the spectators, from the fact, for which I am not able to account, that, undoubtedly, the prisoners had among themselves, individually and collectively, considerable funds.

'The residents treated the jetsam and flotsam of war with more than forbearance, with genuine liberality and kindness, receiving them into their houses on cordial terms. Soon there was not a festivity in the town at which the French prisoners were not permitted—nay, heartily pressed to attend. How the complacent guests viewed those rejoicings in which the natives, as they frequently did, commemorated British victories over the enemy is not on record.

'But there was no thought of war and its fierce passions among the youth of the company in the simple dinners, suppers, and carpet-dances in private houses. There were congratulations on the abundance of pleasant partners, and the assurance that no girl need now sit out a dance or lack an escort if her home was within a certain limited distance beyond which the prisoners were not at liberty to stray.

'I have heard my mother and a cousin of hers dwell on the courtesy and agreeableness of the outlanders—what good dancers, what excellent company, as the country girls' escorts.... As was almost inevitable, the natural result of such intimacy followed, whether or not it was acceptable to the open-hearted entertainers. Love and marriage ensued between the youngsters, the vanquished and the victors. A Colonel, who was one of the band, married a daughter of the Episcopal clergyman in the town, and I am aware of at least two more weddings which eventually took place between the strangers and the inhabitants. (These occurred at the end of the prisoners' stay.)'

Balass, where the Gibbs lived, was within parole limits. One day Gibb asked the whole lot of the prisoners to breakfast, and forgot to tell Mrs. Gibb that he had done so.

'Happily she was a woman endowed with tranquillity of temper, while the ample resources of an old bountiful farmhouse were speedily brought to bear on the situation, dispensed as they were by the fair and capable henchwomen who relieved the mistress of the house of the more arduous of her duties. There was no disappointment in store for the patient, ingenious gentlemen who were wont to edify and divert their nominal enemy by making small excursions into the fields to snare larks for their private breakfast-tables.

'Another generous invitation of my grandfather's ran a narrow risk of having a tragic end. Not all his sense of the obligation of a host nor his compassion for the misfortunes of a gallant foe could at times restrain race antagonism, and his intense mortification at any occurrence which would savour of national discomfiture. Once, in entertaining some of these foreign officers, among whom was a *maître d'armes*, Harry Gibb was foolish enough to propose a bout of fencing with the expert. It goes without saying that within the first few minutes the yeoman's sword was dexterously knocked out of his hand.... Every other consideration went down before the deadly insult. In less time than it takes to tell the story the play became grim earnest. My grandfather turned his fists on the other combatant, taken unawares and not prepared for the attack, sprang like a wild-cat at his throat, and, if the bystanders had not interposed and separated the pair, murder might have been committed under his own roof by the kindest-hearted man in the countryside.'

This increasing intimacy between the prisoners and the inhabitants displeased the Government, and the crisis came when, in return for the kindness shown them, the prisoners determined to erect a theatre:

'The French prisoners were suffered to play only once in their theatre, and then the rout came for them. Amidst loud and sincere lamentation from all concerned, the officers were summarily removed in a body, and deposited in a town at some distance ... from their former guardians. As a final *gage d'amitié* ... the owners of the theatre left it a a gift to the town.'

Later—in the 'thirties—this theatre was annexed to the Grammar School to make extra class-rooms, for it was an age when Scotland was opposed to theatres.

KELSO[14]

For some of the following notes, I am indebted to the late Mr. Macbeth Forbes, who helped me notably elsewhere, and who kindly gave me permission to use them.

Some of the prisoners on parole at Kelso were sailors, but the majority were soldiers from Spain, Portugal, and the West Indies, and about twenty Sicilians. The inhabitants gave them a warm welcome, hospitably entertained them, and in return the prisoners, many of whom were men of means, gave balls at the inns—the only establishments in these pre-parish hall days where accommodation for large parties could be had—at which they appeared gaily attired with wondrous frills to their shirts, and white stockings.

'The time of their stay', says Mr. Forbes, 'was the gayest that Kelso had ever seen since fatal Flodden.'

Here as elsewhere there were artists among them who painted miniatures and landscapes and gave lessons, plaiters of straw and manufacturers of curious beautiful articles in coloured straw, wood-carvers, botanists, and fishermen. These last, it is said, first introduced the sport of catching fish through holes in the ice in mid-winter. Billiards, also, are said to have been introduced into Scotland by the prisoners. They mostly did their own cooking, and it is noted that they spoiled some of the landladies' tables by chopping up frogs for fricassees. They bought up the old Kelso 'theatre', the occasional scene of action for wandering Thespians, which was in a close off the Horse-Market, rebuilt and decorated it, some of the latter work still being visible in the ceiling of the ironmongery store of to-day. One difficulty was the very scanty dressing accommodation, so the actors often dressed at home, and their passage therefrom to the theatre in all sorts of garbs was a grand opportunity for the gibes of the youth of Kelso. Kelso was nothing if not 'proper', so that when upon one occasion the postmistress, a married woman, was seen accompanying a fantastically arrayed prisoner-actor to the theatre from his lodging, Mrs. Grundy had much to say for some time. On special occasions, such as when the French play was patronized by a local grandee like the Duchess of Roxburgh, the streets were carpeted with red cloth.

Brément, a privateer officer, advertised: 'Mr. Brément, Professor of Belles-Lettres and French Prisoner of War, respectfully informs the ladies and gentlemen of Kelso that he teaches the French and Latin languages. Apply for terms at Mrs. Matheson's, near the Market Place.' He is said to have done well.

Many of the privateersmen spoke English, as might be expected from their constant intercourse with men and places in the Channel.

One prisoner here was suspected of being concerned with the manufacture of forged bank-notes, so rife at this time in Scotland, as he ordered of Archibald Rutherford, stationer, paper of a particular character of which he left a pattern.

Escapes were not very frequent. On July 25, 1811, Surgeon-Major Violland, of the *Hebe* corvette, escaped. So did Ensign Parnagan, of the *Hautpol* privateer, on August 5, and on 23rd of the same month Lieutenant Rossignol got away. On November 11 one Bouchart escaped, and in June 1812 Lieutenant Anglade was missing, and a year later several got off, assisted, it was said, by an American, who was arrested.

In November 1811 the removal of all 'midshipmen' to Valleyfield, which was ordered at all Scottish parole towns, took place from Kelso.

Lieutenant Journeil, of the 27th Regiment, committed suicide in September 1812 by swallowing sulphuric acid. He is said to have become insane from home-sickness. He was buried at the Knowes, just outside the churchyard, it being unconsecrated ground.

A Captain Levasseur married an aunt of Sir George Harrison, M.P., a former Provost of Edinburgh, and the Levasseurs still keep up correspondence with Scotland.

On May 24, 1814, the prisoners began to leave, and by the middle of June all had gone. The *Kelso Mail* said that 'their deportment had been uniformly conciliatory and respectable'.

In Fullarton's *Imperial Gazetteer* of Scotland we read that:

'From November 1810 to June 1814, Kelso was the abode of a body, never more than 230 in number, of foreign prisoners of war, who, to a very noticeable degree, inoculated the place with their fashionable follies, and even, in some instances tainted it with their laxity of morals.'

Another account says:

'Their stay here seems to have been quiet and happy, although one man committed suicide. They carried on the usual manufactures in wood and bone and basket work; gave performances in the local theatre, which was decorated by them; were variously employed by local people, one man devoting his time to the tracking and snaring of a rare bird which arrived during severe weather.'

Rutherford's *Southern Counties Register and Directory* for 1866 says:

'The older inhabitants of Kelso remember the French prisoners of war quartered here as possessed of many amiable qualities, of which "great mannerliness" and buoyancy of spirits, in many instances under the depressing effects of great poverty, were the most conspicuous of their peculiarities; the most singular to the natives of Kelso was their habit of gathering for use different kinds of wild weeds by the road side, and hedge-roots, and killing small birds to eat—the latter a practise considered not much removed from cannibalism. That they were frivolous we will admit, as many of them wore ear-rings, and one, a Pole, had a ring to his nose; while all were boyishly fond of amusement, and were merry, good-natured creatures.'

One memorable outbreak of these spirits is recorded in the *Kelso Mail* of January 30, 1812:

'In consequence of certain riotous proceedings which took place in this town near the East end of the Horn Market on Christmas last, by which the peace of the neighbourhood was very much disturbed, an investigation of the circumstances took place before our respectable magistrate, Bailie Smith. From this it appeared that several of the French prisoners of war here on parole had been dining together on Christmas Day, and that a part of them were engaged in the riotous proceedings.'

These 'riotous proceedings' are said to have amounted to little more than a more or less irregular arm-in-arm procession down the street to the accompaniment of lively choruses. However, the Agent reported it to the Transport Office, who ordered each prisoner to pay £1 1s. fine, to be deducted from their allowance. The account winds up:

'It is only an act of justice, however, to add that in so far as we have heard, the conduct of the French prisoners here on parole has been regular and inoffensive.'

On the anniversary of St. Andrew in 1810, the Kelso Lodge of Freemasons was favoured with a visit from several French officers, prisoners of war, at present resident in the town. The Right Worshipful in addressing them, expressed the wishes of himself and the Brethren to do everything in their power to promote the comfort and happiness of the exiles. After which he proposed the health of the Brethren who were strangers in a foreign land, which was drunk with enthusiastic applause.

There is frequent mention of their appearance at Masonic meetings, when the 'harmony was greatly increased by the polite manners and the vocal power of our French Brethren'.

There are a great many of their signatures on the parchment to which all strangers had to subscribe their names by order of the Grand Lodge.[15]

The only war-prisoner relics in the museum are some swords.

I have to thank Sir George Douglas for the following interesting letters from French prisoners in Kelso.

The first is in odd Latin, the second in fair English, the third in French. The two latter I am glad to give as additional testimonies to the kindly treatment of the enforced exiles amongst us.

The first is as follows:

'Kelso: die duodecima mensis Augusti anni 1811.

'Honorifice Praefecte:

'Monitum te facio, hoc mane, die duodecima mensis Augusti, hora decima et semi, per vicum transeuntem vestimenta mea omnino malefacta fuisse cum aqua tam foetida ac mulier quae jactavit illam.

'Noxia mulier quae vestimenta mea, conceptis verbis, abluere noluit, culpam insulsitate cumulando, uxor est domino Wm. Stuart Lanio [Butcher?]

'Ut persuasum mihi est hanc civitatem optimis legibus nimis constitutam esse ut ille eventus impunitus feratur, de illo certiorem te facio, magnifice Praefecte, ut similis casus iterum non renovetur erga captivos Gallos, quorum tu es curator, et, occurente occasione, defensor.

'Quandoquidem aequitas tua non mihi soli sed cunctis plane nota est, spe magna nitor te jus dicturam expostulationi meae, cogendo praedictam mulierem et quamprimum laventur vestimenta mea. In ista expectatione gratam habeas salutationem illius qui mancipio et nexo, honoratissime praefecte, tuus est.

'MATRIEN.

'Honorato, Honoratissimo Domino Smith,

'Captivorum Gallorum praefecto. Kelso.'

The gist of the above being that Mrs. Stuart threw dirty water over M. Matrien as he passed along the street in Kelso, and he demands her punishment and the cleansing of his clothes.

The second letter runs:

'Paris, on the 6th day of May, 1817.

'Dear Sir,

'I have since I left Kelso wrote many letters to my Scots friends, but I have been unfortunate enough to receive no answer. The wandering life I have led during four years is, without doubt, the cause of that silence, for my friends have been so good to me that I cannot imagine they have entirely forgotten me. In all my letters my heart has endeavoured to prove how thankful I was, but my gratitude is of that kind that one may feel but cannot express. Pray, my good Sir, if you remember yet your prisoner, be so kind as to let him have a few lignes from you and all news about all his old good friends.

'The difficulty which I have to express myself in your tongue, and the countryman of yours who is to take my letter, compel me to end sooner than I wish, but if expressions want to my mouth, be assure in revange that my heart shall always be full of all those feelings which you deserve so rightly.

'Farewell, I wish you all kind of happiness.

'Your friend for ever,

'Le Chevalier Lebas de Ste. Croix.

'My direction: à Monsieur le Chevalier Lebas de Ste. Croix, Capitaine à la légion de l'Isère, caserne de La Courtille à Paris. P.S.—All my thanks and good wishes first to your family, to the family Waldie, Davis, Doctor Douglas, Rutherford, and my good landlady Mistress Elliot.

'To Mister John Smith Esq.,

'bridge street,

'Kelso, Scotland.'

(In Kelso, towards the end of 1912, I had the pleasure of making the acquaintance of Mr. Provost Smith, grandson of the gentleman to whom the foregoing two letters were addressed, and Mr. Smith was kind enough to present me with a tiny ring of bone, on which is minutely worked the legend: 'I love to see you', done by a French officer on parole in Kelso in 1811.)

The third letter is as follows:

'Je, soussigné officier de la Légion d'Honneur, Lieutenant Colonel au 8ᵉ Régiment de Dragons, sensible aux bons traitements que les prisonniers français sur parole en cette ville reçoivent journellement de la part de Mr. Smith, law agent, invite en mon nom et en celui de mes compagnons d'infortune ceux de nos compatriotes entre les mains desquels le hasard de la guerre pourroit faire tomber Mesdemoiselles St. Saure (?) d'avoir pour elles tous les égards et attentions qu'elles méritent, et de nous aider par tous les bons offices qu'ils pourront rendre à ces dames à acquitter une partie de la reconnaissance que nous devons à leur famille.

'Kelso. 7 Avril, 1811.

'DUDOUIT.'

SELKIRK

In 1811, ninety-three French prisoners arrived at Selkirk, many of them army surgeons. Their mile limits from the central point were, on the Hawick road, to Knowes; over the bridge, as far as the Philiphaugh entries; and towards Bridgehead, the 'Prisoners' Bush'. An old man named Douglas, says Mr. Craig-Brown (from whose book on Selkirk, I take this information, and to whom I am indebted for much hospitality and his many pains in acting as my mentor in Selkirk), remembered them coming to his father's tavern at Heathenlie for their morning rum, and astonishing the people with what they ate. 'They made tea out of dried whun blooms and skinned the verra paddas. The doctor anes was verra clever, and some of them had plenty o' siller.'

On October 13, 1811, the prisoners constructed a balloon, and sent it up amidst such excitement as Selkirk rarely felt. Indeed, the Yeomanry then out for their training could not be mustered until they had seen the balloon.

A serious question came up in 1814 concerning the public burden which the illegitimate children of these gentlemen were causing, and complaints were sent to the Transport Office, whose reply was that the fathers of the children were liable to the civil law, and that unless they should provide for their maintenance, they should go to prison.

Two of the prisoners quarrelled about a girl and fought a bloodless duel at Linglee for half an hour, when the authorities appeared upon the scene and arrested the principals, who were sent to jail for a month.

Mr. J. John Vernon wrote:

'In an article upon the old Selkirk Subscription Library, reference is made to the use of the Library by the officers who were confined in Selkirk and district during the Napoleonic wars.

'Historical reference is furnished incidentally in the pages of the Day Book—the register of volumes borrowed and returned. There is no mention of such a privilege being conferred by the members or committee, but, as a matter of fact, all the French officers who were prisoners in Selkirk during the Napoleonic wars were allowed to take books from the Library as freely and as often as they chose. Beginning with April 5th, 1811, and up to May 4th, 1814, there were no less than 132 closely written foolscap pages devoted exclusively to their book-borrowing transactions. They were omnivorous readers, with a *penchant* for History and Biography, but devouring all sorts of literature from the poetical to the statistical. Probably because the Librarian could not trust himself to spell them, the officers themselves entered their names, as well as the names of books. Sometimes, when they made an entry for a comrade they made blunders in spelling the other man's name: that of Forsonney, for instance, being given in four or five different ways. As the total number of prisoners was 94, it can be concluded from the list appended that only two or three did not join the Library.

'Besides the French prisoners, the students attending Professor Lawson's lectures seem to have had the privilege of reading, but for them all about two pages suffice. It is said that, moved by a desire to bring these benighted foreigners to belief in the true faith, Doctor Lawson added French to the more ancient languages he was already proficient in, but the aliens were nearly all men of education who knew their Voltaire, with the result that the Professor made poor progress with his well meant efforts at proselytism, if he did not even receive a shock to his own convictions.'

There were several Masonic Brethren among the foreign prisoners at Selkirk, and it is noteworthy that on March 9, 1812, it was proposed by the

Brethren of this Lodge that on account of the favour done by some of the French Brethren, they should be enrolled as honorary members of the Lodge, and this was unanimously agreed to.

It should be noted that the French Brethren were a numerous body, twenty-three of their names being added to the roll of St. John's; and we find that, as at Melrose, they formed themselves into a separate Lodge and initiated their fellow countrymen in their own tongue.

In what was known as Lang's Barn, now subdivided into cottages, the French prisoners extemporized a theatre, and no doubt some of their decorative work lies hidden beneath the whitewash. The barn was the property of the grandfather of the late Andrew Lang.

The experiences of Sous-lieutenant Doisy de Villargennes, of the 26th French line regiment, I shall now relate with particular pleasure, not only on account of their unusual interest, but because they reflect the brightest side of captivity in Britain. Doisy was wounded after Fuentes d'Oñoro in May 1811, and taken prisoner. He was moved to hospital at Celorico, where he formed a friendship with Captain Pattison, of the 73rd. Thence he was sent to Fort Belem at Lisbon, which happened to be garrisoned by the 26th British Regiment, a coincidence which at once procured for him the friendship of its officers, who caused him to be lodged in their quarters, and to be treated rather as an honoured guest than as a prisoner, but with one bad result—that the extraordinary good living aggravated his healing wound, and he was obliged to return to hospital. These were days of heavy drinking, and Lisbon lay in the land of good and abundant wine; hosts and guest had alike fared meagrely and hardly for a long time, so that it is not difficult to account for the effect of the abrupt change upon poor Doisy. However, he pulled round, and embarked for Portsmouth, not on the ordinary prisoner transport, but as guest of Pattison on a war-ship. Doisy, with sixty other officers, were landed at Gosport, and, contrary to the usual rule, allowed to be on parole in the town previous to their dispatch to their *cautionnement*.

At the Gosport prison—Forton—whither he went to look up comrades, Doisy was overjoyed to meet with his own foster-brother, whom he had persuaded to join his regiment, and whom he had given up as lost at Fuentes d'Oñoro, and he received permission to spend some time with him in the prison. I give with very great pleasure Doisy's remarks upon captivity in England in general, and in its proper place under the heading of Forton Prison (see pp. 217–18) will be found his description of that place, which is equally pleasant reading.

'I feel it my duty here, in the interests of truth and justice, to combat an erroneous belief concerning the hard treatment of prisoners of war in England.... No doubt, upon the hulks they led a very painful existence; execrable feeding, little opportunity for exercise, and a discipline extremely severe, even perhaps cruel. Such was their fate. But we must remember that only refractory prisoners were sent to the hulks.'

(Here we must endorse a note of the editor of Doisy's book, to the effect that this is inaccurate, inasmuch as there were 19,000 prisoners upon the hulks, and they could not all have been 'refractory'.)

'These would upset the discipline of prisons like Gosport. Also we must remember that the inmates of the hulks were chiefly the crews of privateers, and that privateering was not considered fair warfare by England.' (Strange to say, the editor passes over this statement without comment.) 'At Forton there reigned the most perfect order, under a discipline severe but humane. We heard no sobbings of despair, we saw no unhappiness in the eyes of the inmates, but, on the contrary, on all sides resounded shouts of laughter, and the chorus of patriotic songs.'

In after years, when Germain Lamy, the foster-brother, was living a free man in France, Doisy says that in conversation Lamy never alluded to the period of his captivity in England without praising warmly the integrity and the liberality of all the Englishmen with whom as a prisoner-trader he had business relations. 'Such testimonies,' says Doisy, 'and others of like character, cannot but weaken the feelings of hatred and antagonism roused by war between the two nations.'

In a few days Doisy was marched off to Odiham, but, on account of the crowded state of the English parole towns, it was decided to send the newcomers to Scotland, and so, on October 1, 1811, they landed at Leith, 190 in number, and marched to Selkirk, via Edinburgh and the dépôt at Penicuik.

There was some difficulty at first in finding lodgings in the small Scottish town for so large a number of strangers, but when it was rumoured that they were largely gentlemen of means and likely to spend their money freely, accommodation was quickly forthcoming.

Living in Scotland Doisy found to be very much cheaper than in England, and the weekly pay of half a guinea, regularly received through Coutts, he found sufficient, if not ample. His lodging cost but half a crown a week, and as the prisoners messed in groups, and, moreover, had no local hindrance to the excellent fishing in Ettrick and Tweed, board was probably proportionately moderate. As the French prisoners in Selkirk spent upon an average £150 a week in the little town, and were there for two years and a half, no less a sum than £19,500 was poured into the local pocket.

The exiles started a French café in which was a billiard table brought from Edinburgh, to which none but Frenchmen were admitted; gathered together an orchestra of twenty-two and gave Saturday concerts, which were extensively patronized by the inhabitants and the surrounding gentry; and with their own hands built a theatre accommodating 200 people.

'Les costumes,' said Doisy, 'surtout ceux des rôles féminins, nous nécessitaient de grands efforts d'habilité. Aucun de nous n'avait auparavant exercé le métier de charpentier, tapissier, de tailleur, ou... fait son apprentissage chez une couturière. L'intelligence, toutefois, stimulée par la volonté, peut engendrer de petits miracles.'

They soon had a répertoire of popular tragedies and comedies, and gave a performance every Wednesday.

On each of the four main roads leading out of the town there was at the distance of a mile a notice-board on which was inscribed: 'Limite des Prisonniers de Guerre.' As evidence of the goodwill generally borne towards the foreigners by the country folk, when a waggish prisoner moved one of these boards a mile further on, no information was lodged about it, and although a reward of one guinea was paid to anybody arresting a prisoner beyond limits, or out of his lodgings at forbidden hours, it was very rarely claimed. Some of the prisoners indeed were accustomed daily to go fishing some miles down the rivers.

The French prisoners did not visit the Selkirk townsfolk, for the 'classy' of the latter had come to the resolution not to associate with them at all; but the priggish exclusiveness or narrow prejudice, or whatever it might have been, was amply atoned for by the excellent friendships formed in the surrounding neighbourhoods. There was Mr. Anderson, a gentleman farmer, who invited the Frenchmen to fish and regaled them in typical old-time Scots fashion afterwards; there was a rich retired lawyer, whose chief sorrow was that he could not keep sober during his entertainment of them: there was Mr. Thorburn, another gentleman farmer, who introduced them to grilled sheep's head, salmagundi, and a cheese of his own making, of which he was particularly proud.

But above all there was the 'shirra', then Mr. Walter Scott, who took a fancy to a bright and lively young Frenchman, Tarnier by name, and often invited him and two or three friends to Abbotsford—Doisy calls it 'Melrose Abbey'. This was in February 1812. Mrs. Scott, whom, Doisy says, Scott had married in *Berlin*—was only seen some minutes before dinner, never at the repast itself. She spoke French perfectly, says Doisy. Scott, he says, was a very different man as host in his own house from what they judged him to be from his appearance in the streets of Selkirk. 'Un homme enjoué, à la physionomie ordinaire et peu significative, à l'attitude même un peu gauche, à la démarche vulgaire et aux allures à l'avenant, causées probablement par sa boiterie.' But at Abbotsford his guests found him, on the contrary, a gentleman full of cordiality and gaiety, receiving his friends with amiability and delicacy. The rooms at Abbotsford, says Doisy, were spacious and well lighted, and the table not sumptuous, but refined.

Doisy tells us that what seemed to be the all-absorbing subject of conversation at the Abbotsford dinner-table was Bonaparte. No matter into what other channel the talk drifted, their host would hark back to Bonaparte, and never wearied of the anecdotes and details about him which the guests were able to give. Little did his informants think that, ten years later, much that they told him would appear, as Doisy says, in a distorted form rarely favourable to the great man, in Scott's *Life of Bonaparte*. He quotes instances, and is at no pains to hide his resentment at what he considers a not very dignified or proper proceeding on the part of Sir Walter.

Only on one prominent occasion was the friendly feeling between the prisoners and the Selkirk people disturbed.

On August 15, 1813, the Frenchmen, in number ninety, united to celebrate the Emperor's birthday at their café, the windows of which opened on to the public garden. They feasted, made speeches, drank numberless toasts, and sang numberless patriotic songs. As it was found that they had a superabundance of food, it was decided to distribute it among the crowd assembled in the public garden, but with the condition that every one who accepted it should doff his hat and cry 'Vive l'Empereur Napoléon!' But although a couple of Frenchmen stood outside, each with a viand in one hand and a glass of liquor in the other, not a Scotsman would comply with the condition, and all went away. One man, a sort of factotum of the Frenchmen, who made a considerable deal of money out of them in one way and another, and who was known as 'Bang Bay', from his habit, when perplexed with much questioning and ordering, of replying 'by and by', did accept the food and drink, and utter the required cry, and his example was followed by a few others, but the original refusers still held aloof and gathered together in the garden, evidently in no peaceable mood.

Presently, as the feast proceeded and the celebrants were listening to a song composed for the occasion, a stone was thrown through the window, and hit Captain Gruffaud of the Artillery. He rushed out and demanded who had thrown it. Seeing a young man grinning, Gruffaud accused him, and as the youth admitted it, Gruffaud let him have the stone full in the face. A disturbance being at once imminent, the French officers broke up chairs, &c., to arm themselves against an attack, and the crowd, seeing this, dispersed. Soon after, the Agent, Robert Henderson, hurried up to say that the crowd had armed themselves and were re-assembling, and that as the Frenchmen were in the wrong, inasmuch as they had exceeded their time-limit, nine o'clock, by an hour, he counselled them to go home quietly. So the matter ended, and Doisy remarks that no evil resulted, and that Scots and French became better comrades than ever.

Another event might have resulted in a disturbance. At the news of a victory by Wellington in Spain, the Selkirk people set their bells ringing, and probably rejoiced with some ostentation. A short time after, says Doisy, came the news of a great French victory in Russia (?). The next day, Sunday, some French officers attended a Quakers' meeting in their house, and managed to hide themselves. At midnight a dozen of their comrades were admitted through the window, bringing with them a coil of rope which they made fast to that of the meeting-house bell, and rang vigorously, awakening the town and bringing an amazed crowd to the place, and in the confusion the actors of the comedy escaped. Then came the Peace of 1814, and the Frenchmen were informed that on April 20 a vessel would be at Berwick to take them to France. The well-to-do among them proposed to travel by carriage to Berwick, but it was later decided that all funds should be united and that they should go on foot, and to defray expenses £60 was collected. Before leaving, it was suggested that a considerable increase might be made to their exchequer if they put up to auction the structure of the theatre, as well as the properties and dresses, which had cost £120. Tarnier was chosen auctioneer, and the bidding was started at £50, but in spite of his eloquence the highest bid was £40. So they decided to have some fun at the last. All the articles were carried to the field which the prisoners had hired for playing football, and a last effort was made to sell them. But the highest bid was only £2 more than before. Rather than sell at such a ridiculous price, the Frenchmen, armed with sticks and stones, formed a circle round the objects for sale, and set fire to them, a glorious bonfire being the result.

The day of departure came. Most of the Frenchmen had passed the previous night in the Public Garden, singing, and drinking toasts, so that all were up betimes, and prepared for their tramp. Their delight and astonishment may be imagined when they beheld a defile of all sorts of vehicles, and even of saddle-horses, into the square, and learned that these had been provided by the people of Selkirk to convey them to Kelso, half way to Berwick.

Says Doisy: 'Nous nous séparâmes donc de nos amis de Selkirk sans garder d'une part et d'autre aucun des sentiments de rancune pouvant exister auparavant'.

Mr. Craig-Brown relates the following anecdote:

'Many years after the war, in the Southern States of America, two young Selkirk lads were astonished to see themselves looked at with evident earnestness by two foreigners within earshot of them. At last one of the latter, a distinguished-looking elderly gentleman, came up and said: "Pardon, I think from your speech you come from Scotland?"

"'We do."

"'Perhaps from the South of Scotland?"

"'Yes, from Selkirk."

"'From Selkirk! Ah! I was certain: General! It is true. They are from Selkirk." Upon which his companion came up, who, looking at one of the lads for a while, exclaimed:

"'I am sure you are the son of ze, ze, leetle fat man who kills ze sheep!"

"'Faith! Ye're recht!" said the astonished Scot. "My father was Tudhope, the flesher!"

'Upon which the more effusive of the officers fairly took him round the neck, and gave him a hearty embrace. Making themselves known as two of the old French prisoners, they insisted on the lads remaining in their company, loaded them with kindness, and never tired of asking them questions about their place of exile, and all its people, particularly the sweethearts they and their comrades had left behind them.'

PEEBLES

Although Peebles was not established as a parole town until 1803, a great many French prisoners, not on parole, were here in 1798–9, most of them belonging to the thirty-six-gun frigates *Coquille* and *Résolue*, belonging to the Brest squadron of the expedition to Ireland, which was beaten by Sir John Warren. They were probably confined in the town jail.

The first parole prisoners were Dutch, Belgians, and Danes, 'all of whom took to learning cotton hand-loom weaving, and spent their leisure time in fishing', says Mr. W. Chambers. In 1810 about one hundred French, Poles, and Italians came: 'Gentlemanly in manner, they made for themselves friends in the town and neighbourhood, those among them who were surgeons occasionally assisting at a medical consultation. They set up a theatre in what is now the public reading-room, and acted Molière and Corneille. In 1811 all the "midshipmen" (gardes-marines) among them were suddenly called to the Cross, and marched away to Valleyfield, possibly an act of reprisal for Bonaparte's action against English midshipmen.'[16]

Shortly after their removal, all the other prisoners were sent away from Peebles, chiefly to Sanquhar. This removal is *said* to have been brought about by the terror of a lady of rank in the neighbourhood at so many enemies being near Neidpath Castle, where were deposited the arms of the Peeblesshire Militia.

Mr. Sanderson, of the Chambers Institute at Peebles, my indefatigable conductor about and around the pleasant old Border town, told me that there is still in Peebles a family named Bonong, said to be descended from a French prisoner; that a Miss Wallink who went to Canada some years ago as Mrs. Cranston, was descended from a Polish prisoner; that there was recently a Mr. Lenoir at the Tontine Hotel (traditionally the 'hotle' which was Meg Dodd's bugbear in *St. Ronan's Well*), and that a drawing master named Chastelaine came of French prisoner parentage.

In the Museum of the Chambers Institute are four excellent specimens of French prisoner-made ship models, and on the plaster walls of a house are a couple of poorly executed oil frescoes said to have been painted by prisoners.

I have the kind permission of Messrs. Chambers to quote the following very complete descriptions of French prisoner life at Peebles from the *Memoirs of William and Robert Chambers* by Mr. William Chambers.

'1803. Not more than 20 or 30 of these foreign exiles arrived at this early period. They were mostly Dutch and Walloons, with afterwards a few Danes. These men did not repine. They nearly all betook themselves to learn some handicraft to eke out their scanty allowance. At leisure hours they might be seen fishing in long leather boots as if glad to procure a few trout and eels. Two or three years later came a *détenu* of a different class. He was seemingly the captain of a ship from the French West Indies, who brought with him his wife and a negro servant-boy named Jack. Black Jack, as we called him, was sent to the school, where he played with the other boys on the town green, and at length spoke and read like a native. He was a good-natured creature, and became a general favourite. Jack was the first pure negro whom the boys at that time had ever seen.

'None of these classes of prisoner broke his parole, nor ever gave any trouble to the authorities. They had not, indeed, any appearance of being prisoners, for they were practically free to live and ramble about within reasonable bounds where they liked.

'In 1810 there was a large accession to this original body of prisoners on parole. As many as one hundred and eleven were already on their way to the town, and might be expected shortly. There was speedily a vast sensation in the place. The local Militia had been disbanded. Lodgings of all sorts were vacant. The new arrivals would on all hands be heartily welcomed. On Tuesday, the expected French prisoners in an unceremonious way began to drop in. As one of several boys, I went out to meet them coming from Edinburgh. They came walking in twos and threes, a few of them lame. Their appearance was startling, for they were in military garb in which they had been captured in Spain. Some were in light blue hussar dress, braided, with marks of sabre wounds. Others were in dark blue uniform. Several wore large cocked hats, but the greater number had undress caps. All had a gentlemanly air, notwithstanding their generally dishevelled attire, their soiled boots, and their visible marks of fatigue.

'Before night they had all arrived, and, through the activity of the Agent appointed by the Transport Board, they had been provided with lodgings suitable to their slender allowance. This large batch of prisoners on parole were, of course, all in the rank of naval or military officers. Some had been pretty high in the service and seen a good deal of fighting. Several were doctors, or, as they called themselves, *officiers de santé*. Among the whole there were, I think, about half a dozen midshipmen. A strange thing was their varied nationality. Though spoken of as French, there was in the party a mixture of Italians, Swiss, and Poles; but this we found out only after some intercourse. Whatever their origin, they were warm adherents of Napoleon, whose glory at this time was at its height. Lively in manner, their minds were full of the recent struggle in the Peninsula.

'Through the consideration of an enterprising grocer, the prisoners were provided with a billiard table at which they spent much of their time. So far well. But how did these unfortunate exiles contrive to live? How did they manage to feed and clothe themselves, and pay for lodgings? The allowance from Government was on a moderate scale. I doubt if it was more than one shilling per head per diem. In various instances two persons lived in a single room, but even that cost half-a-crown per week. The truth is they must have been half starved, but for the fortunate circumstance of a number of them having brought money—foreign gold-pieces, concealed about their persons, which stores were supplemented by remittances from France; and in a friendly way, at least as regards the daily mess, or *table d'hôte*, the richer helped the poorer, which was a good trait in their character. The messing together was the great resource, and took place in a house hired for the purpose, in which the cookery was conducted under the auspices of M. Lavoche, one of the prisoners who was skilled in *cuisine*. My brother and I had some dealings with Lavoche. We cultivated rabbits in a hutch built by ourselves in the backyard, and sold them for the Frenchmen's mess; the money we got for them, usually eighteenpence a pair, being employed in the purchase of books.

'Billiards were indispensable, but something more was wanted. Without a theatre, life was felt to be unendurable. But how was a theatre to be secured? There was nothing of the kind in the place. The more eager of the visitors managed to get out of the difficulty. There was an old and disused ball-room. It was rather of confined dimensions, and low in the roof, with a gallery at one end, over the entrance, for the musicians.... Walter Scott's mother, when a girl, (I was told,) had crossed Minchmoor, a dangerously high hill, in a chaise, from the adjacent country, to dance for a night in that little old ball-room. Now set aside as unfashionable, the room was at anybody's service, and came quite handily for the Frenchmen. They fitted it up with a stage at the inner end, and cross benches to accommodate 120 persons, independently of perhaps 20 more in the musicians' gallery. The thing was neatly got up with scenery painted by M. Walther and M. Ragulski, the latter a young Pole. No licence was required for the theatre, for it was altogether a private undertaking. Money was not taken at the door, and no tickets were sold. Admission was gained by complimentary billets distributed chiefly among persons with whom the actors had established an intimacy.

'Among these favoured individuals was my father, who, carrying on a mercantile concern, occupied a prominent position. He felt a degree of compassion for these foreigners, constrained to live in exile, and, besides welcoming them to his house, gave them credit in articles of drapery of which they stood in need; and through which circumstance they soon assumed an improved appearance in costume. Introduced to the family circle, their society was agreeable, and in a sense instructive. Though with imperfect speech, a sort of half-English, half-French, they related interesting circumstances in their careers.

'How performances in French should have had any general attraction may seem to require explanation. There had grown up in the town among young persons especially, a knowledge of familiar French phrases; so that what was said, accompanied by appropriate gestures, was pretty well guessed at. But, as greatly contributing to remove difficulties, a worthy man, of an obliging turn and genial humour, volunteered to act as interpreter. Moving in humble circumstances as hand-loom weaver, he had let lodgings to a French captain and his wife, and from being for years in domestic intercourse with them, he became well acquainted with their language. William Hunter, for such was his name, besides being of ready wit, partook of a lively musical genius. I have heard him sing *Malbrook s'en va t'en guerre* with amazing correctness and vivacity. His services at the theatre were therefore of value to the natives in attendance. Seated conspicuously at the centre of what we may call the pit, eyes were turned on him inquiringly when anything particularly funny was said requiring explanation, and for general use he whisperingly communicated the required interpretation. So, put up to the joke, the natives heartily joined in the laugh, though rather tardily.... As for the French plays, which were performed with perfect propriety, they were to us not only amusing but educational. The remembrance of these dramatic efforts of the French prisoners of war has been through life a continual treat. It is curious for me to look back on the performances of the pieces of Molière in circumstances so remarkable.

'My mother, even while lending her dresses and caps to enable performers to represent female characters, never liked the extraordinary intimacy which had been formed between the French officers and my father. Against his giving them credit she constantly remonstrated in vain. It was a tempting but perilous trade. For a time, by the resources just mentioned, they paid wonderfully well. With such solid inducements, my father confidingly gave extensive credit to these strangers—men who, by their positions, were not amenable to the civil law, and whose obligations, accordingly, were altogether debts of honour. The consequence was that which might have been anticipated. An order suddenly arrived from the Government commanding the whole of the prisoners to quit Peebles, and march chiefly to Sanquhar in Dumfriesshire: the cause of the movement being the prospective arrival of a Militia Regiment.

'The intelligence came one Sunday night. What a gloom prevailed at several firesides that evening!

'On their departure the French prisoners made many fervid promises that, should they ever return to their own country, they would have pleasure in discharging their debt. They all got home in the Peace of 1814, but not one of them ever paid a farthing, and William Chambers was one of the many whose affairs were brought to a crisis therefrom.'

It will be seen later that this was not the uniform experience of British creditors with French debtors.

CHAPTER XXIV
PAROLE PRISONERS IN SCOTLAND (*continued*)

SANQUHAR

The first prisoners came here in March 1812. They were chiefly some of those who had been hurried away from Wincanton and other towns in the west of England at the alarm that a general rising of war-prisoners in those parts was imminent, and on account of the increasing number of escapes from those places; others were midshipmen from Peebles. In all from sixty to seventy prisoners were at Sanquhar. A letter from one of the men removed from Peebles to Mr. Chambers of that town says that they were extremely uncomfortable; such kind of people as the inhabitants had no room to spare; the greater part of the Frenchmen were lodged in barns and kitchens; they could get neither beef nor mutton, nothing but salted meat and eggs. They applied to the Transport Office, in order to be removed to Moffat.

The prisoners at Sanquhar left behind them, when discharged at the Peace of 1814, debts amounting to £160, but these were paid by the French Commissioners charged with effecting the final exchanges in that year.

One duel is recorded. It was fought on the Washing Green, and one of the combatants was killed. Mr. Tom Wilson, in his *Memorials of Sanquhar Kirkyard*, identifies the victim as Lieutenant Arnaud, whose grave bears the inscription:

'In memory of J. B. Arnaud, aged 27 years, Lieutenant in the French Navy, prisoner of war on parole at Sanquhar. Erected by his companions in arms and fellow prisoners as a testimony of their esteem and attachment. He expired in the arms of friendship, 9th November, 1812.'

It had been announced that he died of small-pox, but Mr. Wilson thinks this was put out as a blind.

Some changes of French names into English are to be noted here as elsewhere. Thus, Auguste Gregoire, cabin boy of the *Jeune Corneille* privateer, captured in 1803, was confined at Peebles, and later at Sanquhar. He married a Peebles girl, but as she absolutely refused to go with him to France when Peace was declared in 1814 he was obliged to remain, and became a teacher of dancing and deportment under the name of Angus MacGregor. So also one Etienne Foulkes became Etney Fox; Baptiste became Baptie, and Walnet was turned into Walden.

There was a Masonic Lodge at Sanquhar—the 'Paix Désirée'.

The banks of Crawick were a favourite resort of the prisoners, and on a rock in the Holme Walks is cut 'Luego de Delizia 1812', and to the right, between two lines, the word 'Souvenir'. The old bathing place of the prisoners, behind Holme House, is still known as 'The Sodger's Pool'.

Hop-plants are said to have been introduced hereabouts by the prisoners—probably Germans.

Mr. James Brown thus writes about the prisoners at Sanquhar:

'They were Frenchmen, Italians and Poles—handsome young fellows, who had all the manners of gentlemen, and, living a life of enforced idleness, they became great favourites with the ladies with whose hearts they played havoc, and, we regret to record, in some instances with their virtue.'

'This', says the Rev. Matthew Dickie, of the South United Free Church, Sanquhar, 'is only too true. John Wysilaski, who left Sanquhar when quite a youth and became a "settler" in Australia, was the illegitimate son of one of the officers. This John Wysilaski died between 25 and 30 years of age, and left a large fortune. Of this he bequeathed £60,000 to the Presbyterian Church of Victoria, and over £4,000 to the church with which his mother had been connected, viz. the South Church, Sanquhar, and he directed the interest of this sum to be paid to the Minister of the South Church over and above his stipend. The same Polish officer had another son by another woman, Louis Wysilaski, who lived and died in his native town. I remember him quite well.'

DUMFRIES

The first detachment of officer-prisoners arrived at Dumfries in November 1811, from Peebles, whence they had marched the thirty-two miles to Moffat, and had driven from there. The agent at Dumfries was Mr. Francis

Shortt, Town Clerk of the Burgh, and brother of Dr. Thomas Shortt, who, as Physician to the British Forces at St. Helena, was to assist, ten years later, at the post-mortem examination of Bonaparte.

At first the prices asked by the inhabitants for lodgings somewhat astonished the prisoners, being from fifteen to twenty-five shillings a week, but in the end they were moderately accommodated and better than in Peebles. Their impressions of Dumfries were certainly favourable, for not only had they in Mr. Shortt a just and kindly Agent, but the townsfolk and the country gentry offered them every sort of hospitality. In a letter to Mr. Chambers of Peebles, one of them says: 'The inhabitants, I think, are frightened with Frenchmen, and run after us to see if we are like other people; the town is pretty enough, and the inhabitants, though curious, seem very gentle.'

Another, after a visit to the theatre, writes in English:

'I have been to the theatre of the town, and I was very satisfied with the actors; they are very good for a little town like Dumfries, where receipts are not very copious, though I would have very much pleasure with going to the play-house now and then. However, I am deprived of it by the bell which rings at five o'clock, and if I am not in my lodging by the hour appointed by the law, I must at least avoid to be in the public meeting, at which some inhabitants don't like to see me.'

It was long before the natives could get used to certain peculiarities in the Frenchmen's diet, particularly frogs. A noted Dumfries character, George Hair, who died a few years ago, used to declare that 'the first siller he ever earned was for gatherin' paddocks for the Frenchmen', and an aged inmate of Lanark Poorhouse, who passed his early boyhood at Dumfries, used to tell a funny frog story. He remembered that fifteen or sixteen prisoners used to live together in a big house, not far from his father's, and that there was a meadow near at hand where they got great store of frogs. Once there was a Crispin procession at Dumfries, and a Mr. Renwick towered above all the others as King.

'The Crispin ploy, ye ken, cam frae France, an' the officers in the big hoose askit the King o' the cobblers tae dine wi' them. They had a gran' spread wi' a fine pie, that Maister Renwick thocht was made o' rabbits tosked up in some new fangled way, an' he didna miss tae lay in a guid stock. When a' was owre, they askit him how he likit his denner, an' he said "First rate". Syne they lauched and speered him if he kent what the pie was made o', but he said he wasna sure. When they tell't him it was paddocks, it was a' ane as if they had gien him a dose of pizzen. He just banged up an' breenged oot the hoose. Oor bit winnock lookit oot on the Frenchmen's backyaird, an' we saw Maister Renwick sair, sair forfochen, but after a dainty bit warsle, he an' the paddocks pairtit company.'

It is recorded that the French prisoners considered a good fat cat an excellent substitute for a hare.

At a fire, two French surgeons who distinguished themselves in fighting it, were, on a petition from the inhabitants to the Transport Board, alowed to return immediately to France. But another surgeon who applied to be sent to Kelso as he had a relative there, was refused permission—a refusal, which, it is quite possible, was really a compliment, for the records of parole life in Britain abound with evidence of the high estimation in which French prisoner-surgeons were held in our country towns.

Between thirty and forty officers tried to escape from Dumfries during the three years of its being a Parole Town; most of these were recaptured, and sent to Valleyfield Prison. Four officers took advantage of the fishing-licence usually extended to the officers on parole here, by which strict adherence to the mile limit was not insisted upon, and gradually got their belongings away to Lochmaben, eight miles distant, where were also parole prisoners. One of them actually wrote to the Colonel of the Regiment stationed in Dumfries, apologizing for his action, explaining it, promising that he would get an English officer-prisoner in France exchanged, and that he would not take up arms against her, and that he would repay all the civilities he had received in Scotland. But all were recaptured and sent to Valleyfield.

As instances of the strictness with which even a popular agent carried out his regulations, may be cited that of the officer here, who was sent to Valleyfield because he had written to a lady in Devonshire, enclosing a letter to a friend of his. a prisoner on parole there, without first showing it to the Agent. In justice to Mr. Shortt, however, it is right to say that had the letter been a harmless one, and not, as was generally the case, full of abuse of the Government and the country, so extreme a view would not have been taken of the breach. Another instance was the refusal by the Agent of a request in 1812 from the officers to give a concert. In this case he was under orders from the Transport Office.

In March 1812, a number of the prisoners had at their own request copies of the Scriptures supplied them in English, French, German, Italian, and Spanish.

That the French officers on parole in Britain politically arranged their allegiance to the Powers that were, is exemplified by the following incidents at Dumfries. On the re-establishment of the Bourbon Dynasty, the following address was drawn up and sent to the French Commissioners for the release of prisoners:

'Dumfries, le 6 Mai 1814.

'Les officiers détenus sur parole donnent leur adhésion aux actes du Gouvernement Français qui rappelle l'illustre sang des Bourbons, au trône de ses ancêtres. Puissent les Français compter une longue suite de rois du sang de Saint Louis et de Henri IV, qui a toujours fait leur gloire et assuré leur bonheur! Vive Louis XVIII! Vivent les Bourbons!'

On the 24th of the same month a French officer, seeing in the window of a bookseller's shop a ludicrous caricature of Bonaparte, went into the shop in a violent passion, bought two copies, and tore them in pieces before a crowd of people, uttering dreadful imprecations against those who dared to insult 'his Emperor'. The fact is that the army to a man was Bonapartist at heart, as after events showed, but at Dumfries, as elsewhere, personal interests rendered it politic to assume loyalty and devotion to the re-established Royalty. Most of the prisoners, however, who elected to remain in Britain after the Declaration of Peace were unswerving Royalists. Lieutenant Guillemet at Dumfries was one of these. He became a professor of French at Dumfries Academy and also gave lessons in fencing, and was a great favourite with his pupils and the public. His son was for many years a chemist at Maxwelltown.

The average number of prisoners was about 100: they were mostly soldiers, and not sailors, on account of the proximity of Dumfries to the sea. I cannot refrain from adding to the frequent testimonies I have quoted as illustrating the good understanding which existed between captors and captives in Scotland, the following extract from a Farewell Letter which appeared in the *Dumfries Courier*, April 26, 1814, contributed by Lieutenant De Montaignac of the 'Parisian Guard'.

'I should indeed be very ungrateful were I to leave this country without publicly expressing my gratitude to the inhabitants of Dumfries. From the moment of my arrival in Scotland, the vexations indispensable in the situation of a prisoner have disappeared before me. I have been two years and five months in this town, prisoner on my parole of honour; and it is with the most lively emotion that I quit a place where I have found so many alleviations to my melancholy situation. I must express my thanks to the generous proceedings with which I have been loaded by the most part of the inhabitants of Dumfries during my captivity, proceedings which cannot but give an advantageous opinion of the Scottish nation. I will add that the respectable magistrates of this town have constantly given proofs of their generous dispositions to mitigate the situation of the prisoners; and that our worthy Agent, Mr. Shortt, has always softened our lot by the delicate manner in which he fulfilled the duty of his functions. It is then with a remembrance full of gratitude, esteem, and consideration for the honest inhabitants of Dumfries, that I quit the charming banks of the Nith to return to the capital of France, my beloved country, from which I have been absent seven years.'

For the following romantic incidents I am indebted to Mr. William McDowell's *Memorials of St. Michael's, Dumfries*.

Polly Stewart, the object of one of Burns's minor poems, married a Dumfries prisoner of war. She lived at Maxwelltown, and her father was a close friend of Burns. A handsome young Swiss prisoner, Fleitz by name, loved her and married her, and when Louis XVIII came to the French throne, he, being in the Swiss Guard, took her to France. When Louis Philippe became king, the Swiss body-guard was disbanded, and Mr. and Mrs. Fleitz went to Switzerland. It is said that poor Polly had an unhappy married life, but at any rate nothing was heard of her for thirty years, when she returned to Scotland, and not long after her husband died and she went to a cousin in France. Here her mind gave way, and she was placed in an asylum, where she died in 1847, aged 71.

On the tombstone, in St. Michael's churchyard, of Bailie William Fingass, who died in 1686, is an inscription to a descendant, Anna Grieve, daughter of James Grieve, merchant, who died in 1813, aged 19, with the following lines subjoined:

'Ta main, bienfaisante et chérie,

D'un exil vient essuyer les pleurs,

Tu me vis loin de parens, de patrie,

Et le même tombeau, lorsque tu m'as ravie,

Renferme nos deux cœurs.'

The story is this. One of the French prisoners on parole at Dumfries fell in love with pretty Anna Grieve, and she regarded his suit with kindness. Had she lived they would probably have been married, for he was in a good position and in every way worthy of her hand. When she died in the flower in her youth, he was overwhelmed with grief, and penned the above-quoted epitaph. After a lapse of about forty-six years, a gentleman of dignified bearing and seemingly about seventy years old, entered St. Michael's churchyard, and in broken English politely accosted Mr. Watson, who was busy with his chisel on one of the monuments. He asked to be shown the spot where Mademoiselle Grieve was buried, and on being taken to it exhibited deep emotion. He read over the epitaph, which seemed to be quite familiar to him, and it was apparent that it was engraved upon the tablets of his memory, he being none other than the lover of the lady who lay below, and for whom, although half a century had elapsed, he still retained his old attachment.

(I should say here that for many of the details about Sanquhar and Dumfries I am indebted in the first place to Mrs. Macbeth Forbes, for permission to make use of her late husband's notes on the prisoner-life at these places, and in the second to the hon. secretary of the Dumfriesshire and Galloway Natural History and Antiquarian Society, for the use of a résumé by him of those notes.)

Melrose

In the life of Dr. George Lawson, of Selkirk, the French prisoners on parole at Melrose are alluded to. The doctor astonished them with his knowledge of the old-world French with which they were unacquainted, and several pages of the book are devoted to the eloquent attempts of one of the prisoners to bring him to the Roman Catholic communion.

Appended to the minutes of the Quarterly Meeting of the Melrose Freemasons on September 25, 1813, in an account of the laying the foundation-stone of a public well, there is the following reference to the French prisoners interned at Melrose (the minutes of the Kelso, Selkirk, and other lodges record the fraternal exchange of courtesies, and the reception of these alien Brethren into the lodges, but at Melrose it would seem that these Brethren held a lodge of their own, which they no doubt worked in their native tongue and style, by leave and warrant of the Melrose Lodge):

'The French Brethren of the Lodge of St. John under the distinctive appellation of *Benevolence* constituted by the French prisoners of war on parole here, were invited to attend, which the Master, office-bearers, and many of the Brethren accordingly did.'

The lodge has preserved in its archives a document with the names of the French prisoners, adhibited to an expression of their appreciation of the kindness they had received during their sojourn at Melrose, which was given to the Brethren at the conclusion of the war when they were permitted to return to their own country and homes.

Jedburgh

Mr. Maberley Phillips, F.S.A., from whose pamphlet on prisoners of war in the North I shall quote later (pp. 388–9) a description of an escape of paroled prisoners from Jedburgh, says:

'Jedburgh had its share of French prisoners. They were for the most part kindly treated, and many of them were permitted a great amount of liberty. One of these had a taste for archaeology and visited all the ruins within the precincts of his radius, namely, a mile from the Cross. There is a tradition that on one of his excursions, he was directed to a ruin about a quarter of a mile beyond his appointed mark, which happened to be a milestone. He asked the Provost for permission to go beyond; that worthy, however, refused, but he quietly added: "If Mr. Combat did walk a short distance beyond the mile and nobody said anything, nothing would come of it." But the Frenchman had given his word of honour, and he could not break it. A happy thought struck him. He borrowed a barrow one afternoon, and with it and the necessary implements proceeded out to the obnoxious milestone. Having "unshipped" the milestone, he raised it on to the barrow, and triumphantly wheeled it to the required distance, where he fixed it.... For a generation the stone stood where the Frenchman placed it, no one being any the worse for the extra extent of the Scotch mile.'

Many of the prisoners were naval officers and were deeply versed in science, including navigation and astronomy. A favourite resort of these was Inchbonny, the abode of James Veitch, the self-taught astronomer. Inchbonny is situated up the Jed about half a mile from Jedburgh. Among the prisoners who made a point of visiting Veitch's workshop we may mention Scot, an old naval lieutenant, who with a long grey coat was to be seen at every gleam of sunshine at the Meridian line with compasses in hand, resolving to determine the problem of finding the longitude, and M. Charles Jehenne, who belonged to the navy, and who was captured at the battle of Trafalgar. He on that memorable day from the masthead of his vessel observed the British fleet under Nelson bearing down upon the French and Spanish vessels. 'They saw us', he was wont to say, 'before we saw them.' He was a constant visitor to the workshop, and constructed a telescope there for his own use. He was most agreeable in his manner, and careful not to give any trouble when doing any work for himself with Veitch's tools. He also was an astronomer, and would often stay out at Inchbonny, in order to view the stars through Veitch's telescopes, until long after the tolling of the bell which warned the prisoners that the daily period of liberty had again expired. In order that he might escape being noticed by the observant eyes of any who might be desirous of obtaining the reward given for a conviction, he usually got the loan of Veitch's plaid, and, muffled in this, reached his quarters undetected.

JEDBURGH ABBEY, 1812

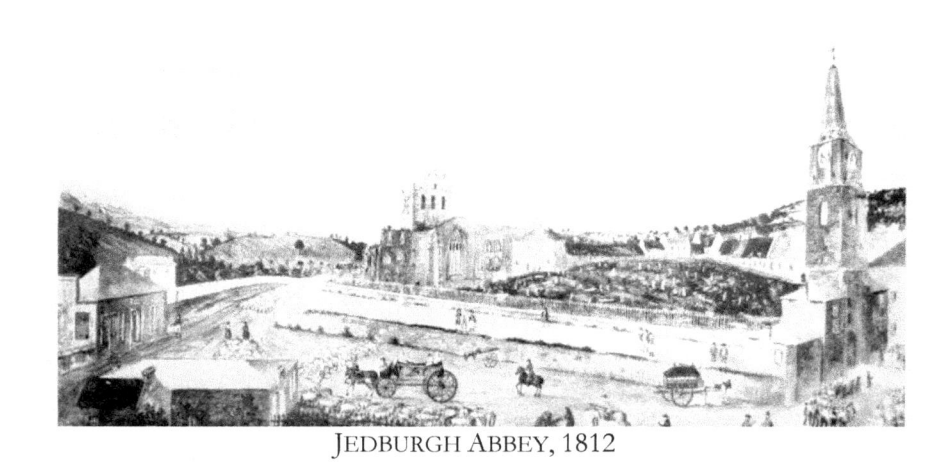

From a painting by Ensign Bazin, a French prisoner of war

Billeted along with Jehenne, and staying in the same room, was Ensign Bazin, of St. Malo, a man of quiet demeanour, captured on the *Torche* corvette in 1805. He was very talented with his pencil, and fond of drawing sketches of Jedburgh characters, many of which are preserved at Inchbonny. He made a painting of Jedburgh Abbey, which he dedicated to Mr. Veitch, dated 1812. In this picture the French prisoners are seen marching on the ramparts, and, in the original, their faces and forms, as also those of many local characters, are so admirably sketched as to be easily recognizable. A duplicate of this picture he sent home to his mother. Mrs. Grant of Laggan perhaps had Bazin in view when in her *Memoir of a Highland Lady*, she wrote:

'A number of French prisoners, officers, were on parole at Jedburgh. Lord Buchanan, whom we met there, took us to see a painting in progress by one of them; some battlefield, all the figures portraits from memory. The picture was already sold and part paid for, and another ordered, which we were very glad of, the handsome young painter having interested us much.'

In October 1813, Bazin received a pass to be sent to Alresford, and he was noted, 'to be exchanged at the first opportunity. Has been long imprisoned, and is a great favourite.' He was of wealthy parents, and got back to France some time before his fellow prisoners were released.

Mrs. Grant thus spoke of the Jedburgh prisoners:

'The ingenuity of the French prisoners of all ranks was amazing, only to be equalled by their industry; those of them unskilled in higher arts earned for themselves most comfortable additions to their allowance by turning bits of wood, bones, straw, almost anything in fact, into neat toys of many sorts, eagerly bought up by all who met with them.'

At Mr. Veitch's house, Inchbonny, may be seen by those fortunate enough to have a personal introduction, much of the French prisoner handiwork—sketches, telescopes, and an electric machine with which the poor fellows had much fun, connecting it with wires to a plate on the window-sill below, whereto they would invite passers-by—generally girls—for a chat and a joke, the result being a shock which sent them flying.

It is stated that when the word came that the Frenchmen were to be allowed to return to their native land, they caused their manufactures and other articles to be 'rouped'. One of the prisoners whose knowledge of the English language, even after his prolonged stay in this quarter, was very limited, was delegated to obtain the sanction of the Provost of the Burgh to hold such roup. He who at this time graced the office of provostship had a draper's shop in Canongate, and hither the Frenchman went on his errand. His lack of knowledge of the popular tongue, however, proved to be an inconvenience, for, on arriving at the shop, he could only request 'A rope! A rope!' The draper had his customary supply of old ropes, and, willing to oblige, brought them out, to the perplexity of the visitor, and commenced to 'wale out the best of them'. Seeing that his would-be benefactor was obviously mistaken, the French envoy reiterated his former request, and supplemented this by adding in a style which would have done credit to any auctioneer, 'One, Two, Tree!' Light dawned upon the Provost's comprehension, and the necessary permission was not long in being granted.

Many of the prisoners are supposed to have rejoined Bonaparte on his return from Elba, and to have fallen at Waterloo.

The officers were billeted among private citizens, says Mr. Forbes, while several occupied quarters immediately under the Clock Tower. Being young and lusty, they were dowered with an exceedingly good appetite, and as they got little to eat so far as their allowance went, some of them used to have a pulley and hoist their loaves of bread to near the ceiling to prevent themselves from devouring them all, and to ensure something being left over for next repast.

The prisoners were not commonly spoken of by name, but were known by the persons with whom they resided, e.g., 'Nannie Tamson's Frenchman', 'Widow Ross's Frenchman'. The boys were a great plague to the Frenchmen, for when a great victory was announced their dominie gave them a holiday, and the youngsters celebrated it too frequently by jeering the prisoners, and by shouting and cheering. The boys at a school then beside the road at No. 1 Milestone, were prominent in these triumphant displays, and sometimes pelted the prisoners with stones.

The manners of the Jedburgh prisoners are thus alluded to in the *False Alarm*, a local pamphlet:

'They were very polite, and not infrequently put us rough-spun Scotchmen to the blush with their polished manners. They came in course of time to be liked, but it seems some of the older members of the community could never be brought to fraternize with them. One old man actually pointed his gun at them, and threatened to fire because they had exceeded their walking limit.'

An aged Jedburgh lady's reminiscences are interesting. She says:

'Among the officers was M. Espinasse, who settled in Edinburgh after the Peace and engaged in teaching; Baron Goldshord or Gottshaw, who married a Jedburgh lady, a Miss Waugh; another, whose name I do not remember, married a Miss Jenny Wintrope, who went with him to the South of France. There was a Captain Rivoli, also a Captain Racquet, and a number of others who were well received by the townspeople, and frequently invited to parties in their homes, to card-clubs, etc. They were for the most part pleasant, agreeable gentlemen, and made many friends. Almost all of them employed themselves in work of some kind, besides playing at different kinds of games, shooting small birds, and fishing for trout. They much enjoyed the liberty granted them of walking one mile out of the town in any direction, as within that distance there were many beautiful walks when they could go out one road, turn, and come back by another. During their stay, when news had been received of one great British victory, the magistrates permitted rejoicing, and a great bonfire was kindled at the Cross, and an effigy of Napoleon was set on a donkey and paraded round the town by torchlight, and round the bonfire, and then cast into the flames. I have often heard an old gentleman, who had given the boots and part of the clothing, say he never regretted doing anything so much in his life, as helping on that great show, when he saw the pain it gave to these poor gentlemen-prisoners, who felt so much at seeing the affront put upon their great commander.

'The French prisoners have always been ingenious in the use they made of their meat bones ... they took them and pounded them into a powder which they mixed with the soft food they were eating. It is even said that they flourished on this dissolved phosphate of lime and gelatine.

'There was an old game called "cradles" played in those days. Two or three persons clasp each other's hands, and when their arms are held straight out at full length, a person is placed on these stretched hands, who is sent up in the air and down again, landing where he started from. A farmer thought he would try the experiment on the Frenchmen. Some buxom lassies were at work as some of them passed, and he gave the girls the hint to treat the foreigners to the "cradles". Accordingly two of them were jerked well up in the air to fall again on the sturdy hands of the wenches. The experiment was repeated again and again until the Frenchmen were glad to call a halt.'

Parole-breaking was rather common, and began some months after the officers arrived in the town. A party of five set out for Blyth in September 1811, but were brought to Berwick under a military escort, and lodged in jail. Next day they were marched to Penicuik under charge of a party of the Forfarshire Militia. Three of them were good-looking young men; one in particular had a very interesting countenance, and, wishing one day to extend his walk, in order to get some watercress for salad, beyond the limit of the one-mile stone, uprooted it, and carried it in his arms as far as he wished to go.

Three other officers were captured the same year, and sent to Edinburgh Castle, and in 1813 occurred the escape and capture to be described later (p. 388).

The highest number of prisoners at Jedburgh was 130, and there were three deaths during their stay.

HAWICK

I owe my best thanks to Mr. J. John Vernon, hon. secretary of the Hawick Archaeological Society, for the following note on Hawick:

'Not many of Napoleon's officers were men of means, so to the small allowance they received from the British Government, they were permitted to eke out their income by teaching, sketching, or painting, or by making little trifles which they disposed of as best they could among the townspeople. At other times they made a little money by giving musical and dramatic entertainments, which proved a source of enjoyment to the audience and of profit to themselves.

'Though "prisoners", they had a considerable freedom, being allowed to go about as they pleased anywhere within a radius of a mile from the Tower Knowe. During their residence in Hawick they became very popular among all classes of the people and much regret was expressed when the time came for their returning to the Continent. Hawick society was decidedly the poorer by their departure. Paradoxical it may seem, but most of those who were termed "French Prisoners" were in reality of German extraction: Fifteen of their number became members of the Freemasons, St. John's Lodge, No. 111. They were lodged in private houses throughout the towns. No. 44 High Street was the residence of a number of them, who dwelt in it from June 1812 to June 1814.'

Speaking of Freemasonry in Hawick, Mr. W. Fred Vernon says:

'Each succeeding year saw the Lodge more thinly attended. An impetus to the working and attendance was given about 1810 by the affiliation and initiation of several of the French prisoners of war who were billeted in the town, and from time to time to the close of the war in 1815, the attendance and prosperity of the Lodge was in striking contrast to what it had been previously.'

The following extracts are from a book upon Hawick published by Mr. J. John Vernon in November 1911.

'One of Bonaparte's officers, compelled to reside for nearly two years in Hawick, thus expressed himself regarding the weather during the winter, and at the same time his opinion of the people. In reply to a sympathetic remark that the weather must be very trying to one who had come from a more genial climate, the officer said:

"'It is de devil's wedder, but you have de heaven contré for all dat. You have de cold, de snow, de frozen water, and de sober dress; but you have de grand constitution, and de manners and equality that we did fight for so long. I see in your street de priest and de shoemaker; de banker and de baker, de merchant and de hosier all meet together, be companions and be happy. Dis is de equality dat de French did fight for and never got, not de ting de English newspapers say we want. Ah! Scotland be de fine contré and de people be de wise, good men.... De English tell me at Wincanton dat de Scots be a nation of sauvages. It was a lie. De English be de sauvages and de Scots be de civilized people. De high Englishman be rich and good; de low Englishman be de brute. In Scotland de people be all de same! Oh! Scotland be a fine contré!

'The fact that so many of the French prisoners of war were quartered in Hawick from 1812–14 did much towards brightening society during that time. Pity for their misfortunes prevailed over any feeling that the name "Frenchman" might formerly have excited, and they were welcomed in the homes of the Hawick people. It heartened them to be asked to dinner; as one of them remarked: "De heart of hope do not jump in de hungry belly", and many valued friendships were thus formed.'

'The presence of so many well-dressed persons for so long a period produced a marked reform in the costume of the inhabitants of Hawick,' says James Wilson in his *Annals of Hawick*.

The first prisoners came to Hawick in January 1812. Of these, thirty-seven came from Wincanton, forty-one came direct from Spain a little later, thirty-seven from Launceston. The prisoners had been sent hither from such distant places as Launceston and Wincanton on account of the increasing number of escapes from these places, the inhabitants of both of which, as we have seen, were notoriously in sympathy with the foreigners. Two surgeons came from the Greenlaw dépôt to attend on them. Mr. William Nixon, of Lynnwood, acted as agent, or commissary, and by the end of 1812 he had 120 prisoners in his charge. A few of the Hawick prisoners were quite well-to-do. There is a receipt extant of a Captain Grupe which shows that he had a monthly remittance from Paris of £13 4s. 6d., in addition to his pay and subsistence money as a prisoner of war.

In the *Kelso Mail* of June 20, 1814, is the following testimony from the prisoners, on leaving, to the kind and hospitable treatment they had so generally received:

'Hawick, May 2, 1814.

'The French officers on parole at Hawick, wishing to express their gratitude to the inhabitants of the town and its vicinity for the liberal behaviour which they have observed to them, and the good opinion which they have experienced from them, unanimously request the Magistrates and Mr. Nixon, their Commissary, to be so kind as to allow them to express their sentiments to them, and to assure them that they will preserve the remembrance of all the marks of friendship which they have received from them. May the wishes which the French officers make for the prosperity of the town and the happiness of its inhabitants be fully accomplished. Such is the most ardent wish, the dearest hope of those who have the honour to be their most humble servants.'

In some cases intercourse did not cease with the departure of the prisoners, and men who had received kindnesses as aliens kept up correspondence with those who had pitied and befriended them.

On May 18, 1814, the officers at Hawick, mostly, if not entirely, Bonaparte's soldiers, drifted with the Royalist tide, and sent an address to Louis XVIII, conceived in much the same terms as that from Dumfries already quoted, speaking of 'the happy events which have taken place in our country, and which have placed on the throne of his ancestors the illustrious family of Bourbon', and adding, 'we lay at the feet of the worthy descendant of Henry IV the homage of our entire obedience and fidelity'.

The prisoners were always welcome visitors at the house of Goldielands adjoining the fine old peel tower of that name, and I give the following pleasant testimony of one of them:

'To Mr. Elliott of Goldielands:

'SIR,

'Very sorry that before my leaving Scotland I could not have the pleasure of passing some hours with you. I take the liberty of addressing you these few lines, the principal object of which is to thank you for all the particular kindness and friendship you honoured me with during my stay in this country. The more lively I always felt this your kindness since idle prejudices had not the power over you to treat us with that coldness and reserve which foreigners, and the more so, prisoners of war in Britain, so often meet with.

'If in the case only that my conduct whilst I had the honour of being acquainted with you, has not met with your disapproval, I pray you to preserve me, even so far off, your friendship. To hear sometimes of you would certainly cause me great pleasure.

'Pray acquaint Mrs. Elliott and the rest of your family of the high esteem with which I have the honour to be, Sir,

'Your humble servant,

'G. DE TALLARD, Lieut.

'Hawick, March 11, 1814.'

LAUDER

I am indebted to the late Mr. Macbeth Forbes for these notes.

There hangs in one of the rooms of Thirlestane Castle, the baronial residence of the Earls of Lauderdale, an oil-painting executed by a French prisoner of war, Lieutenant-Adjutant George Maurer of the Hesse-Darmstadt Infantry. He is described in the Admiralty Records as a youth of twenty, with hazel eyes, fresh complexion, five feet nine and three-quarter inches in height, well made, but with a small sword scar on his left cheek. Although his production is by no means a striking work of art, it is nevertheless cherished as a memento of the time when—a hundred years ago—French prisoners were billeted in Lauder, Berwickshire, and indulged in pleasant intercourse with the inhabitants of this somewhat remote and out-of-the-way country town. In the left corner of the painting, which represents Lauder as seen from the west, is a portrait, dated August 1813, of the artist decked in a sort of Tam-o'-Shanter bonnet, swallow-tailed coat, and knee breeches, plying his brush.

The average number of prisoners at Lauder was between fifty and sixty, and the average age was twenty-six. They appear to have conducted themselves with great propriety in the quiet town; none of them was ever sent to the Tolbooth. They resided for the most part with burgesses, one of whom was James Haswell, a hairdresser, whose son remembered two of the prisoners who lived in his father's house, and who made for him and his brothers, as boys, suits of regimentals with cocked hats, and marched them through the town with bayonets at their sides.

About the end of January 1812, Captain Pequendaire, of *L'Espoir* privateer, escaped. At Lauder he never spoke a word of English to any one, and about six weeks after his arrival he disappeared. It came out that he had walked to Stow, near Lauder, and taken the coach there, and that he had got off because he spoke English so perfectly as to pass for a native!

Angot, second captain of *L'Espoir*, was released upon the representation of inhabitants of St. Valery, that he with others had saved the lives of seventy-nine British seamen wrecked on the coast.

A duel took place on a terrace on the east side of Lauderdale Castle between two prisoners armed with razors fastened to the end of walking-sticks. No harm was done on this occasion.

The prisoners were always kindly and hospitably treated by the inhabitants. On one occasion some of them were at a dinner-party at Mr. Brodie's, a farmer of Pilmuir. The farm was beyond the one-mile limit, but no notice would have been taken if the prisoners had duly reported themselves and enabled the Agent to make the necessary declaration, but, unfortunately, a heavy snowstorm prevented them from getting back to Lauder, and the report went in that So-and-so had not appeared. The Transport Board at once dealt with the matter, and the parish Minister, the Rev. Peter Cosens, who had been one of the party at Pilmuir, wrote to the authorities by way of explaining, and the reply received was very severe, the authorities expressing surprise that one in his position should have given countenance to, and should seek to palliate or excuse, the offence. The result to the prisoners is not known, but they were probably let off with a fine stopped out of their allowance.

Many of the prisoners knew little or no English when they came to Lauder. On the occasion of a detachment coming into the town, some of the baggage had not arrived, and the interpreter of the party appeared before the Agent, and made a low bow, and held up a finger for each package that was wanting, and uttered the only appropriate English word he knew, 'Box'. Another, who wished to buy eggs, went into a shop, and, drawing his cloak around him, sat down and clucked like a hen.

Many of the prisoners in the Scottish towns were Germans in French service. In January 1813, the Lauder St. Luke's Lodge of Freemasons admitted eight Germans and one Frenchman, and it is related that on the occasion of their induction, when the time for refreshments after business came, the foreign installations delighted the company with yarns of their military experiences. When the great movement for German liberty got into full swing, Britain encouraged the French prisoners of German nationality to fight for their own country. Accordingly the eleven German prisoners in Lauder, belonging to the Hesse-Darmstadt regiment, received £5 each at the end of February 1814, to pay their expenses to Hawick, whence to proceed to the seat of war. It is related that the joy they felt at their release was diminished by their regret at leaving the town where they had been treated by the inhabitants with so much marked hospitality and kindness. The evening previous to their departure, the magistrates gave them an entertainment at the *Black Bull* Inn, and wished them all success in their efforts to restore liberty and prosperity. The remaining twenty-two prisoners finally left Lauder, June 3, 1814; others having been previously removed to Jedburgh, Kelso, and Dumfries. While they were in Lauder some of the merchants gave them credit, and they were honourably repaid on the prisoners' return to their own country. Maurer, the artist before alluded to, often revisited his friends in Lauder, and always called on and dined with the Agent, and talked over old times.

Lockerbie and Lochmaben

About a score of prisoners were at each of these places, but as the record of their lives here is of very much the same character as of prisoner life elsewhere, it hardly makes a demand upon the reader's attention. In both places the exiles conducted themselves peaceably and quietly, and they, especially the doctors, were well liked by the inhabitants.

CHAPTER XXV
PRISONERS OF WAR IN WALES

IN MONTGOMERYSHIRE

I am indebted to Canon Thomas of Llandrinio Rectory, Llanymynech, for information which led me to extract the following interesting details from the Montgomeryshire Archaeological Collections.

Batches of French officers were on parole during the later years of the Napoleonic wars at Llanfyllin, Montgomery, Bishop's Castle, Newtown, and Welshpool.

Llanfyllin

About 120 French and Germans were quartered here during the years 1812 and 1813. Many of them lived together in a large house, formerly the Griffith residence, which stood where is now Bachie Place. Others were at the 'Council House' in High Street. In a first-floor room of this latter may still be seen thirteen frescoes in crayon executed by the prisoners, representing imaginary mountain scenery. Formerly there were similar frescoes in a neighbouring house, once the *Rampant Lion* Inn, now a tailor's shop, but these have been papered over, and according to the correspondent who supplies the information, 'utterly destroyed'. These prisoners were liberally supplied with money, which they spent freely. An attachment sprang up between a prisoner, Captain Angerau, and the Rector's daughter, which resulted in their marriage after the Peace of 1814. It is interesting to note that in 1908 a grandson of Captain Angerau visited Llanfyllin.

The following pleasing testimony I take from *Bygones*, October 30, 1878:

'The German soldiers from Hessia, so well received by the inhabitants of Llanfyllin during their captivity, have requested the undersigned to state that the kindness and the favour shewn them by the esteemed inhabitants of Llanfyllin will ever remain in their thankful remembrance.

'C. W. WEDIKIND.

'Newtown, June 17, 1817.'

Montgomery

A correspondent of the *Gentleman's Magazine* contributed a notice of the death at Montgomery of an old gentleman named Chatuing who had been nearly four years a prisoner in that town, and who had preferred to remain there after the Peace of 1814.

Occasionally we come across evidence that there were men among the prisoners on parole who were not above acting as Government spies among their fellows. One Beauvernet at Montgomery was evidently one of these, for a Transport Office letter to the Agent in that town in 1806 says:

'Mr. Beauvernet may rest perfectly satisfied that any information communicated by him will not in any way be used to his detriment or disadvantage.'

Allen, the Montgomery Agent, is directed to advance Beauvernet £10, as part of what ultimately would be given him. One Muller was the object of suspicion, and he was probably an escape agent, as in later letters Beauvernet is to be allowed to choose where he will 'work', and eventually, on the news that Muller has gone to London, is given a passport thither, and another £10. Of course it does not follow from this that Beauvernet was actually a prisoner of war, and he may have been one of the foreign agents employed by Government at good pay to watch the prisoners more unostentatiously than could a regular prisoner agent, but the opening sentence of the official letter seems to point to the fact that he was a prisoner.

A French officer on parole at Montgomery, named Dumont, was imprisoned for refusing to support an illegitimate child, so that it came upon the rates. He wrote, however, to Lady Pechell, declaring that he was the victim 'of a sworn lie of an abandoned creature', complaining that he was shut up with the local riff-raff, half starved, and penniless, and imploring her to influence the Transport Board to give him the subsistence money which had been taken from him since his committal to prison to pay for the child. What the Transport Board replied does not appear, but from the frequency of these complaints on the part of prisoners, there seems no doubt that, although local records show that illicit amours were largely indulged in by French and other officers on parole, in our country towns, much advantage of the sinning of a few was taken by unprincipled people to blackmail others.

In the *Cambrian* of May 2, 1806, is the following:

'At the last Quarter Sessions for Montgomeryshire, a farmer of the neighbourhood of Montgomery was prosecuted by order of the Transport Office for assaulting one of the French prisoners on parole, and, pleading guilty to the indictment, was fined £10, and ordered to find sureties for keeping the peace for twelve months. This is the second prosecution which the Board has ordered, it being determined that the prisoners shall be protected by Government from insult while they remain in their unfortunate position as Prisoners of War.'

Bishop's Castle

At Bishop's Castle there were many prisoners, and in *Bygones* Thomas Caswell records chats with an old man named Meredith, in the workhouse, who had been servant at the *Six Bells*, where nine officers were quartered. 'They cooked their own food, and I waited upon them. They were very talkative ... they were not short of money, and behaved very well to me for waiting upon them.'

The attempted escape of two Bishop's Castle prisoners is described on page 391.

Newtown

'Mr. David Morgan of the Canal Basin, Newtown, who is now (February 1895) 81 years of age, remembers over 300 prisoners passing through Kerry village on their way from London via Ludlow, to Newtown. He was then a little boy attending Kerry school, and the children all ran out to see them. All were on foot, and were said to be all officers. A great number of them were billeted at various public-houses, and some in private houses in Newtown. They exerted themselves greatly in putting out a fire at the *New Inn* in Severn Street, and were to be seen, says my informant, an aged inhabitant, "like cats about the roof ". When Peace was made, they returned to France, and many of them were killed at Waterloo. The news of that great battle and victory reached Newtown on Pig Fair Day, in June 1815. I have a memorandum book of M. Auguste Tricoche, one of the prisoners, who appears to have served in the French fleet in the West Indies, and to have been taken prisoner at the capture of Martinique in 1810.'

Welshpool

'On the occasion of a great fire at the corner shop in December 1813, there was a terrific explosion of gunpowder which hurled portions of timber into the Vicarage garden, some distance off. The French prisoners were very active, and some of them formed a line to the Lledan brook (which at that time was not culverted over), whence they conveyed water to the burning building to others of their comrades who courageously entered it.

'Dr. P. L. Serph, one of the prisoners, settled down at Welshpool, where he obtained a large practice as a physician and surgeon, and continued to reside there until the time of his death. Dr. Serph married Ann, the daughter of John Moore, late of Crediton in the county of Devon, gentleman, by Elizabeth his wife. Mrs. Serph died in 1837, and there is a monument to their memory in Welshpool churchyard.

'There is at Gungrog a miniature of Mrs. Morris Jones painted by a French prisoner; also a water colour of the waterfall at Pystyl Rhaiadr, which is attributed to one of them. I recollect seeing in the possession of the late Mr. Oliver E. Jones, druggist, a view of Powis Castle, ingeniously made of diverse-coloured straws, the work of one of the prisoners.

'It is said that French blood runs in the veins of some of the inhabitants of each of these towns where the prisoners were located.

'R. WILLIAMS.'

IN PEMBROKESHIRE

Pembroke

In 1779 Howard the philanthropist visited Pembroke, and reported to this effect:

He found thirty-seven American prisoners of war herded together in an old house, some of them without shoes or stockings, all of them scantily clad and in a filthy condition. There were no tables of victualling and regulations hung up, nor did the prisoners know anything more about allowances than that they were the same as for the French prisoners. The floors were covered with straw which had not been changed for seven weeks. There were three patients in the hospital house, in which the accommodation was very poor.

Fifty-six French prisoners were in an old house adjoining the American prison. Most of them had no shoes or stockings, and some had no shirts. There was no victualling table and the prisoners knew nothing about their allowance. Two or three of them had a money allowance, which should have been 3/6 per week each, for aliment, but from this 6*d.* was always deducted. They lay on boards without straw, and there were only four hammocks in two rooms occupied by thirty-six prisoners. There was a court for airing, but no water and no sewer. In two rooms of the town jail were twenty French prisoners. They had some straw, but it had not been changed for many weeks. There was no supply of water in the jail, and as the prisoners were not allowed to go out and fetch it, they had to do without it. On one Sunday morning they had had no water since Friday evening. The bread was tolerable, the beer very small, the allowance of beef so scanty that the prisoners preferred the allowance of cheese and butter. In the hospital were nine French prisoners, besides five of the *Culloden's* crew, and three Americans. All lay on straw with coverlets, but without sheets, mattresses, or bedsteads.

This was perhaps the worst prison visited by Howard, and he emphatically recommended the appointment of a regular inspector. In 1779 complaints came from Pembroke of the unnecessary use of fire-arms by the militiamen on guard, and that 150 prisoners were crowded into one small house with an airing yard twenty-five paces square—this was the year of Howard's visit. His recommendations seem to have had little effect, for in 1781 twenty-six prisoners signed a complaint that the quantity and the quality of the provisions were deficient; that they had shown the Agent that the bread was ill-baked, black, and of bad taste, but he had taken no notice; that he gave them cow's flesh, which was often bad, thinking that they would refuse it and buy other at their own expense; that he vexed them as much as he could, telling them that the bread and meat were too good for

Frenchmen; that on their complaining about short measure and weight he refused to have the food measured and weighed in their presence in accordance with the regulations; that he tried to get a profit out of the straw supplied by making it last double the regulation time without changing it, so that they were obliged to buy it for themselves; and that he had promised them blankets, but, although it was the raw season of the year, none had yet been issued.

In 1797 the Admiralty inspector reported that the condition of the dépôt at Pembroke was very unsatisfactory; the discipline slack, as the Agent preferred to live away at Hubberstone, and only put in an occasional appearance; and that the state of the prisoners was mutinous to a dangerous degree.

The Fishguard affair of 1797

If the Great Western Railway had not brought Fishguard into prominence as a port of departure for America, it would still be famous as the scene of the last foreign invasion of England. On February 22, 1797, fifteen hundred Frenchmen, half of whom were picked men and half galley slaves, landed from four vessels, three of which were large frigates, under an Irish General Tate, at Cerrig Gwasted near Fishguard. They had previously been at Ilfracombe, where they had burned some shipping. There was a hasty gathering of ill-armed pitmen and peasants to withstand them, and these were presently joined by Lord Cawdor with 3,000 men, of whom 700 were well-trained Militia. Cawdor rode forward to reconnoitre, and General Tate, deceived, as a popular legend goes, into the belief that he was opposed by a British military force of great strength, by the appearance behind his lordship of a body of Welshwomen clad in their national red 'whittles' and high-crowned hats, surrendered.

Be the cause what it might, by February 24, without a shot being fired, 700 Frenchmen were lodged in Haverfordwest Jail, 500 in St. Mary's Church, and the rest about the town. Later on, for security, 500 Frenchmen were shut up in the Golden Tower, Pembroke, and with this last body a romance is associated. Two girls were daily employed in cleaning the prison, and on their passage to and fro became aware of two handsome young Frenchmen among the prisoners selling their manufactures at the daily market, who were equally attracted by them. The natural results were flirtation and the concoction of a plan of escape for the prisoners. The girls contrived to smuggle into the prison some shin bones of horses and cows, which the prisoners shaped into digging tools, and started to excavate a passage sixty feet long under the prison walls to the outer ditch which was close to the harbour, the earth thus dug out being daily carried away by the girls in the pails they used in their cleaning operations. Six weeks of continuous secret labour saw the completion of the task, and all that now remained was to secure a vessel to carry the performers away. Lord Cawdor's yacht at anchor offered the opportunity. Some reports say that a hundred prisoners got out by the tunnel and boarded the yacht and a sloop lying at hand; but at any rate, the two girls and five and twenty prisoners secured the yacht, and, favoured by a thick fog, weighed anchor and got away. For three days they drifted about; then, meeting a brig, they hailed her, represented themselves as shipwrecked mariners, and were taken aboard. They learned that a reward of £500 was being offered for the apprehension of the two girls who had liberated a hundred prisoners, and replied by clapping the brig's crew under hatches, and setting their course for St. Malo, which they safely reached.

The girls married their lovers, and one of them, Madame Roux, ci-devant Eleanor Martin, returned to Wales when peace was declared, and is said to have kept an inn at Merthyr, her husband getting a berth at the iron-works.

Another of General Tate's men, a son of the Marquis de Saint-Amans, married Anne Beach, sister-in-law of the Rev. James Thomas, Vicar of St. Mary's, Haverfordwest, and head master of the Grammar School. General Tate himself was confined in Portchester Castle.

IN MONMOUTHSHIRE

Abergavenny

There were some two hundred officers on parole here, but the only memory of them extant is associated with the Masonic Lodge, 'Enfants de Mars et de Neptune', which was worked by them about 1813–14. Tradition says that the officers' mess room, an apartment in Monk Street, remarkable for a handsome arched ceiling, also served for Lodge meetings. De Grasse Tilly, son of Admiral De Grasse, who was defeated by Rodney in the West Indies, was a prominent member of this Lodge. At the present 'Philanthropic' Lodge, No. 818, Abergavenny, are preserved some collars, swords, and other articles which belonged to members of the old French prisoners' Lodge.

In Brecknockshire

Prisoners were at Brecon; tombs of those who died may be seen in the old Priory Churchyard, and 'The Captain's Walk' near the County Hall still preserves the memory of their favourite promenade.

In 1814 the Bailiff of Brecon requested to have the parole prisoners in that town removed. The reason is not given, but the Transport Office refused the request.

CHAPTER XXVI
ESCAPE AGENTS AND ESCAPES

To the general reader some of the most interesting episodes of the lives of the paroled prisoners of war in Britain are those which are associated with their escapes and attempts to escape. Now, although, as has been already remarked, the feeling of the country people was almost unanimously against the prisoners during the early years of the parole system, that is, during the Seven Years' War, from 1756 to 1763, during the more tremendous struggles which followed that feeling was apparently quite as much in their favour, and the authorities found the co-operation of the inhabitants far more troublous to combat than the ingenuity and daring of the prisoners. If the principle governing this feeling among the upper classes of English society was one of chivalrous sympathy with brave men in misfortune, the object of the lower classes—those most nearly concerned with the escapes—was merely gain.

There were scores of country squires and gentlemen who treated the paroled officers as guests and friends, and who no doubt secretly rejoiced when they heard of their escapes, but they could not forget that every escape meant a breach of solemnly-pledged honour, and I have met with very few instances of English ladies and gentlemen aiding and abetting in the escapes of paroled prisoners.

So profitable an affair was the aiding of a prisoner to escape that it soon became as regular a profession as that of smuggling, with which it was so intimately allied. The first instance I have seen recorded was in 1759, when William Scullard, a collar-maker at Liphook, Hampshire, was brought before the justices at the Guildford Quarter Sessions, charged with providing horses and acting as guide to assist two French prisoners of distinction to escape—whence is not mentioned. After a long examination he was ordered to be secured for a future hearing, and was at length committed to the New Jail in Southwark, and ordered to be fettered. The man was a reputed smuggler, could speak French, and had in his pocket a list of all the cross-roads from Liphook round by Dorking to London.

In 1812 Charles Jones, Solicitor to the Admiralty, describes the various methods by which the escapes of paroled prisoners are effected. They are of two kinds, he says:

'1. By means of the smugglers and those connected with them on the coast, who proceed with horses and covered carriages to the dépôts and by arrangement rendezvous about the hour of the evening when the prisoners ought to be within doors, about the mile limit, and thus carry them off, travelling through the night and in daytime hiding in woods and coverts. The horses they use are excellent, and the carriages constructed for the purpose. The prisoners are conveyed to the coast, where they are delivered over to the smugglers, and concealed until the boat is ready. They embark at night, and before morning are in France. These escapes are generally in pursuance of orders received from France.

'2. By means of persons of profligate lives who, residing in or near the Parole towns, act as conductors to such of the prisoners as choose to form their own plan of escape. These prisoners generally travel in post-chaises, and the conductor's business is to pay the expenses and give orders on the road to the innkeepers, drivers, &c., to prevent discovery or suspicion as to the quality of the travellers. When once a prisoner reaches a public-house or inn near the coast, he is considered safe. But there are cases when the prisoners, having one among themselves who can speak good English, travel without conductors. In these cases the innkeepers and post-boys alone are to blame, and it is certain that if this description of persons could be compelled to do their duty many escapes would be prevented.... The landlord of the *Fountain* at Canterbury has been known to furnish chaises towards the coast for six French prisoners at a time without a conductor.'

The writer suggested that it should be made felony to assist a prisoner to escape, but the difficulty in the way of this was that juries were well known to lean towards the accused. In the same year, 1812, however, this came about. A Bill passed the Commons, the proposition being made by Castlereagh that to aid in the escape of a prisoner should cease to be misdemeanour, and become a felony, punishable by transportation for seven or fourteen years, or life. Parole, he said, was a mere farce; bribery was rampant and could do anything, and an organized system existed for furthering the escape of prisoners of rank. Within the last three years 464 officers on parole had escaped, but abroad *not one British officer* had broken his parole. The chief cause, he continued, was the want of an Agent between the two countries for the exchange of prisoners, and it was an extraordinary feature of the War that the common rules about the exchange of prisoners were not observed.

The most famous escape agent was Thomas Feast Moore, *alias* Maitland, *alias* Herbert, but known to French prisoners as Captain Richard Harman of Folkestone. He was always flush of money, and, although he was known to be able to speak French very fluently, he never used that language in the presence of Englishmen. He kept a complete account of all the dépôts and parole places, with the ranks of the principal prisoners thereat, and had an agent at each, a poor man who was glad for a consideration to place well-to-do prisoners in communication with Harman, and so on the road to escape. Harman's charge was usually £100 for four prisoners. As a rule he got letters of recommendation from the officers whose escapes he safely negotiated, and he had the confidence of some of the principal prisoners in England and Scotland. He was generally in the neighbourhood of Whitstable and Canterbury, but, for obvious reasons, owned to no fixed residence. He seems to have been on the whole straight in his dealings, but once or twice he sailed very closely in the track of rascally agents who took money from prisoners, and either did nothing for them, or actually betrayed them, or even murdered them.

On March 22, 1810, General Pillet, 'Adjudant Commandant, Chef de l'État-Major of the First Division of the Army of Portugal,' and Paolucci, commander of the *Friedland*, taken by H.M.S. *Standard* and *Active* in 1808, left their quarters at Alresford, and were met half a mile out by Harman with a post-chaise, into which they got and drove to Winchester, alighting in a back street while Harman went to get another chaise. Thence they drove circuitously to Hastings via Croydon, Sevenoaks, Tunbridge, Robertsbridge, and Battle, Harman saying that this route was necessary for safety, and that he would get them over, as he had General Osten, in thirty-four hours.

They arrived at Hastings at 7 p.m. on March 23, and alighted outside the town, while Harman went to get lodgings. He returned and took them to the house of Mrs. Akers, a one-eyed woman; they waited there four days for fair weather, and then removed to the house of one Paine, for better concealment as the hue and cry was after them. They hid here two days, whilst the house was searched, but their room was locked as an empty lumber room. Pillet was disgusted at the delays, and that evening wanted to go to the Mayor's house to give himself up, but the landlord brought them sailor clothes, and said that two women were waiting to take them where they pleased. They refused the clothes, went out, met Rachael Hutchinson and Elizabeth Akers, and supposed they would be taken to the Mayor's house, but were at once surrounded and arrested. All this time Harman, who evidently saw that the delay caused by the foul weather was fatal to the chance that the prisoners could get off, had disappeared, but was arrested very shortly at the inn at Hollington Corner, three miles from Hastings. He swore that he did not know them to be escaped prisoners, but thought they were Guernsey lace-merchants.

During the examination which followed, the Hastings town crier said that he had announced the escape of the prisoners at forty-three different points of the eight streets which composed Hastings.

Pillet and Paolucci were sent to Norman Cross, and Harman to Horsham jail.

At the next examination it came out that Harman had bought a boat for the escape from a man who understood that it was to be used for smuggling purposes by two Guernsey lace men. The Mayor of Hastings gave it as his opinion that no Hastings petty jury would commit the prisoners for trial, although a grand jury might, such was the local interest in the escape-cum-smuggling business. However, they were committed. At Horsham, Harman showed to Jones, the Solicitor to the Admiralty, an iron crown which he said had been given him by the French Government for services rendered, but which proved to have been stolen from Paolucci's trunk, of which he had the key.

Harman, on condition of being set free, offered to make important disclosures to the Government respecting the escape business and its connexion with the smugglers, but his offer was declined, and, much to his disgust, he was sent to serve in the navy. 'He could not have been disposed of in a way less expected or more objectionable to himself,' wrote the Admiralty Solicitor, Jones, to McLeay, the secretary.

But Harman's career was by no means ended. After serving on the *Enterprise*, he was sent to the *Namur*, guardship at the Nore, but for a year or more a cloud of mystery enveloped him, and not until 1813 did it come out that he must have escaped from the *Namur* very shortly after his transfer, and that during the very next year, 1811, he was back at his old calling.

A man giving the name of Nicholas Trelawney, but obviously a Frenchman, was captured on August 24, 1811, on the Whitstable smack *Elizabeth*, lying in Broadstairs Roads, by the *Lion* cutter. At his examination he confessed that he was a prisoner who had broken parole from Tiverton, and got as far as Whitstable on July 4. Here he lodged at an inn where he met Mr. 'Feast' of the hoy *Whitstable*. In conversation the Frenchman, not knowing, of course, who Mr. 'Feast' really was, described himself as a Jerseyman who had a licence to take his boat to France, but she had been seized by the Customs, as she had some English goods in her. He told 'Feast' that he much wanted to get to France, and 'Feast' promised to help him, but without leading the Frenchman to suppose that he knew him to be an escaped prisoner of war.

He paid 'Feast' £10 10*s.*, and went on board the *Elizabeth* to get to Deal, as being a more convenient port for France. 'Feast' warned him that he would be searched, and persuaded him to hand over his watch and £18 for safe keeping. He saw nothing more of Mr. 'Feast' and was captured.

When the above affair made it clear that Harman, alias Feast Moore, was at work again, a keen servant of the Transport Office, Mantell, the Agent at Dover, was instructed to get on to his track. Mantell found that Harman had been at Broadstairs, to France, and in Dover, at which place his well-known boat, the *Two Sisters*, was discovered, untenanted and with her name obliterated. Mantell further learned that on the very night previous to his visit Harman had actually been landed by Lieutenant Peace of the armed cutter *Decoy*, saying that he bore important dispatches from France for Croker at the Admiralty. The lieutenant had brought him ashore, and had gone with him to an inn whence he would get a mail-coach to London. Mantell afterwards heard that Harman went no farther than Canterbury.

Mantell described Harman's usual mode of procedure: how, the French prisoners having been duly approached, the terms agreed upon, and the horses, chaises, boats with sails, oars, charts and provisions arranged for, he would meet them at a little distance outside their place of confinement after dark, travel all night, and with good luck get them off within two days at the outside. Mantell found out that in August 1811 Harman got four prisoners away from Crediton; he lived at Mr. Parnell's, the *White Lion*, St. Sidwell's, under the name of Herbert, bought a boat of Mr. Owen of Topsham, and actually saw his clients safe over Exmouth bar.

His manner, said Mantell, was free and open; he generally represented his clients to be Guernseymen, or *émigrés*, or Portuguese, and he always got them to sign a paper of recommendation.

In July 1813 news came that Harman was at work in Kelso, Scotland. A stranger in that town had been seen furtively carrying a trunk to the *Cross Keys* inn, from which he presently went in a post-chaise to Lauder. He was not recognized, but frequent recent escapes from the town had awakened the vigilance of the Agent, and the suspicious behaviour of this stranger at the inn determined that official to pursue and arrest him. The trunk was found to belong to Dagues, a French officer, and contained the clothes of three other officers on parole, and from the fact that the stranger had made inquiries about a coach for Edinburgh, it was clear that an arrangement was nipped in the bud by which the officers were to follow, pick up the trunk at Edinburgh, and get off from Leith.

Harman was disguised, but the next morning the Kelso Agent saw at once that he answered the description of him which had been circulated throughout the kingdom, and sent him to Jedburgh Jail, while he communicated with London.

The result of Harman's affair was that the Solicitor-General gave it as his opinion that it was better he should be detained as a deserter from the navy than as an aider of prisoners to escape, on the ground that there were no sufficiently overt acts on the parts of the French prisoners to show an intention to escape! What became of Harman I cannot trace, but at any rate he ceased to lead the fraternity of escape agents.

Waddell, a Dymchurch smuggler, was second only to Harman as an extensive and successful escape agent. In 1812 he came to Moreton-Hampstead, 'on business', and meeting one Robins, asked him if he was inclined to take part in a lucrative job, introducing himself, when in liquor afterwards at the inn, as the author of the escape of General Lefebvre-

Desnouettes and wife from Cheltenham, for which he got £210, saying that while in France he engaged to get General Reynaud and his aide-de-camp away from Moreton-Hampstead for £300 or 300 guineas, which was the reason of his presence there. He added that he was now out on bail for £400 about the affair of Lefebvre-Desnouettes, and was bound to appear at Maidstone for trial. If convicted he would only be heavily fined, so he was anxious to put this affair through.

Robins agreed, but informed the Agent, and Waddell was arrested. As regards General Reynaud, above alluded to, that officer wrote to the Transport Office to say that the report of his intention to abscond was untrue. The Office replied that it was glad to hear so, but added, 'In consequence of the very disgraceful conduct of other French officers of high rank, such reports cannot fail to be believed by many.'

As a rule the prisoners made their way to London, whence they went by hoy to Whitstable and across the Channel, but the route from Dymchurch to Wimereux was also much favoured. Spicer of Folkestone, Tom Gittens (known as Pork Pie Tom), James King, who worked the western ports; Kite, Hornet, Cullen, Old Stanley, Hall, Waddle, and Stevenson of Folkestone; Yates, Norris, Smith, Hell Fire Jack, old Jarvis and Bates of Deal; Piper and Allen of Dover; Jimmy Whather and Tom Scraggs of Whitstable, were all reported to be 'deep in the business', and Deal was described as the 'focus of mischief'. The usual charge of these men was £80 per head, but, as has been already said, the fugitives ere they fairly set foot on their native soil were usually relieved of every penny they possessed.

An ugly feature about the practice of parole-breaking is that the most distinguished French officers did not seem to regard it seriously. In 1812 General Simon escaped from Odiham and corresponded with France; he was recaptured, and sent to Tothill Fields Prison in London, and thence to Dumbarton Castle, where two rooms were furnished for him exactly on the scale of a British field officer's barrack apartment; he was placed on the usual parole allowance, eighteenpence per day for himself, and one shilling and threepence per day for a servant, and he resented very much having to give up a poniard in his possession. From Dumbarton he appears to have carried on a regular business as an agent for the escape of paroled prisoners, for, at his request, the Transport Office had given permission for two of his subalterns, also prisoners on parole, Raymond and Boutony by name, to take positions in London banks as French correspondents, and it was discovered that these men were actually acting as Simon's London agents for the escape of prisoners on parole. It was no doubt in consequence of this discovery that in 1813 orders were sent to Dumbarton that not only was Simon to be deprived of newspapers, but that he was not to be allowed pens and ink, 'as he makes such a scandalous and unbecoming use of them.'

In May 1814 Simon, although he was still in close confinement, was exchanged for Major-General Coke, it being evidently considered by the Government that he could do less harm fighting against Britain than he did as a prisoner.

The frequent breaches of parole by officers of distinction led to severe comments thereon by the Transport Board, especially with regard to escapes. In a reply to General Privé, who had complained of being watched with unnecessary rigour, it was said: 'With reference to the "eternal vigilance" with which the officers on parole are watched, I am directed to observe that there was a little necessity for this, as a great many Persons who style themselves Men of Honour, and some of them members of the Legion of Honour, have abandoned all Honour and Integrity by running from Parole, and by bribing unprincipled men to assist in their Escape.'

Again:

'Certain measures have been regarded as expedient in consequence of the very frequent desertions of late of French officers, not even excepting those of the highest rank, so that their Parole of Honour has become of little Dependence for their Security as Prisoners of War. Particularly do we select General Lefebvre-Desnouettes, an officer of the Legion of Honour, a General of Division, Colonel commanding the Chasseurs à cheval de la Garde. He was allowed unusually great privileges on parole—to reside at Cheltenham, to go thence to Malvern and back to Cheltenham as often as he liked; his wife was allowed to reside with him, and he was allowed to have two Imperial Guardsmen as servants. Yet he absconded, May 1, 1812, with his servants and naval lieutenant Armand le Duc, who had been allowed as a special favour to live with him at Cheltenham.'

Lord Wellington requested that certain French officers should be given their parole, but in reply the Transport Office declined to consent, and as a reason sent him a list of 310 French officers who had broken their parole during the current year, 1812.

The *Moniteur* of August 9, 1812, attempted to justify these breaches of parole, saying that Frenchmen only surrendered on the condition of retaining their arms, and that we had broken that condition.

At the Exeter Assizes, in the summer of 1812, Richard Tapper of Moreton-Hampstead, carrier, Thomas and William Vinnacombe of Cheriton Bishop, smugglers, were convicted and sentenced to transportation for life for aiding in the attempted escape of two merchant captains, a second captain of a privateer, and a midshipman from Moreton-Hampstead, from whom they had received £25 down and a promise of £150. They went under Tapper's guidance on horseback from Moreton to Topsham, where they found the Vinnacombes waiting with a large boat. They started, but grounded on the bar at Exmouth, and were captured.

In the same year, acting upon information, the Government officers slipped quietly down to Deal, Folkestone, and Sandgate, and seized a number of galleys built specially for the cross-Channel traffic of escaped prisoners. They were beautifully constructed, forty feet long, eight-oared, and painted so as to be almost invisible. It was said that in calm weather they could be rowed across in *two hours*!

The pillory was an additional punishment for escape-aiders. Russel, in his *History of Maidstone*, says that 'the last persons who are remembered to have stood in the pillory were two men, who in the first decade of the present (nineteenth) century, had assisted French prisoners of War to escape while on Parole'.

But I find that in 1812, seven men were condemned at Maidstone, in addition to two years' imprisonment, to stand in the pillory on every market-day for a month, for the same offence. In this year, Hughes, landlord of the *Red Lion* and postmaster at Rye, Hatter, a fisherman, and Robinson, of Oswestry, were sentenced to two years in Horsham Jail, and in the first month to be pilloried on Rye Coast, *as near France as possible*, for aiding in the escape of General Phillipon and Lieutenant Garnier.

Men, not regular escape agents, as well as the latter, often victimized the poor Frenchmen under pretence of friendship.

One Whithair, of Tiverton, was accused, at the Exeter Summer Assizes of 1812, by French prisoners of having cheated them. He had obtained £200 from six officers on parole at Okehampton—he said to purchase a boat to get them off, and horses to carry them to the coast—through the medium of Madame Riccord, the English wife of one of the French officers. Whithair had also persuaded them to send their trunks to Tiverton in readiness. They waited four months, and then suspected that Whithair was tricking them, and informed the Agent. Whithair was arrested, and condemned to pay £200, and to be imprisoned until he did so. Later, Whithair humbly petitioned to be released from Newgate on the plea that during his imprisonment he would have no chance of paying the fine, and the Superintendent recommended it.

It may be imagined that the profession of escape-aiding had much the same fascination for adventurous spirits as had what our forefathers called 'the highway'. So we read of a young gentleman of Rye, who, having run through a fortune, determined to make a trial of this career as a means of restoring his exchequer, but he was evidently too much of an amateur in a craft which required the exercise of a great many qualities not often found in one man's composition. His very first venture was to get off two officers of high rank from Reading, for which he was to receive three hundred guineas, half paid down. He got them in a post-chaise as far as the inn at Johns Cross, Mountfield, about fourteen miles from Hastings, but here the Excise officers dropped upon them, and there was an end of things.

At Ashbourne in Derbyshire, a young woman was brought up on March 13, 1812, charged with aiding prisoners on parole to escape, and evidently there had been hints about improper relationship between her and the Frenchmen, for she published the following:

'*To the Christian Impartial Reader.*

'I the undernamed Susanna Cotton declares she has had nothing to do with the escape of the French prisoners, although she has been remanded at Stafford, and that there has been no improper relationship as rumoured.

'Judge not that ye be not judged. Parents of female children should not readily believe a slander of their sex, nor should a male parent listen to the vulgar aggravation that too often attends the jocular whispering report of a crime so important. For it is not known what Time, a year or a day, may bring forth.

'Misses Lomas and Cotton take this opportunity (tho' an unpleasant one) of returning their grateful acknowledgement of Public and Individual Favours conferred on them in their Business of Millinery, and hope for a continuance of them, and that they will not be withheld by reason of any Prejudices which may have arisen from the Slander above alluded to.'

The prosecution was withdrawn, although Miss Cotton's denials were found to be untrue.

CHAPTER XXVII
ESCAPES OF PRISONERS ON PAROLE

The newspapers of our forefathers during the eighteenth and early nineteenth centuries contained very many advertisements like the two following. The first is from the *Western Flying Post*, of 1756, dated from Launceston, and offering Two Guineas reward for two officers, who had broken their parole, and were thus described:

'One, Mons. Barbier, a short man, somewhat pock-marked, and has a very dejected look, and wore a snuff-coloured coat; the other, Mons. Beth, a middle-aged man, very strongly set, wore his own hair and a blue coat. The former speaks no English, but the latter very well. They were both last seen near Exeter, riding to that city.'

The second is from the London *Observer* of April 21, 1811:

BREACH OF PAROLE OF HONOUR.—Transport Office, April 12, 1811.

'Whereas the two French Officers, Prisoners of War, named and described at the foot hereof, have absconded from Chesterfield in violation of their Parole of Honour; the Commissioners for conducting His Majesty's Transport Service, etc., do hereby offer a Reward of Five Guineas for the recapture of each of the said Prisoners, to any Person or Persons who shall apprehend them, and deliver them at this office, or otherwise cause them to be safely lodged in any of the Public Gaols. Joseph Exelman, General of Brigade, age 36, 5 feet 11½ inches high, stout, oval visage, fresh complexion, light brown hair, blue eyes, strong features.

'Auguste de la Grange, Colonel, age 30, 6 feet high, stout, round visage, fair complexion, brown hair, dark eyes, no mark in particular.'

Excelmans was one of Bonaparte's favourites. He and De la Grange induced Jonas Lawton, an assistant to Doctor John Elam, the surgeon at Chesterfield, to make the necessary arrangements for escape, and to accompany them. They left Chesterfield concealed in a covered cart, and safely reached Paris. Here Lawton was liberally rewarded, and provided with a good post as surgeon in a hospital, and retained the position long after the conclusion of peace.

Merely escaping from the parole town did not become frequent until it was found necessary to abolish virtually the other method of returning to France which we allowed. By this, an officer on parole upon signing a declaration to the effect that unless he was exchanged for a British officer of similar rank by a certain date he would return to England on that date, was allowed to go to France, engaging, of course, not to serve against us. But when it became not a frequent but a universal rule among French officers to break their honour and actually to serve against us during their permitted absence, the Government was obliged to refuse all applications, with the result that to escape from the parole town became such a general practice as to call into existence that profession of escape-aiding which was dealt with in the last chapter.

The case of Captain Jurien, now to be mentioned, is neither better nor worse than scores of others.

On December 10, 1803, the Transport Office wrote to him in Paris:

'As the time allowed for your absence from this Kingdom expired on November 22nd, and as Captain Brenton, R.N., now a prisoner of war in France, has not been released in exchange for you agreeably to our proposal, you are hereby required to return to this country according to the terms of your Parole Agreement.'

But on March 16, 1804, Jurien had not returned. One result was that when a Colonel Neraud applied to be sent to France upon his giving his word to have a British officer exchanged for him, the Transport Office reminded him that Jurien had been released on parole, August 22, 1803, on the promise that he would return in three months, if not exchanged for Captain Brenton, and that seven months had passed and he was still away. They added that the French Government had not released one British officer in return for 500 French, who had been sent on parole to France, some of whom, furthermore, in violation of their parole, were in arms against Britain. 'Hence your detention is entirely owing to the action of your own Government.'

As time went on, and Jurien and the others did not return, the Transport Office, weary of replying to the frequent applications of French officers to go to France on parole, at last ceased to do so, with the result that attempted escapes from parole places became frequent.

At the same time it must not be understood that laxity of honour as regards parole obligation of this kind was universal. When in 1809 the Transport Office, in reply to a request by General Lefebvre to be allowed to go to France on parole, said that they could not accede inasmuch as no French officer thus privileged had been *allowed* to return, they italicized the word 'allowed', and cited the case of General Frescinet, 'who made most earnest but ineffectual Intreaty to be allowed to fulfil the Parole d'Honneur' he had entered into, by returning to this country.

Thame seems to have been a particularly turbulent parole town, and one from which escapes were more than usually numerous. One case was peculiar. Four prisoners who had been recaptured after getting away justified their attempt by accusing Smith, the Agent, of ill-behaviour towards them. Whereupon the other prisoners at Thame, among them Villaret-Joyeuse, testified against them, and in favour of Smith.

The experiences of Baron Le Jeune are among the most interesting, and his case is peculiar inasmuch as although he was nominally a prisoner on parole, he was not so in fact, so that his escape involved no breach. In 1811 he was taken prisoner by Spanish brigands, who delivered him to the English garrison at Merida. Here he was treated as a guest by Major-General Sir William Lumley and the officers, and when he sailed for England on H.M.S. *Thetis* he had a state-cabin, and was regarded as a distinguished passenger. On arriving at Portsmouth his anxiety was as to whether the hulks were to be his fate. 'And our uneasiness increased', he writes in the *Memoirs*, whence the following story is taken, 'when we passed some twenty old vessels full of French prisoners, most of them wearing only yellow vests, whilst others were perfectly naked. At this distressing sight I asked the captain if he was taking us to the hulks. To which he replied with a frown: "Yes, just as a matter of course." At the same moment our boat drew up alongside the *San Antonio*, an old 80–gun ship. We ascended the side, and there, to our horror, we saw some five to six hundred French prisoners, who were but one-third of those on board, climbing on to each other's shoulders, in the narrow space in which they were penned, to have a look at the newcomers, of whose arrival they seemed to have been told. Their silence, their attitude, and the looks of compassion they bestowed on me as I greeted them *en passant* seemed to me omens of a terrible future for me.'

The captain of the hulk apologized to the baron for having no better accommodation. Le Jeune, incredulous, made him repeat it, and flew into a rage. He snatched a sword from an Irishman and swore he would kill any one who would keep him on a hulk. The French prisoners shouted: 'Bravo! If every one behaved as you do, the English would not dare treat us so!'

The captain of the hulk was alarmed at the possible result of this with 1,500 desperate prisoners, and hurried the baron into his boat.

Thus Baron Le Jeune escaped the hulks!

He was then taken to the Forton Dépôt, where he remained three days, and was then ordered to Ashby-de-la-Zouch. So rapidly was he hurried into a coach that he had not time to sign his parole papers and resolved to profit by the omission. He passed many days on a very pleasant journey via Andover and Blenheim, for he paused to see all that was interesting on the way, and even went to theatres. He found about a hundred French prisoners at Ashby (some of whom, he says, had been there fifteen years!), and reported himself to the Agent, Farnell, a grocer, 'certainly the tallest, thinnest, most cadaverous seller of dry goods in the world.'

At Ashby he found old friends, and passed his time with them, and in learning English. He was invited to Lord Hastings' house about a mile from Ashby. Hastings was brother to Lord Moira, a friend of the Prince of Wales, and here he met the orphan daughter of Sir John Moore. He was most kindly treated, and Lord Hastings said he would try to get leave for him to live in London.

Then came a change.

'A man came to me one morning, and said to me privately that the Duke of Rovigo, minister of Police in France, authorized by the Emperor, had sent him to propose to me that I should let him arrange for me to get out of England, and return to France. I distrusted him, for I had heard of the tricks of escape Agents, and said I would first consult my friend, Colonel

Stoffel. I did so. Stoffel said it was a *bonâ fide* offer, but the emissary had brought no money with him, and it would cost probably 200 guineas.'

Where was the baron to get such a sum? He went to Baudins, a merchant, and asked him for a loan, and at a ball that night Baudins signalled that the loan was all right. Farnell was at the ball, and the baron describes his comical assumption of dignity as the guardian of the French prisoners. Baudins lent Baron Le Jeune the money in gold without asking interest on it.

'I was invited to a grand dinner by General Hastings the very evening we were to start, and I duly appeared at it. The evening passed very brightly, and at dessert, after the ladies had retired, the men remained behind to drink wine together, beginning with a toast to the ladies. As a matter of taste, as well as of design, I kept my head clear, and when my companions were sufficiently exhilarated by the fumes of the claret they had drunk, they returned with somewhat unsteady steps to the drawing-room, where tea had been prepared by the ladies.'

The baron won the goodwill of all and was invited to return the next day.

At 11 p.m., it being very dark, he slipped out through the park to meet Colonel Stoffel and a guide. He waited an hour, but at last they arrived in a post-chaise, and they drove off. Passing through Northants, North Middlesex [*sic*], London, and Reigate, they came to Hythe, where they stopped the next night. They pretended to be invalids come for a course of sea baths, and the baron was actually assisted out of the carriage by Custom-house officers. The chaise dismissed, tea was ordered while the guide went to make inquiries about Folkestone. He returned with a horror-struck face, and wrote on a slate: 'Pay at once and let us be off.' Le Jeune gave the girl of the house a guinea, and told her to keep the change, which made her look suspicious, as if the money had not been honestly come by. No time was to be lost, for Hythe was full of troops. The guide advised the baron to drop the erect bearing of a soldier, and assume a stoop. They got away, and hid in a wheat-field during the day while the guide again went into Folkestone. He was away seventeen hours. At length they got to

Folkestone, and Le Jeune was introduced to a smuggler named Brick, a diabolical-looking man, who said he would take them safely over to France.

Brick asked the Baron for 200 guineas, and got them. The wind was contrary, he said, but he would lodge them well. A decent room was hired with a trap-door under the bed for escape, and here they remained thirteen days. Le Jeune became impatient, and at last resolved to risk weather and everything else and go. 'Well! follow me! like the others!' growled Brick ferociously to the sailor with him. But the woman of the house implored Le Jeune and Stoffel not to go with Brick: they remained determined, but she persisted and held them back, and so, now persuaded that she had good reasons for her action, and she seeming a decent body, they remained. Later on they learned how close to danger they had been, for the woman told them that Brick had taken the money of a score of fugitives like themselves, promising to land them in France, hiding them under nets to avoid the coast-guard, and as soon as they were well out, murdering them and flinging their bodies overboard with stones tied to them, knowing that transportation awaited him if he was caught aiding prisoners to escape.

They asked the woman to help them, for now they had no money. The baron told the sailor that he would give him fifty livres at Boulogne, if he landed them there. He was an honest fellow, brought them a sailor's clothes, and went along the beach with them, replying, 'Fishermen' to the many challenges they got. Finding a small boat, they shoved it off, and got in, so as to board a fishing-smuggling smack riding outside. It was a foul night, and three times they were hurled back ashore, wet to the skin; so they returned. The next day the weather moderated and they got off, under the very lee of a police boat, which they deceived by pretending to get nets out. In six hours they were within sight of Boulogne, but were obliged to keep off or they would be fired upon, until they had signalled and were told to come in.

At this time England sent by smugglers a quantity of incendiary pamphlets which the French coast-guard had orders to seize, so that Le Jeune and Stoffel were searched and, guarded by armed men, marched to the Commissary of Police, 'just as if', Le Jeune said, 'we were infected with the plague.'

Luckily, the Commissary was an old friend of the baron, so they had no further trouble, but paid the sailor his fifty livres, and went to Paris. At an interview with the Emperor, the latter said to Le Jeune, 'And did you see Lefebvre-Desnouettes?'

'No, sire, but I wrote to him. He is extremely anxious to get back to you, and is beginning to lose hope of being exchanged. He would do as I have done if he were not afraid of your Majesty's displeasure.'

'Oh! Let him come! Let him come! I shall be very glad to see him,' said the Emperor.

'Does your Majesty give me leave to tell him so in your name?'

'Yes, yes. Don't lose any time.'

So Madame Lefebvre-Desnouettes got a passport, and went over to England, and her presence did much to distract the attention of the general's guardians, and made his escape comparatively easy. The general, as a German or Russian Count, Madame in boy's clothes as his son, and an A.D.C. got up as a valet-de-chambre, went in a post-chaise from Cheltenham to London, where they rested for a couple of hours at Sablonière's in Leicester Square, then at midnight left for Dover and thence to Paris.

General Osten, second in command at Flushing, on parole at Lichfield, was another gentleman who was helped to get off by a lady member of his family. His daughter had come with him from Flushing, and in December 1809 went away with all her father's heavy baggage. In February 1810, Waddell, the escape agent, met the general and two other officers in Birmingham, and forty-six hours later landed with them in Holland.

In this year, 1810, the escapes were so numerous by boats stolen from the shores that the Admiralty issued a warning that owners of boats on beaches should not leave masts, oars, and tackle in them, and in 1812 compensation was refused to a Newton Abbot and to a Paignton fisherman, because prisoners had stolen their boats, which had been left with their gear on the beach, despite warning, and when the prisoners were recaptured it was found that they had destroyed the boats.

In October 1811, six French officers—Bouquet, army surgeon, Leclerc, lieutenant of hussars, Denguiard, army surgeon, Jean Henry, 'passenger' on privateer, Gaffé, merchant skipper, and Glenat, army lieutenant, under the guidance of one Johns, left Okehampton, crossed the moor to Bovey

Tracey, where they met a woman of whom they asked the way to Torbay. She replied, and while they consulted together, gave the alarm so that the villagers turned out and caught three of the runaways. The other three ran and were pursued. Johns turned on the foremost pursuer and stabbed him so that he died, and two others were wounded by the Frenchmen, but the latter were caught at Torquay. Johns got off, but on November 2 was seen at Chesterfield, where he got work on a Saturday; instead of going to it on Monday morning, however, he decamped, and was seen on the Manchester road, eight miles from Chesterfield. In 1812 a man named Taylor, of Beer Alston, said to be Johns, was arrested, but proved an alibi and was discharged.

In 1812 General Maurin, who may be remembered in connexion with the Crapper trouble at Wantage, escaped with his brother from Abergavenny, whither he had been sent, the smuggler Waddell being paid £300 for his help. At the same time General Brou escaped from Welshpool. Both these officers had been treated with particular leniency and had been allowed unusual privileges, so that the Transport Office comments with great severity upon their behaviour.

On November 8, 1812, a girl named Mary Clarke went in very foggy weather from Wolverhampton to Bridgnorth to meet a friend. She waited for some time, but he did not come; so she turned back towards her inn, where her chaise was waiting. Here was Lieutenant Montbazin, a French naval officer, who had broken his parole from Lichfield, who politely accosted her and asked her if she was going to Wolverhampton. She replied that she was. Was she going to walk? No; she had her chaise. Would she let him have a seat if he paid half expenses? She agreed, and went back for the chaise while he walked on, and she picked him up half a mile on, between some rocks by the roadside. So they went on to Wolverhampton—and to Birmingham. In the meantime he had been missed at Lichfield, and followed, and in the back parlour of the *Swan* at Birmingham was arrested with the girl.

This was Mary Clarke's evidence in court.

In defence, Montbazin said that he had been exchanged for four British seamen, who had been landed from France, but that the Transport Office had refused to let him go, so he had considered himself absolved from his parole.

It is hardly necessary to say that the girl's story was concocted, that her meeting with Montbazin was part of a prearranged plan, and the Court emphasized their opinion that this was the case by sending the lieutenant to a prison afloat, and Mary Clarke to one ashore.

In October 1812, eight French officers left Andover quietly in the evening, and, a mile out, met two mounted escape-aiders. Behind each of them a prisoner mounted, and all proceeded at a walk for six miles, when they met another man with three horses. On these horses the remaining six prisoners mounted, and by daybreak were at Ringwood, thirty-six miles on their road to liberty. All the day they remained hidden in the forest, living upon bread, cheese, and rum, which their guides procured from Ringwood. At nightfall they restarted, passed through Christchurch to Stanpit, and thence to the shore, where they found a boat waiting for them; but the wind being contrary and blowing a gale, they could not embark, and were obliged to remain hidden in the woods for three days, suffering so much from exposure and want that they made a bargain with a Mrs. Martin to lodge in her house for £12 until the weather should moderate sufficiently for them to embark. They stayed here for a week, and then their suspense and anxiety, they knowing that the hue and cry was after them, became unbearable, and they gave the smuggler-skipper of the *Freeholder* a promissory note for six hundred guineas to hazard taking them off. He made the attempt, but the vessel was driven ashore, and the Frenchmen were with difficulty landed at another spot on the coast; here they wandered about in the darkness and storm, until one of them becoming separated from the others gave himself up, and the discovery of his companions soon followed.

The result of the trial was that the officers were, of course, sent to the hulks, the master of the *Freeholder* was transported for life, four of his men for seven years, and the *aiders acquitted*. This appears curious justice, which can only be explained by presuming that the magistrates, or rather the Admiralty, often found it politic to get escape-aiders into their service in this way.

Of course, all 'escapes' were bad offences from an honourable point of view, but some were worse than others. For instance, in 1812, the Duc de Chartres wrote a strong letter of intercession to the Transport Office on behalf of one Du Baudiez. This man had been sent to Stapleton Prison for having broken his parole at Odiham, and the duke asked that his parole should be restored him. The Transport Office decidedly rejected the application, and in their reply to the duke quoted a letter written by Du Baudiez to his sister in France in which he says that he has given his creditors in Odiham bills upon her, but asks her not to honour them, because 'Les Anglais nous ont agonis de sottises, liés comme des bêtes sauvages, et traités toute la route comme des chiens. Ce sont des Anglais; rien ne m'étonne de ce qu'ils ont fait ... ce sont tous des gueux, des scélérats depuis le premier jusqu'au dernier. Aussi je vous prie en grâce de protester ces billets ... je suis dans la ferme résolution de ne les point payer.'

On one occasion an unexpected catch of 'broke-paroles' was made. The Revenue Officers believed that two men who were playing cards in an inn near Canterbury were escaped prisoners, and at 8 p.m. called on a magistrate to get help. The magistrate told them that it was of no use to get the constable, as at that hour he was usually intoxicated, but authorized them to get the military.

This they did, but the landlord refused to open the door and, during the parleying, two men slipped out by the back door, whom the officers stopped, and presently two others, who were also stopped. All four were French 'broke-paroles' from Ashby-de-la-Zouch, and the card-players within were not prisoners at all. The captured men said that on Beckenham Common they had nearly been caught, for the driver of the cart stopped there at 10 p.m. to rest the horse. The horse-patrol, passing by, ordered him to move on. As he was putting the horse to the Frenchmen, all being at the back of the cart, tilted it up and cried out. However, the horse-patrol had passed on and did not hear.

In the two next cases English girls play a part. In 1814 Colonel Poerio escaped from Ashbourne with an English girl in male attire, but they were captured at Loughborough. At the trial an Ashbourne woman said that one day a girl came and asked for a lodging, saying that she was a worker at 'lace-running'; she seemed respectable, and was taken in, and remained some days without causing any suspicion, although she seemed on good terms with the French prisoners on parole in the town. One evening the woman's little girl met the lodger coming downstairs, and said: 'Mam! *she* has got a black coat on!' When asked where she was going, she replied, 'To

Colonel Juliett's. Will be back in five minutes.' (Colonel Juliett was another prisoner.) She did not return, and that was the last witness saw of her.

Upon examination, the girl said that she kept company with Poerio, but as her father did not approve of her marrying him she had resolved to elope. She took with her £5, which she had saved by 'running' lace. They were arrested at the *Bull's Head*, Loughborough, where the girl had ordered a chaise. Counsel decided that there was no case for prosecution!

I am not sure if this Colonel Poerio is identical with the man of that name who, in 1812, when on a Chatham hulk, applied to be put on parole, the answer being a refusal, inasmuch as he was a man of infamous character, and that when in command of the island of Cerigo he had poisoned the water there in order to relieve himself of some 600 Albanian men, women, and children, many of whom died—a deed he acknowledged himself by word and in writing.

Colonel Ocher in 1811 got off from Lichfield with a girl, was pursued by officers in a chaise and four, and was caught at Meriden, on the Coventry road, about two miles beyond Stone Bridge. Upon examination, Ann Green, spinster, lodging at 3, Newman Street, Oxford Street, London, said that she came to Birmingham by the 'Balloon' coach, according to instructions she had received from a Baron Ferriet, whom she knew. He had given her £6, paid her fare, and sent her to the *Swan with two Necks* in Ladd Lane, where she was given a letter, which, as she could not read, the waiter read to her. The letter told her to go to Lichfield to the *St. George* hotel, as the baron had business to attend to which kept him in London. At the Lichfield hotel there was a letter which told her to go to Mr. Joblin's, where Colonel Ocher lodged. Here she left word she would meet him in the fields, which she did at 9 p.m., when they went off, and were captured as above.

In defence, 'Baron Ferriet' told a strange story. He said he had been in the British Secret Service in France. He lived there in constant danger as there was a reward of 40,000 francs offered for him by the French Government. At Sables d'Olonne, Colonel Ocher's family had hidden him when the authorities were after him, and had saved him, and Madame Ocher had looked after his wife and family. So, in a long letter he explains in very fair English that he determined to repay the Ochers in France for their kindness to him by procuring the escape of General Ocher, a prisoner on parole in England, and regarded him as 'his property'.

Although the prisoners on parole had no lack of English sympathizers, especially if they could pay, a large section of the lower class of country folk were ever on the alert to gain the Government reward for the detection and prevention of parole-breaking. The following is a sample of letters frequently received by the 'Sick and Hurt' Office and its agents:

'MY LORDS AND GENTLEMEN,

'This informs your lordships that on ye 30th July 1780, I was on Okehampton road leading to Tavistock, saw four French prisoners, on horseback without a guide. They signified to me that they had leave to go to Tavistock from there company at Okehampton. After I was past Tavistock four miles they came galloping on towards Buckland Down Camp. I kept in sight of them and perceived them to ride several miles or above out of the Turnpike Road taking of what view they could of Gentlemen's seats, and ye Harbour and Sound and Camp, and I thought within myself it was very strange that these profest Enemies should be granted such Libertys as this, by any Company whatever. Accordingly came to a Resolution as soon as they came within the lines of the Camp ride forward and stopt them and applyd to the Commanding Officer which was Major Braecher of the Bedfordshire Militia, who broke their letter, and not thinking it a proper Passport the Major ordered them under the care of the Quarter Guard.

[Winds up with a claim for reward.]

'JOSEPH GILES,

'Near ye P.O., Plymouth Dock.'

It turned out in this case that the Agent at Okehampton had given the Frenchmen permission to go to Tavistock for their trunks, so they were released and returned. The 'Sick and Hurt' Office said that to allow these prisoners to ride unguarded to Tavistock was most improper, and must, under no circumstances, be allowed to occur again.

From a paper read by Mr. Maberley Phillips, F.S.A., before the Newcastle Society of Antiquaries, I take the following instances of escapes of parole prisoners in the North.

In 1813 there were on parole at Jedburgh under the Agent, George Bell, about a hundred French prisoners. At the usual Saturday muster-call on June 1, all were present, but at that of June 4, Benoît Poulet and Jacques Girot were missing. From the evidence at the trial of the accomplices in this escape, all of whom except the chief agent, James Hunter of Whitton, near Rothbury, were arrested, and three of whom turned King's evidence, the story was unfolded of the flight of the men—who were passed off as Germans on a fishing excursion—across the wild, romantic, historic fell-country between the Border and Alwinton on the Coquet; and so by Whitton, Belsay, and Ponteland, to the *Bird in Bush* inn, Pilgrim Street, Newcastle; whence the Frenchmen were supposed to have gone to Shields, and embarked in a foreign vessel for France.

I quote this and the following case as instances of the general sympathy of English country people with the foreign prisoners amongst them. The *Courant* of August 28, 1813, says: 'The trial of James Hunter occupied the whole of Monday, and the court was excessively crowded; when the verdict of Not Guilty was delivered, clapping of hands and other noisy symptoms of applause were exhibited, much to the surprise of the judge, Sir A. Chambers, who observed that he seemed to be in an assembly of Frenchmen, rather than in an English court of justice. The other prisoners charged with the same offence, were merely arraigned, and the verdict of acquittal was recorded without further trial.'

Hunter had been arrested in Scotland, just before the trial. Quoting from Wallace's *History of Blyth*, Mr. Phillips says:

'One Sunday morning in the year 1811, the inhabitants were thrown into a state of great excitement by the startling news that five Frenchmen had been taken during the night and were lodged in the guard-house. They were officers who had broken their parole at Edinburgh Castle [? Jedburgh], and in making their way home had reached the neighbourhood of Blyth; when discovered, they were resting by the side of the Plessy wagon-way beside the "Shoulder of Mutton" field.

'A party of countrymen who had been out drinking, hearing some persons conversing in an unknown tongue, suspected what they were, and determined to effect their capture. The fugitives made some resistance, but in the end were captured, and brought to Blyth, and given into the charge of the soldiers then quartered in the town. *This act of the countrymen met with the strongest reprobation of the public* (the italics are mine). 'The miscarriage of the poor fellows' plan of escape through the meddling of their captors, excited the sympathy of the inhabitants; rich and poor vying with each other in showing kindness to the strangers. Whatever was likely to alleviate their helpless condition was urged upon their acceptance; victuals they did not refuse, but though money was freely offered them, they steadily refused to accept it. The guard-house was surrounded all day long by crowds anxious to get a glimpse of the captives. The men who took the prisoners were rewarded with £5 each, but doubtless it would be the most unsatisfactory wages they ever earned, for long after, whenever they showed their faces in the town, they had to endure the upbraiding of men, women, and children; indeed, it was years before public feeling about this matter passed away.'

The continuance and frequency of escapes by prisoners on parole necessitated increased rigidity of regulations. The routes by which prisoners were marched from place to place were exactly laid down, and we find numberless letters of instruction from the Transport Office like this:

'Colonel X having received permission to reside on parole at Ashby-de-la-Zouch, his route from Chatham is to be: Chatham, Sevenoaks, Croydon, Kingston, Uxbridge, Wendover, Buckingham, Towcester, Daventry, and Coleshill.'

The instructions to conductors of prisoners were as follows:

Prisoners were to march about twelve miles a day. Conductors were to pay the prisoners sixpence per day per man before starting. Conductors were to ride ahead of prisoners, so as to give notice at towns of their coming, and were to see that the prisoners were not imposed upon. Conductors (who were always mounted), were to travel thirty miles a day on the return journey, and to halt upon Sundays.

Of course, it was in the power of the conductors to make the journeys of the prisoners comfortable or the reverse. If the former, it was the usual custom to give a certificate of this kind:

'*April 1798.* This is to certify that Mr. Thomas Willis, conductor of 134 Dutch and Spanish prisoners of war from the *Security* prison ship at Chatham, into the custody of Mr. Barker, agent for prisoners of war at Winchester, has provided us with good lodgings every night, well littered with straw, and that we have been regularly paid our subsistence every morning on our march, each prisoner sixpence per day according to the established allowance.

'(Signed).'

The ill-treatment of prisoners on the march was not usual, and when reported was duly punished. Thus in 1804 a Coldstream guardsman on escort of prisoners from Reading to Norman Cross, being convicted of robbing a prisoner, was sentenced to 600 lashes, and the sentence was publicly read out at all the dépôts.

In 1811 posters came out offering the usual reward for the arrest of an officer who had escaped from a Scottish parole town, and distinguished him as lacking three fingers of his left hand. A year later Bow Street officers Vickary and Lavender, 'from information received', followed a seller of artificial flowers into a public-house in 'Weston Park, Lincolns Inn Fields.' The merchant bore the distinctive mark of the wanted foreigner, and, seeing that the game was up, candidly admitted his identity, said that he had lived in London during the past twelve months by making and selling artificial flowers, and added that he had lost his fingers for his country, and would not mind losing his head for her.

In the same year a militia corporal who had done duty at a prisoner dépôt, and so was familiar with foreign faces, saw two persons in a chaise driving towards Worcester, whom he at once suspected to be escaped prisoners. He stopped the chaise, and made the men show their passports, which were not satisfactory, and, although they tried to bribe him to let them go, he refused, mounted the bar of the chaise, and drove on. One of the men presently opened the chaise-door with the aim of escaping, but the corporal presented a pistol at him, and he withdrew. At Worcester they confessed that they had escaped from Bishop's Castle, and said they were Trafalgar officers.

In 1812 prisoners broke their parole in batches. From Tiverton at one time, twelve; from Andover, eight (as recorded on pp. 384–5); from Wincanton, ten; and of these, four were generals and eighteen colonels.

In the *Quarterly Review*, December 1821, the assertion made by M. Dupin, in his report upon the treatment of French prisoners in Britain, published in 1816, and before alluded to in the chapter upon prison-ships, that French officers observed their parole more faithfully than did English, was shown to be false. Between May 1803, and August 1811, 860 French officers had attempted to escape from parole towns. Of these, 270 were recaptured, and 590 escaped. In 1808 alone, 154 escaped. From 1811 to 1814, 299 army officers escaped, and of this number 9 were generals, 18 were colonels, 14 were lieutenant-colonels, 8 were majors, 91 were captains, and 159 were lieutenants. It should be noted that in this number are not included the many officers who practically 'escaped', in that they did not return to England when not exchanged at the end of their term of parole.

From the Parliamentary Papers of 1812, I take the following table:

Transport Office, June 25, 1812.

	Total No. Com. Officers on parole	No. that broke parole	Been retaken	Escaped
Year ending 31 June 1810	1,685	104	47	57
Year ending 31 June 1811	2,087	118	47	71
Year ending 31 June 1812	2,142	242	63	179
	5,914	464	157	307
		218	85	133
		682	242	440

Besides the above, the following officers prisoners of rank, entitled to be on parole, have broken it during the three years above mentioned.

N.B. The numbers stated in this account exclude those persons only who are actually discarded from the places appointed for their residence, a considerable number of officers have been obliged to close confinement, in various other breaches of their parole engagements.

(Signed)
Rea. Grasson
J. Bowen
R. Thomson.

During the above-quoted period, between 1803 and 1811, out of 20,000 British *détenus*, not prisoners of war, in France, it cannot be shown that more than twenty-three broke their parole, and even these are doubtful.

Sometimes the epidemic of parole-breaking was severe enough to render drastic measures necessary. In 1797 orders were issued that all French prisoners, without distinction of rank, were to be placed in close confinement.

In 1803, in consequence of invasion alarms, it was deemed advisable to remove all prisoners from the proximity of the coast to inland towns, the Admiralty order being:

'At the present conjunction all parole prisoners from the South and West towns are to be sent to North Staffordshire, and Derbyshire—that is, to Chesterfield, Ashbourne, and Leek.'

General Morgan at Bishop's Waltham resented this removal so far away, in a letter to the Transport Office, to which they replied:

'This Board has uniformly wished to treat Prisoners of War with every degree of humanity consistent with the public safety: but in the present circumstances it has been judged expedient to remove all Prisoners of War on Parole from places near the Coast to Inland towns. You will therefore observe that the order is not confined to you, but relates generally to all Prisoners on Parole: and with regard to your comparison of the treatment of prisoners in this country with that of British prisoners in France, the Commissioners think it only necessary to remark that the distance to which it is now proposed to remove you does not exceed 170 miles, whereas British prisoners in France are marched into the interior to a distance of 500 miles from some of the ports into which they are carried.'

Morgan was allowed eventually his choice of Richmond or Barnet as a place of parole, a privilege accorded him because of his kindness to a Mr. Hurry, during the detention of the latter as a prisoner in France.

In 1811, so many prisoners escaped from Wincanton that all the parole prisoners in the place were marched to London to be sent thence by sea to

Scotland for confinement. 'Sudden and secret measures' were taken to remove them, all of the rank of captain and above, to Forton for embarkation, except General Houdetôt, who was sent to Lichfield. From Okehampton sixty were sent to Ilfracombe, and thence to Swansea for Abergavenny, and from Bishop's Waltham to Oswestry in batches of twelve at intervals of three days.

Many parole towns petitioned for the retention of the prisoners, but all were refused; the inhabitants of some places in Devon attempted to detain prisoners for debts; and Enchmarsh, the Agent at Tiverton, was suspended for not sending off his prisoners according to orders. Their departure was the occasion in many places for public expressions of regret, and this can be readily appreciated when it is considered what the residence of two or three hundred young men, some of whom were of good family and many of whom had private means, in a small English country town meant, not merely from a business but from a social point of view.

In *The Times* of 1812 may be read that a French officer, who had been exchanged and landed at Morlaix, and had expressed disgust at the frequent breaches of parole by his countrymen, was arrested and shot by order of Bonaparte. I merely quote this as an example that even British newspapers of standing were occasionally stooping to the vituperative level of their trans-Channel *confrères*.

CHAPTER XXVIII
COMPLAINTS OF PRISONERS

It could hardly be expected that a uniform standard of good and submissive behaviour would be attained by a large body of fighting men, the greater part of whom were in vigorous youth or in the prime of life, although, on the whole, the conduct of those who honourably observed their parole seems to have been admirable—a fact which no doubt had a great deal to do with the very general display of sympathy for them latterly. In some places more than others they seem to have brought upon themselves by their own behaviour local odium, and these are the places in which were quartered captured privateer officers, wild, reckless sea-dogs whom, naturally, restraint galled far more deeply than it did the drilled and disciplined officers of the regular army and navy.

In 1797, for instance, the inhabitants of Tavistock complained that the prisoners went about the town in female garb, after bell-ringing, and that they were associated in these masquerades with women of their own nation. So they were threatened with the Mill Prison at Plymouth.

In 1807 complaints from Chesterfield about the improper conduct of the prisoners brought a Transport Office order to the Agent that the strictest observation of regulations was necessary, and that the mere removal of a prisoner to another parole town was no punishment, and was to be discontinued. In 1808 there was a serious riot between the prisoners and the townsfolk in the same place, in which bludgeons were freely used and heads freely broken, and from Lichfield came complaints of the outrageous and insubordinate behaviour of the prisoners.

In 1807 Mr. P. Wykeham of Thame Park complained of the prisoners trespassing therein; from Bath came protests against the conduct of General Rouget and his A.D.C.; and in 1809 the behaviour of one Wislawski at Odiham (possibly the 'Wysilaski' already mentioned as at Sanquhar) was reported as being so atrocious that he was at once packed off to a prison-ship.

In 1810, at Oswestry, Lieutenant Julien complained that the Agent, Tozer, had insulted him by threatening him with his cane, and accusing him of drunkenness in the public-houses. Tozer, on the other hand, declared that Julien and others were rioting in the streets, that he tried to restore order, and raised his cane in emphasis, whereupon Julien raised his with offensive intent.

Occasionally we find complaints sent up by local professionals and tradesmen that the prisoners on parole unfairly compete with them. Here it may be remarked that the following of trades and professions by prisoners of war was by no means confined to the inmates of prisons and prison-ships, and that there were hundreds of poor officers on parole who not only worked at their professions (as Garneray the painter did at Bishop's Waltham) and at specific trades, but who were glad to eke out their scanty subsistence-money by the manufacture of models, toys, ornaments, &c.

In 1812 a baker at Thame complained that the prisoners on parole in that town baked bread, to which the Transport Office replied that there was no objection to their doing it for their own consumption, but not for public sale. It is to be hoped the baker was satisfied with this very academic reply!

So also the bootmakers of Portsmouth complained that the prisoners on parole in the neighbourhood made boots for sale at lower than the current rates. The Transport Office replied that orders were strict against this, and that the master bootmakers were to blame for encouraging this 'clandestine trade.'

In 1813 the doctors at Welshpool complained that the doctors among the French parole prisoners there inoculated private families for small-pox. The Transport Office forbade it.

In the same year complaints came from Whitchurch in Shropshire of the defiant treatment of the limit-rules by the prisoners there; to which the Transport Office replied that they had ordered posts to be set up at the extremities of the mile-limits, and printed regulations to be posted in public places; that they were fully sensible of the mischief done by so many prisoners being on parole, but that they were unable to stop it.

Still in 1813, the Transport Office commented very severely upon the case of a Danish officer at Reading who had been found guilty of forging a 'certificate of succession', which I take to be a list of prisoners in their order for being exchanged. I quote this case, as crimes of this calibre were hardly known among parole prisoners; for other instances, see pages 320 and 439.

Many complaints were made from the parole towns about the debts left behind them by absconded prisoners. The Transport Office invariably replied that such debts being private matters, the only remedy was at civil law.

When we come to deal with the complaints made by the prisoners—be they merely general complaints, or complaints against the people of the country—the number is so great that the task set is to select those of the most importance and interest.

Complaints against fellow prisoners are not common.

In 1758 a French doctor, prisoner on parole at Wye in Kent, complains that ten of his countrymen, fellow prisoners, wanted him to pay for drinks to the extent of twenty-seven shillings. He refused, so they attacked him, tore his clothes, stole thirty-six shillings, a handkerchief, and two medals. He brought his assailants before the magistrates, and they were made to refund twenty-five shillings. This so enraged them that they made his life a burden to him, and he prayed to be removed elsewhere.

In 1758 a prisoner on parole at Chippenham complained that he was subjected to ill treatment by his fellow prisoners. The letter is ear-marked:

'Mr. Trevanion (the local Agent) is directed to publish to all the prisoners that if any are guilty of misbehaviour to each other, the offenders will immediately be sent to the Prison, and particularly that if any one molests or insults the writer of this letter, he shall instantly be confined upon its being proved.'

Later, however, the writer complains that the bullying is worse than ever, and that the other prisoners swear that they will cut him in pieces, so that he dare not leave his lodgings, and has been besieged there for days.

In the same year Dingart, captain of the *Deux Amis* privateer, writes from confinement on the *Royal Oak* prison-ship at Plymouth that he had been treated unjustly. He had, he says, a difference with Feraud, Captain of *Le Moras* privateer, at Tavistock, during which the latter struck him, ran away, and kept out of sight for a fortnight. Upon his reappearance, the complainant returned him the blow with a stick, whereupon Feraud brought him up for assault before the Agent, Willesford, who sent him to a prison-ship.

At Penryn in the same year, Chevalier, a naval lieutenant, complained of being insulted and attacked by another prisoner with a stick, who, 'although only a privateer sailor, is evidently favoured by Loyll' (Lloyd?) the Agent.

In 1810 one Savart was removed from Wincanton to Stapleton Prison at the request of French superior officers who complained of his very violent conduct.

These complaints were largely due to the tactless Government system of placing parole prisoners of widely different ranks together. There are many letters during the Seven Years' War period from officers requesting to be removed to places where they would be only among people of their own rank, and not among those 'qui imaginent que la condition de prisonnier de guerre peut nous rendre tous égaux.'

Nor was this complaint confined to prisoners on parole, but even more closely affected officers who, for breaches of parole, were sent to prisons or to prison-ships. There are strong complaints in 1758 by 'broke-paroles', as they were termed, of the brutal class of prisoners at Sissinghurst with whom they were condemned to herd; and in one case the officer prisoners actually petitioned that a prison official who had been dismissed and punished for cutting and wounding an ordinary prisoner should be reinstated, as the latter richly deserved the treatment he had received.

Latterly the authorities remedied this by setting apart prison-ships for officers, and by providing separate quarters in prisons. Still, in dealing with the complaints, they had to be constantly on their guard against artifice and fraud, and if the perusal of Government replies to complaints makes us sometimes think that the complainants were harshly and even brutally dealt with, we may be sure that as a rule the authorities had very sufficient grounds for their decisions. For example, in 1804, Delormant, an officer on parole at Tiverton, was sent to a Plymouth hulk for some breach of parole. He complained to Admiral Colpoys that he was obliged there to herd with the common men. Colpoys wrote to the Transport Board that he had thought right to have a separate ship fitted for prisoner officers, and had sent Delormant to it. Whereupon the Board replied that if Admiral Colpoys had taken the trouble to find out what sort of a man Delormant really was, he would have left him where he was, but that *for the present* he might remain on the special ship.

One of the commonest forms of complaint from prisoners was against the custom of punishing a whole community for the sins of a few, or even of a single man. In 1758 a round-robin signed by seventy-five prisoners at Sissinghurst protested that the whole of the inmates of the Castle were put upon half rations for the faults of a few 'impertinents'.

At Okehampton in the same year, upon a paroled officer being sent to a local prison for some offence, and escaping therefrom, the whole of the other prisoners in the place were confined to their lodgings for some days. When set free they held an indignation meeting, during which one of the orators waved a stick, as the mayor said, threateningly at him. Whereupon he was arrested and imprisoned at 'Coxade', the 'Cockside' prison near Mill Bay, Plymouth.

We see an almost pathetic fanning and fluttering of that old French aristocratic plumage, which thirty years later was to be bedraggled in the bloody dust, in the complaints of two highborn prisoners of war in 1756 and 1758. In the former year Monsieur de Béthune strongly resented being sent on parole from Bristol into the country:

'Ayant appris de Mr. Surgunnes (?) que vous lui mandé par votre lettre du 13 courant si Messire De Béthune, Chevalier de St. Simon, Marquis d'Arbest, Baron de Sainte Lucie, Seigneur haut, et bas justicier des paroisses de Chateauvieux, Corvilac, Lâneau, Pontmartin, Neung et autres lieux, étoit admis à la parole avec les autres officiers pour lesquels il s'intéresse, j'aurai l'avantage de vous répondre, qu'un Grand de la trempe de Messire De Béthune, qui vous adresse la présente, n'est point fait pour peupler un endroit aussi désert que la campagne, attendu qu'allié du costé paternel et maternel à un des plus puissans rois que jamais terre ait porté, Londres, comme Bristol ou autre séjour qu'il voudra choisir, est capable de contenir celui qui est tout à vous.

'De Bristol; le 15 Xbre. 1756.'

Later he writes that he hears indirectly that this letter has given offence to the gentlemen at the 'Sick and Hurt' Office on Tower Hill, but maintains that it is excusable from one who is allied to several kings and sovereign princes, and he expects to have his passport for London.

The Prince de Rohan, on parole at Romsey, not adapting himself easily to life in the little Hampshire town, although he had the most rare privilege of a six-mile limit around it, wrote on July 4, 1758, requesting permission for self and three or four officers to go to Southampton once a week to make purchases, as Romsey Market is so indifferent, and to pass the night there. The six-mile limit, he says, does not enable him to avail himself of the hospitality of the people of quality, and he wants leave to go further with his suite. He adds a panegyric on the high birth and the honour of French naval officers, which made parole-breaking an impossibility, and he resents their being placed in the same category with privateer and merchant-ship captains.

However, the Commissioners reply that no exceptions can be made in his favour, and that as Southampton is a sea-port, leave to visit it cannot be thought of.

In 1756 twenty-two officers on parole at Cranbrook in Kent prayed to be sent to Maidstone, on the plea that there were no lodgings to be had in Cranbrook except at exorbitant rates; that the bakers only baked once or twice a week, and that sometimes the supply of bread ran short if it was not ordered beforehand and an extra price paid for it; that vegetables were hardly to be obtained; and that, finally, they were ill-treated by the inhabitants. No notice was taken of this petition.

In 1757 a prisoner writes from Tenterden:

'S'il faut que je reste en Angleterre, permettez-moi encore de vous prier de vouloir bien m'envoyer dans une meilleure place, n'ayant pas déjà lieu de me louer du peuple de ce village. Sur des plaintes que plusieurs Français ont portées au maire depuis que je suis ici, il a fait afficher de ne point insulter aux Français, l'affiche a été le même jour arrachée. On a remis une autre. Il est bien désagréable d'être dans une ville où l'on est obligé de défendre aux peuples d'insulter les prisonniers. J'ai ouï dire aux Français qui ont été à Maidstone que c'était très bien et qu'ils n'ont jamais été insultés ... ce qui me fait vous demander une autre place, c'est qu'on déjà faillit d'être jeté dans la boue en passant dans les chemins, ayant eu cependant l'intention de céder le pavé.'

In reply, the Commissioners of the 'Sick and Hurt' Office ask the Agent at Tenterden why, when he heard complaints, he did not inform the Board. The complainant, however, was not to be moved, as he had previously been sent to Sissinghurst for punishment.

In 1758, twenty officers at Tenterden prayed for removal elsewhere, saying that as the neighbourhood was a residential one for extremely rich people, lodgings at moderate prices were not to be had, and that the townspeople cared so little to take in foreign guests of their description, that if they were taken ill the landlords turned them out. This application was ear-marked for inquiry.

No doubt the poor fellows received but scanty courtesy from the rank and file of their captors, and the foreigner then, far more than now, was deemed fair game for oppression and robbery. In support of this I will quote some remarks by Colonel Thierry, whose case certainly appears to be a particularly hard one.

Colonel Thierry had been sent to Stapleton Prison in 1812 for having violated his parole by writing from Oswestry to his niece, the Comtesse de la Frotté, without having submitted the letter, according to parole rule, to the Agent. He asks for humane treatment, a separate room, a servant, and liberty to go to market.

'Les vexations dont on m'a accablé en route sont révoltantes. Les scélérats que vos lois envoyent à Tyburn ne sont pas plus mal traités; une semblable conduite envers un Colonel, prisonnier de guerre, est une horreur de plus que j'aurai le droit de reprocher aux Anglais pour lesquels j'ai eu tant de bontés lorsqu'ils sont tombés en mon pouvoir. Si le Gouvernement français fût instruit des mauvais traitements dont on accable les Français de touts grades, et donnait des ordres pour user de représailles envers les Anglais détenus en France ... le Gouvernement anglais ordonnerait-il à ses agents de traiter avec plus d'égards, de modération, d'humanité ses prisonniers.'

In a postscript the Colonel adds that his nephew, the Comte de la Frotté, is with Wellington, that another is in the Royal Navy, and that all are English born. One is glad to know that the Colonel's prayer was heard, and that he was released from Stapleton.

In 1758 a prisoner writes from Tenterden:

'Last Thursday, March 16th, towards half-past eight at night, I was going to supper, and passed in front of a butcher's shop where there is a bench fixed near the door on which three or four youths were sitting, and at the end one who is a marine drummer leaning against a wall projecting two feet on to the street. When I came near them I guessed they were talking about us Frenchmen, for I heard one of them say: "Here comes one of them," and when I was a few paces beyond them one of them hit me on the right cheek with something soft and cold. As I entered my lodging I turned round and said: "You had better be careful!" Last Sunday at half-past eight, as I was going to supper, being between the same butcher's shop and the churchyard gate, some one threw at me a stick quite three feet long and heavy enough to wound me severely....'

Also at Tenterden, a prisoner named D'Helincourt, going home one night with a Doctor Chomel, met at the door of the latter's lodging a youth and two girls, one of whom was the daughter of Chomel's landlord, 'avec laquelle il avait plusieurs fois poussé la plaisanterie jusqu'à l'embrasser sans qu'elle l'eût jamais trouvé mauvais, et ayant engagé M. Chomel à l'embrasser aussi.' But the other girl, whom they would also kiss, played the prude; the youth with her misunderstood what D'Helincourt said, and hit him under the chin with his fist, which made D'Helincourt hit him back with his cane on the arm, and all seemed at an end. Not long after, D'Helincourt was in the market, when about thirty youths came along. One of them went up to him and asked him if he remembered him, and hit him on the chest. D'Helincourt collared him, to take him to the Mayor, but the others set on him, and he certainly would have been killed had not some dragoons come up and rescued him.

Apparently the Agents and Magistrates were too much afraid of offending the people to grant justice to these poor strangers.

At Cranbrook a French officer was assaulted by a local ruffian and hit him back, for which he was sent to Sissinghurst.

In 1808 and 1809 many complaints from officers were received that their applications to be allowed to go to places like Bath and Cheltenham for the benefit of their health were too often met with the stereotyped reply that 'your complaint is evidently not of such a nature as to be cured by the waters of Bath or Cheltenham'. Of course, the Transport Office knew well enough that the complaints were not curable by the *waters* of those places, but by their life and gaiety: by the change from the monotonous country town with its narrow, *gauche* society, its wretched inns, and its mile limit, to the fashionable world of gaming, and dancing, and music, and flirting; but they also knew that to permit French officers to gather at these places in numbers would be to encourage plotting and planning, and to bring together gentlemen whom it was desirable to keep apart.

So in the latter year the Mayor of Bath received an order from the Earl of Liverpool that all prisoners of war were to be removed from the city except those who could produce certificates from two respectable doctors of the necessity of their remaining, 'which must be done with such caution as, if required, the same may be verified on oath.' The officers affected by this order were to go to Bishop's Waltham, Odiham, Wincanton, and Tiverton.

Of complaints by prisoners on parole against the country people there must be many hundreds, the greater number of them dating from the period of the Seven Years' War. During this time the prisoners were largely distributed in Kent, a county which, from its proximity to France, and its consequent continuous memory of wrongs, fancied and real, suffered at the hands of Frenchmen during the many centuries of warfare between the two countries, when Kent bore the brunt of invasion and fighting, may be understood to have entertained no particular affection for Frenchmen, despite the ceaseless commerce of a particular kind which the bitterest of wars could not interrupt.

A few instances will suffice to exemplify the unhappy relationship which existed, not in Kent alone, but everywhere, between the country people and the unfortunate foreigners thrust among them.

In 1757 a prisoner on parole at Basingstoke complained that he was in bed at 11 p.m., when there came '7 ou 8 drôles qui les défièrent de sortir en les accablant d'injures atroces, et frappant aux portes et aux fenêtres comme s'ils avoient voulu jeter la maison en bas.' Another prisoner here had stones thrown at him 'd'une telle force qu'elles faisoient feu sur le pavé,' whilst another lot of youths broke windows and almost uprooted the garden.

From Wye in Kent is a whole batch of letters of complaint against the people. One of them is a round-robin signed by eighty prisoners complaining of bad and dear lodgings, and praying to be sent to Ashford, which was four times the size of Wye, and where there were only forty-five prisoners, and lodgings were better and cheaper.

At Tonbridge, in the same year, two parole officers dropped some milk for fun on the hat of a milk-woman at the door below their window. Some chaff ensued which a certain officious and mischief-making man named Miles heard, who threatened he would report the Frenchmen for *improper conduct*, and get them sent to Sissinghurst! The authors of the 'fun' wrote to the authorities informing them of the circumstances, and asking for forgiveness, knowing well that men had been sent to Sissinghurst for less. Whether the authorities saw the joke or not does not appear.

The rabble of the parole towns had recourse to all sorts of devices to make the prisoners break their paroles so that they could claim the usual reward of ten shillings. At Helston, on August 1, 1757, Hingston, the Parole Agent, sent to Dyer, the Agent at Penryn, a prisoner named Channazast, for being out of his lodgings all night. At the examination, Tonken, in whose house the man was, and who was liable to punishment for harbouring him, said, and wrote later:

'I having been sent for by the mayor of our town this day to answer for I cannot tell what, however I'll describe it to you in the best manner I am able. You must know that last Friday evening, I asked Monsieur Channazast to supper at my house who came according to my request. Now I have two Frenchmen boarded at my house, so they sat down together till most ten o'clock. At which time I had intelligence brought me that there was a soldier and another man waiting in the street for him to come out in order to get the ten shillings that was orders given by the Mayor for taking up all Frenchmen who was seen out of their Quarters after 9 o'clock. So, to prevent this rascally imposition I desired the man to go to bed with his two countrymen which he did accordingly altho' he was not out of my house for the night——'

Reply: 'Make enquiries into this.'

From Torrington in the same year eighteen prisoners pray to be sent elsewhere:

'Insultés à chaque instant par mille et millions d'injures ou menaces, estre souvent poursuivis par la popullace jusqu'à nos portes à coups de roches et coups de bâtons. En outre encore, Monseigneur, avant hier il fut tirré un coup de fusil à plomb à cinque heures apres midy n'etant distant de notre logement que d'une portée de pistolet, heureusement celuy qui nous l'envoyoit ne nous avoit point assez bien ajusté . . . qu'il est dans tous les villages des hommes proposés pour rendre justice tres surrement bien judicieux mais il est une cause qui l'empeche de nous prouver son equité comme la crainte de detourner la populasce adverse . . . nous avons été obligés de commettre à tous moments à suporter sans rien dire ce surcrois de malheurs. . . .'

Two more letters, each signed by the same eighteen prisoners, follow to the same intent. The man who fired the shot was brought up, and punishment promised, but nothing was done. Also it was promised that a notice forbidding the insulting of prisoners should be posted up, but neither was this done. The same letters complain also of robbery by lodging keepers, for the usual rate of 4*s*. a week was raised to 4*s*. 6*d*., and a month later to 5*s*. One prisoner refused to pay this. The woman who let the lodging complained to 'Enjolace,' the Agent, who tells the prisoner he must either pay what is demanded, or go to prison.

A prisoner at Odiham in the same year complained that a country girl encouraged him to address her, and that when he did, summoned him for violently assaulting her. He was fined twelve guineas, complains that his defence was not heard, and that ever since he had been insulted and persecuted by the country people.

In 1758 a letter, signed by fifty-six prisoners at Sevenoaks, bitterly complains that the behaviour of the country people is so bad that they dare not go out. In the same year a doctor, a prisoner in Sissinghurst Castle, complains of a grave injustice. He says that when on parole at Sevenoaks he was called in by a fellow countryman, cured him, and was paid his fee, but that 'Nache', the Agent at Sevenoaks, demanded half the fee, and upon the prisoner's refusal to pay him, reported the case to the Admiralty, and got him committed to Sissinghurst.

A disgraceful and successful plot to ruin a prisoner is told from Petersfield in 1758.

Fifteen officers on parole appealed on behalf of one of their number named Morriset. He was in bed on December 22, at 8 a.m., in his lodging at one 'Schollers', a saddler, when Mrs. 'Schollers' came into the room on the pretext of looking for a slipper, and sat herself on the end of the bed. Suddenly, in came her husband, and, finding his wife there, attacked Morriset cruelly. Morriset to defend himself seized a knife from a waistcoat hanging on the bed, and 'Schollers' dropped his hold of him, but took from the waistcoat three guineas and some 'chelins', then called in a constable, accused Morriset of behaving improperly with his wife, and claimed a hundred pounds, or he would summons him. Morriset was brought up before the magistrates, and, despite his protestations of innocence, was sent to Winchester Jail. In reply to the appeal, the Commissioners said that they could not interfere in what was a private matter.

In the same year a prisoner wrote from Callington:

'Lundy passé je fus attaqué dans mon logement par Thomas, garçon de Mr. Avis qui, après m'avoir dit toutes les sottises imaginables, ne s'en contenta pas, sans que je luy répondis à aucune de ses mauvaises parolles, il sauta sur moy, et me frapa, et je fus obligé de m'en défendre. Dimance dernier venant de me promener à 8 heures du soir, je rancontray dans la rue près de mon logement une quarantaine d'Anglois armés de bâtons pour me fraper si je n'avois peu me sauver à la faveur de mes jambes. Mardy sur les 7 heures de soir je fus attaqué en pleine place par les Anglois qui me donnèrent beaucoup de coups et m'étant défait d'eux je me sauvai à l'oberge du *Soleil* ou j'ai été obligé de coucher par ordre de Mr. Ordon, veu qu'il y avoit des Anglois qui m'attendoient pour me maltraiter.'

But even in 1756, when the persecution of prisoners by the rural riff-raff was very bad, we find a testimony from the officers on parole at Sodbury in Gloucestershire to the kindly behaviour of the inhabitants, saying that only on holidays are they sometimes jeered at, and asking to be kept there until exchanged.

Yet the next year, eighteen officers at the same place formulate to the Commissioners of the Sick and Wounded the following complaints:

1. Three Englishmen attacked two prisoners with sticks.

2. A naval doctor was struck in the face by a butcher.

3. A captain and a lieutenant were attacked with stones, bricks, and sticks, knocked down, and had to fly for safety to the house of Ludlow the Agent.

4. A second-captain, returning home, was attacked and knocked down in front of the *Bell* inn by a crowd, and would have been killed but for the intervention of some townspeople.

5. Two captains were at supper at the *Bell*. On leaving the house they were set on by four men who had been waiting for them, but with the help of some townspeople they made a fight and got away.

6. Between 10 and 11 p.m. a lieutenant had a terrible attack made on his lodging by a gang of men who broke in, and left him half dead. After which they went to an inn where some French prisoners lodged, and tried to break in 'jusqu'au point, pour ainsy dire, de le demolir,' swearing they would kill every Frenchman they found.

From Crediton a complaint signed by nearly fifty prisoners spoke of frequent attacks and insults, not only by low ruffians and loafers, but by people of social position, who, so far from doing their best to dissuade the lower classes, rather encouraged them. Even Mr. David, a man of apparently superior position, put a prisoner, a Captain Gazeau, into prison, took the keys himself, and kept them for a day in spite of the Portreeve's remonstrance, but was made to pay damages by the effort of another man of local prominence.

The men selected as agents in the parole towns too often seem to have been socially unfitted for their positions as the 'guides, philosophers, and friends' of officers and gentlemen. At Crediton, for instance, the appointment of a Mr. Harvey called forth a remonstrance signed by sixty prisoners, one of whom thus described him:

'Mr. Harvey à son arrivée de Londres, glorieux d'être exaucé, n'eut rien de plus pressé que de faire voir dans toutes les oberges et dans les rues les ordres dont il était revetu de la part des honorables Commissaires; ce qui ne pourra que nous faire un très mauvais effet, veu que le commun peuple qui habite ce pays-ci est beaucoup irrité contre les Français, à cause de la Nation et sans jusqu'au présent qu'aucun Français n'est donné aucun sujet de plainte.'

Again, in 1756 the *aumonier* of the Comte de Gramont, after complaining that the inhabitants of Ashburton are 'un peuple sans règle et sans éducation', by whom he was insulted, hissed, and stoned, and when he represented this to the authorities was 'garrotté' and taken to Exeter Prison, ridicules the status of the agents—here a shoemaker, here a tailor, here an apothecary, who dare not, for business reasons, take the part of the prisoners. He says he offered his services to well-to-do people in the neighbourhood, but they were declined—deceit on his part perhaps being feared.

From Ashford, Kent, a complainant writes, in 1758, that he was rather drunk one evening and went out for a walk to pick himself up. He met a mounted servant of Lord Winchilsea with a dog. He touched the dog, whereupon the servant dismounted and hit him in the face. A crowd then assembled, armed with sticks, and one man with a gun, and ill-treated him until he was unconscious, tied his hands behind him, emptied his pockets, and took him before Mr. Tritton. Knowing English fairly well, the prisoner justified himself, but he was committed to the *cachot*. He was then accused of having ill-treated a woman who, out of pity, had sent for her husband to help him. He handed in a certificate of injuries received, signed by Dr. Charles Fagg. His name was Marc Layne.

Complaints from Goudhurst in Kent relate that on one occasion three men left their hop-dressing to attack passing prisoners. Upon another, the French officers were, *mirabile dictu*, playing 'criquet', and told a boy of ten to get out of the way and not interfere with them, whereupon the boy called his companions, and there ensued a disturbance. A magistrate came up, and the result was that a Captain Lamoise had to pay £1 1*s*. or go to Maidstone Jail.

That the decent members of the community reprobated these attacks on defenceless foreigners, although they rarely seem to have taken any steps to stop them, is evident from the following story. At Goudhurst, some French prisoners, coming out of an inn, were attacked by a mob. Thirty-seven paroled officers there signed a petition and accompanied it with this testimony from inhabitants, dated November 9, 1757:

'We, the inhabitants of the Parish of Goudhurst, certifie that we never was insulted in any respect by the French gentlemen, nor to their knowledge have they caused any Riot except when they have been drawn in by a Parcel of drunken, ignorant, and scandalous men who make it their Business to ensnare them for the sake of a little money.

(Signed.)

STEPHEN OSBOURNE. THOS. BALLARD. JOHN SAVAGE.

JASPER SPRANG. RICHARD ROYSE. J. DICKINSON.

W. HUNT. JOHN BUNNELL. ZACH. SIMS.'

The complainants made declaration:

1. That the bad man Rastly exclaimed he would knock down the first Frenchman he met.

2. Two French prisoners were sounding horns and hautboys in the fields. The servant of the owner ordered them to go. They went quietly, but the man followed them and struck them. They complained to Tarith, the Agent, but he said that it did not concern him.

3. This servant assembled fifteen men with sticks, and stopped all exit from Bunnell's inn, where five French prisoners were drinking. The prisoners were warned not to leave, and, although 'remplis de boisson', they kept in. Nine o'clock, ten o'clock came; they resolved to go out, one of them being drunk; they were attacked and brutally ill-used.

The Agent assured them that they should have justice, but they did not get it.

As physical resistance to attacks and insults would have made matters worse for the Frenchmen, besides being hopeless in the face of great odds of numbers, it was resolved in one place at any rate, the name of which I cannot find, to resort to boycotting as a means of reprisal. I give the circulated notice of this in its original quaint and illiterate French:

'En conséquence de la délibération faite et teneu par le corps de François deteneus en cette ville il a esté ordonné qu'après qu'il aura cette Notoire, que quelque Marchand, Fabriquant, Boutiquier etcetera de cette ville aurons insulté, injurié, ou comis quelque *aiesais* (?) au vis à vis de quelque François tel que puis être, et que le fait aura été averée, il sera mis une affiche dans les Lieus les plus aparants portant proscription de sa Maison, Boutique, Fabrique etcetera, et ordonné et defendeu à tout François quelque qualité, condition qu'il soy sous Paine d'être regardé et déclaré traité à la Patrie et de subire plus grande Punition suivent l'exsigence du cas et qu'il en sera decidé.

'LA FRANCE.'

The above is dated 1758.

In 1779 the parole prisoners at Alresford complained of being constantly molested and insulted by the inhabitants, and asked to be sent elsewhere. Later, however, the local gentry and principal people guarantee a cessation of this, and the prisoners pray to be allowed to stay. The officer prisoners asked to be allowed to accept invitations at Winchester, but were refused. In the same year prisoners at Redruth complained of daily insults at the hands of an uncivilized populace, and from Chippenham twenty-nine officers signed a complaint about insults and attacks, and stated that as a result one of them was obliged to keep his room for eight days.

On the other hand, prisoners under orders to leave Tavistock for another parole town petition to be allowed to remain there, as the Agent has been so good to them; and as a sign that even in Kent matters were changing for the better, the prayer of some parole prisoners at Tenterden to be sent to Cranbrook on account of the insults by the people, is counterbalanced by a petition of other prisoners in the same town who assert that only a few soldiers have insulted them, and asking that no change be made, as the inhabitants are hospitable and kindly, and the Agent very just and lenient.

Much quiet, unostentatious kindness was shown towards the prisoners which has not been recorded, but in the Memoir of William Pearce of Launceston, in 1810, it is written that he made the parole prisoners in that town the objects of his special attention; that he gave them religious instruction, circulated tracts among them in their own language, and relieved their necessities, with the result that many reformed and attended his services. One prisoner came back after the Peace of 1815, lived in the service of the chapel, and was buried in its grave-yard. *En parenthèse* the writer adds that the boys of Launceston got quite into the habit of ejaculating 'Morbleu!' from hearing it so constantly on the lips of the French prisoners.

In the *Life of Hannah More*, written by William Roberts, we read:

'Some French officers of cultivated minds and polished manners being on their parole in the neighbourhood of Bristol, were frequent guests at Mr. More's house, and always fixed upon Hannah as their interpreter, and her intercourse with their society is said to have laid the ground of that free and elegant use of their language for which she was afterwards distinguished.'

CHAPTER XXIX
PAROLE LIFE. SUNDRY NOTES

In this and the succeeding chapter I gather together a number of notes connected with the life of the paroled prisoners in Britain, which could not conveniently be classed under the headings of previous chapters.

BEDALE, YORKSHIRE

During the Seven Years' War prisoners were on parole at Bedale in Yorkshire. The following lines referring to them, sent to me by my friend, Mrs. Cockburn-Hood, were written by Robert Hird, a Bedale shoemaker, who was born in 1768:

'And this one isle by Frenchmen then in prisoners did abound,

'Twas forty thousand Gallic men. Bedale its quota found:

And here they were at liberty, and that for a long time,

Till Seventeen Hundred and Sixty Three, they then a Peace did sign,

But though at large, they had their bound, it was a good walk out,

Matthew Masterman in their round, they put him to the rout;

This was near to the Standing Stone: at Fleetham Feast he'd been,

And here poor Matthew they fell on. He soon defeated them;

His arms were long, and he struck hard, they could not bear his blows,

The French threw stones, like some petard; he ran, and thus did lose.

James Wilkinson, he lived here then, he'd sons and daughters fair,

Barber he was in great esteem, the Frenchmen oft drew there.'

To this the sender appended a note:

'In the houses round Bedale there are hand-screens decorated with landscapes in straw, and I have a curious doll's chair in wood with knobs containing cherry stones which rattle. These were made by French prisoners, according to tradition.'

DERBY

I am indebted to Mr. P. H. Currey, F.R.I.B.A., of Derby, for the following extract, dated June 20, 1763, from All Saints' Parish Book, quoted in Simpson's *History of Derby*:

'These men (the prisoners during the Seven Years' War), were dispersed into many parts of the nation, 300 being sent to this town on parole about July 1759, where they continued until the end of the War in 1763. Their behaviour at first was impudent and insolent, at all times vain and effeminate, and their whole deportment light and unmanly, and we may venture to say from our observation and knowledge of them, that in any future war this nation has nothing to fear from them as an enemy. During their abode here, the road from this place to Nottingham was by act of Parliament repaired, the part from St. Mary's Bridge (which by reason of the floods was impassable) being greatly raised. Numbers of these people were daily employed, who worked in their *bag-wigs*, *pig-tails*, *ruffles*, etc., etc., a matter which afforded us much merriment. But, to their honour let it be remembered, that scarce *one* act of fraud or theft was committed by any of them during their stay among us. These men were allowed 6*d.* a day each by the British Government.'

We read that an Italian prisoner on parole at Derby in 1797 went to Leicester and bought a pair of pistols, thus committing a double breach of his parole by going beyond the limit, and by possessing himself of arms. 'It is presumed,' remarks the chronicler, 'from the remarkable anxiety he showed to procure possession of these offensive weapons, that he has some particular object to accomplish by them—perhaps his liberation.'

It is much more likely that his object was to fight a duel.

ASHBOURNE, DERBYSHIRE

Mr. Richard Holland, of Barton under Needwood, Staffordshire, has favoured me with this note about Ashbourne.

'Here in 1803 were Rochambeau and 300 of his officers. The house where the general resided is well known, and a large building was erected in which to lodge the prisoners who could not afford to find their own houses or apartments. I have heard that the limit of parole was two miles.... I never heard of any breaches of parole or crimes committed by the prisoners....

I have often heard that the prisoners made for sale many curious articles, models, etc., ... but I remember a fine drawing of a man-of-war on the outside wall of the prison referred to, which now happens to belong to me.... Even fifty years ago very little was remembered of the prisoners. One of them was a famous runner, and I knew an old man who told me he ran a race with the Frenchman, and beat him too!'

In 1804 General Pageot was on parole at Ashbourne. Here he seems to have been received, like so many of his countrymen prisoners, on a footing of friendship at the houses of the neighbouring gentry, for he received permission to live for eight days at Wooton Lodge, the seat of Colonel Wilson. In granting this unusual indulgence the Commissioners remark that 'as our people are very strictly treated in France, it is improper that unusual indulgences be given to French prisoners, and we hope that no other applications will be made'.

Later on the Commissioners wrote to Colonel Wilson:

'As it appears by letters between General Pageot and some of his countrymen that he is paying his addresses to a Lady of Respectability in or near Ashbourne, the Board think it proper that you should be informed that they have good authority for believing that he is actually a married man, and has a family in France.'

Still later, writing to Mr. Bainbrigge, the Commissioners say that General Pageot has been sent to Montgomery, and they recommend Mr. Bainbrigge to take measures to prevent him having any communication with the lady, Mr. Bainbrigge's niece.

Say they:

'From Motives of Public Duty the Commissioners, when they first heard of the intended connexion between General Pageot and Miss Bainbrigge, they caused such suspicious circumstances respecting the General as came to their knowledge to be communicated to the young lady's mother, and that it affords them very much satisfaction now to find that her Friends are disposed to prevent an union which could promise very little comfort to her or Honour to her Family.'

CHESTERFIELD

My best thanks are due to Mr. W. Hawkesly Edmunds, Scarsdale House, Chesterfield, for these notes:

'Mrs. Roberts, widow of Lieutenant Roberts, R.N., left some interesting reminiscences among her papers. She says:

'Different indeed was the aspect of the town from what one sees to-day. Grim visages and whiskered faces met one at every turn, to say nothing of moustaches, faded uniforms, and rusty cocked hats. At certain hours of the day it was difficult to walk along the High Street or the middle Causeway, for these were the favourite promenades of the officers on parole. When the weather permitted, they assembled each morning and evening to the number of 200 to exchange friendly greetings with all the extravagance of gesture and high-pitched voice for which the Frenchman is remarkable.'

The French prisoners in Chesterfield in the years around 1806 were for the most part, if not wholly, officers and their servants, and their treatment by the English Government was liberal and mild. All officers down to the rank of Captain, inclusive, were allowed ten shillings per week, and all below that rank, seven shillings each. On giving their parole they were allowed the greatest freedom; had permission to walk one mile from the town in any direction, but had to be in their lodgings at 8 each evening. At that hour a bell rang, known as the Frenchman's Bell. It was, in fact, the very bell in the tower of the church formerly used as the curfew bell. It was in connexion with this mile regulation that a little fraud was perpetrated by Sir Windsor Hunloke, Bart., which was winked at by the authorities. Wingerworth Hall, the residence of Sir Windsor, was just outside the mile limit, but with the desire that many of the prisoners, who, like himself, were Roman Catholics, should visit him, he caused the milestone to be removed along the road to the other side of the hall, and so brought his residence within the mile limit. This old milestone is still to be seen.

The prisoners were first in charge of a Commissary, a local solicitor, Mr. John Bower, of Spital Lodge, but later the Government appointed superannuated lieutenants in the Navy. The first of these, Lieutenant Gawen, found that there had been so many escapes during Mr. Bower's kindly but lax régime that he instituted more stringent regulations, and mustered the men twice a week instead of once, and he inspected all correspondence both to and from the prisoners. The first detachment of prisoners arrived in 1803, officers both of the Army and Navy; most of them had undergone the greatest privations. These were the prisoners from San Domingo, whose sufferings during the sieges of the blacks, and from sickness, famine, and sword, are matters of history. Indeed, had not the British squadron arrived, it is certain all their lives would have been sacrificed by the infuriated blacks in revenge for the barbarities practised on them by the French Commander-in-Chief General Rochambeau, who, with Generals D'Henin, Boyer, and Lapoype, Commodore Barré, and the other naval officers, with the staffs of the generals, were all at Chesterfield.

The successes of Wellington in Spain brought many more prisoners to Chesterfield, and a great number captured at San Sebastian and Pampeluna.

Most of the prisoners in the town managed to add to the Government allowance by teaching languages, drawing, and music. Others produced various articles for sale. Many of them were excellent ornamental workers in hair and bone, and there were not a few who were adept wood-carvers. Making bone models of men-of-war was a favourite occupation, and the more elaborate of these models were disposed of by means of lotteries. Another of their industries was the working of straw, which they dyed in gay colours, or plaited. Silk-hat making and silk-weaving they are said to have introduced into the town. They were also experts at making woollen gloves, &c., with a bone crook. One Bourlemont opened a dépôt for British wines. One prisoner got employment as a painter, but another had to seek work as a banksman at the Hady coal-pits.

Several of the prisoners were surgeons, and practised in the town, and it is reported that so great were the services some of these gentlemen rendered the poor of the town gratuitously, that representations were made to the Government, and they were given free pardons and safe-conducts back to France.

Some prisoners married, one the daughter of Turner the Parish Clerk, but generally beneath them.

BONE MODEL OF H.M.S. *PRINCE OF WALES*

Made by prisoners of war

The Abbé Legoux tried to have religious services in a private house, but they were poorly attended, the Republicans nearly all being atheists, and preferring to pass their Sundays at card-tables and billiards.

Mrs. Roberts thus describes some peculiarities of the prisoners' dress and manners:

'Their large hooped gold ear-rings, their pink or sky-blue umbrellas, the Legion of Honour ribbons in their button holes; their profuse exchange of embraces and even kisses in the public street; their attendant poodles carrying walking-sticks in their mouths, and their incessant and vociferous talking. A great source of amusement was the training of birds and dogs.

'There were few instances of friction between the prisoners and the townsfolk, but there was one angry affray which led to six of the prisoners being sent to Norman Cross to be kept in close confinement. The wives of some of the prisoners had permission to join their husbands in confinement, but "they were very dingy, plain-looking women."

'Colonel Fruile married a Miss Moore, daughter of a Chesterfield cabinet maker, and she, like the English wives of other of the prisoners, went to France when Peace was proclaimed. Rank distinctions between officers were rigidly observed, and the junior officers always saluted their superiors who held levées on certain days of the week. The fortunes of Napoleon were closely followed; defeats and victories being marked. During the sojourn of the French prisoners at Chesterfield, took place the battles of Wagram, Jena, Vienna, Berlin, and the Russian campaign. The news of Trafalgar produced great dismay, and the sight of rejoicings—of sheep and oxen roasted whole, of gangs of men yoked together bringing wood and coals for bonfires, was too much to bear, and most of them shut themselves up in their lodgings until the rejoicings were over.

'After the Peace a few of the prisoners remained in Chesterfield, and some of their descendants live in the town to-day. Many died, and were buried in the "Frenchmen's Quarter" of the now closed Parish churchyard.'

OSWESTRY

Oswestry, in Shropshire, was an important parole town. In 1803, when rumours were afloat that a concerted simultaneous rising of the French prisoners of war in the Western Counties was to be carried out, a hurried transfer of these latter was made to the more inland towns of Staffordshire and Shropshire. and it has been stated that Oswestry received no less than 700, but this has been authentically contradicted, chiefly by correspondents to *Bygones*, a most complete receptacle of old-time information concerning Shropshire and the Welsh border, access to which I owe to the kindness of Mr. J. E. Anden of Tong, Shifnal.

Among the distinguished prisoners at Oswestry were the Marquis d'Hautpol, on whose *Memories of Captivity in England* I have already drawn largely; General Phillipon, the able defender of Badajos, who escaped with Lieut. Garnier from Oswestry; and Prince Arenburg, who was removed thither to Bridgnorth upon suspicion of having aided a fellow prisoner to escape.

The prisoners were, as usual, distributed in lodgings about the town; some were at the *Three Tuns* inn, where bullet marks in a wall are said to commemorate a duel fought between two of them.

From the *London Chronicle* of May 20, 1813, I take the following:

'There is in this town (Oswestry) a French officer on parole who is supposed by himself and countrymen to possess strength little inferior to Samson. He is Monsieur Fiarsse, he follows the profession of a fencing-master, and is allowed to have considerable skill in that way. He had been boasting that he had beat every Englishman that opposed him in the town where he was last on parole (in Devonshire), and he sent a challenge the other day to a private of the 64th Regiment to a boxing-match. It was accepted. The Frenchman is a very tall, stout-built man, of a most ferocious countenance; the soldier is a little, round-faced man, as plump as a partridge. Five rounds were fought; the first, I understand, the Frenchman threw a blow at his adversary with all his strength which brought him down; he rose, however, in a moment, and played his part so well that I think M. Fiarsse will never like to attack a British soldier again! The little fellow made him spin again, he dealt his blows with such judgement. After the fifth round, Fiarsse said: "It is 'nough! I vill no moe!"'

There were French Royalist refugees at Oswestry as elsewhere, and one of the hardest tasks of local parole agents was to prevent disturbances between these men and their bitter opponents the Bonapartist officer prisoners, dwelling in the same towns. In fact, the presence of large numbers of French Royalists in England, many of them very highly connected, brought about the very frequent attacks made on them in contemporary French literature and journalism for playing the parts of spies and traitors, and originated the parrot-cry at every French diplomatic or military and naval reverse, 'Sold by the princes in England!'

There are graves of French prisoners in Oswestry churchyard. Upon one is 'Ci-gît D. J. J. J. Du Vive, Capitaine-Adjudant aux États-Majors généraux: prisonnier de guerre sur parole; né à Pau, Dép^t des Basses-Pyrénées, 26 Juillet 1762; décédé à Oswestry, 20 Juillet 1813.'

Leek

Leek, in Staffordshire, was also an important parole centre.

'The officer prisoners at Leek received all courtesy and hospitality at the hands of the principal inhabitants, with many of whom they were on the most intimate terms, frequenting the assemblies, which were then as gay and as well attended as any within a circuit of 20 miles. They used to dine out in full uniform, each with his body-servant behind his chair.' (Sleigh's *History of Leek.*)

The first prisoners came here in 1803 from San Domingo. In 1809 and 1812 many more arrived—some accounts say as many as 200, and one fact considered worthy of record is that they were to be met prowling about early in the morning in search of snails!

A correspondent to *Notes and Queries* writes:

'All accounts agree that these unfortunates conducted themselves with the utmost propriety and self-respect during their enforced sojourn among us; endearing themselves to the inhabitants generally by their unwonted courtesy and strictly honourable behaviour. But as to their estimate of human life, it was unanimously remarked that they seemed to value it no more than we should crushing a fly in a moment of irritation.'

The Freemasons had a Lodge 'Réunion Désirée,' and a Chapter 'De l'Amitié,' working at Leek in 1810–11.

Alresford

At Alresford the prisoners were at first unpopular, but their exertions at a fire in the town wrought a change of feeling in their favour. It is interesting to note that when the Commune in Paris in 1871 drove many respectable people abroad, quite a number came to Alresford (as also to Odiham), from which we may deduce that they were descendants of men who had handed down pleasant memories of parole life in these little Hampshire towns.

The Rev. Mr. Headley, Vicar of Alresford, kindly allowed me to copy the following from his Parish Records:

'1779. The Captain and officers of the Spanish man-of-war who behaved so gallantly in the engagement with the *Pearl*, and who are prisoners of war at Alresford, lately gave an elegant entertainment and ball in honour of Capt. Montagu and his officers, in testimony of the high sense they entertain of the polite and most generous treatment they received after their capture. Capt. Montagu and his officers were present, also Capt. Oates and officers of the 89th Regiment, and many of the most respectable families from the neighbourhood of Alresford.'

I am indebted also to Mr. Headley for the following entries in the registers of his church:

Burials.

1794.

July 21. St. Aubin, a French prisoner on parole.

1796.

July 11. Baptiste Guillaume Jousemme; aged 21, born at Castillones in France. A prisoner on parole.

1803.

June 27. Thomas Monclerc. Aged 42. A French servant.

1809.

Dec. 12. Jean Charbonier. A French prisoner.

1810.

Dec. 14. Hypolite Riouffe. A French prisoner.

1811.

Aug. 2. Pierre Garnier. A French prisoner.

1811.

Dec 25. Ciprian Lavau. A French prisoner. Aged 29.

1812.

Feb. 7. Louis de Bousurdont. A French prisoner. Aged 44.

1812.

April 13. Marie Louise Fournier. A French prisoner. Aged 44.

1812.

Aug. 8. Jean de l'Huille. A French prisoner. Aged 51.

Mr. Payne of Alresford told me that the clock on the church tower, which bears the date 1811, is said to have been presented by the French prisoners on parole in the town in gratitude for the kindly treatment they received from the inhabitants.

THAME

At Thame, in 1809, Israel Eel was charged at the Oxford Quarter Sessions with assaulting Ravenau, a French prisoner on parole. To the great surprise of all, *not a true bill* was returned.

Some of the prisoners at Thame were lodged in a building now called the 'Bird Cage', once an inn. A memory of the prisoners lingers in the name of 'Frenchman's Oak' still given to a large tree there, it having marked their mile boundary.

General Villaret-Joyeuse, Governor of Martinique, was one of the many prisoners of fame or rank at Thame. He brought upon himself a rebuke from the Transport Office in 1809, for having said in a letter to his brother, 'Plusieurs Français se sont détruits ne pouvant supporter plus longtemps l'humiliation et l'abjection où ils étaient réduits.' The Transport Office told him that he had been grossly misinformed, and that during the past war only two prisoners were known to have destroyed themselves: one was supposed to have done so in consequence of the deranged state of his account with the French Government, and the other, having robbed his brother prisoner of a large amount, when detected, dreading the consequence. 'When you shall have better informed yourself and altered the said letter accordingly, it will be forwarded to France.'

General Privé, one of Dupont's officers, captured at Baylen, was called to order for making false statements in a letter to the French minister of war, in an offensive manner: 'The Board have no objection of your making representations you may think proper to your Government respecting the Capitulation of Baylen, and transmitting as many Truths as you please to France, but indecent Abuse and reproachful Terms are not to be suffered.'

WINCANTON

To Mr. George Sweetman I am indebted for some interesting particulars about parole prisoner life at Wincanton in Somersetshire. The first prisoners came here in 1804, captured on the *Didon*, and gradually the number here rose to 350, made up of Frenchmen, Italians, Portuguese, and Spaniards. In 1811 the census showed that nineteen houses were occupied by prisoners, who then numbered 297 and 9 women and children. An 'oldest inhabitant', Mr. Olding, who died in 1870, aged eighty-five, told Mr. Sweetman that at one time there were no less than 500 prisoners in Wincanton and the adjacent Bayford. Some of them were men of good family, and were entertained at all the best houses in the neighbourhood.

'After the conquest of Isle of France,' said Mr. Olding, 'about fifty French officers were sent here, who were reputed to have brought with them half a million sterling.... They lived in their own hired houses or comfortable lodgings. The poorer prisoners took their two meals a day at the *Restaurant pour les Aspirants*. The main staple of their diet was onions, leeks, lettuce, cucumbers, and dandelions. The richer, however, ate butchers' meat plentifully.'

Altogether the establishment of Wincanton as a parole town must have been of enormous benefit to a linen-weaving centre which was feeling severely the competition of the great Lancashire towns, and was fast losing its staple industry.

Mr. Sweetman introduces an anecdote which illustrates the great trading difficulties which at first existed between foreigners who knew nothing of English, and natives who were equally ignorant of French.

One of the many butchers who attended the market had bought on one occasion some excellent fat beef to which he called the attention of a model French patrician, and, confusing the Frenchman's ability to understand the English language with defective hearing, he shouted in his loudest tones, which had an effect contrary to what he expected or desired. The officer (noted for his long pig-tail, old round hat, and long-waisted brown coat), to all the jolly butcher's earnest appeals to him to buy, answered nothing but 'Non bon, non bon!'

'Well, Roger,' said a brother butcher, 'If I were you, he should have bone enough next time!'

'So he shall,' said Roger, and on the next market-day he brought a fine neck and chine of bull beef, from which lots of steaks were cut, and soon sold.

Presently the old officer came by, and Roger solicited his custom for his fine show of bones. The indignant Frenchman again exclaimed, 'Non bon! non bon!'

'Confound the fellow,' said Roger, 'what can he want, why, 'tis a'al booin, idden it?'

Both men were becoming really angry, when a boy standing by, who had speedily acquired some knowledge of French, explained the matter to both men. When at length they understood each other they both laughed heartily at the misunderstanding, but the incident became a standing joke against Roger as long as he lived.

The mile boundaries of the prisoners were Bayford Elm on the London road; Anchor Bridge on the Ilchester road; Abergavenny Gate on the Castle Cary road; and Gorselands on the Bruton road. The prisoners frequently promenaded the streets in great numbers, four abreast. The large rooms in the public-houses were often rented for holding meetings of various kinds. On one occasion the large room at the *Swan* Inn was used for the lying in state of a Freemason, who was buried in a very imposing manner. Two other great officers lay in state at the *Greyhound* and *The Dogs*. Many died from various causes incidental to captivity. They were buried in the churchyard, and a stone there marks the resting-place of a Russian or a Pole who was said to have died of grief.[17] One of them committed suicide. Another poor fellow became demented, and every day might have been heard playing on a flute a mournful dirge, which tune he never changed. Others bore their estrangement from home and country less sorrowfully, and employed their time in athletic sports or in carving various articles of different kinds of wood and bone. Some were allowed to visit friends at a distance, always returning faithfully to their parole.

During the winter months they gave, twice a week, musical and theatrical entertainments. Many of the captives, especially those of the upper ranks, were good musicians. These held concerts, which were attended by the people of the town.

Sunday was to them the dullest day of the week; they did not know what to make of it. Some of them went to the parish church and assisted in the instrumental part of the service. A few attended the Congregational, or as it was then called, the Independent Chapel. The majority of them were, in name at least, Roman Catholics; whatever they were, they spent Sundays in playing chess, draughts, cards and dominoes,—indeed, almost anything to while the time away.

The prisoners used to meet in large rooms which they hired for various amusements. Some of them were artists, and Mr. Sweetman speaks of many rooms which they decorated with wall-pictures. In one—the 'Orange Room' at *The Dogs* in South Street—may still be seen wall-paintings done by them; also in the house of Mr. James, in the High Street, three panels of a bedroom are painted with three of the Muses. Miss Impey, of Street, has some drawings done by a prisoner, Charles Aubert, who probably did the paintings above alluded to.

As time went on and the prisoners became more homesick and more impatient of restraint, desertions became frequent, and it was necessary to station a company of infantry in Wincanton, and they were 'kept lively'. One night a party was escaping and the constable of the town, attempting to prevent them, was roughly handled. The soldiers were on guard all night in the streets, but nevertheless some prisoners managed even then to escape.

'In 1811', said the *Salisbury Journal*, 'Culliford, a notorious smuggler, was committed to Ilchester Gaol for conveying from Wincanton several of the prisoners there to the Dorsetshire coast, whence they crossed to Cherbourg. Culliford was caught with great difficulty, and then only because of the large reward offered.'

There was at Wincanton, as in other parole towns, a Masonic Lodge among the prisoners; it was called (as was also the Lodge at Sanquhar) 'La Paix Désirée'. There were English members of it. Mr. Sweetman reproduces, in the little book upon which I have drawn for my information, the certificate of Louis Michel Duchemin, Master Mason in 1810. This M. Duchemin married Miss Clewett of Wincanton, and settled in England, dying in Birmingham in 1854 or 1855. His widow only survived him a week, but he left a son who in 1897 lived in Birmingham, following his father's profession as a teacher of French. M. Duchemin was evidently much esteemed in Wincanton, as the following testimonial shows:

'Wincanton, June 1821.

'I, the undersigned, having been His Majesty's Agent for Prisoners of War on Parole in this place during the late war, do certify that Monsr. L. M. Duchemin was resident for upwards of six years on his Parole of Honour in this Town, from the time [1805] of the capture of the French frigate *La Torche* to the removal of the Prisoners to Scotland, and that in consequence of his universal good conduct, he was excepted (on a memorial presented by Inhabitants to the Commissioners of H. M. Transport Service) from a previous Order of Removal from this place with other prisoners of his rank. Monsr. Duchemin married while resident in this place into a respectable family, and, having known him from 1806 to the present time, I can with much truth concur in the Testimonial of his Wells friends.

'G. MESSITER.'

This Mr. George Messiter, a solicitor, was one of the best sort of parole agents, and is thus eulogized by Mr. Sweetman:

'He was a gentleman well qualified for the office he held: of a noble mien, brave, and held in respect by all who knew him. Under his direction the captives were supplied with every accommodation he could give them. Several years after his death one of the survivors, an army surgeon, came to the scene of his former captivity, when he paid a high tribute to the Commissary, and spoke in terms of affection of the townspeople amongst whom he had sojourned.'

When it is remembered that Messiter had to deal with such troublesome fellows as Generals Rochambeau and Boyer (who were actually sent away from Wincanton, as they had already been sent away from other parole places, on account of their misdeeds), the worth of this testimony may be appreciated.

Not many marriages between prisoners and Englishwomen are recorded at Wincanton, for the same reason that ruled elsewhere—that the French law refused to regard such marriages as valid.

Alberto Bioletti, an Italian servant to a French officer, married and settled in the town as a hairdresser. He married twice, and died in 1869, aged ninety-two. William Bouverie, known as 'Billy Booby', married and settled here. John Peter Pichon is the very French name of one who married Dinah Edwards, both described as of Wincanton, in 1808. In 1809 Andrée Joseph Jantrelle married Mary Hobbs.

Mr. Sweetman says:

'Here, as in all other parole towns, a large number of children were born out of wedlock whose fathers were reputed to be our visitors. Some indeed took French names, and several officers had to pay large sums of money to the parish authorities before they left. One of the drawbacks to the sojourn of so many strangers among us was the increase of immorality. One informant said: "Not the least source of attraction to these gallant sons of France, were the buxom country maidens, who found their way into the town, but lost their way back. I regret to say that our little town was becoming a veritable hotbed of vice."'

The prisoners were suddenly withdrawn from Wincanton, on account of the alarm, to which I have alluded elsewhere, that a general rising of the prisoners of war all over England, but chiefly in the west, had been concerted, and partly on account of the large numbers of escapes of prisoners, favoured as they were by the proximity of the Dorsetshire coast with its gangs of smugglers.

Mr. Sweetman continues:

'In February 1812, a company of infantry and a troop of cavalry arrived at the South Gate, one morning at roll-call time. Before the roll had been completed the troop entered the town and surrounded the captives. The infantry followed, and those who had not presented themselves at roll-call were sent for. So sudden had been the call, that although many had wished for years to leave, they were unprepared when the time came. At 4 o'clock those who were ready departed; some had not even breakfasted, and no one was allowed to have any communication with them. They were marched to Mere, where they passed the night in the church. Early next morning, those who were left behind, after having bestowed their goods (for many of them had furnished their own houses), followed their brethren, and, joining them at Mere, were marched to Kelso. Deep was the regret of many of the inhabitants at losing so many to whom they had become endeared by ties of interest and affection. A great gap was made in the life of the town which it took years to fill.'

Seventeen burials are recorded in the Wincanton registers from the end of July 1806 to the end of May 1811.

Prominent prisoners at Wincanton were M. de Tocqueville, Rear-Admiral de Wailly-Duchemin, and Rochambeau, whom Sir Arthur Quiller-Couch, in his story *The Westcotes*, the scene of which he lays at 'Axcester'—i.e. Wincanton—paints as quite an admirable old soldier. It was the above-named rear-admiral who, dying at Wincanton, lay in state in the panelled 'Orange Room' of *The Dogs*. This is now the residence of Dr. Edwards, who kindly allowed me to inspect the paintings on the panels of this and the adjoining room, which were executed by French officers quartered here, and represent castles and landscapes, and a caricature of Wellington, whose head is garnished with donkey's ears.

The 'Orange Room' is so called from the tradition that Dutch William slept here on his way from Torbay to London to assume the British crown.

Later on a hundred and fifty of the French officers captured at Trafalgar and in Sir Richard Strachan's subsequent action, were quartered here, and are described as 'very orderly, and inoffensive to the inhabitants'.

The suicide mentioned above was that of an officer belonging to a highly respectable family in France, who, not having heard from home for a long time, became so depressed that he went into a field near his lodgings, placed the muzzle of a musket in his mouth, and pushed the trigger with his foot. The coroner's jury returned a verdict of 'Lunacy'.

I have said that the frequency of escapes among the prisoners was one of the causes of their removal from Wincanton. The Commissary, Mr. George Messiter, in November 1811 asked the Government to break up the Dépôt, as, on account of the regularly organized system established between the prisoners and the smugglers and fishermen of the Dorsetshire coast, it was impossible to prevent escapes. Towards the close of 1811 no fewer than twenty-two French prisoners got away from Wincanton. The Commissary's request was at once answered, and the *Salisbury Journal* of December 9, 1811, thus mentions the removal:

'On Saturday last upwards of 150 French prisoners lately on their parole at Wincanton were marched by way of Mere through this city under an escort of the Wilts Militia and a party of Light Dragoons, on their way to Gosport, there to be embarked with about 50 superior officers for some place in Scotland. Since Culliford, the leader of the gang of smugglers and fishermen who aided in these escapes, was convicted and only sentenced to six months' imprisonment, they have become more and more daring in their violations of the law.'

Ashby-de-la-Zouch

Ashby occupies an interesting page in that little-known chapter of British history which deals with the prisoners of war who have lived amongst us, and I owe my cordial thanks to the Rev. W. Scott, who has preserved this page from oblivion, for permission to make use of his pamphlet.

In September 1804, the first detachment of prisoners, forty-two in number, reached Ashby, and this number was gradually increased until it reached its limit, 200. The first arrivals were poor fellows who had to board and lodge themselves on about ten shillings and sixpence a week; but the later officers from Pampeluna had money concealed about their clothing and in the soles of their boots.

On the whole, Mr. Scott says, they seem to have had a tolerably good time in Ashby. Their favourite walk was past the Mount Farm near the Castle, along the Packington Road, then to the left to the Leicester Road, across the fields even now sometimes called 'The Frenchman's Walk', but more generally, Packington Slang. The thirty-shilling reward offered to any one who should report a prisoner as being out of bounds was very rarely claimed, for the officers were such general favourites that few persons could be found who, even for thirty shillings, could be base enough to play the part of informer.

An indirect evidence of the good feeling existing between the townspeople and their guests is afforded by the story of two dogs. One of these, named Mouton, came with the first prisoners in 1804, spent ten years in Ashby, and returned with the men in 1814. The other dog came with the officers from Pampeluna, and was the only dog who had survived the siege. Both animals were great pets with the people of Ashby.

There seem to have been at least two duels. Mr. Measures, a farmer of Packington, on coming to attend to some cattle in Packington Slang, saw a cloak lying on the ground, and upon removing it was horrified to see the body of a French officer. It proved to be that of Captain Colvin. He was buried in the churchyard of Packington, and, honour being satisfied, the man who had slain him was one of the chief mourners. There is a brief entry of another duel in Dr. James Kirkland's records: 'Monsieur Denègres, a French prisoner, killed in a duel, Dec. 6th, 1808.'

Good friends as the prisoners were with the male inhabitants of the town, and with the neighbouring farmers, who on more than one occasion lent horses to officers who wished to escape, it was with the ladies that they were prime favourites. One of the prisoners, Colonel Van Hoof, was the admirer of Miss Ingle, the reigning beauty of Ashby. The courtesy and good nature of the prisoners bore down all obstacles; and the only ill-wishers they had were the local young dandies whose noses they put out of joint. The married dames were also pleased and flattered: many of the prisoners were excellent cooks, and one who made a soup which was the envy and despair of every housekeeper in Ashby, when asked by a lady the secret of it, said: 'I get some pearl barley and carry it here several days,' placing his hand melodramatically over his heart.

In spite of the mile-limit regulation, they went to picnics in Ashby Old Parks, riding in wagons, and going along the tram road which ran from Willesley to Ticknall. On these occasions the officers were accompanied by the better class girls of the town and their admirers. Music was supplied by one of the Frenchmen who played a violin. For this or for some other reason he seems to have been a first favourite. When passing through the tunnel underneath Ashby Old Parks Hill, it was no unusual thing for him to lay aside his fiddle to kiss the girls. Of course, they always asked him to play while in the tunnel in order to keep him from obliging them in this manner, and of course he would know what they meant.

The permanent result of this love-making is shown by the parish register of Ashby; from 1806 to June 1, 1814, the following weddings took place between local girls and French 'Prisoners of War resident in this Parish', or 'on parole in this Parish':

1806.

Francis Robert to Jane Bedford.

〃

Pierre Serventie to Elizabeth Rowbottom.

〃

Anthony Hoffmann to Elizabeth Peach.

1809.

Louis Jean to Elizabeth Edwards.

1810.

Francis Picard to Charlotte Bedford.

〃

Henry Antoine to Sarah Roberts.

〃

Pierre Geffroy to Phillis Parkins

1812.

Casimir Gantreuil to Elizabeth Adcock.

〃

Louis François Le Normand Kegrist to Mary Ann Kirkland.

〃

Louis Adoré Tiphenn to Ann Vaun.

〃

Frederic Rouelt to Ann Sharp.

1813.

Auguste Louis Jean Segoivy to Elizabeth Bailey.

„

Francis Peyrol to Martha Peach.

1814.

Francis Victor Richard Ducrocq to Sarah Adcock.

„

Richard le Tramp to Mary Sharpe.

Two Masonic Lodges and a Rose Croix Chapter were established in Ashby—the above-mentioned Louis Jean was a member of the 'Vrais Amis de l'Ordre' Lodge, and four relics of his connexion are still preserved. Tradition says that the constitution of the Lodge was celebrated by a ball given by the French officers, the hosts presenting to each lady two pairs of white gloves, one pair long, the other short.

The second Lodge was 'De la Justice et de l'Union'.

When Peace was declared, the French Masons at Ashby disposed of their Lodge furniture to the 'Royal Sussex', No. 353, of Repton, in Derbyshire. In 1869 the Lodge removed to Winshill, Burton-on-Trent, where the furniture is still used.

There is the register of three burials:

1806.

Étienne Lenon.

1807.

François Rabin.

1808.

Xavier Mandelier.

Here, as elsewhere, the Frenchmen gave proofs of their skill in fine handiwork. They did ornamental work in several new houses; they taught the townsfolk the art of crochet-work (I quote from Mr. Scott); they were artists, carvers, &c. Some of the officers worshipped in the Baptist Church, and became members of it. The conversion of Captain Le Jeune is an interesting little story. Shocked by certain phases and features of the Roman Catholic religion, he became a deist and finally an atheist, and during the

Revolution joined readily in the ill-treatment of priests. At San Domingo he was taken prisoner in 1804, and sent to Ashby on parole. Four years later the death of his father very deeply impressed him, and he began to think seriously about the existence of God. A fellow prisoner, De Serre, a member of the Baptist Church in Ashby, a devout Christian, became intimate with him, persuaded him to join the Church, and he finally became an active and zealous missionary in his own country; and until his death corresponded with the Ashby pastors, and particularly with the Rev. Joseph Goadly, who exercised an wholesome and powerful influence among the French prisoners of war.

CHAPTER XXX
PAROLE LIFE: SUNDRY NOTES (*continued*)

ASHBURTON, DEVON

Mr. J. H. Amery says in *Devon Notes and Queries*:

'We can hardly credit the fact that so little reliable information or even traditional legend, remains in the small inland market towns where so many officers were held prisoners on parole until as recently as 1815. It certainly speaks well for their conduct, for had any tragedy been connected with their stay, tradition would have preserved its memory and details. For several years prior to 1815 a number of educated foreigners formed a part of the society of our towns. At one time they were lively Frenchmen, at others sober Danes or spendthrift Americans. They lodged and boarded in the houses of our tradesmen; they taught the young people modern languages, music and dancing; they walked our streets and roads, and took a general interest in passing events; yet to-day hardly a trace can be discovered of their presence beyond a few neglected mile-stones on our country roads, and here and there a grave in our Parish churchyards. This is particularly the case with Ashburton.'

He goes on to say that he got more information about the American prisoners at Ashburton from a Bostonian who was at the post-office there, making inquiries, than from anyone else. This Bostonian's grandfather was a naval surgeon who had been captured on the *Polly*; had been sent to Dartmoor, but was released on parole to Ashburton.

Mr. Amery gives as an instance of this local indifference to the past the fact that the family of Mr. Joseph Gribble, solicitor and county coroner, who had been prisoner agent at Ashburton, had lived opposite to the entrance to the vicarage until 1899, but that by that time everything about the prisoners had been forgotten by them.

Mr. Amery writes to me:

'I have heard our people say that my great-uncle who lived here at that time used to have open house for the prisoners on parole. The French were very nice and gentlemanly, but the Americans were a much rougher lot, and broke up things a good deal. The French used to teach French and dancing in the town.'

The following Masonic Petition from Ashburton is interesting:

'Ashburton, April 6, 1814, of our Lord, and in Masonry 5814. To the Grand Master, Grand Wardens, and Members of the Grand Lodge, London.

'BRETHREN,

'We, the undersigned, being Ancient York Masons, take the liberty of addressing you with this Petition for our Relief, being American prisoners of war on parole at this place. We are allowed 10*s*. 6*d.* per week for our support. In this place we cannot get lodgings for less than 3*s*. per week, and from that to 5*s*. per week. Meat is constantly from 9*d.* to 1*s*. per lb., and other necessaries in proportion. Judge, brethren, how we live, for none of us have any means of getting money. Our clothes are wearing out, and God knows how long we shall be kept here; many of us have been captured 9 or 10 months, as you will see opposite our signatures. We form a body in this place by ourselves for the purpose of lecturing each other once a week, and have had this in contemplation for some time, but have deferred making application until absolute want has made it necessary. We therefore pray that you will take into consideration and provide some means for our relief. You will please address your letter to Edwin Buckannon.

'We humbly remain your pennyless brethren.

'EDWIN BUCKANNON. G. W. BURBANK. PIERSON BALDWIN. WM. MILLER. ARCHD. TAYLOR, JUNR. EZRA OBER. WM. SMITH. JAMES LANS. JOHN SCHERS.'

There was also a French Lodge at Ashburton, 'Des Amis Réunis', but the only record of its existence is a certificate granted to Paul Carcenac, an initiate. It is roughly drawn by hand on parchment, and is entirely in

French, and, as the recipient is under obligation to affiliate himself to some regularly warranted French Lodge immediately on his return to his native land, it would seem that the Lodge at Ashburton was only of a temporary or irregular character.

The foregoing references to Freemasonry remind us that this universal brotherhood was the occasion of many graceful acts during the Great Wars between men of opposing sides.

TAVISTOCK

There were upon an average 150 prisoners here. The Prison Commissioners wrote:

'Some of them have made overtures of marriage to women in the neighbourhood, which the magistrates very properly have taken pains to discourage.'

This, of course, refers to the ruling of the French Government that it would regard such marriages as invalid. That French women sometimes accompanied their husbands into captivity is evident from not infrequent petitions such as this:

'The French woman at Tavistock requests that Sir Rupert George (Chairman to the Transport Office) will interest himself to procure rations for her child who was born at the Dépôt, and is nearly five months old.'

OKEHAMPTON

Here, very little information is obtainable, as very few of the 'oldest inhabitant' type are to be found, and there are very few residents whose parents have lived there for any length of time—a sign of these restless, migrating days which makes one regret that the subject of the foreign prisoners of war in Britain was not taken up before the movement of the rural world into large towns had fairly set in. One old resident could only say that his father used to talk of from five to six hundred prisoners being at Okehampton, but in the rural mind numbers are handled as vaguely as is time, for assuredly in no single parole town in Britain were there ever so many prisoners. Another aged resident said:

'They were all bettermost prisoners: the rough ones were kept at Princetown, but these were quartered in various houses, and paid very well for it. Their bounds were a mile out of town, but I have heard they were very artful, and shifted the milestones and borough stones. My father told me that one escaped, but he was shot down in the neighbourhood of the Bovey Clay Works. There was a riot in the town one day amongst them, and old Dr. Luxmoore, who was a big, tall man, mounted his big horse, and, armed with his hunting whip, rode down through the prisoners, who were fighting in the town, and with the cracks of it dispersed them in every direction.... The Mess Room was the St. James' Street schoolroom, and stood opposite the South entrance of the Arcade which was pulled down a few years ago. In their spare time the prisoners made many small articles such as cabinets, chairs, cribbage-boards, and various models of churches and houses. Some taught their languages to the inhabitants.'

ODIHAM

General Simon was at Odiham. We have had to do with him before, and he seems to have been thoroughly bad. He had been concerned with Bernadotte and Pinoteau in the Conspiracy of Rennes against Bonaparte's Consular Government, had been arrested, and exiled to the Isle of Rhé for six years. When Bonaparte became emperor he liberated Simon and gave him a command. At the battle of Busaco, September 27, 1810, Simon's brigade led the division of Loison in its attack on the British position, and Simon was first man over the entrenchments. 'We took some prisoners,' says George Napier, 'and among them General Simon. He was horribly wounded in the face, his jaw being broken and almost hanging on his chest. Just as myself and another officer came to him a soldier was going to put his bayonet into him, which we prevented, and sent him up as prisoner to the General.'

Simon reached England in October 1810, and was sent on parole to Odiham. The prisoners lived in houses in Bury Square, opposite the stocks and the church, and some old redbrick cottages on the brink of the chalk-pit at the entrance to the town, all of which are now standing. They naturally made the fine old *George* Inn their social centre, and to this day the tree which marked their mile limit along the London road is known as

'Frenchman's Oak'. Simon absconded from Odiham, and the advertisement for him ran:

'One hundred pounds is offered for the capture of the French general Simon, styled a baron and a chevalier of the Empire, who lately broke his parole and absconded from Odiham.'

The Times of Jan. 20, 1812, details his smart capture by the Bow Street officers. They went first to Richmond, hearing that two foreigners of suspicious appearance were there. The information led to nothing, so they went on to Hounslow, thinking to intercept the fugitives on their way from Odiham to the Kent Coast, and here they heard that two Frenchmen had hired a post-chaise to London. This they traced to Dover Street, Piccadilly, but the clue was lost. They remembered that there was a French doctor in Dover Street, but an interview with him revealed nothing. On they went to the house of a Madame Glion, in Pulteney Street, late owner of a Paris diligence, and, although their particular quarry was not there, they 'ran in' three other French 'broke-paroles'. Information led them to Pratt Street, Camden Town. A female servant appeared in the area of No. 4 in reply to their knocks, denied that there was any one in the house, and refused them admittance. The officers, now reinforced, surrounded the house, and some men were seen sitting in a back-parlour by candle-light. Suddenly the candles were put out. Lavender, the senior officer, went again to the front door and knocked. The servant resisted his pretext of having a letter for a lady in the house, and he threatened to shoot her if she still refused admission. She defied him. Other officers had in the meanwhile climbed over the back garden wall and found Simon and another officer, Surgeon Boiron, in the kitchen in darkness.

The mistress and servant of the house were both Frenchwomen, and they were carried off with Simon and Boiron: altogether a capital haul, as the women were found upon examination to be 'deep in the business' of aiding and abetting in the escape of prisoners. With Simon's subsequent career I have dealt in the chapter upon Escapes and Escape Agents.

LEICESTER

To Mr. John Thorp of this town I am indebted for the following notes:

'In 1756 Count Benville and 30 other French officers were on parole at Leicester. Most of them were men of high rank, and were all well received by the townpeople.[18] They were polite and agreeable in manner, and as they expended about £9,000 during their stay in the town it was of benefit to a large part of the inhabitants.

'A number of French prisoners came from Tavistock in 1779, and remained in the town about six months. They behaved well and produced agreeable impressions upon the inhabitants by their light-hearted and amiable manners, and, in consequence, were very civilly treated. They were free from boasting, temperate, and even plain in living, and paid the debts they had contracted during their residence in the town.'

Tragic Events

Tragic events were by no means so common among the prisoners on parole as in the prisons, no doubt because of the greater variety in their lives, and of their not being so constantly in close company with each other.

A French officer, on parole at Andover in 1811, at what is now Portland House in West Street, fell in love with the daughter of his host, and upon her rejection of his suit, retired to a summer-house in the garden, opened a vein in his arm, and bled to death.

Duels were frequent, and not only would there have been more, had weapons of offence been procurable, but the results would have been more often fatal.

In 1812 two French officers at Reading fought in a field near the *New Inn* on the Oxford road. They could not get pistols, but one gun. They tossed for the first shot with it at fifty paces, and the winner shot his opponent through the back of the neck so that he died.

At Leek in Staffordshire in the same year, a Captain Decourbes went out fishing and came in at curfew. At 8 p.m. in the billiard-room of the *Black's Head*, a Captain Robert chaffed him about his prowess as an angler, words were exchanged, and Robert insulted and finally struck him. Decourbes, of course, challenged him. The only weapon they could get was a cavalry horse-pistol which they borrowed from a yeomanry trooper. They met at Balidone on October 17. Decourbes won the toss for first shot and hit

Robert in the breech. Robert, who had come on to the ground on crutches, then fired and hit Decourbes in the nape of the neck. Decourbes managed to walk back to Leek, but he died in ten days.

A very different version of this affair was given in a contemporary *Times*. According to this, Decourbes, about ten days before the duel, was out of his lodgings after the evening bell had rung, and the boys of Leek collected and pelted him with stones. His behaviour caused one of his brother officers to say that he was 'soft' and would faint at the sight of his own blood. Decourbes gave him the lie, the other struck him, and the result was a challenge and the duel as described. But the verdict, 'Died by the visitation of God,' was questioned, and the writer of a letter to *The Times* declared that there was no evidence of a duel, as Decourbes' body was in a putrid state, and that three French and two English surgeons had declared that he had died from typhus.

In 1807 a tragedy was enacted at Chesterfield which caused much stir at the time. Colonel Richemont and Captain Méant were fellow prisoners, released from the Chatham hulks, and travelling together to Chesterfield where they were to live on parole. On the road thither they slept at Atherstone. When Richemont arrived at the Falcon Hotel at Chesterfield he found that his trunk had been robbed of a quantity of gold dust, a variety of gold coins, and of some gold and silver articles. Suspecting that it had been done at the inn in Atherstone, he caused inquiry to be made, but without result. He then suspected his fellow traveller Méant, caused his box to be searched, and in it found silver spoons and other of his missing property.

Méant, on being discovered, tried to stab himself, but, being prevented, seized a bottle of laudanum and swallowed its contents. Then he wrote a confession, and finding that the laudanum was slower in action than he expected, tried to stab himself again. A struggle took place; Méant refused the emetic brought, and died. Méant's brother-in-law brought an action against Richemont, declaring that the latter in reality owed the dead man a large sum of money, and that Méant had only taken his due. During the trial Colonel Richemont was very violent against the British, and especially when the jury decided the case against him, and found that the dead man was his creditor, although, of course, the means he employed to get what was his were illegal.

Méant was buried, according to usage, at the union of four cross roads just outside the borough boundary, with a stake driven through his body. The funeral took place on a Sunday, and great crowds attended.

On April 13, 1812, Pierre de Romfort or De la Roche, a prisoner on parole at Launceston, was hanged at Bodmin for forgery. 'He behaved very penitently, and was attended to at the last moment by Mr. Lefers, a Roman Catholic priest living at Lanhearne.'

I quote this because it is one of the very few instances of this crime being committed by a prisoner on parole.

INTERNATIONAL COURTESIES

It is gratifying to read testimonies such as the following, taken out of many, to chivalry and kindness on the part of our enemies, and to note practical appreciations of such conduct.

In 1804 Captain Areguandeau of the *Blonde* privateer, captured at sea and put on the parole list, was applied for by late British prisoners of his to whom he had been kind, to be returned to France unconditionally. The Commissioners of the Transport Board regretted that under existing circumstances they could not accede to this, but allowed him a choice of parole towns—Tiverton, Ashbourne, Chesterfield, Leek, or Lichfield.

In 1806, Guerbe, second captain of a transport, was allowed to be on parole although he was not so entitled by his rank, because of his humane treatment of Colonel Fraser and other officers and men, lately his prisoners.

Lefort, on parole at Tiverton, was allowed to go to France on parole because of his kindly treatment of the wounded prisoners on the *Hannibal* (which, after a heroic resistance, ran aground in 1801 at Algeciras and was captured).

In 1813 Captain Collins of H.M.S. *Surveillante* successfully obtained the unconditional release of Captain Loysel because of the splendid manner in which the latter had risked his life in protecting two British officers, who were wounded in the unsuccessful first attack on San Sebastian, from being killed by some drunken or infuriated French soldiers.

A French marine officer named Michael Coie, a prisoner on parole, died at Andover, November 9, 1813. It happened that the 2nd battalion, 5th

Regiment was halting on the march in the town, and the commanding officer, Captain Boyle, at once offered to attend the funeral, with the battalion, the regimental band at the head. This was done, all the French officers in Andover being present. The act of grace was much appreciated by the prisoners.

So also when General Rufin—a great favourite of Bonaparte, captured at Barossa in 1811—died in the May of that year on his passage to England, his body was interred in the Garrison Chapel at Portsmouth, with every rank of honour and distinction, minute guns, flags half-mast high, and three rounds of nine pieces of cannon at the close.

In 1814, an officer on parole at Oswestry was liberated for having rescued an infant from the paws of a lion.

The following is pleasing reading:

General Barraguay-Hilliers, who with his suite was captured in the *Sensible* by H.M.S. *Seahorse* in June 1798, arrived at Portsmouth in August, and on the very day after his arrival was allowed to go on parole to France with his aides-de-camp, Lamotte and Vallie. But before they could get out of England an amusing incident occurred which afforded an English gentleman an opportunity for displaying a graceful courtesy. The officers reached Lewes *en route* for Dover, where they hoped to get a neutral vessel to France, but, as Brighton races were on, not for love or money could they get a conveyance to carry them on their journey. None of them could speak English; they were not allowed by the terms of their parole to go to London, which they might have done by mail-coach, so they resolved to send their baggage on by cart, and themselves proceed on foot. Sir John Shelley of Maresfield Park heard of their predicament, and at once sent carriages to take them on to Dover.

It is also pleasant to read that at Tiverton the French officers on parole there, with scarcely an exception, conducted themselves in such a way as to win the esteem and regard of their hosts, and in many cases lasting friendships were formed with them. After the establishment of Peace in 1815, some, rather than return to France, remained. Among these was M. Alexandre de la Motte, who lived at Tiverton, acquired property there, and gained much respect as French master at Blundell's School.

That so gregarious a race as the French should form clubs and associations for social purposes among themselves in all circumstances can be readily understood, and in almost every parole town some such institution existed, and in no small degree contributed to the enlivenment of local social life. There were also no less than twenty-five lodges and chapters of Freemasons in England, and others in Scotland. Still, the Government, from politic motives, warned their Agents to keep these institutions under observation, and were disposed to regard with suspicion such clubs as the 'Des Amis Réunis' at Ashburton and Plymouth, the 'Enfants de Mars et de Neptune' at Abergavenny and Tiverton, and others of like character, as being institutions for the fomentation *sub rosâ* of agitation and disaffection. For the same reasons all amusements which gathered crowds were discouraged among the prisoners.

CHAPTER XXXI
VARIORUM

(1) Some Distinguished Prisoners of War

When the roll of the 46th Regiment (or, as it was, the 46th demi-brigade), of the French Army is called, the name of La Tour d'Auvergne brings forward the sergeant-major of the Grenadier Company, who salutes and replies: 'Dead upon the field of honour!'

This unique homage to Théophile de La Tour d'Auvergne—who won the distinguishing title of 'First Grenadier of the Republican Armies' in an age and an army crowded with brave men, quite as much, so says history, by his modesty as by his bravery in action—was continued for some time after his death in 1800, was discontinued, was revived in 1887, and has been paid ever since.

In 1795, after the taking of San Sebastian by the French, he applied for leave of absence on account of his health, and started by sea for his native Brittany, but the ship in which he sailed was captured by British cruisers. He was brought to England and sent to Bodmin on parole. Here he insisted upon wearing his Republican cockade, a silly, unnecessary act of bravado which so annoyed some English soldiers that they mobbed him, and, as he showed a disposition to resent the attack, matters would have gone hard with him but for timely rescue. (I reproduce a picture of one of these attacks from his biography by Montorgueil, not on account of its merit, but of its absurdity. La Tour d'Auvergne, it will be noted, uses his sword toasting-fork wise. Not even the most distinguished of parole prisoners was ever allowed to wear his sword, although some were not required to give them up according to rule.) This inspired the following letter from him to the Agent at Bodmin:

LA TOUR D'AUVERGNE DEFENDING HIS COCKADE AT BODMIN

'1st October, 1795.

'SIR,

'I address myself to you as the Agent entrusted by your Government with the immediate care of the French prisoners at Bodmin, to acquaint you with the outrage just perpetrated upon me by some soldiers of the garrison in this town, who, on their return from drill, attacked me with their arms, and proceeded to violent extremes with the object of depriving me of my cockade, a distinctive part of my military uniform. I have always worn it during my detention in England, just as your officers, prisoners in my country, have always worn theirs without being interfered with. It is impossible, Sir, that such behaviour towards an officer of the French Republic should have been encouraged by your Government, or that it should countenance any outrage upon peaceable prisoners who are here under your protection. Under these circumstances, Sir, I beg you without delay to get to the root of the insult to which I have been subjected, so that I may be able to adapt my conduct in future accordingly. Into whatever extremity I may find myself reduced by my determination not to remove my distinctive badge, I shall never regard as a misfortune the ills and interferences of which the source will have been so honourable to me.'

The reply of the Agent was probably much the same as the Transport Office made in 1804 to a letter from the Agent at Leek, in Staffordshire, to whom a French midshipman had complained of similar interference.

'We think the French midshipman very imprudent in wearing his Cockade, as it could answer no good purpose, and might expose him to evils greater than he has already experienced from the rage of the populace, and you are to inform him if he persists he must not expect protection from the consequences.'

In 1797 the inhabitants of Bishop's Waltham complained of the constant wearing by the prisoners there of Republican cockades, and the reply was exactly as above.

In Cornwall La Tour d'Auvergne occupied himself with literary pursuits, especially with philology, and was pleased and interested to find how much there was in common between phrases and words of Cornwall, and those of Brittany. Concerning his captivity he wrote thus to Le Coz, Archbishop of Besançon:

'I will not bother you with an account of all I have had to suffer from the English during a year of captivity, they being no doubt egged on by our French é[migrés] and p[rinces]. My Republican spirit finds it hard to dissemble and to adapt itself to circumstances, so I shall show myself to be what I always have been, Frenchman and patriot. The revered symbol of my nation, the tricolour cockade, was always on my hat, and the dress I wore *dans les fers* was that which I wore in battle. Hence the hatred let loose against me and the persecutions which I have had to endure.'

He returned to France from Penryn, February 19, 1796, and was killed at Oberhausen in Bavaria in June 1800.

From the following extract from Legard's biography, and from the phrase *dans les fers* which I have italicized above, La Tour d'Auvergne would seem to have been in prison, possibly for persistent adherence to cockade-wearing:

'It was horrible to see the misery of so many brave Frenchmen, crammed into unwholesome dungeons, struggling against every sort of want, exposed to every rigour and every vexation imaginable, and devoured by cruel maladies. La Tour d'Auvergne kept up their courage, helped them in every way, shared his money with them, and was indignant to hear how agents of the Government tried to seduce them from their fidelity, corrupt them, and show them how hateful was the French Government.'

After Trafalgar the Spanish prisoners were confined at Gibraltar, the French, numbering 210 officers and 4,589 men, were brought to England. The rank and file who were landed at Portsmouth were imprisoned at Forton, Portchester, and in seven hulks; those at Plymouth in the Millbay Prison and eight hulks; those at Chatham in four hulks. The officers from the captured ships *Fougueux*, *Aigle*, *Mont-Blanc*, *Berwick*, *Scipion*, *Formidable*, *Intrépide*, *Achille*, and *Duguay Trouin*, were sent to Crediton and Wincanton.

Admiral Villeneuve and his suite were first at Bishop's Waltham, where he was bound by the ordinary rules of a prisoner on parole, except that his limits were extended; he was allowed to visit Lord Clanricarde, and to retain, but not to wear, his arms.

He had asked to be sent to London, but, although this was not granted him, he was allowed to choose any town for parole, north or west of London, but not within thirty miles.

He had leave to visit any of the neighbouring nobility and gentry, and his lieutenants could go three miles in any direction. He chose Reading, which was not then a regular parole town, although it became one later. Hither he went with Majendie, his captain, whose third experience it was of captivity in England (he had been actually taken prisoner five times, and had served two years, one month, twenty-five days as prisoner in England), Lucas of the *Redoutable*, and Infernet of the *Intrépide*. Villeneuve and Majendie attended Nelson's funeral in London, and a little later Majendie had permission to go to France to try to arrange some definite system of prisoner-exchange between the two countries. In March 1806 Villeneuve was exchanged for four post-captains, and went to France with his officers and suite on the condition that once in every two months he gave notice to a British agent of his place of residence, and was not to change the same without notifying it.

Upon his arrival in Paris Villeneuve found that Lucas and Infernet had been much honoured by Bonaparte and made rear-admirals. No notice was taken of him by Bonaparte, who had always disliked and despised him, and one day he was found stabbed at the Hôtel de la Patrie, Rennes. Bonaparte was suspected of foul play, and again was heard the saying, 'How fortunate Napoleon is! All his enemies die of their own accord!' At St. Helena, however, Bonaparte strenuously denied the imputation.

Lucas, captain of the *Redoutable*, the ship whence Nelson received his death-shot, was at Tiverton. His heroic defence, his fight against the *Téméraire* and the *Victory* at the same time, resulting in a loss out of 645 men of 300 killed and 222 wounded, are among the immortal deeds of that famous day. Only 169 of his men were made prisoners, and of these only 35 came to England; the rest, being wounded, went down with the ship.

Villeneuve said when he wrote to congratulate Lucas upon being honoured by Bonaparte:

'Si tous les capitaines de vaisseaux s'étaient conduits comme vous, à Trafalgar, la victoire n'eût pas été un instant indécisive, certainement personne ne le sait aussi bien que moi.'

His conduct was so much appreciated in England, that at a supper given him by Lady Warren his sword was returned to him.

Rear-Admiral Dumanoir of the *Formidable* was also at Tiverton. Although he fought at Trafalgar, he was not captured there, as it was thought in many quarters he should have been or have died with his ship. From Tiverton he wrote, with permission, under date of January 2, 1806, to *The Times*, replying to some rather severe remarks which had been made in that paper concerning his behaviour at Trafalgar, tantamount to saying that during the greater part of the battle he had remained a mere passive spectator. It is not necessary to relate the facts, which are fully given by James, the naval historian.

In 1809 he had special leave to go on parole to France to defend himself, but the Transport Office refused to allow three captains and two adjutants to go with him, because of the continual refusal of the French Government to release British prisoners. At first he was not allowed to take even his secretary, a non-combatant, but later this was permitted. The Court Martial in France acquitted him, and in 1811 he was made a vice-admiral and Governor of Danzig, and behaved with great credit during the siege of that city by the Allies in 1814. In connexion with this, it is interesting to note that the only British naval flag trophy at the Invalides in Paris was captured by Dumanoir at Danzig.

It is not out of place here to note that Cartigny, the last French survivor of Trafalgar, who died at Hyères in 1892, aged 101, had a considerable experience of war-prisoner life, for, besides having been on a Plymouth hulk, he was at Dartmoor and at Stapleton. He attended the Prince Imperial's funeral at Chislehurst in 1879.

Marienier, a black general, captured at San Domingo, was, with his four wives, brought to Portsmouth. The story is that, being entitled to parole by his rank, when the Agent presented him the usual form for signature, he said: 'Je ne connais pas le mystère de la plume; c'est par ceci (touching the hilt of his sword) que je suis parvenu au grade que je tiens. Voilà mon aide-de-camp; il sait écrire, et il signera pour moi.'

Tallien, Revolutionist writer, prominent Jacobin, agent of the Terror in Bordeaux, and largely responsible for the downfall of Robespierre, was captured on his way home from Egypt, whither he had gone with Bonaparte's expedition. As he was a non-combatant he was only a prisoner a short time, and went to London, where he was lionized by the Whig party. He married Madame de Fontenai, whose salon in Paris was the most brilliant of the Directory period, and where Bonaparte first met Madame de Beauharnais.

In 1809 François, nephew of the great actor Talma, was taken prisoner. He was nobody in particular, but his case is interesting inasmuch as his release on January 1, 1812, was largely brought about by the interest of Talma's great friend, John Kemble.

Admiral Count Linois was as worthy a prisoner as he had proved himself many times a worthy foe. A French writer describes him as having displayed during his captivity a philosophic resignation; and even the stony-hearted Transport Board, in acceding to his request that his wife should be allowed to join him at Bath, complimented him on his behaviour 'which has formed a very satisfactory contrast to that of many officers of high rank, by whom a similar indulgence has been abused.'

Lucien, Bonaparte's second brother, was a prisoner in England, but very nominally, from 1810 to 1814. He could not fall in with the grand and ambitious ideas of his brother so far as they touched family matters. Bonaparte, having made his brothers all princes, considered that they should marry accordingly. Lucien married the girl he loved; his brother resented it, and passed the Statute of March 30, 1806, by which it was enacted that 'Marriages of the Imperial Family shall be null and void if contracted without the permission of the Emperor, as the princes ought to be devoted without reserve to the great interests of the country, and the glory of our house.' He wanted Lucien to marry the Queen of Etruria, widow of Louis I, Prince of Parma, a match which, when Tuscany should be annexed to the Empire, would mean that their throne would be that of Spain and the Indies.

So Lucien sailed for the United States, but was captured by a British cruiser carried to Malta, and thence to England. He was sent on parole to Ludlow, where he lived at Dinham House. Then he bought Thorngrove, near Worcester, where he lived until 1814, and where he wrote *Charlemagne, ou l'Église sauvée*.

Cambronne, wounded at the head of the Imperial Guard at Waterloo, and reputed author of a famous *mot* which he never uttered, was for two hours on a Portsmouth hulk, but was soon placed on parole, and was at Ashburton in Devonshire until November 1815. The grand-daughter of Mrs. Eddy, at whose house Cambronne lodged, still preserves at the *Golden Lion* a portrait of the general, given by him to Mrs. Eddy. From England he wrote to Louis XVIII, professing loyalty, and offering his services, but on his arrival in Paris was brought up for trial on these counts:

(1) Having betrayed the King. (2) Having made an armed attack on France. (3) Having procured aid for Bonaparte by violence. He was adjudged Not Guilty on all three.

Admiral De Winter, Commander of the Dutch fleet at Camperdown, was a prisoner for a year in England, but I cannot learn where. It is gratifying to read his appreciation of the kindly treatment he received, as expressed in his speech at his public entry into Amsterdam after his release in December 1798.

'The fortune of war previously forced me to live abroad, and, being since then for the first time vanquished by the enemy, I have experienced a second state of exile. However mortifying to the feelings of a man who loves his country, the satisfactory treatment I met with on the part of the enemy, the English, and the humane and faithful support and assistance they evinced towards my worthy countrymen and fellow sufferers, have considerably softened the horrors of my situation. Nay! Worthy burghers! I must not conceal from you that the noble liberality of the English nation since this bloody contest justly entitles them to your admiration.'

De Winter's flag-ship, the *Vryheid*, was for many years a hulk at Chatham.

(2) SOME STATISTICS

Statistics are wearisome, but, in order that readers may form some idea of the burden cast on the country by the presence of prisoners of war, I give a few figures.

During the Seven Years' War the annual average number of prisoners of war in England was 18,800, although the total of one year, 1762, was 26,137. This, it must be remembered, was before the regular War Prison became an institution, so that the burden was directly upon the people among whom the prisoners were scattered. Of these, on an average, about 15,700 were in prisons healthy, and 1,200 sick; 1,850 were on parole healthy, and 60 sick. The total net cost of these prisoners was £1,174,906. The total number of prisoners brought to Britain between the years 1803 and 1814 was 122,440. Of these 10,341 died whilst in captivity, and 17,607 were exchanged or sent home sick or on parole. The cost of these was £6,800,000.

The greatest number of prisoners at one time in Britain was about 72,000 in 1814.

The average mortality was between one and three per cent., but epidemics (such as that which at Dartmoor during seven months of 1809 and 1810 caused 422 deaths—more than double the total of nineteen ordinary months—and that at Norman Cross in 1801 from which, it is said, no less than 1,000 prisoners died) brought up the percentages of particular years very notably. Thus, during the six years and seven months of Dartmoor's existence as a war-prison, there were 1,455 deaths, which, taking the average number of prisoners as 5,600, works out at about four per cent., but the annual average was not more than two and a quarter per cent., except in the above-quoted years. The average mortality on the prison ships was slightly higher, working out all round at about three per cent., but here again epidemics made the percentages of particular years jump, as at Portsmouth in 1812, when the average of deaths rose to about four per cent.

Strange to say, the sickness-rate of officers on parole was higher than that of prisoners in confinement. Taking at random the year 1810, for example, we find that at one time out of 45,940 prisoners on the hulks and in prisons, only 320 were in hospital, while at the same time of 2,710 officers on parole no less than 165 were on the sick-list. Possibly the greater prevalence of duels among the latter may account for this.

(3) EPITAPHS OF PRISONERS

I do not claim completeness for the following list, for neglect has allowed the obliteration of many stones in our churchyards which traditionally mark the last resting-places of prisoners of war.

At New Alresford, Hampshire, on the west side of the church:

'Ici repose le corps de M. Joseph Hypolite Riouffe, enseigne de vaisseau de la Marine Impériale et Royale qui mourut le 12 Dec. 1810, âgé 28 ans. Il emporta les regrets de tous ses camarades et personnes qui le connurent.'

'Ci-gît le corps de M. P^re Garnier, sous-lieut. au 66me régiment d'Infanterie Française, né le 14 Avril 1773, mort le 31 Juillet 1811.'

'Ci-gît le corps de M. C. Lavau, officier de commerce, décédé le 25 de Xbre 1811, et la 29 de son âge.'

'Ici est le corps de Marie Louise Vve Fournier, épouse de François Bertet, capitaine au Corps Impérial d'Artillerie Française, décédée le 11me Avril 1812, âgée de 44 ans.'

'Ci-gît Jean de l'Huille, lieutenant d'Artillerie Française, décédé le 6 Avril 1812, âgé de 51.'

At Leek, Staffordshire:

'Çy-gît Jean Marie Claude Decourbes, enseigne de vaisseau de la Marine Impériale de France, décédé 17 Octobre 1812, âgé de 27 ans—Fidelis Decori Occubuit Patriaeque Deoque.'

'Jean-Baptiste Milloy. Capitaine 72me cavalerie, décédé 2 Sept. 1811, âgé de 43 ans.'

'Joseph Debec, Capitaine du navire "La Sophie" de Nantes. Obiit Sept. 2me 1811, âgé de 54 ans.'

'Charles Luneaud, Capitaine de la Marine Impériale. Mort le 4me Mars 1812.'

There also died at Leek, but no stones mark their graves, General Brunet (captured at San Domingo, with his A.D.C. Colonel Degouillier, and his Adjutant-General, Colonel Lefevre), Colonel Félix of the Artillery, Lieut.-Col. Granville, Captain Pouget, Captain Dupuis of the 72nd Infantry, Captain François Vevelle (1809), Lieut. Davoust of the Navy, son of the General, and Midshipmen Meunier, Berthot, and Birtin—the last-named was a prisoner eleven years, and 'behaved extremely well'. Also there are registered the burials of Jean le Roche, in 1810, aged 44, J. B. Lahouton, died 1806, aged 28; 'C.A.G. A French Prisoner' in 1812, aged 62; and Alexander Gay, in 1850.

At Okehampton, Devon:

'Cette pierre fut élevée par l'amitié à la mémoire d'Armand Bernard, né au Havre en Normandie, marié à Calais à Mlle Margot; deuxième officier de commerce, décédé Prisonnier de Guerre à Okehampton, le 26 Oct. 1815. Agé 33 ans.

A l'abri des vertus qui distinguaient la vie,

Tu reposes en paix, ombre tendre et chérie.'

'Ci-gît Adelaïde Barrin de Puyleanne de la Commune de Montravers, Dép^t des Deux-Sèvres, née le 21 Avril 1771, décédée à Okehampton le 18 Fév. 1811. Ici repose la mère et l'enfant.'

In the churchyards of Wincanton and Andover are stones to the memories of Russian and Polish officers.

In the churchyard at Tenterden, Kent, there is a tomb upon which is carved a ship and a recumbent figure, with the epitaph:

'Hier Legt Begraven Schipper Siebe Nannes, Van de Jower in Vriesland, is in den Heere Gernstden, 8 November, 1781. Oudt 47 Jaren.' On the other side is inscribed:

'As he's the first, the neighbours say, that lies

First of War captives buried in this place:

So may he hope to be the first to rise

And gain the Mansions of Eternal Peace.'

By the way, it may be remarked, in association with the above Dutch burial, that there are to-day in Tenterden work-people named Vanlanschorten, who are said to be descended from a prisoner of war.

At Bishop's Castle church, in Montgomeryshire, there is a stone opposite the belfry door inscribed:

'A la Mémoire de Louis Pages, Lieut.-Col. des chevaux-légers; chevalier des ordres militaires des Deux Siciles et d'Espagne. Mort à Bishop's Castle le 1er Mai 1814, âgé de 40 ans.'

In the Register of the same church is recorded the baptism of a son of Antoine Marie Jeanne Ary Bandart, Captain of the 4th Regiment of Light Infantry, Member of the Legion of Honour, a prisoner of war; and fifteen months later the burial of the child. These are in 1813 and 1814. In the latter year also is recorded the baptism of a son of Joseph and Maria Moureux.

In the churchyard of Moreton-Hampstead, Devon, are ranged against the wall stones with the following epitaphs:

'A la mémoire de Louis Ambroise Quanti, Lieut, du 44 Rég^t du Corps Impérial d'Artillerie de Marine. Agé de 33 ans. Décédé le 29 Avril 1809.' The Masonic compass and dividers follow the inscription.

'Ici repose le corps de M. Armand Aubry, Lieut, du 70me Rég^t d'Infanterie de Ligne. Agé de 42 ans. Décédé le 10 Juin 1811. Priez Dieu pour le repos de son âme.' This is followed by two crossed swords.

'A la mémoire de Jean François Roil; Aspirant de la Marine Impériale, âgé de 21 ans. Décédé le 22 Janvier 1811.' This has as emblem a sword and anchor crossed.

There are still in Moreton-Hampstead two shops bearing the name of Rihll. To the register-entries of two of the above deaths is added: 'These were buried in Wooling, according to Act of Parliament.'

In the churchyard of Ashburton, Devon, is a stone thus inscribed:

'Ici

Repose François Guidon natif de Cambrai en France, Sous-Lieutenant au 46me Rég^t de Ligne. Décédé le 18 7bre 1815. Agé de 22 ans. Requiescat in Pace.'

At East Dereham, Norfolk:

'In memory of Jean de la Narde, son of a notary public of Saint Malo, a French prisoner of war, who, having escaped from the bell tower of this Church, was pursued and shot by a soldier on duty. October 6th, 1799. Aged 28.'

Mr. Webb, of Andover, sends me the following registrations of death:

J. Alline. Prisoner of War. March 18, 1802.

Nicholas Ockonloff. Prisoner of War. March 19, 1808.

Michael Coie. Prisoner of War. November 9, 1813. [For an account of his funeral see pp. 439–40.]

At Odiham, in Hampshire, are the graves of two French prisoners of war. When I visited them in August 1913, the inscriptions had been repainted and a memorial wreath laid upon each grave. The inscriptions are as follows:

'Cy-gît Piere Feron, Capitaine au 66e Régiment de Ligne, Chevalier de l'Empire Français, né à Reims, Départ^t de la Marne, le 15 Août 1766, décédé à Odiham le 8 Mai 1810.'

'Pierre Julian Jonneau, son of Jean Joseph Jonneau, de Daure, and of Marie Charlotte Franquiny de Feux, officer in the administration of the French Navy. Born in the Isle of Rhé. Died at Odiham, September 4th, 1809, in the 29th year of his age.

'"He was a Prisoner of War. Death hath made him free."'

During the Communist trouble in France in 1871, quite a large number of French people came over to Odiham until order should be restored, and it was during their stay here, but not by them, that the above-mentioned graves were put in order. The old houses facing the Church and the stocks in Bury Close, and those by the large chalk-pit at the entrance to the town, remain much as when they were the lodgings of the prisoners of war.

Milton Keynes UK
Ingram Content Group UK Ltd.
UKHW030631061024
449204UK00012B/422